ANTIQUITIES

OF THE

SOUTHERN INDIANS,

PARTICULARLY OF THE

GEORGIA TRIBES

ANTIQUITIES

OF THE

SOUTHERN INDIANS,

PARTICULARLY OF THE

GEORGIA TRIBES

CHARLES C. JONES, Jr.

GYAN

Published by

Gyan Publishing House
5, Ansari Road
Daryaganj, New Delhi-110002
Phone: 011-47034999, 9811692060
E-mail: books@gyanbooks.com

Distribution Network
gyanbooks.com
India, USA, Canada, UK, Australia, France

ISBN: 978-81-212-9069-2 (PB)
First Published, 1873

2nd Impression 2023

Printed at: Gyan Press, Delhi.

ANTIQUITIES OF THE SOUTHERN INDIANS, PARTICULARLY OF THE GEORGIA TRIBES

AUTHOR: CHARLES C. JONES

ANTIQUITIES

OF THE

SOUTHERN INDIANS,

PARTICULARLY OF THE

GEORGIA TRIBES.

BY

CHARLES C. JONES, Jr.

NEW YORK:
D. APPLETON AND COMPANY,
549 & 551 BROADWAY.
1873.

TO

THE STATE OF GEORGIA,

THIS VOLUME IS AFFECTIONATELY INSCRIBED

BY

ONE OF HER SONS.

PREFACE.

ALTHOUGH the title intimates that our investigations have been directed principally to an examination of the antiquities of a single State, the present work will be found to embrace within its scope a much more extended field of observation. In prosecuting the proposed inquiries, it appeared both unnecessary and improper narrowly to observe the boundary-lines which separate modern States. It will be remembered, moreover, that the original grant from the British crown conveyed to the Trustees of the Colony of Georgia a territory greater by far than that now embraced within the geographical limits accorded to her as a State. A striking similarity exists among the customs, utensils, implements, and ornaments of all the Southern Indians: consequently, in elucidating the archæology of a region often occupied in turn by various tribes, it seemed appropriate to mention and contrast the antiquities of Virginia, the Carolinas, Florida, Alabama, Mississippi, Louisiana, and Tennessee.

Our object has been, from the earliest and most authentic sources of information at command, to convey a correct impression of the location, characteristics, form of government, social relations, manufactures, domestic economy, diversions, and customs of the Southern Indians, at the time of primal contact between them and the Europeans. This introductory part of the work is followed by an examination of tumuli, earthworks, and various relics obtained from burial-mounds, gathered amid refuse-piles, found in ancient graves, and picked up in cultivated fields and on the sites of old villages and fishing-resorts. Whenever these could be interpreted in the light of early recorded observations, or were capable of explanation by customs not obsolete at the dawn of the historic period, the authorities relied upon have been carefully noted.

The accompanying plans of mounds were prepared from personal surveys, and nearly every typical object used in illustration may be seen in the author's collection. Most of these relics were obtained by me *in situ*. They are now figured for the first time.

To the friends who have kindly aided me in gathering together a cabinet which so fully and beautifully represents the arts and the manufactures of these primitive peoples, I here renew my cordial and grateful acknowledgments.

Prepared at irregular intervals and in odd moments as they could be borrowed from the exacting and ever-recurring engagements of an active professional life, these pages, with their manifest shortcomings, are offered in the hope that they will, at least in some degree, minister to the information and pleasure of those who are not incurious with regard to the subject of American archæology.

CHARLES C. JONES, JR.

NEW YORK, *April* 10, 1873.

CONTENTS.

CHAPTER I.

Location of Tribes.—Physical Characteristics of the Southern Indians.—System of Government.—The Mico.—The Head War-Chief.—Public Buildings in a Creek Village.—Mode of Warfare.—Office of High-Priest.—Sun-Worship.—Offering of the Stag.—Idol-Worship.—Religious Ideas.—The Sun among the Natchez.—The Cacica of Cutifachiqui.—Mausoleum of Talomeco.—Tombs of the Virginia Kings, ... Page 1

CHAPTER II.

Office of the Conjurer or Medicine-man.—Treatment of the Sick.—Medicinal Plants.—Towns and Private Houses.—Tenure of Property.—Agricultural Pursuits.—Town Plantations and Private Gardens.—Public Granaries.—Animal and Vegetable Food.—Mechanical Labors.—Early Mining in Duke's-Creek Valley.—Manufacture of Canoes, Pottery, Copper Implements, Gold, Silver, Shell, and Stone Ornaments.—Various Implements and Articles of Stone, Bone, and Wood.—Trade Relations, ... 28

CHAPTER III.

Marriage and Divorce.—Punishment of Adultery.—Costume and Ornaments.—Skin-painting and Tattooing.—Manufacture of Carpets, Feather-shawls, and Moccasins.—Weaving, ... 65

CHAPTER IV.

Music and Musical Instruments.—Dancing.—Games.—Gambling.—Festivals.—Divisions of the Year.—Counting.—Funeral Customs, ... 90

CHAPTER V.

General Observations on Mound-Building.—Bartram's Account of the Georgia Tumuli.—Absence of Megalithic Monuments and Animal-shaped Mounds.—Distribution of the Ancient Population.—Few Sepulchral Mounds erected since the Advent of Europeans.—Antiquity of the Tumuli, . PAGE 118

CHAPTER VI.

Mounds on the Etowah River.—Temple for Sun-worship.—Stone Images.—Fish-Preserves.—Tumuli in the Valley of Little Shoulder-bone Creek.—Circular Earthwork on the Head-waters of the Ogeechee.—Stone Tumulus near Sparta.—Mounds on the Savannah River.—Meeting between the Cacica of the Savannah and De Soto, ... 136

CHAPTER VII.

Tumuli on the Ocmulgee River, opposite Macon.—Brown's Mount.—Mound on Messier's Plantation, in Early County, ... 158

CHAPTER VIII.

Chunky-Yards.—Elevated Spaces.—Mounds of Observation and Retreat.—Tumuli on Woolfolk's Plantation.—Sepulchral Tumuli.—Chieftain-Mounds.—Custom of burying Personal Property with the Dead.—Savannah owes a Monument to Tomo-chi-chi.—Family or Tribal Mounds.—Cremation, . . 178

CHAPTER IX.

Shell-Mounds.—Tumulus on Stalling's Island.—Shell-Heaps and their Contents.—Rock-Piles.—Indian Affection for the Graves of their Departed.—Ancient Burial-Ground on the Coast.—Rock-Walls, Embankments, and Defensive Enclosures.—Stone Mountain.—Fortified Towns of the Southern Indians, 195

CHAPTER X.

Stone Graves in Nacoochee Valley and elsewhere.—Copper Implements and the Use of that Metal among the Southern Indians.—Cane-Matting.—Shell Drinking-Cups.—Shell Pins.—Age of Stone Graves.—Evidence of Commerce among the Aborigines, ... 213

CHAPTER XI.

Arrow and Spear Heads.—Use of the Bow.—Skill in Archery.—Manufacture and General Distribution of Arrow and Spear Points.—Various Forms of these Implements.—Stone Dagger.—Flint Sword, ... 240

CHAPTER XII.

Grooved Axes.—Hand and Wedge-shaped Axes or Celts.—Perforated and Ornamental or Ceremonial Axes.—Chisels.—Gouges.—Scrapers.—Flint Knives.—Awls, or Borers.—Leaf-shaped Implements.—Smoothing-Stones.—Drift-Implements, ... PAGE 269

CHAPTER XIII.

Agriculture and Agricultural Implements.—Ceremony of the Busk.—Cultivation of Maize.—Mortars and Pestles.—Crushing-Stones.—Nut-Stones.—Use of Walnut and Hickory-nut Oil, ... 296

CHAPTER XIV.

Fishing.—Wears.—Nets.—Net-sinkers.—Plummets, ... 321

CHAPTER XV.

Discoidal Stones.—Chungke-Game, ... 341

CHAPTER XVI.

Stone Tubes, ... 359

CHAPTER XVII.

Stones for rounding Arrow-shafts.—Whetstones or Sharpeners.—Pierced Tablets.—Pendants.—Slung-stones.—Amulets.—Stone Plate.—Mica Mirrors.—Sculptured Rocks, ... 366

CHAPTER XVIII.

Pipes.—The Use of Tobacco.—Idol Pipes.—Calumets.—Common Pipes. . 383

CHAPTER XIX.

Idol-Worship among the Southern Indians.—Stone and Terra-Cotta Images, 413

CHAPTER XX.

Pottery, ... 441

CHAPTER XXI.

The Use of Pearls as Ornaments among the Southern Indians, . . 467

CHAPTER XXII.

Primitive Uses of Shells.—Shell-Money.—Shell Ornaments.—Personal Decorations.—Conclusion, ... 495

LIST OF ILLUSTRATIONS.

PLATE I. (*To face page* 136.)

Tumuli and Fish-Preserves in the Etowah Valley, Georgia.

PLATE II. (*To face page* 144.)

Figs. 1 and 2. Tumuli in the Valley of Little Shoulder-bone Creek.
3. Enclosed Work.
4. Circular Earthwork on the Head-waters of the Ogeechee.
5. Stone Tumulus near Sparta, Georgia.

PLATE III. (*To face page* 152.)

Tumuli on the Savannah River, below Augusta.

PLATE IV. (*To face page* 158.)

Tumuli on the Ocmulgee River, opposite the City of Macon.

PLATE IV., A. (*To face page* 160.)

Fig. 1. Skull of a Creek Indian.
2 and 3. Two Views of the Skull of an Ancient Mound-builder.

PLATE V. (*To face page* 168.)

Mound on Messier's Plantation, in Early County.

PLATE VI. (*To face page* 224.)

Relics found in Stone Graves in Nacoochee Valley.
Fig. 1. Cane Matting.
2–7. Copper Implements.
8 and 9. Shell Pins.
10. Soapstone Pin.
11 and 12. Stone Beads.

PLATE VII. (*To face page* 252.)

Figs. 1 and 2. Large Flint Spear-heads.
3 and 5. Flint Daggers.
4. Serrated Flint Sword.

PLATE VIII. (*To face page* 254.)

Figs. 1–12. Typical Forms of Flint Spear-heads.

PLATE IX. (*To face page* 256.)

Figs. 1–41. Typical Forms of Arrow-points.

PLATE X. (*To face page* 274.)

Figs. 1–7. Typical Forms of Grooved Stone Axes.
8. Stone Adze.

PLATE XI. (*To face page* 278.)

Figs. 1–6. Typical Forms of Polished Stone Celts.

PLATE XII. (*To face page* 280.)

Stone Axe from Tennessee.

PLATE XIII. (*To face page* 282.)

Figs. 1–5. Typical Forms of Perforated and Ornamental or Ceremonial Hatchets.
6. Hammer-Stone.

PLATE XIV. (*To face page* 286.)

Figs. 1–4. Stone Chisels.
5–7. Stone Gouges.
8. Bone Gouge.
9–14. Typical Forms of Stone Scrapers.

PLATE XV. (*To face page* 290.)

Figs. 1–9. Flint Knives and Leaf-shaped Implements.

PLATE XVI. (*To face page* 292.)

Fig. 1. Bone Awl.
2–5. Stone Borers.
6–9. Smoothing-Stones.
10. Drift Implement.

PLATE XVII. (*To face page* 302.)

Fig. 1. Stone Hoe.
2. Stone Spade.
3–5. Flint Agricultural Implements.

PLATE XVIII. (*To face page* 312.)

Figs. 1–3. Stone Mortars.
4–5. Stone Pestles.
6 and 8. Maize-crushers or Triturating Stones.
7. Stone upon which Nuts were cracked.

PLATE XIX. (*To face page* 338.)

Figs. 1–6. Perforated Stone Net-sinkers.
7–11. Grooved " "
12. Fishing Plummet.

PLATE XX. (*To face page* 348.)

Figs. 1–13. Discoidal Stones.

PLATE XXI. (*To face page* 358.)

Figs. 1–6. Stone Tubes.

PLATE XXII. (*To face page* 366.)

Fig. 1. Stone for rounding Arrow-shafts.
2 and 3. Pierced Tablets.
4. Slung-stone.
5. Amulet.
6. Stone Plate.
7. Whetstone.

PLATE XXIII. (*To face page* 404.)

Figs. 1–9. Typical Forms of Calumets.

PLATE XXIV. (*To face page* 410.)

Figs. 1–7. Typical Forms of Common Clay and Stone Pipes.

PLATE XXV. *To face page* 430.)

Figs. 1–9. Clay Images.

PLATE XXVI. (*To face page* 432.)

Figs. 1–3. Front, Side and Rear Views of the Stone Image found in the Etowah Valley, Georgia.

PLATE XXVII. (*To face page* 454.)

Fig. 1. Burial-Urn.
2. Large Earthen Pot.
3 and 4. Jars.
5–7. Pots with Ears.
8. Pot with Legs.
9 and 10. Bowls.

PLATE XXVIII. (*To face page* 456.)

Fig. 1. Jar.
2. Burial-Urn.
3 and 4. Vessels with Narrow Necks.
5–10. Pottery from Stone Graves of Tennessee.

PLATE XXIX. (*To face page* 458.)

Figs. 1–32. Sherds, showing the Ornamentation of Primitive Pottery.

PLATE XXX. (*To face page* 502.)

Figs. 1 and 2. Wampum or Shell Money.
3 and 4. Shell Gorgets.
5–7. Shell Pins.
8. The Oliva as a Shell Bead.
9. The Marginella as a Shell Bead.
10–12. Imperforate Columns of Sea-Shells as Articles of Commerce.
13. Bone Bead.
14–19. Typical Forms of Shell Beads.

WOODCUTS.

1. Buried Canoe from the Savannah-River Swamp, . . PAGE 53
2. Bartram's Plan of the "Chunk-Yard" of the Muscogulges or Creeks, 179
3. Two Views of a Sculptured Rock in Forsyth County, Georgia, . 378

ANTIQUITIES

OF THE

SOUTHERN INDIANS.

CHAPTER I.

Location of Tribes.—Physical Characteristics of the Southern Indians.—System of Government.—The Mico.—The Head War-Chief.—Public Buildings in a Creek Village.—Mode of Warfare.—Office of High-Priest.—Sun-Worship.—Offering of the Stag.—Idol-Worship.—Religious Ideas.—The Sun among the Natchez.—The Cacica of Cutifachiqui.—Mausoleum of Talomeco.—Tombs of the Virginia Kings.

By letters patent, dated the 9th of June, 1732, King George II. incorporated the trustees for establishing the colony of Georgia in America, and conveyed to them and their successors "seven-eighths of all that territory lying between the Savannah and Alatamaha Rivers, and westwardly from the heads of the said rivers respectively, in direct lines, to the south seas." In this alienation were embraced all islands within twenty leagues of the coast. Including a large portion of the present States of Alabama and Mississippi, this grant claimed an extension, in a westerly direction, as indefinite as was then the geographical knowledge of the region intended to be comprised in the royal feofment.

Of the Indian nations, east of the Mississippi River, occupying and living adjacent to this territory about the beginning of the eighteenth century, the dominant peoples were the Uchees, Lower, Middle, and Upper Creeks—constituting the formidable MUSCOGEE CONFEDERACY—the Yamasees, the Cherokees, the Chickasaws, the Choctaws, the Natchez and the Seminoles.[1] East of the Savannah River resided the Catawbas, the Savannahs, and the Westoes—the latter tribe including the Stonoes and the Edistoes—cruel and hostile peoples, between whom and the Carolina colonists early and prolonged warfare ensued. The Yamasees are mentioned by Governor Archdale[2] as living about eighty miles from Charleston, and extending their hunting excursions nearly to St. Augustine. This was in 1695. Between the Westoes and the Savannahs—both potent tribes and numbered by "many thousands"—a violent civil strife arose, in consequence of which they were greatly reduced in population and resources. This contest resulted in the final overthrow and expulsion of the Westoes—"the more cruel of the two"—the Savannahs continuing "good friends and useful neighbors to the English."[3] Smallpox and other unusual sicknesses are said, at an early period of the English colonization of Carolina, to have wrought sad havoc among the natives.

Surveyor-General Lawson describes the Savannahs as a "famous, warlike, friendly nation of *Indians* liv-

[1] *See* Bowen's map of Georgia, etc. London, 1764. Jeffery's map of Florida. London, 1773. Gallatin's map. "Archæologia Americana," vol. ii., p. 265.

The Chickasaws are described by Captain Romans[1] as a fierce, cruel, insolent, and haughty race, corrupt in morals, filthy in discourse, lazy, powerful, and well-made, expert swimmers, good warriors and excellent hunters. The Choctaws, on the contrary, he praises as a nation of farmers, inclined to peace and industry.

[2] "Description of Carolina," etc., p. 19. London, 1707.

[3] Archdale's "Description of Carolina," p. 3. London, 1707.

---

[1] "Concise Natural History of East and West Florida," pp. 59–67, 71. New York, 1775.

ing to the *south* end of Ashly River."[1] They probably derived their name from the river whose banks they inhabited, and it is Mr. Gallatin's opinion[2] that they and the Yamasees were one and the same people, the latter being the true Indian name.

These Yamasees and their confederates were, in 1715, routed by Governor Craven and driven across the Savannah River into the arms of the Spaniards in Florida. It is not improbable that the Yamacraws, who were occupying the present site of the city of Savannah when General Oglethorpe landed and established the colony of Georgia, were a remnant of this tribe. Among the allies of the Yamasees the Uchees were numbered, and they, too, after this signal discomfiture, contented themselves with a residence in the everglades of Florida. Theirs, of all the Indian languages of this region, was the most uncouth and guttural. Bartram asserts that their national language was radically different from the Muscogulgee tongue. He was informed by the traders that their dialect was the same as that of the Shawnees. Although at one time confederated with the Creeks, they refused to mix with them and excited the jealousy of that whole nation.

The Chickasaws at one period occupied the left bank of the Savannah River opposite Augusta.[3]

About the date of the colonization of Georgia, the territory of the Creek Confederacy—including lands inhabited by the Seminoles—was bounded on the west by Mobile River and by the ridge separating the waters of the Tombigbee from those of the Alabama (the latter being the contested boundary-line be-

[1] "History of Carolina," p. 42. London, 1714.

[2] Synopsis of the Indian Tribes, "Archæologia Americana," vol. ii., p. 84.

[3] Haywood's "Aboriginal History of Tennessee," p. 290.

tween the Creeks and the Choctaws), on the north by the Cherokees, on the northeast by the Savannah River, and on every other side by the Atlantic Ocean and the Gulf of Mexico. It is believed, at the end of the seventeenth century, that south of the thirty-fourth degree of north latitude the Creeks occupied the eastern as well as the western bank of the Savannah. It cannot now be ascertained with certainty when the consolidation of this confederacy was effected. "It is probable," says Mr. Gallatin, "that the appellation of Appalachians was geographical, and applied to the Indians living on the Appalachicola or Chattahoochee River, as the name of Creeks seems to have been given from an early time to those inhabiting generally the country adjacent to the Savannah River." Of the Creek Confederacy, by far the most numerous and powerful nation was the Muscogee.[1] The Hitchittees, who resided on the Chattahoochee and Flint Rivers, although a distinct tribe, spoke a dialect of the Muscogee. The Seminoles, or Isty-semole (wild men), inhabiting the peninsula of Florida, were pure Muscogees, and received that name because they subsisted principally by hunting and devoted but little attention to agriculture.[2]

When questioned as to their origin, the Muscogees responded that the prevailing tradition among them was, that their progenitors had issued out of a cave near the Alabama River. The account given by the Hitchittees of their beginning was scarcely less fanciful. They claimed that their ancestors had fallen from the sky.

[1] "Concise Natural History of East and West Florida," etc., by Captain Bernard Romans. New York, 1775.

[2] Gallatin's Synopsis of the Indian Tribes. "Archæologia Americana," vol. ii., p. 94.

"The Chactaws," says Captain Romans, "have told me of a hole between their nation and the Chicasaws, out of which their whole, very numerous nation, walked forth at once, without so much as warning any neighbor."[1]

The Uchees and the Natchez both acknowledged allegiance to the Creek Confederacy. The original seats of the Uchees are thought to have been east of the Coosa, and probably of the Chattahoochee. They declared themselves the most ancient inhabitants of the country, and it has been suggested that they were the peoples called Appalaches by the historians of De Soto's expedition. Their country was mentioned as a land abounding in towns and subsistence. Early in the eighteenth century, they occupied the western bank of the Savannah River; and, as late as 1736, claimed the country both above and below Augusta. The name of at least one creek in Columbia County perpetuates at once their memory and the fact of their former occupancy of this region.

A residue of the Natchez forsook their old habitat on the banks of the Mississippi, and, journeying eastward, associated themselves with the Creeks less than one hundred and fifty years ago. The principal towns of the Creeks were Cussetah, Cowetah, Tukawbatchie, and Oscoochee.[2] The Muscogee, the Hitchittee, the Uchee, the Natchez, and the Alibamon or Coosada, were the principal languages spoken by the various tribes composing the Creek Confederacy. On the 12th of March, 1733, General Oglethorpe mentions the Lower and Upper Creeks, and the Uchees, as the three

[1] "Concise Natural History of East and West Florida," p. 58. New York, 1775.

[2] "Archæologia Americana," vol. ii., p. 95.

most powerful Indian nations in Georgia between the mountains and the coast. The Lower Creeks consisted of nine towns or cantons, and their warriors were estimated by him at one thousand. The military strength of the Upper Creeks he computes at eleven hundred men capable of bearing arms, while it was supposed that the Uchees were at that time unable to bring into the field more than two hundred bow-men. This estimate is evidently too small, and was vaguely formed. De Brahm,[1] at a later date, reckons the population of the Upper and Lower Creeks at fifteen thousand men, women, and children, and rates their warriors and gunmen above three thousand. To Colonel Hawkins[2] we are indebted for a very valuable sketch of the Creek country in 1798 and 1799.

The Creeks are described as powerful warriors, great politicians, and full of jealousy. They were a terror to the Cherokees and to the various Indian nations with whom they waged ceaseless wars.[3]

Captain Romans[4] enumerates remnants of the Cawittas, Talepoosas, Coosas, Apalachias, Conshacs, or Coosades, Oakmulgis, Oconis, Okchoys, Alibamons, Natchez, Weetumkus, Pakanas, Taënsas, Chacsihoomas, Abékas, and of other tribes, whose names he did not recollect, all calling themselves *Muscokees*, and constituting what was known as the *Creek Confederacy*.

"The territories of the Cherokees, Chelakees, or more properly, Tsalakies," says Mr. Gallatin, "extended

[1] "History of the Province of Georgia," etc., p. 55. Wormsloe, 1849.

[2] "Collections of the Georgia Historical Society," vol. iii., part 1., p. 18, *et seq.* Savannah, 1848. *See*, also, "A Voyage to Georgia," begun in the year 1735, by Francis Moore, p. 61. London, 1744.

[3] "History of the Province of Georgia," by De Brahm, p. 55. Wormsloe, 1849. Adair's "History of the North-American Indians," p. 257, *et seq.* London, 1775. "Travels," etc., by William Bartram, p. 461, *et seq.* London, 1792.

[4] "Concise Natural History of East and West Florida," etc., p. 90. New York, 1775.

north and south of the southwesterly continuation of the Appalachian Mountains, embracing on the north the country on Tennessee or Cherokee River and its tributary streams, from their sources down to the vicinity of the Muscle Shoals, where they were bounded on the west by the Chicasas. The Cumberland mountain may be considered as having been the boundary on the north; but, since the country has been known to us, no other Indian nation, except some small bands of Shawnoes, had any settlement between that mountain and the Ohio." On the west side of the Savannah, the Cherokees were confronted on the south by the Creeks, the division-line being Broad River and generally along the thirty-fourth parallel of north latitude. East of the Savannah, their original seats embraced the upper waters of that river, of the Santee, and, probably, of the Yadkin, but could not have extended as far south as the thirty-fourth degree of north latitude. They were bounded on the south, probably, by Muskhogee tribes in the vicinity of the Savannah, and, farther east, by the Catawbas.[1]

Between the Shawnoes and the Cherokees prolonged strife occurred, which resulted in the expulsion of the former from the country south of the Ohio. With the Creeks also the Cherokees were constantly at variance. When in 1730 the whites interposed their good offices to bring about a pacification between the Tuscaroras and the Cherokees, the latter responded: "We cannot live without war; should we make peace with the Tuscaroras, with whom we are at war, we must immediately look out for some other with whom we can be engaged in our beloved occupation."[2]

[1] "Archæologia Americana," vol. ii., p. 90.

[2] Haywood's "Natural and Aboriginal History of Tennessee," p. 238. Nashville, 1823.

The history of the Cherokees is marked by continued and prolonged struggles. Their country being strong, their men trained to arms, and the integrity of the nation at all times wonderfully preserved, these peoples do not appear, in their territorial possessions, to have been materially injured by their frequent contests with adjacent tribes. In 1762 Adair estimated the number of their warriors at three thousand two hundred, and adds, he was informed that, forty years before, they had at least six thousand men capable of bearing arms.[1]

In perpetuating his impressions of the PHYSICAL CHARACTERISTICS of the Southern Indians, Mr. Bartram[2] writes: "The males of the Cherokees, Muscogulgees, Siminoles, Chicasaws, Chactaws, and confederate tribes of the Creeks, are tall, erect, and moderately robust; their limbs well shaped, so as generally to form a perfect human figure; their features regular and countenance open, dignified, and placid; yet the forehead and brow so formed as to strike you instantly with heroism and bravery; the eye, though rather small, active and full of fire; the iris always black, and the nose commonly inclining to the aquiline. Their countenance and actions exhibit an air of magnanimity, superiority, and independence. Their complexion of a reddish brown or copper color; their hair long, lank, coarse, and black as a raven, and reflecting the like lustre at different exposures to the light. The women of the Cherokees are tall, slender, erect, and of a delicate frame; their features formed with perfect symmetry, their countenance cheerful and friendly; and they move with a becoming grace and dignity.

[1] "History of the American Indians," p. 227. London, 1775.

[2] "Travels through North and South Carolina, Georgia," etc., p. 481. London, 1792.

"The Muscogulgee women, though remarkably short of stature, are well formed; their visage round, features regular and beautiful, the brow high and arched; the eye large, black, and languishing, expressive of modesty, diffidence, and bashfulness; these charms are their defensive and offensive weapons; and they know very well how to play them off; and, under cover of these alluring graces, are concealed the most subtle artifices; they are, however, loving and affectionate; they are, I believe, the smallest race of women yet known, seldom above five feet high, and I believe the greater number never arrive to that stature; their hands and feet not larger than those of Europeans of nine or ten years of age; yet the men are of gigantic stature, a full size larger than Europeans; many of them above six feet, and few under that, or five feet eight or ten inches. Their complexion much darker than any of the tribes to the north of them that I have seen. This description will, I believe, comprehend the Muscogulges, their confederates, the Chactaws, and, I believe, the Chicasaws (though I have never seen their women), excepting some bands of the Siminoles, Uches, and Savaunucas, who are rather taller and slenderer and their complexion brighter.

"The Cherokees are yet taller and more robust than the Muscogulges, and by far the largest race of men I have seen; their complexions brighter and somewhat of the olive cast, especially the adults; and some of their young women are nearly as fair and blooming as European women.

"The Cherokees, in their dispositions and manners, are grave and steady; dignified and circumspect in their deportment; rather slow and reserved in conversation; yet frank, cheerful, and humane; tenacious of the liberties and natural rights of man; secret, deliberate, and determined in their councils; honest, just, and liberal, and ready always to sacrifice every pleasure and gratification, even their blood and life itself to defend their territory and maintain their rights. . . .

"The national character of the Muscogulges, when considered in a political view, exhibits a protraiture of a great or illustrious hero. A proud, haughty, and arrogant race of men, they are brave and valiant in war, ambitious of conquest, restless and perpetually exercising their arms, yet magnanimous and merciful to a vanquished enemy when he submits and seeks their friendship and protection; always uniting the vanquished tribes in confederacy with them: when they immediately enjoy, unexceptionably, every right of free citizens, and are, from that moment, united in one common band of brotherhood. They were never known to exterminate a tribe, except the Yamasees, who would never submit on any terms, but fought it out to the last, only about forty or fifty of them escaping at the last decisive battle, who threw themselves under the protection of the Spaniards, at St. Augustine. . . . The Muscogulges are more volatile, sprightly, and talkative, than their northern neighbors, the Cherokees."

The SYSTEM OF GOVERNMENT obtaining among these Southern nations seems, in its general features, to have been quite similar. In the Muscogulgee confederacy every town or village was regarded as an independent nation or tribe having its own mico or chief. In the soil and in the hunting privileges of the region each inhabitant had an equal right. Private property in habitations and in planting-grounds, however, was conceded and respected.

The MICO[1] was considered the first man, in dignity and power, in his nation or town. He was the supreme civil magistrate, and presided over the national council. His executive power was not independent, however, of the council, which convened every day, in the forenoon, in the public square. This office of mico or king was elective. The advancement to this supreme dignity was always conferred upon the person most worthy of it.

Next in the order of dignity and power was the GREAT WAR-CHIEF. He led the army. In council his seat was nearest the mico, on his left, and at the head of the most celebrated warriors. On the right of the mico sat the second head-man of the tribe, and below him the younger warriors of the nation.

When assembled in the Great Rotunda, or Winter Council-House, for the purpose of deliberating upon matters of general concern, the most profound respect and homage were paid by every one to the mico. To him the members of the council bowed very low, almost to his feet, when the cup-bearer handed him the shell filled with the black-drink.[2] This decoction of the leaves and tender twigs of the *cassine* or *ilex yupon* was freely used by the natives upon occasions of solemn deliberation. Being a most active and powerful diuretic, its purgative influences were invoked to free their bodies from all hinderance to thought; and, thus prepared for careful discussion, they entered upon the consideration of the important matters presented for the action of council. De Bry presents us with a spirited sketch of the king and warriors in convention

[1] "Transactions of the American Ethnological Society," vol. iii., part 1, p. 23. Compare Lawson's "History of Carolina," p. 195. London, 1714.

[2] "Brevis Narratio," plate xxix. Francoforti ad Mœnum, De Bry. Anno 1591.

assembled, drinking freely of this cassine from shell-cups and listening to the animated address of one of the principal men. When out of the council-house, and unemployed in public affairs, the intercourse between the mico and the common people was cordial and free from restraint. If we may credit the representations of De Bry,[1] no little ceremony was observed when the kings and queens of the Florida tribes appeared in public. The mico alone had the disposal of the corn and fruits collected in the public granary. These general storehouses, circular in form—their walls constructed of stone and earth, and their roofs fashioned with the branches of trees, grass, clay, and palmetto-leaves—were located in the neighborhood of streams and in retired spots where they were protected from the direct rays of the sun. They were built and furnished by the common labor of the tribe, and in them were stored corn, various fruits, and the flesh of fishes, deer, alligators, snakes, dogs, and other animals, previously smoked and dried on a scaffold.[2]

With the first fruits of the season was the king complimented. It was his province to give audience to ambassadors, deputies, and strangers, and to him were public presents offered. He alone had the privilege of giving a general feast to an entire village, on which occasion the king's standard was displayed in front of his house, a flag hoisted in the public square, drums beat about the town, and the inhabitants busily engaged in painting and dressing themselves for the festivities. In the sixteenth century, the Florida warriors, when about to set out on a hostile expedition,

[1] "Brevis Narratio," plates xxxvii., xxxviii., and xxxix. Francoforti ad Mœnum. Anno 1591.

[2] *See* plates xxii., xxiii., and xxiv., of the "Brevis Narratio."

assembled round their king, who, taking a dipper of water and sprinkling them, exclaimed, "As I have scattered this water, so do you cause the blood of your enemies to flow freely." Then, with water from another vessel, extinguishing a fire kindled in the circle, he added, "As I have put out this flame, so may you vanquish and destroy your antagonists."[1]

It would appear that, on some occasions, the king, when about to enter into battle, was borne upon a platform elevated upon the heads and shoulders of his men.[2]

The care and protection of widows, whose husbands had fallen in battle or perished by disease, devolved upon the king.[3]

Capital punishment was meted out in the presence of the mico and council seated in a semicircle, the victim kneeling in the centre, and the executioner, his left foot upon the back of the criminal, with a stout, paddle-shaped club made of hard wood, striking him upon the top of the head with such violence as to split the skull.[4]

The custom obtained among some of the Southern nations of sacrificing to the king the first-born male child.[5]

The office of king was for life, or during good behavior.

It cannot be denied that to the kingly office, among most of the Southern tribes, appertained despotic powers. Especially was this the fact at the period of our first acquaintance with the form of government dominant among these peoples. By at least

[1] "Brevis Narratio," plate xi. [2] Ibid., plate xiii. [3] Ibid., plate xxiii. [4] Ibid., plate xxxii. [5] Ibid., plate xxxiii.

one of the early historians are we assured that, in saluting a cacique, the subject used gestures, somewhat modified in degree, but similar in form to those employed in the adoration of the sun. The intimation is that in his person and position were recognized a superiority, a dignity, and an authority near akin, but subordinate to those which inhered in the celestial luminary—the most potent and admirable representative of the goodness and supremacy of the Great Spirit.

Colonel Hawkins[1] thus epitomizes the duties of the Creek mico in 1798: The mico of the town superintends all public and domestic concerns, receives all public characters, hears their talks, lays them before the town and delivers the talks of his town. The mico of a town is always chosen from some one family. The mico of Tuck-au-bat-che is of the eagle tribe (Lum-ul-gee). After he is chosen and put on his seat, he remains for life. On his death, if his nephews are fit for the office, one of them takes his place as his successor; if they are unfit, one is chosen of the next of kin, the descent being always in the female line.

When a mico, from age, infirmity, or any other cause, wants an assistant, he selects a man who appears to him the best qualified, and proposes him to the councillors and great men of the town, and, if he is approved by them, they appoint him as an assistant in public affairs.

The mico, councillors, and warriors, meet every day in the public square, sit and drink ā-cee—a strong decoction of the cassine yupon, called by the traders

[1] "Sketch of the Creek Country." Collections of the Georgia Historical Society, vol. iii., part i., p. 69. Savannah, 1848.

black-drink—talk of news, the public and domestic concerns, smoke their pipes and play thla-chal-litch-cau. They have a regular ceremony for making as well as delivering the ā-cee to all who attend the square. In all transactions which require secrecy the rulers meet in the chooc-ofau-thluc-co—the *rotunda* or *assembly-room* called by the traders *hot-house*—kindle the spiral fire, deliberate, and decide. When they have decided on any case of death or whipping, the mico appoints the warriors who are to carry it into effect, or he gives the judgment to the great warrior (tustunnuggee-thluc-co) and leaves to him the time and manner of executing it.

War is always determined on by the great warrior. If the mico and warriors are of opinion that the town has been injured, it is the province of the former to lift the hatchet against the offending nation. Even after a declaration of war, however, the mico and councillors may interpose and proceed to adjust the misunderstanding by negotiations.

Peace is concluded by the mico and councillors, and peace-talks are always addressed to the cabin of the mico. It is the privilege of the mico and councillors to fix the precise time for the celebration of the annual festival of the Boos-ke-tau.

Of the buildings which formed the public square in the Creek villages, the first in rank was the mic-ul-gee-in-too-pau, or mico's cabin. It fronts the east. The centre of this building is occupied by the mico, the right division by the mic-ug-gee and the councillors, and the left division by the people second in command, who have the direction of the public works appertaining to the town.

Second in rank is the tus-tun-nug-ul-gee-in-too-pau,

or warrior's cabin. This fronts the south. At the west end of this cabin sits the head-warrior. In this division are seated also the great warriors. The next in rank sit in the centre division, and the young warriors in the third. These warriors rise by merit, and the great-warrior is selected by the mico and councillors as the most noted of all the warriors. The cabin of the beloved men—is-te-chăguc-ul-gee-in-too-pau—fronts north and is erected for the accommodation of those who have been war-leaders and who have rendered themselves distinguished by a long course of valuable public service. Last in rank is hut-te-mau-hug-gee-in-too-pau—the cabin of the young people and their associates. This fronts the west. To these may be added the chooc-ofau-thluc-co—the rotunda, or assembly-room, called by the traders *hot-house.* In the centre of this is the spiral fire. This is the assembly-room for all people, old and young. Here they congregate every night, and amuse themselves with dancing, singing, or conversation. In this building sometimes, in very cold weather, the old and naked sleep.

In the absence of the mico, the GREAT WAR-CHIEF[1] represented him in council, and his voice was of the greatest weight in military affairs. His authority was independent of the mico, although, should the mico enter upon a military expedition, he was entitled to the command. Subordinate to the great war-captain were leaders of parties—elderly men distinguished for valor, strategy and intrepidity. Of such were their dignified and venerable councils composed.

Having by fasts and purifications prepared themselves for the expedition, having consulted the high-

[1] "Bartram's Travels," p. 494. London, 1792.

priest,[1] with regard to the success of the enterprise, and obtained from him a favorable response, fantastically painted and plumed, each carrying a small bag of parched corn, and armed with a long bow and quiver of arrows suspended from the right hip, and frequently with a formidable club made of hard wood, and a spear,[2] the warriors set off from the village with a great noise and defiant shouts. The head-warrior, taking the lead, was followed by the rest in single file. When near the hostile town or in the vicinity of the spot where a meeting with the enemy was anticipated, the most profound silence and careful circumspection were observed. Their conduct then resembled the action of the concealed lynx waiting for an opportunity to pounce upon its prey in an unguarded moment. A sudden attack, a fearful succession of wild yells, an indiscriminate massacre, and the demolition by fire of the habitations of their enemies, and then a hasty return with captives and bloody trophies of the pillage and butchery—these constituted, as a general rule, the sum total of a successful military excursion. "Their maner of warres," says Thomas Hariot,[3] "amongst themselues is either by sudden surprising one an other most commonly about the dawning of the day, or moone light; or els by ambushes, or some suttle deuises: Set battels are very rare, except it fall out where there are many trees, where eyther part may haue some hope of defence, after the deliuerie of euery arrow, in leaping behind some or other." The Southern Indians are said

[1] "Brevis Narratio," plate xii. [2] Ibid., plate xiv.

[3] "A Briefe and True Report of the New-found-land of Virginia," etc., p. 25. Francoforti ad Mœnum. De Bry, anno 1590. Compare also Du Pratz's "History of Louisiana," chapter iii., book iv., sec. vii., vol. ii., p. 242, *et seq.* London, 1763. Smith's "History of Virginia," Richmond reprint, 1819, vol. i., p. 132.

to have dealt less cruelly with their captives than did their Northern neighbors. The Spaniards found to their cost that the natives were very ready with their weapons.

Says the Gentleman of Elvas,[1] "The Indians are so warlike and nimble that they have no fear of footmen; for if these charge them, they flee, and when they turn their backs they are presently upon them. They avoid nothing more easily than the flight of an arrow. They never remain quiet, but are continually running, traversing from place to place, so that neither cross-bow nor arquebuse can be aimed at them. Before a Christian can make a single shot with either, an Indian will discharge three or four arrows, and he seldom misses of his object. Where the arrow meets with no armour, it pierces as deeply as the shaft from a cross-bow. Their bows are very perfect; the arrows are made of certain canes, like reeds, very heavy, and so stiff that one of them, when sharpened, will pass through a target. Some are pointed with the bone of a fish, sharp and like a chisel; others with some stone, like a point of diamond: of such, the greater number, where they strike upon armour, break at the place where the parts are put together; those of cane split, and will enter a shirt of mail, doing more injury than when armed."

A public declaration of war was sometimes made by planting arrows along the pathway leading to the principal village of the enemy.[2] They also were able, by means of ignited tufts of dried moss and grass, attached to the heads of their arrows, to set fire to the thatched cabins located in the fortified towns of their

[1] "Narratives of the Career of Hernando de Soto in the Conquest of Florida," translated by Buckingham Smith, p. 26. New York, 1846.

[2] "Brevis Narratio," plate xxxii.

adversaries.[1] The wretched cruelties visited even upon the dead bodies of the hostile slain are shockingly portrayed by De Bry in plate xv. of the "Brevis Narratio."

Courage, craft, perseverance, physical endurance, stoicism, ability to counsel with wisdom and eloquence, experience in combat, and activity and skill in the use of weapons, must all have been acquired and exhibited in a marked manner before the Southern Indian came to be regarded as a leading warrior in his nation. His honor and love of country he esteemed of far greater value than life; and the most exquisite tortures failed to compel him to surrender and compromise the one, or renounce the other. In the arts of strategy, ambuscade, deception, and personal concealment, they excelled. Mr. Adair,[2] in his general observations on the North American Indians, presents us with a detailed account of the martial spirit, devotion to country, caution in war, method of fighting, cruelty to captives, fortitude in view of death, and the triumphs accorded to successful warriors, as they existed among the Southern Indians during the period of his residence among them, which, did the limits of this general sketch permit, we would gladly here reproduce.

A person of great power and consequence was the Ancient High-Priest. He presided in spiritual affairs; and, in military matters, his influence was most potent. Never did the council determine upon a hostile expedition without his counsel and sanction.[3] To him was accorded the ability to hold personal communion with invisible spirits capable of exerting a con-

[1] "Brevis Narratio," plate xxxi.

[2] "History of the American Indians," etc., pp. 377, *et seq.* London, 1775.

[3] "Brevis Narratio," plate xii.

trolling influence over human plans. Through him the elements were propitiated, and his capability to foresee the result of an enterprise was unquestioned.

So great, remarks Mr. Bartram,[1] is the influence of these high-priests, that they have been frequently known to stop and turn back an army after a march of several hundred miles, and when it had approached within a day's journey of the enemy. Their predictions were frequently surprising. They pretended, moreover, to foretell the coming of a drought, and to be able to bring rain upon the thirsty zea, to cure diseases, invoke or expel the presence of evil spirits, cause the tempest to cease, and direct the thunder and lightning. It was their office to mediate between the beloved red-people and the bountiful, holy spirit of Fire. With their advice the season was set for planting, and occasions were designated for the solemnization of the public religious festivals. In every town they had their juniors or graduates learned in the conjurer's and medicine-man's arts.

Among the Southern tribes the sun was regarded as the symbol of the power and beneficence of the Great Spirit, the Supreme God, or Creator, the soul and governor of the universe, the giver and taker-away of the breath of life. Hence, to this celestial luminary did they pay profound homage as to the visible minister and representative of the author of life, and light, and heat. To it their vows were offered as they puffed the smoke from the great calumet toward the heavens. With reverence did they look upon the face of this God of Day, as they deliberated in council, or set out upon the war-path. Fire,

[1] "Travels," etc., p. 495. London, 1792. "Transactions of the American Ethnological Society," vol. iii., part i., p. 24.

as an emanation from this celestial source, they venerated and propitiated with mysterious rites and ceremonies. Temples were erected at great cost of material and labor for this sun-worship, in which priests officiated. Their province it was to guard the Eternal Fire in the Rotunda; and, in the solemn, annual festival of the Busque, when all the fires of the nation were extinguished, the high-priest alone—ministering between the Great Spirit and man—was commissioned, in the temple, to reproduce the celestial spark and give new fire to the community.

Believing in the immortality of the soul, in a future state of rewards and punishments, acknowledging the supreme power and control of one great, invisible, supreme spirit, these Southern Indians were plagued with an apprehension of visions, dreams, trances, and malign influences of lesser divinities, which afforded ample scope for the operation by priests and conjurers using incantations, charms, and mysterious appliances upon their hopes and fears, credulity, and superstitions. Upon the death of a high-priest, the entire community united in paying the fullest funeral honors, and heaped above him the conical earth-mound.[1]

If we may credit the assertion of the Gentleman of Elvas,[2] some of the Florida tribes worshipped the devil, and made offerings of human sacrifices to the spirit of evil.

Toward the latter part of February in each year, the Indians of Florida, taking the skin of the largest stag they had killed, stuffed it with the choicest fruits and matters which chiefly delighted them. The horns,

[1] "Brevis Narratio," plate xl.

[2] "Narratives of the Career of Hernando de Soto," etc., translated by Buckingham Smith, p. 31. New York, 1866.

neck, and body were encircled with vines and fruits most rare. Thus attired, the stag, with music and parade, was carried and placed upon the top of a tall tree, with its head and breast turned full toward the rising sun. By the king and high-priest—who stationed themselves nearest the tree—prayers were addressed to this celestial luminary, and petitions offered that he would be pleased to reproduce the good gifts which were then presented. The members of the tribe assembled in a circle, and, at a little remove, repeated these supplications. When they were finished, all having saluted the sun, departed, leaving the stuffed and garlanded stag until the recurrence of the same season, when, on each ensuing year, similar ceremonies were observed.[1]

It is probable that some of the larger terraced mounds and truncated pyramids were temples erected in honor of, and devoted to the worship of the sun.

Within the historic period idol-worship existed, at least to a limited extent, among the Southern Indians. We will have occasion, however, in a subsequent chapter, to consider this interesting subject somewhat at length.

Among the Natchez the machinery of temples, idols, priests, keepers of sacred things, and sundry religious festivals, was most elaborate. The preservation of the eternal fire engaged their utmost solicitude. The Sun ruled with despotic power, and seemed in his person to unite the privileges of king and high-priest. Here were observed more emphatically than among any other Southern tribes the distinctions of rank. The common people—or Miche-Miche-Quipy (Stinkards) —were, to the last degree, submissive to the nobility,

[1] "Brevis Narratio," plate xxv.

consisting of Suns, nobles, and men of rank. These Suns claimed to be the descendants of the man and woman who came down from the sun; and their children, to the remotest degree, were distinguished above the bulk of the nation and enjoyed an exemption from capital punishment. By them it was ordained that nobility should be transmitted only through the women. Upon the death of a Sun, many subjects, both male and female, were sacrificed. No greater calamity could befall the nation than the extinction of the eternal fire.[1]

The great chief of the Natchez bore the appellation of THE SUN. He was succeeded in the kingly office by the son of the woman who was most nearly related to him.[2] To this woman the title of *woman chief* was given. Great honors were paid to her, although she meddled not in affairs of state. Like the great chief, she possessed the power of life and death over the common people, and did not hesitate to order her guards to slay any who offended her.

Every morning, says Father Charlevoix,[3] as soon as the sun appears, the great chief comes to the door of his cabin, turns himself to the east, and howls three times, bowing down to the earth. Then they bring him a calumet, which is used only for this purpose. This he smokes, and blows the smoke of the tobacco first toward the sun, and then toward the other three cardinal points. He acknowledges no superior other than the sun. From this luminary he claims to

[1] *See* Du Pratz's "History of Louisiana," vol. ii., chap. iii., sec. 2–4, pp. 170, 222. London, 1763.

[2] Among the Carolina Indians the succession fell not to the king's son, but to his sister's son (Lawson's "History of Carolina," p. 195. London, 1714), and it appears that a similar rule obtained among other Southern tribes.

[3] "Voyage to North America," etc., vol. ii., p. 196. Dublin, 1766.

derive his origin. Over his subjects he exercises unlimited power, can dispose at pleasure of their property and lives, and pays no recompense for any labors he may demand of them.

The death of a great chief costs the lives of his guards, and sometimes of more than a hundred persons. At one time very few of the principal personages died without being escorted to the country of souls by some of their relations, friends, or servants. Suspecting the death of De Soto, the Cacique of Guachoya ordered two well-proportioned young Indian men to be brought, saying it was the usage of the country, when any lord died, to kill some persons who might accompany and serve him on the way to the spirit-land. He, therefore, ordered their heads to be struck off, and it was only after much persuasion, and upon the emphatic statement that the governor was not dead but had only gone on a visit to the heavens, attended by a suitable number of soldiers, that Luys de Moscoso succeeded in effecting the release of these young Indians.[1]

The tribes encountered by De Soto during his march east of the Mississippi were ruled over by caciques to whom their subjects yielded implicit obedience. The province of Cutifachiqui, however, was governed by a cacica who welcomed the Spanish adventurer right royally, and extended to him the hospitalities of her kingdom. The stern of her canoe was covered with an awning, and she sat upon cushions. The country was delightful and fertile, and here were found, in the possession of the natives and in the barbacoas, large quantities of clothing, and shawls

[1] "Narratives of the Career of Hernando De Soto," translated by Buckingham Smith, p. 148. New York, 1866.

made of fibres of the bark of trees and of feathers richly colored in white, gray, vermilion, and yellow, suitable for winter wear—well-dressed deer-skins with various designs depicted upon them—and many pearls. The inhabitants, says the Gentleman of Elvas, were brown of skin, well formed and admirably proportioned. He distinctly affirms that they were more civilized than any peoples he had seen in all the territories of Florida, and that they wore clothes and shoes. To this cacica her subjects paid great respect, and her niece was at first commissioned to meet De Soto and assure him of the good-will of the queen. Mention is also made of the queen-mother, a widow, who, reposing upon her dignity, refused to hold converse with the strangers.

At Talomeco was a mausoleum a hundred paces in length and forty in breadth, with lofty roofs of reed. The entrance to this temple was guarded by gigantic wooden statues, carved with considerable skill, the largest of them being twelve feet high. Armed with various weapons, they stood in threatening attitudes and with ferocious looks. Within were statues of various shapes and sizes. Around the sepulchre were benches upon which, in wooden chests skilfully wrought, but without locks or hinges, reposed the bodies of the departed caciques, priests, and chieftains of Cutifachiqui. Beside these were smaller chests, and cane baskets filled with valuable furs, robes of dressed skins, and mantles made of the inner rind of trees and of a species of grass which, when beaten, closely resembled flax. There were coverings formed of feathers of various colors, which the natives wore in winter. This temple also contained great store of pearls.

Adjacent to this grand sepulchral receptacle were

several buildings which served as armories. In them weapons of various sorts were carefully arranged and kept in order by numerous attendants.[1] The erection of temples or buildings, and their dedication to the preservation of the bodies of their chiefs obtained also among other Southern tribes. Thus, in plate xxii. of the "Admiranda Narratio," we have a representation of one of these sepulchres as it existed among the Virginia Indians in the sixteenth century. The explanatory note is thus quaintly "made in English" by Thomas Hariot, servant to Sir Walter Raleigh:

THE TOMBE OF THEIR WEROWANS OR CHEIFF LORDES.

"The builde a Scaffolde 9 or 10 foote hihe as is expressed in this figure under the tóbs of theit Weroans, or cheefe lordes which they couer with matts, and lai the dead corpses of their weroans thereuppon in manner followinge. First the bowells are taken forthe. Then layinge down the skinne, they cutt all the flesh cleane from the bones, which the drye in the sonne, and well dryed the inclose in Matts and place at their feete. Then their bones (remaininge still fastened together with the ligaments whole and vncorrupted) are couered agayne with leather, and their carcase fashioned as yf their flesh wear not taken away. They lapp eache corps in his owne skinne after the same in thus handled, and lay yt in his order by the corpses of the other cheef lordes. By the dead bodies they sett their idol Kiwasa, whereof we spake in the former chapiter. For they are persuaded that the same doth kepe the dead bodyes of their cheefe lordes that nothinge may hurt them. Moreouer under the foresaid scaffolde some on of their

[1] Irving's "Conquest of Florida," chapter xlviii.

preists hath his lodginge, which Mumbleth his prayers nighte and day, and hath charge of the corpses. For his bedd he hath two deares skinnes spredd on the growndе, yf the wether bee cold hee maketh a fyre to warme by withall. Thes poore soules are thus instructed by natute to reuerence their princes euen after their death."[1]

Caves were sometimes dedicated to similar uses.

[1] "A Briefe and True Report of the New-found-land of Virginia, etc., made in English by Thomas Hariot." Plate xxii. and explanatory note. Francoforti ad Mœnum. De Bry. Anno 1590.

CHAPTER II.

Office of the Conjurer or Medicine-man.—Treatment of the Sick.—Medicinal Plants.—Towns and Private Houses.—Tenure of Property.—Agricultural Pursuits.—Town Plantations and Private Gardens.—Public Granaries.—Animal and Vegetable Food.—Mechanical Labors.—Early Mining in Duke's-Creek Valley.—Manufacture of Canoes, Pottery, Copper Implements, Gold, Silver, shell, and Stone Ornaments.—Various Implements and Articles of Stone, Bone, and Wood.—Trade Relations.

ANOTHER important person in every community was the CONJURER, who generally united in himself the offices of priest, physician, and fortune-teller. He was supposed to possess unusual powers because of his constant communion with and influence over evil spirits. Various and extravagant were his incantations, his charms mysterious and unexplained, and his contortions, when engaged in the practice of his arts, prolonged and violent. His knowledge of medicinal herbs and simples gave him a decided advantage over the unlearned. Encouraging the superstitions of his patients, he pretended to work wonderful cures, and acquired wherever he went an influence most marked in its character. In the explanatory note accompanying plate xx. of the "Brevis Narratio," we are made acquainted with several methods adopted by the Florida Indians in their treatment of the sick. One remedy consisted in scarifying the forehead of the patient with a shell, and sucking therefrom the blood and humors which were supposed to contain the seeds of the disease. Others, suffering from different maladies, were compelled to lie upon their stomachs with their heads over pans, from which they inhaled, through their mouths and nostrils, the fumes of certain medicinal plants in a state of ignition. Tobacco-smoking was also employed as a means of expelling disease. To Coreal[1] we are indebted for the following interesting account of the office of the medicine-men among the Florida tribes:

"When they are sick they have not a vein opened, according to our practice, but send for their *Jaoünas* who are their priests and physicians. The latter suck that part of the body which causes the patient the greatest pain, and this they do with the mouth, and sometimes also by means of a kind of shepherd's flute (une espèce de chalumeau), after having made a small incision near some vein. They also make incisions in the suffering parts of those who submit to their treatment. Previous to the ceremony, and also after the operation, the jaoüna utters some words. Whether the patient dies or recovers, the jaoüna's gravity remains unaffected. This behavior constitutes a part of his professional art. The respect and confidence with which the savages regard these men remain the same, no matter what the result may be.

"The jaoünas also understand how to make their patients vomit by means of a powder which they prepare from calcined shells. One must be a Floridian or the devil to resist the violence of this emetic, for I doubt whether there exists a more efficient prescription for sending a European to the other world. They

[1] "Voyages de François Coreal, aux Indes Occidentales (1660–1697)." Amsterdam, 1722. Vol. i., pp. 39–41.

also bathe their sick, and when all remedies are exhausted, and no hope remains, they expose them before their cabins to the rising sun, imploring and conjuring that luminary to cure them. In all diseases the method of treatment (or succession of remedies) is the same. They begin by sucking and making incisions, after which they resort to bathing, etc., until recovery or death occurs. In all these proceedings they preserve well their presumption, which they conceal from these poor people under an affected modesty and feigned abstinence. It is true, however, that they go through a rough and long apprenticeship under the old *jaoünas*, who are the chiefs of the sect, and this doubtless enhances the confidence which the Floridians repose in these priests and physicians. These jaoünas are clad in long robes made of various skins cut into unequal bands. These robes are fastened by girdles of deerskin, to which they attach their pouches filled with herbs. Over the robe they wear, after the fashion of a cloak, the hide of some wild animal. Their feet and arms are uncovered, and they have on their heads a skin cap terminating in a point."

Of the Virginia conjurers, Hariot[1] says, they use strange gestures and are often contrary to Nature in their enchantments. They be "verye familiar with deuils, of whom they enquier what their enemys doe, or other suche thinges. They shaue all their heads sauinge their creste, which they weare as other doe, and fasten a small black birde aboue one of their ears as a badge of their office. They weare nothinge but a skinne, which hangeth downe from their gyrdle and couereth their priuityes. They weare a bagg by their

[1] "A Briefe and True Report of the New-found-land of Virginia," etc. Francoforti ad Mœnum. De Bry. Anno 1590, plate xi.

side. The Inhabitants giue great credit vnto their speeche, which oftentimes they finde to bee true."

The Natchez jugglers not only pretended to cure the sick, but also professed to procure rain and seasons favorable for the fruits of the earth. Their incantations were often directed to the dispersion of clouds and the expulsion of evil spirits from the bodies of the afflicted. They were a lazy set of fellows, imposing upon the credulity of their countrymen, and receiving rich rewards when their patients recovered.[1] The Alibamons reposed great confidence in their doctors, and regarded the ravings of these quacks and cunning impostors as the utterances of a divine language.[2]

Among the Carolina tribes the priests were the conjurers and doctors of the nation.[3] The theory was that all distempers were caused by evil spirits; consequently, none of their physicians attempted to effect a cure until he had conversed with the good spirit, and ascertained whether his aid could be secured in the effort to exorcise the adverse demon.

"As soon as the Doctor comes into the Cabin," says Surveyor-General Lawson,[4] "the sick Person is sat on a Mat or Skin, stark-naked, lying on his Back, and all uncovered, except some small Trifle that covers their Nakedness when ripe, otherwise in very young Children, there is nothing about them. In this Manner the Patient lies, when the Conjurer appears; and the King of that Nation comes to attend him with a Rattle made

[1] *See* Charlevoix's "Voyage to North America," etc., vol. ii., p. 203. Dublin, 1766.

[2] "Travels through Louisiana, by Captain Bossu," vol. i., p. 264. London, 1771.

[3] Lawson's "History of Carolina," p. 211. London, 1714.

[4] Idem, p. 214.

of a Gourd with Pease in it. This the King delivers into the Doctor's Hand, whilst another brings a Bowl of Water, and sets it down. Then the Doctor begins, and utters some few Words very softly; afterwards he smells of the Patient's Navel and Belly, and sometimes scarifies him a little with a Flint, or an Instrument made of Rattle-Snake's teeth for that Purpose; then he sucks the Patient, and gets out a Mouthful of Blood and *Serum*, but *Serum* chiefly; which, perhaps, may be a better Method in many Cases, than to take away great Quantities of Blood, as is commonly practised; which he spits in the Bowl of Water. Then he begins to mutter and talk apace, and, at last, to cut Capers and clap his Hands on his Breech and Sides, till he gets into a Sweat, so that a Stranger would think he was running mad; now and then sucking the Patient, and so, at times, keeps sucking, till he has got a great Quantity of very ill-coloured Matter out of the Belly, Arms, Breast, Forehead, Temples, Neck, and most Parts, still continuing his Grimaces and antick Postures, which are not to be matched in *Bedlam*. At last you will see the Doctor all over of a dropping Sweat, and scarce able to utter one Word, having quite spent himself; then he will cease for a while, and so begin again till he comes in the same pitch of Raving and seeming Madness as before. (All this time the sick Body never so much as moves, although, doubtless, the Lancing and Sucking must be a great Punishment to them; but they certainly are the patientest and most steady People under any Burden that I ever saw in my Life.) At last the Conjurer makes an end, and tells the Patient's Friends whether the Person will live or die; and then one that waits at this Ceremony takes the Blood away (which remains in a Lump in the middle of the Water), and buries it in the Ground, in a Place unknown to any one but he that inters it."[1] "In Medicine, or the Nature of *Simples*," says Thomas Ash,[2] "some have an exquisite knowledge; and in the Cure of *Scorbutic*, *Venereal*, and *Malignant Distempers*, are admirable. In all *External Diseases* they suck the Part affected with many *Incantations*, *Philtres*, and *Charms*."

These medicine-men also conjured for stolen goods, understood the art of coloring the human hair, cured lingering distempers by wrapping a snake around the body of the afflicted, treated affections of the spleen and of the stomach by hot applications, relieved the toothache, administered ample purges through large draughts of the *Yaupon*, comprehended the medicinal virtues of the sassafras and many native plants, approved of the salutary influences of profuse sweating, rubbed with the fat of animals to render the limbs pliable, and, when wearied, to relieve pains in the joints, administered the juice of the tulip-tree as a remedy for pox, and suggested various specifics for diseases incident to climate and the exposed manner of life.[3]

The office of physician among these primitive peoples, accompanied as it was with authority, notoriety, and emolument, was not exempt from danger. Failure to effect a cure, in some instances, involved as a direct consequence the death of the practitioner. The suggestion of such a penalty at this time, for professional ignorance or malpractice, would most essentially diminish the applications for admission to the degree

[1] Compare Brickell's "Natural History of North Carolina," p. 372. Dublin, 1737.

[2] "Carolina," etc., p. 35. London, 1682.

[3] *See* Lawson's "Carolina," p. 215, *et seq.* London, 1714

of M. D., emphatically thin the ranks of the medical fraternity, and entirely extirpate the race of impudent quacks infesting the country through all its borders.

In the opinion of Mr. Bartram,[1] the Southern Indians, in the treatment of diseases, depended more upon regimen and abstinence than they did upon medicines.

The Cherokees used the *Lobelia syphilitica*, and endeavored to conceal from the whites all knowledge both of its virtues and of the localities in which it grew. A decoction of the *Bignonia crucigera* and of the roots of the *china brier* and the *sassafras* was freely employed for the purification of the blood. The caustic and detergent properties of the roots of the white nettle (*Jatropha urens*) were utilized in cleansing old ulcers and consuming proud flesh, while the dissolvent and diuretant powers of the root of the *Convolvulus panduratus* were highly esteemed as a remedy in nephritic complaints. The emollient and discutient power of the swamp-lily (*Saururus cernuus*) and the virtues of the *hypo* or *may-apple* (*Podophyllum peltatum*) were both communicated to the Europeans by the Indians.

The roots of the *Panax ginseng* and *Norida*, or white-root, were held in the highest esteem among the Cherokees and Creeks. The virtues of the former are well known, and the friendly carminative qualities of the latter were constantly invoked for relieving all disorders of the stomach and intestines. The patient chewed the root and swallowed the juice, or smoked it, when dry, with tobacco. Even the smell of the root exerted a beneficial effect. The Lower Creeks, in whose

[1] "Observations on the Creek and Cherokee Indians." Transactions of the American Ethnological Society, vol. iii., part 1, p. 45, e . New York, 1853.

country it did not grow, gladly exchanged two or three buckskins for a single root of it.[1]

Of the ANCIENT TOWNS of Florida, De Bry has given us several representations.[2] They are all small, circular in outline, and defended by stockades. The dwellings of chiefs, council-houses, public buildings, granaries, and temples, we have considered elsewhere, and it only remains for us, in this connection, to notice the character of the cabins occupied by the common people. These were confined, inconvenient, and ephemeral in their structure. Describing the dwellings of Toalli, the Knight of Elvas remarks that they were roofed with cane after the fashion of tile. They were kept very clean, and their sides, made of clay, looked like tapia. Throughout the cold country, he continues, every Indian has a winter house, plastered inside and out, with a very small door, which is closed at dark. Within, a fire is kindled which heats the building like an oven and renders clothing during the night-time entirely unnecessary. The summer-house was more open, and near it was erected a small kitchen for baking bread. Maize was kept in a house with wooden sides, raised aloft on four posts, with a cane floor. The houses of the principal men or chiefs were larger than those of the subjects, and, in front, had deep balconies furnished with cane seats. There were also large barbacoas filled with maize, deer-skins, and the blankets of the country—the tribute of the common people to their rulers.[3] These private residences were generally

[1] Consult also Adair's "History of the North American Indians," p. 172, *et seq.* London, 1775.

[2] "Brevis Narratio," etc., plates xxx., xxxi., xxxiii., xl. Francoforti ad Mœnum, anno 1591.

[3] *See* "Narratives of the Career of Hernando de Soto," translated by Buckingham Smith, p. 52. New York, 1866.

circular in form, their sides made of upright poles, the interstices filled with clay, and their tops thatched with dry grass, palmetto-leaves, or cane. During the summer months but little covering was needed, and the light, open summer-houses were frequently roofed simply with branches of trees. At a later period the Muscogulgees built houses much more substantial in their character, plastering the walls carefully with red or white clay, and ornamenting them with various drawings of animals, plants, trees, birds, and men.[1]

In the latter part of the sixteenth century the houses of the Virginia Indians were made of poles fastened at the top and covered either with bark or with rush mats. They were from twelve to twenty-four yards in length, and about half as broad. Their towns consisted of a collection of from ten to thirty houses, and were sometimes open, and, in other instances, were protected by stockades not unlike those in use among the Florida tribes. An example of a fortified village is presented in plate xix. of the "Admiranda Narratio." The town of Secota (plate xx.), on the contrary, is entirely unprotected. In the vicinity of this village are seen fields of maize and tobacco. The relative positions of the places of prayer, of feasting, of dancing, of idol-worship, of the spot where the sacred fire is kept burning, of the large building wherein are entombed their kings, and the locality whence they derived their supply of water, are all delineated. When a village was situated at a remove from a stream, spring, or lake, the earliest attention was paid to digging an artificial pond from which a liberal supply of water could at all times be obtained.

[1] Bartram's "Observations on the Creek and Cherokee Indians." Transactions of the American Ethnological Society, vol. iii., part 1, p. 18.

Ribault thus describes a native village on the Florida coast: "Their houses be made of wood fitly and close; set upright and covered with reeds, the most part of them after the fashion of a pavilion. But there was one house among the rest very long and broad, with settles about made of reeds, trimly couched together, which serve them both for beds and seats; they be of height two foot from the ground, set upon great round pillars painted with red, yellow, and blue, well and trimly polished."[1]

Perhaps the most minute and satisfactory description of the dwellings of the Southern Indians is that presented by Mr. Lawson.[2] Referring more particularly to the Carolina tribes, he writes: "These Savages live in *Wigwams* or Cabins built of Bark, which are made round like an Oven, to prevent any Damage by hard Gales of Wind. They make the Fire in the middle of the House, and have a Hole at the Top of the Roof right above the Fire, to let out the Smoke. These Dwellings are as hot as Stoves, where the *Indians* sleep and sweat all Night. The Floors thereof are never paved nor swept, so that they have always a loose Earth on them. They are often troubled with a multitude of Fleas, especially near the Places where they dress their Deer-Skins, because that Hair harbors them; yet I never felt any ill, unsavory Smell in their Cabins, whereas, should we live in our Houses, as they do, we should be poison'd with our own Nastiness; which confirms these *Indians* to be, as they really are, some of the sweetest People in the World.

"The Bark they make their Cabins withal, is generally Cypress, or red or white Cedar; and sometimes,

[1] "The Whole and True Discoverye of Terra Florida," etc. Prynted at London, by Rowland Hall, for Thomas Hackett, 1563.

[2] "History of Carolina," etc., p. 176. London, 1714.

when they are a great way from any of these Woods, they make use of Pine-Bark, which is the worser sort. In building these Fabricks they get very long Poles of Pine, Cedar, Hiccory, or any Wood that will bend; these are the Thickness of the Small of a Man's Leg at the thickest end, which they generally strip of the Bark, and warm them well in the Fire, which makes them tough and fit to bend; afterwards they stick the thickest ends of them in the Ground, about two Yards asunder in a Circular Form, the Distance they design the Cabin to be (which is not always round, but sometimes oval), then they bend the Tops and bring them together, and bind their ends with Bark of Trees, that is proper for that use, as Elm is, or sometimes the Moss that grows on Trees, and is a Yard or two long, and never rots; then they brace them with other Poles to make them strong; afterwards cover them all over with Bark, so that they are very warm and tight, and will keep firm against all the Weathers that blow. They have other sorts of Cabins without Windows, which are for their Granaries, Skins, and Merchandizes; and others that are covered over head; the rest left open for the Air. These have Reed-Hurdles like Tables to lie and sit on, in Summer, and serve for pleasant Banqueting-Houses in the hot Season of the Year. The Cabins they dwell in have Benches all round, except where the Door stands; on these they lay Beasts-Skins and Mats made of Rushes, whereon they sleep and loll. In one of these several Families commonly live, though all related to one another."[1]

[1] Compare Adair's "History of the American Indians," p. 417. London, 1755; Bartram's "Travels," pp. 189, 365, 386, *et aliter*. London, 1792. Romans's "Concise Natural History of East and West Florida," pp. 67, 68. New York, 1775. Smith's "History of Virginia," Richmond reprint, 1819, vol. i., p. 130.

Some fifty years subsequent to the time when this description was furnished by Mr. Lawson, De Brahm thus perpetuated his observations respecting the character of the houses used by the Indians on the coast of South Carolina and Georgia: "The Indian built their houses of posts, on which they lash in and outside canes, and plaster them over with a white clay mixed with small pieces of talk, which, in a sun shiny day gives to these houses, or rather cottages, a splendor of unpolished silver: they are about twelve foot wide, and twenty or more foot long, covered with a clapboard roof, have no windows, but two doors on the opposite sides, sometimes only one door; the fire place is at one end of the house, with two bed states on both sides of the fire; the bed states are made of canes, raised from the ground about two foot, and covered with bear's skins; their corn houses are buit in the same manner, but raised upon four posts, four and five foot high from the ground; its floor is made of round poles on which the corn worms cannot lodge, but fall through, and thus the Indians preserve their corn from being distroyed by the weevils a whole year. Two or more famelies joine together in building a hot-house about thirty foot in diameter, and fifteen foot high, in a form of a cone, with poles and tatched, without any air hole, except a small door about three foot high and eighteen inches wide; in the center of the hot-house they burn fire of well seasoned dry wood; round the inside are bedstades fixed to the studs which support the middle of each post; in these houses they resort with their children in the winter nights. Upon the same plan of these hot-houses (only a greater diameter and perpendicul) their town houses are built, in which the head men assemble to consult in war, peace, or other concerns; and every evening during summer all families of the town meet to dance and divert themselves."[1]

In the vicinity of the Georgia villages, which were usually located upon the banks of streams and in rich valleys, the followers of De Soto often found large fields of maize, and in some instances artificial lakes used as fish-preserves.

With reference to the TENURE OF LAND AND PROPERTY, it may be remarked, generally, that every tribe had its boundary-lines, and each nation or confederacy its own recognized territorial limits. In the public domain, with its rivers, and lakes, and forests, each Indian claimed a right of property for the purposes of travel, hunting, and fishing. All that a man earned or fashioned by his individual labor and industry belonged to himself, and he could dispose of it according to the customs and usages of his people. It was his privilege to clear, settle, and plant as much land as he chose, within the boundaries of his tribe.

In villages the right of personal property was scrupulously observed, and theft was an uncommon occurrence. Every town or community, for the sake of convenience, assigned a parcel of land in its vicinity for agricultural purposes.

This was called the "town plantation,[2] where every family or citizen had his parcel, or lot, according to desire, or convenience, or the largeness of his family." These shares were bounded by a strip of grass, by poles, or some artificial marks. In ancient

[1] "Documents connected with the History of South Carolina, edited by Plowden Charles Jennett Weston," p. 221. London, 1856.

[2] Bartram's "Observations on the Creek and Cherokee Indians." Transactions of the American Ethnological Society, vol. iii., part 1, p. 39.

times, in these corn-fields there were no fences. Each person, however, recognized the limits of his own little farm, and refrained from interfering with his neighbors' rights.[1] The entire plantation, therefore, was simply a collection of lots, adjacent the one to the other, and all embraced in one general enclosure. When the proper season for planting arrived, all the inhabitants, as one family, devoted their attention to the preparation of the ground and the sowing of the seed. In like manner the plants, at proper times, were, by common consent, cultivated. These agricultural labors were superintended by an overseer elected or designated annually for that purpose. During the periods of special labor his province it was to awaken the inhabitants of the town at daybreak with a singularly loud cry, assemble them with their agricultural implements in the public square, and, by sunrise, lead them into the fields where the work was commenced, and under his supervision prosecuted until evening. The women did not march out with the men, but followed in detached parties bearing the provisions of the day. "When the fruits of their labors are ripe and in fit order to gather in," says Mr. Bartram, "they all, on the same day, repair to the plantation; each gathers the produce of his own proper lot, brings it to town, and deposits it in his own *crib*, allotting a certain portion for the public granary, which is called the king's crib, because its contents are at his disposal, though not his private property, but considered as the tribute or free contribution of the citizens of the state, at the disposal of the king.

"The design of the common granary is for the wisest and best of purposes with respect to their people, i. e.,

[1] "Lawson's Carolina," p. 179. London, 1714.

a store or resource to repair to in cases of necessity. Thus, when a family's private stores fall short, in cases of accident or otherwise, they are entitled to assistance and supply from the public granary, by applying to the king. It also serves to aid other towns which may be in want, and affords provisions for their armies, for travellers, sojourners, etc., etc. Thus the mico becomes the provider or *father of his people.*"

Besides the general plantation, each inhabitant of the village enclosed a garden-spot adjoining his cabin, in which he cultivated corn and vegetables, upon which he subsisted before the general harvest was gathered.

Widows with large families were always assisted in planting, working, and gathering their crops.[1]

Throughout the Creek Confederacy there was continual and friendly intercourse between the families constituting the respective tribes. To their doors there were no bolts, and universal hospitality and good feeling prevailed. Ever ready to assist each other, and entertaining an abiding friendship, the one for the other, the members of the various tribes seemed to Mr. Bartram to constitute one great family, holding all their possessions in common. Theft was almost unknown.

The ANIMAL FOOD of the Southern Indians, at the dawn of the historic period, comprised all the wild animals native to the region, among which may be specially enumerated buffaloes, deer, bears, beavers, panthers, raccoons, opossums, wild-cats, rabbits[2] and

[1] Lawson's "History of Carolina," p. 179. London, 1714.

[2] These animals were captured sometimes by means of snares. "Narratives of the Career of Hernando de Soto;" Buckingham Smith's Translation, p. 132. New York, 1866.

squirrels. These were generally killed with the bow and arrow. Certain seasons of the year were set apart for hunting, during which large quantities of meat were obtained, cured, and housed for future consumption. Fawns in the womb were esteemed a great delicacy. All sorts of fishes, turtles, terrapins, oysters, clams, fresh-water mussels, conchs, alligators, and even some varieties of snakes, were eaten, and much time was consumed in the capture of fishes by means of the bow and arrow, spears, nets, baskets, and wears. The bone hook, and line made of deer-thong, or twisted fibre, were used only to a limited extent. Captain John Smith[1] asserts that the Virginia Indian women spun betwixt their hands and thighs the barks of trees, a kind of grass, and deer sinews, out of which they readily made a very even thread. Out of this thread they made garments, nets, and fishing-lines. "Their fish-hooks," he continues, "are either a bone grated as they noch their arrowes, in the forme of a crooked pinne, or of the splinter of a bone tyed to the clift of a little sticke, and with the end of the line they tie on the bate." Young wasps, white in the comb, were regarded as a dainty morsel.[2] Wild-turkeys, water-fowl, and various birds, were eagerly sought after and eaten. In a word, there was but little animal life in the forests or in the waters of the country which the Southern Indian excluded from his food-list. Even

[1] "History of Virginia," Richmond reprint, 1819, vol. i., p. 133.

[2] Lawson's "History of Carolina," p. 178. London, 1714. "Brevis Narratio," plates xxiv., xxv., xxvi. Francoforti ad Mœnum, 1591. "Admiranda Narratio," plates xiii., xiv. Francoforti ad Mœnum, 1590. Ash's "Carolina," p. 36. London, 1682. Bartram's "Observations on the Creek and Cherokee Indians." Transactions of the American Ethnological Society, vol. iii., part i., p. 47. Adair's "History of North American Indians," p. 402, *et seq.* London, 1775. Timberlake's "Memoirs," p. 45. London, 1765. Smith's "History of Virginia," Richmond reprint, 1819, vol. i., p. 133.

upon dogs did they sometimes subsist. The skins of the buffalo, deer, and other animals, were dressed and used as clothing.

Among the vegetables upon which these primitive peoples chiefly relied for sustenance, may be mentioned Indian corn (maize or zea), wild-potatoes, ground-nuts, acorns, walnuts, hickory-nuts, chestnuts, pumpkins, melons, gourds, beans, pulse of various sorts, persimmons, peaches, plums, grapes, and mulberries. The tuberous roots of the smilax (*S. pseudochina*) were dug up, and, while still fresh and full of juice, were chopped up and macerated well in wooden mortars. When thoroughly beaten, this pulpy mass was put in earthen vessels containing clean water. Here it was stirred with wooden paddles or with the hands. The lighter particles, floating upon the top, were poured off. A farinaceous matter was left at the bottom of the vessel; which, when taken out and dried, remained an impalpable powder or farina of a reddish color. Boiled in water, this powder formed a beautiful jelly, which, when sweetened, was both agreeable and nourishing. In combination with corn-flour and when fried in fresh bear's-grease it made excellent fritters.[1]

Tobacco also was regularly and extensively cultivated. The Southern Indians, especially those resident upon the rich valleys of the interior, devoted no little time and attention to agriculture. With them maize was emphatically the staff of life. Upon its nutritious properties they relied both during its milky state and when dry. In the latter condition it was often parched, pounded, moistened with water, and thus eaten. This

[1] Bartram's "Observations on the Creek and Cherokee Indians." Transactions of the American Ethnological Society, vol. iii., part 1, p. 49. New York, 1853.

was the case when the party was on the march or engaged in hunting. Generally beaten in a mortar, it was either boiled for hominy, or, mixed with hickory-nut-milk, walnut-oil, or fresh bear's-fat, was baked into bread or fried as cakes. In a subsequent chapter upon agriculture we will note more carefully the facts connected with the cultivation, preservation, and use of the grain which subserved such important purpose in the domestic economy of these peoples.

Walnuts and hickory-nuts were diligently collected, cracked, and boiled in vessels, when the oil which rose to the surface was skimmed off and carefully preserved in covered earthen jars. This oil was highly esteemed in the preparation of their corn-cakes. Of the seeds of the sunflower, when pounded, they also made bread. The amexias was freely eaten, and ripe persimmons were pressed into cakes and stored away for consumption during the winter months. Grapes were dried in the sun and collected in the public granaries and private store-houses. Wild-honey was also gathered.[1]

Salt was manufactured by the natives. The Knight of Elvas[2] informs us that the natural salt and the sand with which it was intermixed were thrown into baskets made for the purpose. These were large at the mouth and small at the bottom, or, in other words, funnel-shaped. Beneath them—suspended in the air on a ridge-pole—vessels were placed. Water was then poured upon the admixture of sand and salt. The

[1] Consult "Narratives of the Career of Hernando de Soto," etc., translated by Buckingham Smith, pp. 38, 55, 69, 77, 200–202. New York, 1866. "A Briefe and True Report of the New-found Land of Virginia," by Thomas Hariot, pp. 13–16. Francoforti ad Mœnum, 1590. Bossu's "Travels through Louisiana," vol. i., p. 224. Lawson's "History of Carolina," p. 207. London, 1714. "Brevis Narratio," plates xxi., xxii., xxiii.

[2] "Narratives of the Career of Hernando de Soto," etc., p. 124. New York, 1866.

drippings were strained and boiled on the fire until all the water was evaporated, and the salt left in the bottom of the pots.

Captain Romans asserts that the Indians never ate salt meats or boiled their food with salt. Nevertheless they had salt in abundance. When deprived of it for a long time, he says an Indian "will frequently eat a pound of salt without any thing else."[1] To the saline springs of Tennessee and Kentucky the natives constantly resorted from time immemorial, and in large numbers, for the manufacture of this necessary seasoning for food. They also obtained rock-salt from natural deposits near the mouth of the Mississippi River.

Of the MECHANICAL LABORS of the aborigines—aside from the construction of their tumuli, fortifications, fish-preserves, temples, public and private houses, and places for feasting, dancing, and religious exercises—it may be remarked that, in the manufacture of pottery, from its most careless expression in small terra-cotta pans, or gourd-shaped drinking-cups, to its more substantial development in burial-vases, large, ornamented cooking-vessels and well-formed jars for the preservation of fruits and oils, the Southern Indians excelled. They had made further progress in the ceramic art than that attained by the Western and Northern tribes. Their pottery savored less of the archaic type, and in form and ornamentation, as well as in smoothness and homogeneousness of composition, gave evidence of superior taste and skill. The shapes of these fictile wares were also more varied. They understood and practised the art of mixing their well kneaded clay with pounded shells and gravel, so as to impart to the material greater tenacity and dura-

[1] "A Concise Natural History of East and West Florida," p. 42. New York, 1785.

bility. The ornamentation of the rims, necks, and sides of this earthenware was varied, and often tasteful and ingenious. The use of the potter's wheel seems to have been unknown. To the women was chiefly committed the manufacture of this pottery. Soapstone, in many localities, was the favorite material from which, by means of flint implements, were fashioned culinary utensils, both great and small. No implements of iron and bronze existed at this early period, and copper was used only to a limited extent. In its treatment that material was regarded rather in the light of a malleable stone, than as a metal. Its employment was confined almost exclusively to the manufacture of ornamental axes, gorgets, pendants, and spindles, or points for piercing pearls. Procured in a pure, native state—chiefly from the shores of Lake Superior—it was, while cold, hammered out into the desired shape. Heat was never applied, and all the implements and ornaments of this metal, which we have seen, show very plainly a laminated struutcre. Comparatively few copper articles have been found within the limits of Georgia, and most of these, as we shall hereafter observe, were obtained from ancient graves in the valleys of the Chattahoochee, the Etowah, and the Oostenaula.

Gold and silver, to a limited extent, were employed in the fabrication of ornaments. Small masses of these precious metals were picked up by the natives in pockets, or gathered in the beds of streams flowing through auriferous regions, and perforated and worn as pendants. Gold beads—evidently not European in their manufacture—rudely hammered into round and oval shapes, with holes drilled through their centres or upper portions, have been found in the Etowah

Valley, in the vicinity of the large mounds on Colonel Tumlin's plantation. In this connection, it is proper that we allude to the traces of early mining in Cherokee Georgia.

In 1834, Colonels Merriwether and Lumsden, while engaged in digging a canal in Duke's-Creek Valley for the purpose of facilitating their mining operations, unearthed a subterranean village consisting of thirty-four small cabins, located in a straight line extending upward of three hundred feet. They were made of logs hewn at the ends and notched down, after the fashion of the rude log-huts of the present day. This hewing and notching had evidently been done with sharp metallic tools, the marks being such as would have been caused by a chopping axe. Above these little houses—situated from fifty to one hundred yards from the principal channel of the creek, and embedded from seven to nine feet below the surface of the ground—trees were growing from two to three feet in diameter.[1] The estimated age of these trees was somewhat over two hundred years. The violent changes often caused, in their narrow valleys and along their yielding banks, by mountain-streams swollen with rain or engorged by the dissolving snows of winter, may account for the inhumation of these cabins within a comparatively short period after their abandonment.

In Valley-River Valley, the writer is informed,[2] eleven old shafts have been found, varying in depth from ninety to one hundred feet. In 1854, one of them was cleaned out, and at the depth of ninety feet the workmen found a windlass of post-oak, well hewn,

[1] White's "Historical Collections of Georgia," p. 487. Stephenson's "Geology and Mineralogy of Georgia," p. 208. Atlanta, Ga., 1871.

[2] MS. letter from Dr. Stephenson.

with an inch augur-hole bored through each end. Distinct traces appeared where it had been banded with iron. The crank and gudgeon-holes were still in excellent preservation. Another shaft, for twenty-five feet, passed through gneiss-rock. Its sides were scarred by the marks of the sharp tools used in forcing a passage through this hard substance. There were no signs of blasting. Below the water-level the casing-boards and timbers were sound, although discolored by the sulphurets of copper and iron.

Six miles southeast of this locality are five other shafts similar in age and construction. The trees growing in the mouths and upon the edges of these abandoned pits were not less than two hundred years old.

The presence of iron and the marks of sharp metallic tools prove that these ancient mining operations cannot be referred to the labors of the Indians. The narratives of the career of De Soto are filled with accounts furnished by the natives of the presence of gold in certain designated localities, and their exaggerated statements continually inflamed the cupidity of the adventurers who accompanied the Adelantado on his wild march from Puerto del Espíritu Santo to the broad prairies beyond the Mississippi. In plate xli. of the "Brevis Narratio" De Bry presents an extravagant and evidently imaginary illustration of the manner in which the natives gathered gold in the streams issuing from the Apalatcy Mountains. These gold and silver-bearing mountains—if we rightly interpret the confused map accompanying the work to which we have just alluded—were situated somewhere in or near the northeastern part of Georgia. There is every reason to believe that De Soto passed through Nacoochee Valley and thence pursued his wanderings by way of the Oostenaula or Etowah Valley to their confluence. There stood the ancient village of Chiaha, and there now stands the beautiful town of Rome.

While lingering among the mountains and valleys of North Carolina and Georgia, earnest and repeated inquiries were made by the Spanish adventurer respecting the existence of precious metals in that region. Parties were dispatched by him to examine the country and ascertain the precise places where the Indians were said to be engaged in mining. While it does not appear from any of the narratives that De Soto and his followers actually undertook any mining operations—other than perhaps a limited examination of the surface of the ground—or that they had with them tools and mechanical appliances which would have enabled them to have penetrated the bowels of the hills and utilized the ores which they contained, it is quite evident that they recognized this as an auriferous region and were greatly disappointed at their failure to secure a considerable quantity of the coveted treasure.

The question still recurs, Who sunk these shafts, and, in that early day, expended so much labor in earnest quest for gold? Dr. Brinton, in an article published in the *Historical Magazine*,[1] has collected some authorities which suggest a probable response to the inquiry.

So carried away was Luis de Velasco with the representations made by the returned soldiers of De Soto's Expedition, with regard to the gold, silver, and pearls abounding in the province of "Cosa," that he dispatched his general, Tristan de Luna, to open communication with Cosa by the way of Pensacola Bay. Three hun-

[1] First Series, vol. x., p. 137.

dred Spanish soldiers of this expedition penetrated quite to the valley of the Coosa, in Northern Georgia, and there passed the summer of 1560. Juan Pardo was subsequently sent by Aviles—the first Governor of Florida—to establish a fort at the foot of the mountains northwest of St. Augustine, in the province of the chief Coabá. It would seem, therefore, that the Spaniards both knew and endeavored, at this early period, to avail themselves of the gold deposits in Upper Georgia. The German traveller, Johannes Lederer, who visited North Carolina and Virginia in 1669 and 1670, and wrote an account of his adventures in Latin, asserts that the Spaniards were then working gold and silver mines in the Appalachian Mountains. He avers that he saw specimens of the ore among the Western tribes, and brought samples of it back with him. "Had I had with me," he adds, "half a score of resolute youths who would have stuck to me, I would have pushed on to the Spanish mines."

In 1690, while making a journey over the "Apalathean Mountains" for inland discovery and trade with the natives, Mr. James Moore was informed by the Indians that the Spaniards were at work upon mines within twenty miles of the place where he then was. The Indians described to him the bellows and furnaces used by these miners, and offered to conduct him to the spot. A difference between himself and his guides, however, prevented his visiting these mines.[1] Subsequently Mr. Moore volunteered to lead a party to these mines, but the scheme fell through.

These authorities, if they do no more, intimate that in the seventeenth century it was believed that the

[1] "Collections of the South Carolina Historical Society," vol. i., p. 209. Charleston, 1857.

Spaniards were at work in this region seeking earnestly for gold, and enable us to account, with at least some degree of probability, for those physical traces of ancient mining observed by the early settlers of Upper Georgia—operations of no mean significance, and which cannot reasonably be ascribed either to the Indians or to the followers of De Soto.

Returning from this digression, we would state that in the manufacture of articles of stone, bone, shell, wood, skin, and feathers, the ingenuity and skill of the primitive workmen found varied and interesting expression. The stone period is here richly represented. We have both chipped and polished stone implements of unusual diversity, beautiful material, and most creditable workmanship. A comparison between the tastes and labors of the Southern and Northern Indians in this, as well as in almost every other respect, results most favorably to the former. As our attention will, in subsequent chapters, be specially directed to an examination of these various articles and implements, it is necessary here only to allude to the existence of spear and arrow points, pipes—plain, bird, and animal-shaped—axes grooved and ungrooved, perforated and ornamental, chipped and ground—gouges, chisels, awls, knives, scrapers, smoothing-stones, mortars, pestles, crushing-stones, net-sinkers, tubes, pendants, gorgets, pins, sling-stones, discoidal stones, nut-stones, images, and numerous other articles. In their manufacture, flint, jasper, quartz, chalcedony, slate, steatite, hornblende, diorite, greenstone, soapstone, graywacke and hematite were principally employed. Great pains were often expended in their construction. For their pipes and discoidal stones the Cherokees were famous. Many of the axes, and arrow and spear heads, are marvels of symmetry and beauty. The attention of the workers in shell was mainly directed to the manufacture of beads, head-ornaments, gorgets, armlets, wampum, pins and perforated disks. Upon the ornamentation of the gorgets much labor and ingenuity were bestowed. Pearls, obtained from salt-water shells and the fluviatile and lacustrine *unionidæ*, were perforated by means of heated copper spindles, and strung and worn around the neck, arms, wrists, waist and ankles.

Plates of mica were used as looking-glasses, and for the ornamentation of the walls of drinking-cups. In the latter case, circular, square, oval, and diamond-shaped pieces were pressed in the clay while still soft—the edges being slightly embedded. When the vessel became hard, their retention was insured.

Boats—some of them large enough to convey forty persons—were made of the trunks of trees. The tree was felled, cut off at the desired length, and hollowed out by fire. Through its agency also, its sides were shaped, and both the interior and exterior of the canoe scraped and smoothed by means of shells and hand-axes or gouges. Bark canoes were seldom if ever used.[1] They belong to colder waters.

FIG. 1.

In 1845, while digging a canal on one of the rice-plantations, on the Savannah River, located only a few miles distant from the city of Savannah, at a depth of three feet and a half below the surface of the

[1] Smith's "History of Virginia," vol. i., p. 132. Richmond reprint, 1819.

swamp, the workmen came upon a canoe embedded in the soil. It answered to the description of what is familiarly known as a *dug-out*, and had been fashioned from the trunk of a cypress-tree (*see* illustration). About eleven feet long and thirty inches wide, its depth was scarcely more than ten inches. Both bow and stern were strengthened, each by a wooden brace kept in position by wooden pins passing through the sides of the canoe and entering the braces at either end. This boat curved upward at either end, so that the bow and stern rose above the middle portion. Located about three feet from the stern was seat nine inches wide, consisting of a rude cypress-plank. For its reception the sides of the canoe had been notched three inches below the gunwales, and it was further kept in position by four wooden pins—two on each side—driven through the boat and entering the seat at either end as in the case of the bow and stern braces.

The bottom was flat, the sides rounding. No effort had been made to form a keel. The bow and stern were both pointed, and not unlike in their general outlines, the latter being more blunt than the former. At the top the sides were rather more than half an inch in thickness—increasing, however, as they descended and curved below the water-line.

When cleaned and dried, this canoe weighed sixty pounds, and could be transported with the greatest facility by a single individual. The agency of fire had obviously been invoked in the construction of this little boat. While there were no marks of sharp cutting-tools, the evidence appeared conclusive that the charred portions of the wood, both within and without, had been carefully removed by rude incisive implements, probably of shell or stone. The plan of felling the tree and of hollowing out the log, as perpetuated in one of De Bry's illustrations,[1] seems to have been observed in this instance. Regarding the regularity with which the outlines and the relative thicknesses of the sides of this boat had been preserved, one could but admire the care and skill with which that dangerous element, fire, had been made subservient to the uses of the primitive boat-builder. It is entirely probable that the ordinary stone celts, chisels, gouges, scrapers, or simple shells, were the only implements at command for the removal of the charred surface, as the cypress-tree was by degrees converted into the convenient *dug-out.*

In all likelihood, this scraping was done with a shell. Such is the intimation given in an early account of the manufacture of canoes by the Virginia Indians: "Mira est in Virginia cymbas fabricandi ratio; nam cum ferreis instrumentis aut aliis nostris similibus careant, eas tamen parare norunt nostris non minus commodas ad nauiqandum quo lubet per flumina & ad piscandum. Primum arbore aliqua crassa & alta delecta, pro cymbæ quam parare volunt magnitudine, ignem circa eius radices summa tellure in ambitu struunt ex arbore musco bene resiccato & ligni assulis paulatim ignem excitantes, ne flamma altius ascendat & arboris longitudinem minuat. Pæne adusta & ruinam minante arbore, nouum suscitant ignem, quem flagrare sinunt donec arbor sponte cadat. Adustis deinde arboris fastigio & ramis vt truncus instam longitudinem retineat, tignis transuersis supra furcas positis, imponunt, ea altitudine vt commode laborare possint, tunc cortice conchis quibusdam adempto, integriorem trunci partem

[1] "Admiranda Narratio," plate xii.

pro cymbæ inferiore parte seruant, in altera parte ignem secundum trunci longitudinem struunt, prætorquam extremis, quod satis adustum illis videtur, restincto igne cõchis scabunt, & nouo suscitato igne denuo adurunt, atque ita deinceps pergunt, subinde urentes & scabentes, donec cymba necessarium alueum nacta sit. Sic Domini spiritus rudibus hominibus suggerit rationem qua res in suum usum necessarias conficere queant."[1]

This canoe had evidently lain for a very long time in its present position, and seemed to have settled gradually. There was an accumulation of forty inches of mud and soil above it, and around lay the rotting trunks, arms, and roots of forest-trees which, during the lapse of years, had died and become intermingled with the *débris* of the swamp. Above the spot were growing cypress-trees as large and seemingly as old as any in the surrounding forest.

It is difficult to form a satisfactory estimate of the age of this relic. That embedded cypress is, for an almost indefinite period, wellnigh indestructible by ordinary agencies, is capable of proof. We have but to instance the salt-marshes along the line of the Georgia coast, in not a few of which, at the depth of several feet below the surface, may still be found the clearly-defined and well-preserved traces of cypress-forests, consisting of limbs, trunks, knees, and roots. In former years, at least some of these salt-marshes must have been fresh-water swamps; and, without the violent intervention of some marked convulsion of Nature, of which we have no record, and for which no plausible reason can be assigned, centuries must have

[1] "Admiranda Narratio" et cæt., plate xii. Francofurti ad Mœnum. De Bry, anno 1590.

elapsed before a gradual settling of the coast could have occurred to such an extent as to have admitted the influx of tidal waves converting cypress-swamps into extensive, uniform salt-marshes, destroying the original growth, and finally covering the fallen forests with mud to the depth of several feet.

We are not aware that a sufficiently-accurate record has been kept of the annual deposit of mud from the overflowing waters of the Savannah River, to enable us to derive from this source a plausible conjecture as to the age of this canoe. So many uncertainties enter into calculations of this character, that in most instances all attempts to arrive at definite results fall far short of satisfactory conclusions. All we know is, that this Indian canoe is old—older than the barge which conveyed Oglethorpe up the Savannah, when he first selected the home of the Yamacraws as a site for the future commercial metropolis of the colony of Georgia—more ancient, probably, than the statelier craft which carried the fortunes of the discoverer of this Western Continent.

So far as our information extends, this is the first and only well-authenticated instance of the exhumation of an ancient canoe in this country. It is in just such a locality that we might have anticipated with greatest confidence the existence of such a relic. The general employment of bark and skin in the manufacture of their canoes by Northern Indians precludes all reasonable hope of finding ancient specimens made of such perishable materials.

The use of the *dug-out*, like the presence of a stone axe, or a jasper arrow-point, tells a true story of the art-condition of the people by whom it is made. It is the simplest form of water-craft, and evidences the first effort in the way of navigation. Hence, among barbarous tribes, there is no essential diversity either in the shape of these primitive boats or in the methods of their construction.

The [1] Andaman-islanders have single-tree canoes hollowed out with a *p*-shaped axe, and in their labors are assisted by the action of fire. On the northeastern coast of Australia, the natives [2] use boats formed from a single trunk, hollowed out by fire. The Clalan Indians excel in the manufacture of *dug-outs* made from the trunks of cedar-trees. In the days of Columbus the natives [3] of San Salvador fashioned their canoes from the trunks of single trees, hollowing them out by fire and polishing them with primitive adzes of flint or shell. While passing down the Mississippi, Hennepin [4] noted the existence, among the natives, of "*pirogues* or *heavy wooden canows* made of the trunks of trees and hollowed out with fire."

William Bartram [5] says: "These Indians (of Southern Florida) have large, handsome canoes which they form out of the trunks of cypress trees (*cupressus disticha*), some of them commodious enough to accommodate twenty or thirty warriors. In these large canoes they descend the river on trading and hunting expeditions to the sea-coast, neighboring islands and keys, quite to the point of Florida, and sometimes cross the Gulph, extending their navigations to the Bahama islands, and even to Cuba; a crew of these adventurers had just arrived, having returned from Cuba but a few

[1] "Prehistoric Times." Sir J. Lubbock. Second edition. London, 1869, p. 425.

[2] Idem, p. 429.

[3] Wilson's "Prehistoric Man," second edition, p. 99. London, 1865.

[4] "New Discovery," etc., p. 153. London, 1698.

[5] "Travels," etc., p. 225. London, 1792.

days before our arrival with a cargo of spirituous liquors, coffee, sugar, and tobacco. One of them politely presented me with a choice piece of tobacco, which he told me he had received from the Governor of Cuba."

Cabeça de Vaca[1] bears testimony to the presence of wooden canoes in use among the Indians whom he encountered in his wanderings, but does not allude to the manner in which they were made.

In the narratives of the career of Hernando de Soto in the conquest of Florida, as told by the Knight of Elvas, and related by Hernandez de Biedma, mention is made of canoes of considerable size and ornament, but we are not informed as to their precise shape or method of construction. They were evidently, however, fashioned from the trunks of trees.

Ribault states that the Florida Indians made canoes out of single trees, capable of transporting safely fifteen or twenty persons, and that they were propelled by short paddles—the rowers standing upright in the boat.

Lieutenant Timberlake,[2] speaking of the canoes in use among the Cherokees, writes: "They are generally made of a large pine or poplar from thirty to forty feet long, and about two broad, with flat bottoms and sides, and both ends alike; the Indians hollow them now (1761) with the tools they get from the Europeans, but formerly did it by fire." The [3]buried canoes in the valley of the Clyde were generally formed out of a single oak-stem, hollowed out by blunt tools —probably stone axes—aided by the action of fire.

[1] *See* his "Relation," translated by Buckingham Smith, p. 54, *et aliter*. New York, 1871.

[2] "Memoirs," p. 60. London, 1765.

[3] "Antiquity of Man." Sir Charles Lyell. Third edition, p. 49. London, 1863.

A few were "cut beautifully smooth, evidently with metallic tools." "Hence," says Sir Charles Lyell, "a gradation could be traced from a pattern of extreme rudeness to one showing great mechanical ingenuity." Penicaut affirms that the canoes of the Indians of Louisiana were made by setting fire to the foot of a cypress-tree, the fire continuing in the interior until it fell to the ground. "They then burned it off at the desired length. When the tree was burned sufficiently for their purpose, they extinguished the fire with moist earth, and scraped it out with large shells, which are very thick. They then wash them with water in such a manner as to give them a fine polish. These canoes are sometimes twenty-five or thirty feet long, but they make of them various lengths according to the uses for which they are intended."[1]

From Bossu's "Travels" we extract the following account: "Before the French came into Louisiana the Indians constructed their boats in the following manner. They went to the banks of some rivers, which are very numerous in this vast region, and which by their rapidity tear up by the roots the trees which stand on their banks. They took their dimensions for length and breadth, and accordingly chose such a tree as they wanted; after which they set fire to it, and as the tree burnt on they scraped away the live coals with a flint or an arrow, and having sufficiently hollowed it out, they set it afloat. They are very well skilled in constructing these little vessels upon their lakes and rivers. They employ them in time of war, and likewise load them with the furs and dried flesh which they bring back from their hunts."[2]

[1] *See* "Historical Collections of Louisiana and Florida." French's new series. J. Sabin & Sons, New York, 1869.

[2] "Travels through Louisiana," etc., vol. i., pp. 222, 223. London, 1771.

Compared with the boats figured by De Bry,[1] or the *einbaum* of Robenhausen, or that taken from the peat-moor of Mercurango, or that found in the nook of Moringen, as represented in Keller's "Lake Dwellings," the Savannah River canoe is more symmetrical and less trough-shaped than them all, and assimilates more nearly to the form of the modern canoe. The addition of the braces in the bow and stern is unusual, and the presence of the seat is by no means customary.

The primitive river-craft of any people, no matter how low in the scale of civilization, is interesting, and, when the former occupants of the soil have passed away, leaving behind them relics at best but few and frail, we experience a sense of genuine satisfaction as we are thus furnished with the physical proof of the precise manner in which the Indians of Georgia constructed the light barks in which they committed themselves to the waters of the Savannah. This rude boat from the Savannah swamp, perhaps the very first ancient American canoe which has been unearthed, confirms our conjectures, and substantially verifies the earliest and most reliable representations which have been preserved of the Indian canoe of the Southern waters.

Shawls, coverings, and articles of dress, were made of feathers, of buffalo, deer, and bear skins, and the hides of other animals, and were woven by hand out of certain fibres. Fishing lines and nets were formed of the inner bark of trees, and convenient mats and baskets fashioned with split canes, reeds, and rushes.

Some of the feather mantles were beautifully

[1] "Admiranda Narratio," plates xii., xiii. Francoforti ad Mœnum. De Bry, anno 1590. "Brevis Narratio," plates xxii., xlii. Francoforti ad Mœnum. De Bry, anno 1591.

wrought, and upon the well-dressed skins of animals were depicted various designs.

Mortars and pestles, bows, spoons, and platters, seats or benches, ornamental posts used in dancing, and huge images were fashioned of wood.

Shell-beads answered as a medium of exchange or currency. Fire was produced by the vehement collision or rubbing together of two sticks.

They prepared their skins by first soaking them in water. The hair was then removed by the aid of a bone or stone scraper. Deer's brains were next dissolved in water, and in this mixture the skins were allowed to remain until they became thoroughly saturated. They were then gently dried, and, while drying, were continually worked by hand and scraped with an oyster-shell or some suitable stone implement to free them from every impurity and render them soft and pliable. In order that they might not become hard, when exposed to rain, they were cured in smoke, and tanned with the bark of trees. Young Indian-corn, beaten to a pulp, answered the same purpose as the deer's brains.[1]

Laboriously-constructed dams and intricate wears were employed in the capture of fish.

In PAINTING and ROCK-WRITING, the efforts of the Southern Indians were confined to the fanciful and profuse ornamentation of their own persons with various colors, in which red, yellow, and black predominated, and to marks, signs, and figures, depicted on skins and scratched on wood, the shoulder-blade of a buffalo, or on stone. The smooth bark of a standing tree or the face of a rock was used to commemorate some feat of

[1] "Natural History of North Carolina," etc., by John Brickell, M. D., p. 364. Dublin, 1737. Du Pratz's "History of Louisiana," vol. ii., p. 224. London, 1763.

arms, to indicate the direction and strength of a military expedition, or the solemnization of a treaty of peace. High up the perpendicular sides of mountain-gorges, and at points apparently inaccessible, save to the fowls of the air, are seen representations of the sun and moon,[1] accompanied by rude characters, the significance of which is frequently unknown to the present observer. The motive which incited to the execution of work so perilous was, doubtless, religious in its character, and directly connected with the worship of the sun and his pale consort of the night.

Coarsely done and barren of interest, this pictography feebly expresses the rudest attempts at imitation by means of colored chalks and the pointed fragment of a flint. Ignorant of phonetic symbols and of letters, the ideographic characters which they employed were such as are more or less common to all semi-barbarians.[2] This primitive system of *intaglios* and picture-writing—designed to convey intelligence and record events—was supplemented by the use of wampum, of which we will speak more at large hereafter.[3]

The art of dyeing feathers, fibres, rushes, and splints of cane and wood, as well as the quills of birds and animals, to be employed in the manufacture of garments, coverings, mats, baskets, and belts, was generally understood and practised.

The TRADE RELATIONS existing among these primitive peoples were extensive. The principal articles of barter were copper, flint and stone implements, pipes,

[1] Haywood's "Natural and Aboriginal History of Tennessee," p. 113. Nashville, 1823.

[2] *See* Ewbank's "North American Rock-writing," p. 8. Morrisania, N. Y., 1866.

[3] Compare "Ancient Monuments of the Mississippi Valley," chap. xviii. Washington, 1848. "Journal of the Anthropological Institute of New York," vol. i., p. 57, *et seq.* Bradford's "American Antiquities," p. 182. New York, 1843.

shell-ornaments, pearls, and skins. Galena, obsidian, mica, and small masses of native gold and silver also formed subjects of merchandise. Between the coast and the interior a constant interchange of commodities was maintained. The beautiful jasper and flint arrow and spear points, stone pipes, discoidal stones, and various articles manufactured by the dwellers among the mountains, were readily sold to the coast-tribes, who gave in exchange for them shells, pearls, and commodities, native to their region, and held in esteem by those at a distance. The primitive merchantmen engaged in this traffic were held in special repute, were generously treated, and had at all times safe-conduct through the territories even of those who were at war with each other. From the same stone grave in Nacoochee Valley were taken an ornamental copper axe from the shores of Lake Superior, a large cassis from the Gulf of Mexico, and stone weapons made of materials entirely foreign to that locality. The sepulchral mounds and relic beds contain articles brought from a distance, and very frequently the finest specimens are obtained at the farthest remove from the spot whence the material used in their manufacture was procured. In this circumstance we trace the intervention of the merchantman, and his inclination, even at that remote period, to find special favor in the eyes of his customers.

This early commerce among the North American Indians is a subject full of interest, and Prof. C. Rau, in his recent article, entitled "Die Tauschverhältnisse der Eingebornen Nordamerika's," published in the first quarterly number of the fifth volume of the "Archiv für Anthropologie," has bestowed upon its consideration much care and research.

CHAPTER III.

Marriage and Divorce.—Punishment of Adultery.—Costume and Ornaments.—Skin-painting and Tattooing.—Manufacture of Carpets, Feather-shawls, and Moccasins.—Weaving.

THE customs obtaining among the Creeks about the close of the last century, with respect to MARRIAGE and DIVORCE, are thus detailed by Colonel Hawkins:[1] The suitor never applies in person, but sends his sister, mother or other female relative, to the female relations of the woman he desires to secure as his wife. Brothers and uncles on the maternal side, and sometimes the father, are consulted, but this is simply a matter of compliment, as neither their approval nor opposition is of any avail. If the match is regarded with favor, a gracious answer is returned to the woman who made the application. The bridegroom thereupon sends a blanket and such articles of clothing as he possesses to the females of the bride's family. If accepted, the contract of marriage is concluded, and he may enter the house of his future wife as soon as he chooses. Having built himself a cabin, made a crop and gathered it in, hunted and brought home his game and placed every thing in the possession of his

[1] "Sketch of the Creek Confederacy." Collections of the Georgia Historical Society, vol. iii., part 1, p. 73. Savannah, 1848.

wife, the preliminary ceremony ends, and the woman is bound. From the time of his first visit to the house of the woman until the termination of the ceremony, she is completely subject to his will in every particular. A man never marries a member of his own tribe. Marriage gives the husband no right over the property of the wife; and, in case of separation, she keeps the children, and all property belonging to them.

Divorce occurs as a matter of mutual consent, or at the choice of either party—the man having the right to marry again at will, but the woman, except during the continuation of the marriage ceremony, being bound until the feasts of the *Boosketau* of that year are over.

As a general rule, adultery on the part of the female only is punished. The matter is taken in charge by the family or tribe of the husband. The members assemble, consult, and determine upon a course of action. If the proof be clear, and they conclude to punish the offenders, they divide and proceed to apprehend them. One half goes to the woman's house and the remainder to the family house of the adulterer, or they all go together to each place if they have so resolved. If the offenders are apprehended, they are beaten severely with sticks and then cropped. The hair of the woman is carried in triumph to the public square. If only one of the offenders be taken, satisfaction is had of the nearest relative of the party who escaped. If both make their escape, and the family or tribe of the husband return home and lay down the sticks, the crime is forgiven. One family only, the "Wind" (Ho-tul-ul-gee), can take up the sticks a second time. Should the offending parties succeed in absenting themselves until the Boos-ke-tau is over, they are pardoned, because, at that solemn festival, universal forgiveness is proclaimed for all offences save murder.

In a letter dated the 9th of June, 1733, Mr. Oglethorpe, speaking of the Indians in the vicinity of Savannah, says, "They abhor adultery, and do not approve of a plurality of wives." He further states that, where adultery had been committed, the injured husband was entitled to his revenge by cutting off the ears of the adulterer; and, if physically unable to inflict this punishment, he had a right to kill him the first time he could do so with safety. The Rev. Mr. Bolzius[1] records the fact that, on the 26th of March, 1734, an Indian (probably of the Yamacraw tribe) cut off both the ears and the hair of his wife, because she had been too familiar with a white man. This he avers to have been the usual punishment for adultery in vogue among the Indians in Southern Georgia.

Adultery among the Creeks, during Captain Romans's[2] sojourn among them, was punished by severe flagellations, and the loss of the hair, nose, and ears of both parties. Sometimes the man's nose was spared.

Of infidelity in the husband no notice seems to have been taken, except in cases where he had infringed upon the vested rights of another of the same sex; and then he was liable only to such punishment as the anger or ability of the injured husband might lead him to inflict.

These marriage customs varied with almost every nation and tribe.[3] The intervention of a priest to im-

[1] "Extract of the Journals of Mr. Commissary Von Reck," etc., p. 49. London, 1734.

[2] "Concise Natural History of East and West Florida," p. 98. New York, 1775.

[3] *See* Du Pratz's "History of Louisiana," vol. ii., p. 197. London, 1763. Bossu's "Travels," etc., vol. i., p. 232. London, 1771. Bartram's "Travels," p. 512. London, 1792. Lawson's "History of Carolina," p. 185. London, 1714.

part any thing like solemnity to the contubernal relationship, thus established, appears never to have been thought of. The tie—such as it was—originated in the fancy of the male, was at first sanctioned by the female friends of the woman, and in other cases by the cacique or head men of the tribe, and was dissoluble at the option of either party.

The Cherokees in the olden time are said to have had no laws against adultery. Speaking generally, it may be affirmed that the Southern Indians were monogamous[1] for the time being. This, however, was simply a matter of choice, and not of compulsion. The Muscogulges formed a marked exception to this rule. With them polygamy obtained with the utmost latitude—the first wife being esteemed the queen or superior, and the others her hand-maids and associates.[2] While polygamy was allowed among the Creeks, Captain Romans[3] declares that it was not usually practised. The only ceremonies attendant upon their marriages consisted in making some presents to the parents of the bride, and in feasting at the hut of the wife's father.

Intermarriages of first cousins was not permitted. If an Indian debauched his sister or any very near relative, his body was burnt and his ashes thrown into

Brickell's "Natural History of North Carolina," p. 304. Dublin, 1737. Haywood's "Natural and Aboriginal History of Tennessee," p. 276. Nashville, 1823. Adair's "History of the North American Indians," p. 138. London, 1775. Hennepin's "Continuation of the New Discovery," chap. xvii. London, 1698.

[1] "Singuli singulas habent uxores," says De Bry. "Regibus autem binas aut ternas habere permissum: Sola tamen primum ducta colitur & pro Regina agnoscitur."

"Brevis Narratio," p. 4. Francoforti ad Mœnum, anno 1591. Cabeça de Vaca says: "Every man has an acknowledged wife. The physicians are allowed more freedom; they may have two or three wives, among whom exist the greatest friendship and harmony."

[2] Bartram's "Travels," p. 513. London, 1792.

[3] "Concise Natural History of East and West Florida," p. 97. London, 1775.

the river. He was regarded as unworthy to remain upon the earth. Among the Carolina tribes the husband had a right to sell his wife. He changed his wife at pleasure, and had at the same time as many wives as he was able to maintain.[1]

Comparatively little virtue existed among the unmarried women. Their chances of marriage were not diminished but rather augmented by the fact that they had been great favorites, provided they had avoided conception during their years of general pleasure. The husband never pretended to recognize any restraint as imposed by the marital relation, but indulged his fancies as inclination prompted or opportunity offered. The wife, on the contrary, was deterred, by fear of public punishment, from the commission of indiscretions. Although these marriages were in great measure temporary in their character—constituting alliances of fancy and convenience—it was not uncommon for parties to live together until extreme old age in comparative peace and affection. By the side of the aged Mico Tomo-chi-chi, as thin and weak, he lies upon his blanket, hourly expecting the summons of the pale-king, we see the sorrowing form of his old wife, Scenauki, bending over and fanning him with a bunch of feathers.[2]

In all verity could the Indian husband say of his wife, as Petruchio affirmed of Catherine:

> "I will be master of what is mine own;
> She is my goods, my chattels; she is my house,
> My household stuff, my field, my barn,
> My horse, my ox, my ass, my anything."

[1] Lawson's "History of Carolina," p. 187. London, 1714.

[2] Whitefield's "Journal at Savannah," p. 2. London, 1739. "Historical Sketch of Tomo-chi-chi," by Charles C. Jones, Jr., p. 107. Albany, 1868.

Doomed to perpetual drudgery and to that subordinate position to which woman is always consigned where civilization and religion are not, she was little else than a beast of burden, busied with cooking, the manufacture of pottery, mats, baskets, moccasins and tunics, a tiller of the ground, a nurse for her own children, and at all times a servant to the commands and passions of the stronger sex.

Seldom barren, passing with great ease through the perils of childbirth, nourishing her offspring from her own breasts, and permitting the child to suck until it was well grown, with her own hands attending to every want of the infant, and guarding well its cleanliness as it lay lashed to its board cradle, it came to pass that the Indian mother seldom had a lame or deformed or sickly child. At an early age the boys were exercised in running, in playing ball, and in the use of the bow and arrow. Prizes were offered for which they contended; and, while quite young, they were made familiar with the secrets of hunting and fishing.[1]

Protracted ceremonies involving isolation, fasting, purgation, self-denial, and ablution, were religiously observed under the personal supervision of the Is-te-puc-cau-chau-thluc-co, or great leader, before the Creek youth was admitted to the dignity and privileges of manhood. Before going to war the young men were compelled, by the observance of certain formalities and prescribed duties, to prepare themselves to receive the war-physic—a charm against all ills.[2]

Of the COSTUME and ORNAMENTS of the Southern

[1] "Brevis Narratio," plate xxxvi.

[2] *See* Hawkins's "Sketch of the Creek Confederacy." Collections of the Georgia Historical Society, vol. iii., part 1, p. 78. Savannah, 1848.

Indians, the following early accounts furnish general descriptions:

As De Soto neared Coça, the cacique came out to receive him at the distance of two cross-bow shots from the town, borne in a litter on the shoulders of his principal men, seated on a cushion and covered with a mantle of marten-skins of the size and shape of a woman's shawl. On his head he wore a diadem of plumes, and he was surrounded by many attendants singing and playing upon flutes.

At Quizquiz the great cacique Aquisco, accompanied by two hundred canoes filled with armed men, waited upon him. These warriors were painted with ochre, and wore great bunches of white and colored plumes. Standing erect in the canoes, they held in their hands bows and arrows and also feathered shields with which they sheltered the oarsmen on either side. The barge conveying the cacique, and those containing his attendant chiefs, had awnings at the poop under which they sat. The cacica of Cutifachique, when she came out of her town to cross the river and extend to the *Adelantado* the hospitalities of her province, was borne to the water's edge in a chair. There she entered her canoe, over the stern of which was spread an awning. A mat lay extended in the bottom, and above this were two cushions upon which she sat. In the boats which escorted her was carried much clothing of the country, consisting of shawls and skins. These shawls were made, some from the bark of trees and others of feathers, white, gray, vermilion and yellow, rich and suitable for winter. The deer-skins of which moccasins, leggings, and coverings were fabricated, were well dressed and ornamented with many-colored designs. The cacica wore strings of pearls, one of which she threw around De Soto's neck, exchanging with him "many gracious words of friendship and courtesy."[1]

Cabeça de Vaca mentions the visit of an Indian chief clothed in a painted deer-skin, and borne upon the back of another Indian. Multitudes of his people attended him, some walking in advance and playing upon reed flutes.[2]

In plate xxxvii. of the "Brevis Narratio," we have a spirited illustration of the litter in which the chosen queen is being conveyed to the king. The mat, the cushioned seat, the canopy, the long fans of feather, the four chair-bearers with the rods resting upon their shoulders, and forked sticks carried in the hand to serve as supports to the litter when they paused to refresh themselves upon the journey—the company of musicians marching in front, playing upon reed flutes, the retinue of female attendants carrying baskets of fruits, and the plumed warriors with javelins in their hands bringing up and guarding the rear—are all represented with apparent fidelity.[3]

[1] "Narratives of the Career of Hernando de Soto," translated by Buckingham Smith, pp. 62, 75, 103. New York, 1866.

[2] "Relation," etc., translated by Buckingham Smith, p. 31. New York, 1871.

[3] The explanatory text is as follows: "Ducturus uxorem, Rex, ex nobiliorum puellarum cœtu, pulcerrimam maximamque deligere jubet: deinde duobus validis longuriis sede aptata, quæ rarioris alicujus animalis pelle tecta est, & posteriore ejus parte ornata ramis supernè nutantibus, ut sedentis caput tegant, Reginam delectam sedi imponentes, longurios sublevant quatuor viri robusti & humeris sustinent, singuli ligneam furcam manu gerentes, ut longuriis subponant quando quiescendum est; duo alii utrinque ad Reginæ latera progrediuntur rotunda umbracula elegantissimè confecta in oblongis baculis gestantes ad Reginam à Solis ardoribus tuendam: præunt alii tubas ex arboris cortice confectas inflantes supernè angustas, infernè laxiores, duobusque dumtaxat foraminibus, supero & infero, præditæ, quibus appensæ sunt ovales sphærulæ auræ, argentæ, æreæ ad majorem concentum. Pone sequuntur puellæ omnium formosissimæ, eleganter ornatæ torquibus & armillis ex margaritis, singulæ canistrum selectioribus fructibus plenum manu ferentes, & sub umbilicum supraque coxendices cinctæ certarum arborum musco ad obscæna tegendum. Eas sequuntur prætoriani."

The use of this primitive palanquin was commanded only by kings, queens, and the most distinguished personages, and seems to have existed chiefly among the Florida tribes.

While passing through what would now be known as Middle Georgia, De Soto observed blankets among the natives. These, says the Knight of Elvas, resembled shawls. Some of them were made from the inner bark of trees, and others of a grass[1] resembling the nettle, which, when beaten, becomes like flax.

Women used them for a covering, wearing one about the body from the waist downward, and another over the shoulder, with the right arm free, after the manner of the Gypsies. The men, on the contrary, wore but one, which they carried over the shoulder in the same way, the loins being covered with a bragueiro of deerskin, after the style of the woollen breech-cloth once the fashion in Spain. "The skins," continues the relator, "are well dressed—the color being given to them that is wished—and in such perfection that when of vermilion they look like very fine red broadcloth; and when black—the sort in use for shoes—they are of the purest. The same hues are given to blankets."[2]

Cabeça de Vaca[3] describes mantelets of thread with which the women partially covered their persons.

The most elaborate robe is that depicted in plate xxxix. of the "Brevis Narratio," upon the person of the king as he walks abroad attended by his queen. This is said to have been made of the skin of the stag, elegantly prepared and elaborately ornamented with various colors. It is confined in a prominent bow or

[1] Evidently the reference is to silk-grass, so common in this region.

[2] "Narratives of the Career of Hernando de Soto," etc., translated by Buckingham Smith, p. 53. New York, 1866.

[3] "Relation," etc., translated by Buckingham Smith, p. 35. New York, 1871.

knot resting on the top of the right shoulder, and thence falling over the left hip, is supported behind by a train-bearer. The arms and legs are bare. A cap is upon the king's head; his ears are ornamented with inflated fish-bladders; his elbows, wrists, and knees, are encircled by beads of shells and pearls, while from the left shoulder depend three strings of beads of like material reaching down as far as the right hip, crossing the breast and stomach transversely. Aside from her necklace, armlets, and anklets of pearls, and her ear-ornaments, his queen-consort is devoid of every covering save the female breech-clout, which differed from that worn by the men in that it encircled the hips, or depended from one shoulder, passing transversely below the navel and across the opposite hip, thus in each instance covering the person only in its most secret parts. Made of moss, it was more flowing and graceful than the naked flap and band used by the men to conceal their privates.

With the exception of these breech-clouts, the Florida Indians, most of the year, appeared in a state of nudity. The cold of winter necessitated the use of shawls and blankets, to which reference has already been made.

The warriors wore no artificial protection[1] for their bodies, but contented themselves with the most fanciful head-ornaments, and with personal decorations. So painted and ochred were their bodies, legs, and arms, with red, black, white, yellow and vermilion stripes, that, in the eyes of the Gentleman of Elvas, these primitive men-at-arms appeared to have on stockings and doublets. Some wore feathers and

[1] Captain Smith says the Virginia warriors carried round targets made of the bark of trees. "History of Virginia," vol. i., p. 132. Richmond, 1819.

others horns on their heads. Their faces were blackened and the eyes encircled with vermilion to heighten their fierce aspect.[1]

Children were permitted to go about in an entirely nude condition until, at their own suggestion, having attained the age of puberty, they put on the breech-clout. The male breech-clout is thus described by De Bry: "Obscœnas partes tegunt cervina pelle eleganter parata."

The custom of tattooing existed. "Maxima illorum pars corpus, brachia, femora pingit elegantibus & concinnis figuris quarum color numquam obliteratur: in ipsa enim cute sunt impressæ notæ sive puncturæ." Captain Ribault's account of the attire of the Florida Indians is as follows: "The most part of them cover their reins and private parts with fair hart's skinns, painted most commonly with sundry colors; and the fore-part of their bodies and arms be painted with pretty devised works of azure, red and black, so well and so properly, that the best painter in Europe could not amend it. The women have their bodies paintett with a certain herbe like unto morse, whereof the cedar trees, and all other trees, be always covered. The men for pleasure do always twine themselves therewith after sundry fashions. They be of tawny color, hawk-nosed, and of a pleasant countenance."[2]

The coast Indians are represented to have used less covering than the tribes of the interior. The farther south we observe them, during the warm months of the year, the more scanty seems the attire. A com-

[1] "Narratives of the Career of De Soto," etc., p. 99. New York, 1866. Compare plate xiv., "Brevis Narratio." Francoforti ad Mœnum, De Bry, anno 1591.

[2] "The Whole and True Discoverye of Terra Florida," etc., written in Frenche by Captaine Ribaulde, etc., and now newly set forth in the English, the xxx of May, 1563. Prynted at London by Rowland Hall, for Thomas Hackett.

parison of the plates illustrative of the "Admiranda Narratio," with those contained in the "Brevis Narratio," confirms this assertion. Even kings and chief-men among the Florida tribes mingled with their head warriors upon occasions of state and general deliberation, with nothing about their persons save the wretched breech-clout.[1] Among the common people even this was often lacking.

Of the vesture of the Virginia Indians Hariot writes: "They are a people clothed with loose mantles made of deere skins, & aprons of the same, rounde about their middles; all els naked."[2] In the accompanying plates[3] we are made acquainted with the distinctive shapes of the female tunic, the priest's cloak fashioned of quilted rabbit-skins, the aprons and tunics worn by chiefs, the long winter garments of old men, dressed with the hair on and lined inside with furs, the scanty covering of the conjurer, and the small breech-clout of the boat-maker and fisherman. The following interesting account of the clothing of the Virginia Indians is borrowed from that valuable work, "The True Travels, Adventures and Observations of Captaine John Smith:"[4] "For their apparell they are sometimes covered with the skinnes of wilde beasts, which in Winter are dressed with the hayre, but in Summer without. The better sort vse large mantels of Deare skins, not much differing in fashion from the Irish mantels. Some imbroidered with white beads, some with Copper, other painted after their manner. But the common sort haue scarce to cover

[1] Plates xi., xii., xvi., xviii., xxix., xxxiii., "Brevis Narratio."

[2] "A Briefe and True Report of the New-Found Land of Virginia," etc., p. 24. Francoforti ad Mœnum, 1590.

[3] iv., v., vi., viii., ix., xii., xiii., xvi., xviii.

[4] Richmond reprint, 1819, vol. i., p. 129.

their nakednesse but with grasse, the leaues of trees or such like. We haue seene some vse mantels made of Turky feathers, so prettily wrought and woven with threads, that nothing could be discerned but the feathers. That was exceeding warme and very handsome. But the women are alwayes covered about their middles with a skin, and very shamefast to be seene bare. They adorne themselues most with copper beads and paintings. Their women, some haue their legs, hands, breasts and face cunningly imbrodered with divers workes as beasts, serpents, artificially wrought into their flesh with blacke spots. In each eare commonly they haue 3 great holes, whereat they hang chaines, bracelets, or copper. Some of their men weare in those holes a small greene and yellow coloured snake, neare halfe a yard in length, which, crawling and lapping her selfe about his necke, oftentimes familiarly would kisse his lips. Others weare a dead Rat tyed by the taile. Some on their heads weare the wing of a bird or some large feather with a Rattell. Those Rattels are somewhat like the chape of a Rapier, but lesse, which they take from the taile of a snake. Many haue the whole skinne of a Hawke or some strange foule, stuffed with the wings abroad. Others a broad peece of Copper, and some the hand of their enemy dryed. Their heads and shoulders are painted red with the roote *Pocone* brayed to powder, mixed with oyle, this they hold in sommer to preserue them from the heate, and in winter from the cold. Many other formes of paintings they vse, but he is the most gallant that is the most monstrous to behold."

The shoes of the natives were made of buckskin, reinforced at the bottom. They were fastened on with running strings, the skin being drawn together like a purse, on the top of the foot, and tied round the ankle.[1]

During the summer the Louisiana Indians wore but little clothing—that of the men consisting of a small apron of deer-skin dressed white or dyed black, the latter color being reserved exclusively for the chiefs. The cloaks of the women were made of the bark of the mulberry-tree, or of the feathers of swans, turkeys, and ducks. The bark of young mulberry-shoots was first dried in the sun, and then beaten so as to cause all the woody parts to fall off. The remaining threads were then beaten a second time, and bleached by exposure to the dew. When well whitened, they were spun or twisted into thread. Garments were woven in the following manner. Two stakes were planted in the ground about a yard and a half apart. A cord was then stretched from the one to the other, to which were fastened double threads of bark. By hand other threads were curiously interwoven, so as in the end to form a cloak about a yard square, with wrought borders round the edges.

Young boys and girls went quite naked. At the age of eight or ten years the girls put on a little fringed petticoat made of threads of mulberry-bark. The boys remained uncovered until they attained a similar age.

"Some women," says Du Pratz,[2] "even in hot weather, have a small cloak wrapt round like a waist-coat; but when the cold sets in they wear a second, the middle of which passes under the right arm, and the two ends are fastened over the left shoulder, so

[1] Beverly's "History and Present State of Virginia," book iii., chap. i., p. 3. London, 1705.

[2] "History of Louisiana," etc., vol. ii., p. 231. London, 1763.

that the two arms are at liberty and one of the breasts is covered. They wear nothing on their heads; their hair is suffered to grow to its full length, except in the fore-part, and it is tied in a cue behind in a kind of net made of mulberry threads. They carefully pick out all the hairs that grow upon any part of their body."

The shoes of the men and women were fashioned after the same pattern, and were seldom worn except upon a journey. They were made of deer-skin, the sole and upper leather being of the same piece, and sewed together on the upper part of the foot. The moccasin was cut about three inches longer than the foot, and folded over the toes. The quarters were about nine inches high, and fastened round the leg like a buskin. Ear-rings of shell, and necklaces "composed of several strings of longish or roundish kernel-stones, somewhat resembling porcelaine," formed the customary female ornaments. With the smallest of these "kernel-stones" they decorated their furs, garters, and shoes. In early youth, females were tattooed across the nose and often down the middle of the chin. Some were pricked all over the upper part of the body, not excepting from the operation even their sensitive breasts.

During the winter the men covered themselves with a shirt made of two dressed deer-skins, and wore breeches of the same material, which protected the legs. In severe weather a buffalo-skin, dressed with the wool on, was kept next the body to increase the warmth.

The young men were very fond of dress, vying with each other in the decorations upon their vestments, painting themselves profusely with vermilion, wearing bracelets of the ribs of deer—softened in boiling water, then bent into the required shape, and finally polished so that they resembled ivory—fancying necklaces like the women, carrying fans in their hands, clipping off the hair from the crowns of their heads and substituting a piece of swan's-skin with the down upon it, fastening the finest white feathers to the hairs which remained, and suffering a part of their hair to grow long, so that they could weave it into a cue hanging over the left ear. Such is the portrait which has been preserved of the Louisiana youthful swells, more than a hundred years ago.

Warriors who had rendered themselves famous by some gallant exploit, caused a tomahawk to be pricked on the left shoulder. Underneath was indelibly imprinted the hieroglyphic sign of the conquered nation. The figure intended to be pricked was first drawn on the skin, which was then punctured to the depth of the tenth of an inch, and powdered charcoal rubbed in. Marks thus caused were never effaced. Ear-rings were worn by the men; and, fastened to their belts, might be seen gourds with pebbles in them.

The chief ornament of the king was a crown of feathers surmounting a black bonnet of net-work fastened to a red diadem, about two inches broad, embroidered with kernel-stones. The feathers were white, about eight inches tall in front and half as high behind. The women fabricated girdles, garters, and collars for carrying burdens. They also embroidered with porcupine-feathers.

Of the habit of the North Carolina Indians, Mr. Lawson[1] writes: The winter dress of the women is "a hairy Match-coat in the nature of a Plad. . . At other

[1] "History of Carolina," etc., p. 190. London, 1714.

times they have only a sort of Flap or Apron containing two Yards in Length and better than half a Yard deep. Sometimes it is a Deer-Skin dress'd white, and pointed or slit at the bottom, like Fringe. When this is clean, it becomes them very well. . . .

"All of them, when ripe, have a small String round the Waste, to which another is tied and comes between their Legs, where always is a Wad of Moss against the *Os pubis;* but never any Hair is there to be found. Sometimes they wear *Indian* Shooes or Moggizons, which are made after the same manner as the Mens are.

"The Hair of their Heads is made into a long Roll like a Horses Tail, and bound round with *Ronoak* or *Porcelan* which is a sort of Beads they make of the Conk-Shells. Others that have not this, make a Leather-String serve. The *Indian* Men have a Match-coat of Hair, Furs, Feathers, or Cloth, as the Women have. Their Hair is roll'd up on each Ear, as the Womens, only much shorter, and oftentimes a Roll on the Crown of the Head or Temples, which is just as they fancy; there being no Strictness in their Dress. Betwixt their Legs comes a Piece of Cloth,[1] that is tuck'd in by a Belt both before and behind. This is to hide their Nakedness. . . . They wear Shooes of Bucks, and sometimes Bears Skin, which they tan in an Hour or two, with the Bark of Trees boil'd, wherein they put the Leather whilst hot, and let it remain a little while, whereby it becomes so qualify'd as to endure Water and Dirt without growing hard. These have no Heels, and are made as fit for the Feet, as a Glove is for the Hand, and are very easie to travel in when one is a little us'd to them. . . . Their Feather Match-coats are very pretty, especially some of them which are made ex-

[1] Or wad of moss. Lawson, p. 203.

traordinary charming, containing several pretty Figures wrought in Feathers, making them seem like a fine Flower Silk-Shag; and when new and fresh, they become a Bed very well, instead of a Quilt. Some of another sort are made of Hare, Raccoon, Bever or Squirrel-Skins, which are very warm. Others again are made of the green Part of the Skin of a Mallard's Head, which they sew perfectly well together, their Thread being either the Sinews of a Deer divided very small, or Silk-Grass. When these are finish'd they look very finely, though they must needs be very troublesome to make. . . . Their Dress in Peace and War is quite different. Besides, when they go to War, their Hair is comb'd out by the Women, and done over very much with Bears Grease and red Root; with Feathers, Wings, Rings, Copper and *Peak* or *Wampum* in their Ears. Moreover, they buy Vermillion of the *Indian* Traders, wherewith they paint their Faces all over red, and commonly make a Circle of Black about one Eye, and another Circle of White about the other, whilst others bedawb their Faces with Tobacco-Pipe Clay, Lamp-black, black Lead and divers other Colours which they make with the several sorts of Minerals and Earths that they get in different Parts of the Country where they hunt and travel. When these Creatures are thus painted, they make the most frightful Figures that can be imitated by Men, and seem more like Devils than Humane Creatures. You may be sure that they are about some Mischief, when you see them thus painted; for in all the Hostilities which have ever been acted against the *English* at any time, in several of the Plantations of *America*, the Savages always appear'd in this Disguize, whereby they might never after be discover'd or known by any of the Christians that should happen to see them after they had made their Escape; for it is impossible ever to know an *Indian* under these Colours, although he has been at your House a thousand times, and you know him at other times as well as you do any Person living. As for their Women, they never use any Paint on their Faces. . . .

"Some of the *Indians* wear great Bobs in their Ears, and sometimes in the Holes thereof they put Eagles and other Birds Feathers for a Trophy. When they kill any Fowl, they commonly pluck off the downy Feathers and stick them all over their Heads. Some (both Men and Women) wear great Necklaces of their Money, made of Shells. . . . They oftentimes make of this Shell a sort of Gorge, which they wear about their Neck in a String; so it hangs on their Collar, whereon sometimes is engraven a Cross, or some odd sort of Figure which comes next in their Fancy." [1]

De Brahm [2] asserts that the South Carolina tribes, about the middle of the last century, had, among themselves, no distinction of dress. They painted their faces red in token of friendship, and black, in expression of warlike intentions. In common with their more northern and southern neighbors they ornamented their hair, ears, and necks with feathers, bobs and beads, wore mantles and breech-cloths, and used leather macksins. "Their cloathing," says Thomas Ash, consists of the "Skins of the Bear and Deer, the Skin drest after their Country Fashion, sometimes with black and red *Chequers* coloured." [3]

Captain Bernard Romans observed cloth made out

[1] Compare "Natural History of North Carolina," etc., by the wonderful plagiarist, John Brickell, M. D., p. 312, *et seq.* Dublin, 1737.

[2] "Documents connected with the History of South Carolina," edited by Plowden Charles Jennett Weston, p. 220. London, 1856.

[3] "Carolina," etc., by T. A.—, Gent., p. 35. London, 1682.

of the bark of a species of *Morus*, the root of the tree being used to dye it yellow. "Buffaloe's wool," he adds, "furnishes a material for a useful manufacture. They likewise make blankets and other coverings out of the feathers of the breasts of wild turkies by a process similar to that of our wig-makers when they knit hair together for the purpose of making wigs."[1]

During the spring of 1811, embedded in the flooring of a copperas cave, in Warren County, West Tennessee, two human bodies—the one male and the other female—were found. They were evidently Indians, and had been interred in curiously-wrought baskets made of cane, with coverings of the same material fitting over their tops. "The flesh of these persons," says Mr. Haywood,[2] "was entire and undecayed, of a brown, dryish colour produced by time, the flesh having adhered closely to the bones and sinews. Around the female, next her body, was placed a well-dressed deer skin. Next to this was placed a rug, very curiously wrought, of the bark of a tree and feathers. The bark seemed to have been formed of small strands, well twisted. Around each of these strands feathers were rolled, and the whole woven into a cloth of firm texture after the manner of our common coarse fabrics. This rug was about three feet wide and between six and seven feet in length. The whole of the ligaments thus framed of bark were completely covered by the feathers, forming a body of about one-eighth of an inch in thickness, the feathers extending about one-quarter of an inch in length from the strand to which they were confined. The appearance was highly diversified by

[1] "A Concise Natural History of East and West Florida," p. 85. New York, 1775.

[2] "Natural and Aboriginal History of Tennessee," p. 164. Nashville, 1823.

green, blue, yellow and black, presenting different shades of color when reflected upon by the light in different positions. The next covering was an undressed deer skin, around which was rolled, in good order, a plain shroud manufactured after the same order as the one ornamented with feathers. This article resembled very much in its texture the bags generally used for the purpose of holding coffee exported from the Havanna to the United States. The female had in her hand a fan formed of the tail feathers of a turkey. The points of these feathers were curiously bound by a buckskin string, well dressed, and were thus closely bound for about one inch from the points. About three inches from the point they were again bound by another deer skin string, in such a manner that the fan might be closed and expanded at pleasure. Between the feathers and this last binding by the string, were placed, around each feather, hairs which seem to have been taken from the tail of a deer. This hair was dyed of a deep scarlet red, and was one-third, at least, longer than the hairs of deer's tail in this climate generally are.

The male was interred sitting in a basket, after the same manner as the former, with this exception, that he had no feathered rug, neither had he a fan in his hand. The hair, which still remained on their heads, was entire. That of the female was of a yellow cast, *and of a very fine texture*. . . . The female was, when she deceased, of about the age of fourteen. The male was somewhat younger. The cave in which they were found abounded in nitre, copperas, alum and salts. The whole of this covering, with the baskets, was perfectly sound, without any marks of decay."

Thus have the conserving properties of the dust of this cave guarded from disintegration not only the forms, but even the clothing of these primitive peoples, offering them almost unchanged for the inspection of a later and not incurious age, placing in our hands the fabrics they wove, the skins they dressed, the colors and fans in which they delighted, and affording physical confirmation of the fidelity of at least some of the accounts furnished by the early observers.

Referring to the tribes then occupying the territory granted to the colony of Georgia, Mr. Oglethorpe, shortly after the settlement of Savannah, declares that "they, as the ancient Germans did, anoint with oil and expose themselves to the sun, which occasions their skins to be brown of color. The men paint themselves of various colors, red, blue, yellow and black. The men wear generally a girdle with a piece of cloth drawn through their legs and turned over the girdle both before and behind, so as to hide their nakedness. The women wear a kind of petticoat to the knees. Both men and women in the winter wear mantles something less than two yards square, which they wrap round their bodies as the Romans did their toga, generally keeping their arms bare; they are sometimes of woollen bought of the English, sometimes of furs which they dress themselves. They wear a kind of pumps which they call moccasins, made of deer skin, which they dress for that purpose."[1]

"Formerly," says Adair,[2] "the Indians made very handsome carpets. They have a wild hemp that grows about six feet high in open, rich, level lands,

[1] Salmon's "Modern History," fourth edition, vol. iii., p. 770.

[2] "History of the American Indians," p. 422. London, 1775.

and which usually ripens in July; it is plenty on our frontier settlements. When it is fit for use, they pull, steep, peel and beat it; and the old women spin it off the distaffs with wooden machines, having some clay on the middle of them to hasten the motion. When the coarse thread is prepared, they put it into a frame about six feet square, and, instead of a shuttle, they thrust through the thread with a long cane, having a large string through the web, which they shift at every second course of the thread. When they have thus finished their arduous labour, they paint each side of the carpet with such figures of various colours as their fruitful imaginations devise; particularly the images of those birds and beasts they are acquainted with; and likewis eof themselves, acting in their social and martial stations." He was informed that the Muscogees, time out of mind, passed the woof with a shuttle, "having a couple of threddles which they move with the hand so as to enable them to make good dispatch, something after our manner of weaving." The women were the manufacturers of these fabrics. Buffalo's wool was extensively used for spinning and weaving. The Choctaws made "turkey-feather blankets with the long feathers of the neck and breast of that large fowl." The inner end of the feather was twisted and made fast in a strong double thread of hemp or coarse twine made of the inner bark of the mulberry-tree. These threads were then worked together after the manner of a fine netting. The long and glittering feathers imparted to the outside of the blanket a pleasing appearance. Such fabrics were quite warm. This writer also confirms the use of breech-cloths, short petticoats, moccasins, and head-ornaments of feathers.[1]

Various clays, and the juices of roots, barks, berries and plants, were employed in painting their persons and dyeing their manufactures. Tassels of the hair of deer, colored red, were held in special esteem.[2]

Not only were the ears slit for the reception of inflated bladders, eagles' claws, feathers and various ornamental pendants, but in some instances the nipples and under lips were bored so that canes and other matters for personal adornment might be introduced and worn.[3] The nose was perforated to admit of the suspension of ornaments from the cartilaginous wall which separates the nostrils. It would appear that lip-stones (called by the Spanish *bezote* and by the Mexicans *teutetl*) were worn, at least to a limited extent.

Without multiplying these references, we are sufficiently assured of the fact that, in the ornamentation of their skins, in the manufacture of shell, stone, bone, wood, hair, and feather pendants, and in the fabrication of skin garments fringed and curiously colored, and of carpets and shawls made of fibre and feathers, a marked similarity existed among the Southern tribes. It is also evident that the manner of wearing these articles of clothing and of personal adornment was, in its general features, common to them all. We perceive that these Indians had advanced beyond that rudest stage when the undressed hide—stripped from the body of the slain wild animal and thrown around

[1] Compare "Bartram's Travels," pp. 499–502. London, 1792. Hennepin's "Continuation of the New Discovery," p. 79. London, 1698.

[2] "Relation of Cabeça de Vaca," p. 86. New York, 1871.

[3] Ibid., pp. 75–78. New York, 1871.

the shoulders—constituted the only protection against the inclement seasons, and that, in the manufacture of their feather coverings and in the decoration of their persons and garments, considerable taste was sometimes exhibited.

At an early period, the natives recognized the superiority of the European commodities, and eagerly exchanged their coarse fabrics for the strouds, blankets and trinkets exhibited by the white traders.

CHAPTER IV.

Music and Musical Instruments.—Dancing.—Games.—Gambling.—Festivals.—Divisions of the Year.—Counting.—Funeral Customs.

THE Southern Indians were much addicted to GAMES, DIVERSIONS, FESTIVALS, and DANCING. It has been quaintly remarked that man is the only animal that laughs, and we find in all ages, and among all peoples, how limited soever their resources, or narrow their avenues to pleasure, special attention has ever been paid to the subject of pastimes and amusements. During periods when the physical development and active training of the human body were eminently necessary for individual protection, subsistence, and a toleration of the dangers and privations incident to the precarious and exposed mode of life, the games in vogue were decidedly muscular in their character, and were conducted in the open air. On occasions of feasting and dancing, the music, both instrumental and vocal, was of that simple, primitive kind, adapted to mark the time required for the saltatory movements in which the performers indulged. Measured sounds there were, but melody and harmony were wanting. The cane flute, the drum and the rattle, constituted the principal musical instruments in vogue among the Southern tribes. The form of the decorated reed-flute or recorder[1] has been preserved for our information, and we are also familiar with the shape of the hand-rattle.[2] "For their musicke," says Captain John Smith,[3] "they vse a thicke Cane on which they pipe as on a Recorder. For their warres they haue a great deepe platter of wood. They cover the mouth thereof with a skin, at each corner they tie a walnut, which meeting on the backside neere the bottome, with a small rope they twitch them together till it be so taught and stiffe, that they may beat vpon it as vpon a drumme. But their chiefe instruments are Rattles made of small gourds or Pumpeon's shels. Of these they haue Base, Tenor, Countertenor, Meane and Treble. These, mingled with their voyces sometimes twenty or thirtie together, make such a terrible noise as would rather affright then delight any man." Mr. Bartram[4] asserts that the Southern Indians were all fond of music and dancing, the music being both vocal and instrumental. Among the musical instruments he enumerates the tambour, the rattle-gourd, and a kind of flute made of the joint of a reed, or of a deer's tibia. The last he pronounces a howling instrument, producing, instead of harmony, "a hideous, melancholy discord." With the tambour and rattle, however, accompanied by sweet, low voices, he confesses himself well pleased. These gourd-rattles contained corn, beans, or small pebbles, and were shaken by hand or struck against the ornamental posts which marked the dancing-ring, in exact time with the movements of the performers. Large earthen pots, tightly covered[5] with

[1] "Brevis Narratio," plate xxxvii. [2] "Admiranda Narratio," plate xviii.

[3] "True Travels," etc., vol. i., p. 136. Richmond reprint, 1819.

[4] "Travels," etc., p. 502. London, 1792.

[5] Brickell's "Natural History of North Carolina," p. 328. Dublin, 1737. Beverly says that these earthen drums were half-full of water. "History of Virginia," book iii., p 55. London, 1705

dressed deer-skins, answered as drums. The shells of terrapins were also fastened to the ankles or suspended from the waist-belts. These being partially filled with small stones or beans, with every motion of the body, gave utterance to rattling sounds. The leather stockings of the young dancing-women of the Creeks were "hung full of the hoofs of the roe-deer, in form of bells, in so much as to make them sound exactly like castagnettes."

Captain Romans counted four hundred and ninety-three of these horn-bells attached to one pair of stockings. Nine women, whose hose were similarly furnished, were present at the dance. Allowing the same number of these tinkling ornaments to each, we will perceive, by easy calculation, that one thousand one hundred and ten deer must have been killed to furnish these women with their dancing-bells. These musical instruments were supplemented by voices plaintive or vehement, slow or rapid, as best accorded with the character of the dance. Their songs, whether of war or devotion, harvest or hunting, consisted of but few words and scanty intonations, repeated in the most monotonous way. When we turn to the music and poetry of these peoples, we enter indeed upon a barren field, with scarcely any thing to provoke inquiry or reward investigation.

In the vicinity of the village was a spot specially prepared for and devoted to the dance. Here a fire was nightly kindled, and all who had a mind to be merry, assembled each evening.[1]

In plate xviii. of the "Briefe and True Report of the New-found Land of Virginia, made into English by Thomas Hariot," we have a lively representation of a

[1] "Admiranda Narratio," plate xx.

public dance—the occasíon a great and solemn feast, to which the inhabitants of neighboring towns had been invited—the place, a level spot in the midst of a broad plain, circular in shape, about which are planted in the ground posts "carued with heads like to the faces of nonnes couered with theyr vayles," the centre being occupied by "three of the fayrest Virgins of the companie, which, imbrassinge one another, doe, as yt wear, turne abowt in their dancinge." Around these, and following the line of the posts, fancifully attired and bearing in their hands the branches of trees and gourd-rattles, with which they keep time by striking them against the posts, are wildly singing and dancing, in the cool of the evening, the natives assembled for the celebration of this "solemne feaste."

Many of these dances were of a purely social character, and were participated in every night by way of amusement. Others were designed, by violent exercise, to prepare the actors "to endure fatigue, and improve their wind."[1] Others still were had in commemoration of war, of peace and of hunting; others in the early spring when the seed was sown, others when the harvest was ended; others—wild and terrible—in presence of captured victims doomed to torture and death; while others, with slow and solemn movement and carefully-observed ceremonies, were conducted in honor of some religious festival. There was scarce an occurrence of note, or a convocation of moment, which did not receive commemoration by a dance. Every occasion was provocative of this amusement.

Referring to the dancing of the tribes composing

[1] Lawson's "Carolina," p. 175. London, 1714.

the Creek Confederacy, Mr. Bartram[1] writes: "They have an endless variety of steps, but the most common, and that which I term the most civil, and indeed the most admired and practised amongst themselves, is a slow, shuffling, alternate step; both feet move forward, one after the other, first the right foot foremost, and next the left, moving one after the other, in opposite circles, i. e., first a circle of young men, and, within, a circle of young women moving together opposite ways, the men with the course of the sun and the females contrary to it; the men strike their arm with the open hand, and the girls clap hands and raise their shrill, sweet voices answering an elevated shout of the men at stated times of termination of the stanzas; and the girls perform an interlude or chorus separately.

"To accompany their dances they have songs of different classes, as martial, bacchanalian and amorous, which last, I must confess, are extravagantly libidinous;[2] and they have moral songs which seem to be the most esteemed and practised, and answer the purpose of religious lectures."

The Choctaws were distinguished above their neighbors for their poetry and music. Between their towns existed great rivalry in the composition of songs for dances, and each year, upon the solemnization of the Busk, at least one new song was produced.

Captain Smith thus describes a dance made for his entertainment by Pocahontas during the absence of her father: "In a fair, plain Field they made a Fire, before which he sat down upon a Mat, when suddenly amongst the Woods was heard such a hideous Noise

[1] "Travels," etc., p. 503. London, 1792.

[2] Compare Bossu's account of the *dance of impudicity*. "Travels," vol. i., p. 97. London, 1771.

and shrieking that the English betook themselves to their Arms, and seized on two or three Old Men by them, supposing *Powhatan*, with all his Power, was coming to surprize them. But presently *Pocahontas* came, willing him to kill her, if any hurt were intended; and the beholders, which were Men, Women and Children, satisfied the Captain that there was no such matter. Then presently they were presented with this Antick: thirty young Women came naked out of the Woods, only covered behind and before with a few Green Leaves, their Bodies all painted, some of one color, some of another, but all differing; their Leader had a fair pair of Buck's Horns on her Head and an Otter's Skin at her Girdle, and another at her Arm, a Quiver of Arrows at her Back, a Bow and Arrows in her Hand. The next had in her Hand a Sword, another a Club, another a Potstick; all of 'em being Horned alike. The rest were all set out with their several Devices. These Fiends with most Hellish Shouts and Cries, rushing from among the Trees, cast themselves in a Ring about the Fire, Singing and Dancing with most excellent ill variety, oft falling into their infernal passions, and then solemnly betaking themselves again to Sing and Dance; having spent near an hour in this *Mascarado*, as they enter'd, in like manner they departed."

In plate xxxviii. of the "Brevis Narratio," we see nineteen of these dancing-girls moving in a circle and singing the praises of the king and queen. Their steps are more graceful and their motions far less violent and irregular than those practised in religious dances, such, for example, as were observed upon the occasion of the sacrifice of the first-born.[1]

[1] "Brevis Narratio," plate xxxiv.

The great game upon which the Southern Indians staked both personal reputation and property, was the *chungke-game*. It was played by the warriors, and with those discoidal stones, the symmetry and beauty of which have attracted so much attention. So important was this amusement, so general the indulgence in it, and so desperate the betting, that we have deemed it proper to devote a separate chapter to its history and conduct.

In *ball-play* one village or tribe was often arrayed against the other, and the contest, although generally good-natured, was prosecuted with so much vigor and excitement, that the players sometimes encountered blows and tumbles which entailed severe bruises and broken limbs. This game was esteemed noble and manly; and, in its exercise, involved feats of strength and agility. Youths of both sexes were frequently engaged, and the principal matches were had in the fall of the year. One chief challenges another to the contest. They meet and make up the game, each selecting from his own tribe an equal number of contestants. Upon the appointed day the respective parties meet and lay off the ground upon some plain agreed upon, in the vicinity of a town. Much property is staked upon the issue, and this is deposited in a pile. Each party is then addressed by its chief, who admonishes fair play and animates the contestants with the hope and glory of beating their antagonists. The chiefs takē no active part in the sport, but, occupying a suitable position, act as judges. The players arrange themselves in the centre of the ball-ground, and the game proceeds. From several accounts descriptive of the manner in which the game was played, we select the following, furnished by Mr. Adair:[1] "The ball is made of a piece of scraped deer-skin, moistened, and stuffed hard with deer's hair, and strongly sewed with deer's sinews. The ball-sticks are about two feet long, the lower end somewhat resembling the palm of a hand, and which are worked with deer-skin thongs. Between these they catch the ball, and throw it a great distance, when not prevented by some of the opposite party, who fly to intercept them. The goal is about five hundred yards in length; at each end of it they fix two long, bending poles into the ground, three yards apart below, but slanting a considerable way outwards. The party that happens to throw the ball over these, counts one; but if it be thrown underneath, it is cast back and played for as usual. The gamesters are equal in number on each side; and at the beginning of every course of the ball, they throw it up high in the centre of the ground, and in a direct line between the two goals. When the crowd of players prevents the one who catched the ball, from throwing it off with a long direction, he commonly sends it the right course by an artful, sharp twirl. They are so exceedingly expert in this manly exercise, that, between the goals, the ball is mostly flying the different ways, by the force of the playing sticks, without falling to the ground, for they are not allowed to catch it with their hands. It is surprising to see how swiftly they fly, when closely chased by a nimble-footed pursuer; when they are intercepted by one of the opposite party, his fear of being cut by the ball-sticks, commonly gives them an opportunity of throwing it, perhaps a hundred yards; but the antagonist sometimes runs up

[1] "History of American Indians," p. 400. London, 1775.

behind, and by a sudden stroke dashes down the ball. It is a very unusual thing to see them act spitefully in any sort of game, not even in this severe and tempting exercise.

"Once, indeed, I saw some break the legs and arms of their opponents, by hurling them down, when on a descent and running at full speed. But I afterward understood, there was a family dispute of long continuance between them, that might have raised their spleen as much as the high bets they had then at stake, which was almost all they were worth. The Choktah are exceedingly addicted to gaming, and frequently, on the slightest and most hazardous occasions, will lay their all and as much as their credit can procure." The method of playing this game did not materially differ among the Southern nations.[1]

Foot-ball was also a manly and favorite diversion. These games were followed by feasting and dancing in the public square. Trials of skill were had with the bow and arrow, the spear and the club. The Natchez women amused themselves with tossing balls by hand, and in playing a game with bits of cane eight or nine inches long. "Three of these they hold loosely in one hand, and knock them to the ground with another; if two of them fall with the round side undermost, she that played counts one; but if only one, she counts nothing."[2]

Lawson[3] mentions several gambling games, as be-

[1] Compare Romans' "Concise Natural History of East and West Florida," p. 79. New York, 1775. Haywood's "Natural and Aboriginal History of Tennessee," p. 285. Nashville, 1823. Bartram's "Travels," etc., p. 506. London, 1792.

[2] Du Pratz' "History of Louisiana," vol. ii., p. 236. London, 1763.

[3] "History of Carolina," p. 176. London, 1714. Compare Hennepin's "Continuation of the New Discovery," etc., chap. xxi, p. 82. London, 1698.

ing in vogue among the Carolina Indians, some played with split reeds and others with persimmon-stones.

To such a desperate extent was gaming carried, that, having lost all their property, the players would not infrequently stake upon the final issue even their personal liberty, and remain willing servants of the victors until redeemed by relatives and friends.

The great feast of the year, among the Creeks, was the *Boos-ke-tau*. It was celebrated in July or August, and partook of the character of a sacred festival, during which universal thanks were offered to the Great Spirit for the incoming harvest. All fires were then extinguished, and were new lighted from the spark kindled by the high-priest. It was an occasion of general purification and of universal amnesty for all crimes committed during the year, murder excepted.[1]

Almost every month had its peculiar feast or festival. Among the Natchez the year began with our month of March, and was divided into thirteen moons. With each new moon a feast was celebrated, receiving its name from the principal fruits gathered or animals hunted. Thus, the first moon was called the *Deer* moon and was observed with universal joy as the commencement of the year. This was followed by the festival of *strawberries*. The third moon ushered in the *small corn*, and was impatiently expected because the crop of large corn seldom lasted from one harvest to the other.

The *water-melon feast* occurred during the fourth moon, answering to our month of June.

[1] Hawkins' "Sketch of the Creek Country." Collections of the Georgia Historical Society, vol. iii., part 1, p. 75. Savannah, 1848. Bartram's "Travels," etc., p. 507. London, 1792. Adair's "History of American Indians," p. 94. London, 1775. Timberlake's "Memoirs," p. 64. London, 1765.

The fifth moon was that of the *fishes.* At this time grapes were gathered.

The sixth was known as the *mulberry* moon. The *maize* or *Great-Corn* moon succeeded, and was rendered remarkable by the most noted festival of the year. The *Turkey* moon answered to our October, while the ninth and tenth moons were known respectively as the *Buffalo* and *Bear* moons. It was then those animals were hunted. The eleventh month was called the *cold-meal* moon; the twelfth, the *chestnut* moon; and the thirteenth, the *walnut* moon.[1]

If we may believe Adair,[2] the *annual feast of love* was most carefully observed.

There were festivals in honor of war and of peace, feasts of the dead, of marriage, and for curing the sick, and public ceremonies in adoration of the sun and in solemnization of various religious rites. When not actively engaged in hunting, or in warlike pursuits, the time of these primitive peoples was largely spent in feasting and dancing. Beneath mild skies, surrounded by forests yielding many and nutritious fruits, with few wants in the present and little care for the future, their lives were idly given to amusements, and the observance of sundry festivals whose recurrence constituted the epochal events of the year.

When Cabeça de Vaca asserted that the Southern Indians were ignorant of all time, and made no reckoning either by the month or the year, his statement was not entirely correct. We have already seen that they divided the year into thirteen moons. They also recognized four seasons—the return of the sun, summer, the fall of the leaf, and winter. Of the celestial

[1] Du Pratz' "History of Louisiana," vol. ii., p. 185. London, 1763.

[2] "History of American Indians," p. 113. London, 1775.

luminaries they took little note except of "the day-moon or sun," and of the "night-sun, or moon." Three divisions were assigned to the day—morning, or "the sun's coming-out," mid-day, and "the sun fallen into the water."

Arguing from the periodicity of their public religious feasts, Adair advances the idea that they understood the division of weeks into seven days. The year commenced with the first new moon of the vernal equinox. Knots of various colors and notched sticks were used to mark the lapse of time. The Cherokees counted as high as a hundred "by various numeral names," while the nations of East and West Florida "rose no higher than the decimal number, adding units after it by a conjunctive copulative."

We conclude these general observations by an allusion to the FUNERAL RITES observed by the Southern Indians. From the multitude of sepulchral shell and earth mounds still extant along the coast, it is evident that in ancient times the islands and headlands were densely populated. The variant ages of these tumuli, their internal evidence and many physical facts connected with them, give assurance that this Indian occupancy was long continued. Here the small shell-mound formed the common grave of the natives—the larger earth-mounds being generally erected in honor of chief, priest, or some noted person. The common dead were interred in a horizontal position, sometimes singly, but usually in numbers. The corpses or skeletons, with articles of property, were, in not a few instances, burnt upon the spot prior to the erection of the mound-tomb. In the tumuli of chiefs and priests, however, no evidences of cremation appear. In them the corpse was interred in a sitting posture.

A thick covering of tenacious clay—enveloping the body like a great, rude, inverted jar—or a light-wood post, firmly driven into the earth, against which the skeleton or dead body was placed, or to which, when seated on the ground, it was securely lashed with a grape-vine, or cord of some sort, was sometimes employed to keep the corpse in proper position while the earth was gradually accumulated around and above it.

The custom of depositing with the dead articles of personal property, which, it was believed, would prove of service to them both in their journey toward and in the land of spirits, seemingly prevailed from the earliest times. These sepulchral tumuli are located in the vicinity of the ancient villages and fishing-resorts of the natives. The indications are, that the coast was more densely populated than the other portions of the Southern country, excepting, perhaps, the valley-lands of some of the principal streams. It is entirely probable that the natives inhabiting the interior resorted, at certain seasons of the year, in considerable numbers, to the islands and headlands of the Atlantic coast and the Gulf of Mexico, for the purpose of fishing and subsisting upon the various and abundant supplies of food which the salt-water afforded. This the frequency of grave-mounds and relic-beds amply suggests.

As we leave the sea-shore, and until we encounter the rich valleys of more elevated sections, burial-mounds become more infrequent, and those dedicated to the inhumation of the general dead contain a larger number of skeletons than mounds of a similar class located on the coast. In them, so far as our observation extends, evidences of cremation are usually wanting.

Through the pine-barren belt sepulchral tumuli are rarely met with; and such as are found are located in the vicinity of deep swamps or near the rivers where luxuriant forests and abundant waters afforded generous supplies of game and fish. In the beautiful alluvial valleys of Upper Georgia, Tennessee, the Carolinas, Alabama, Mississippi, and Louisiana, we again encounter the physical traces of a permanent and extensive population. Here we are surrounded with monuments attesting the care and labor expended by these primitive peoples in commemoration of the last resting-places of their dead.

These burial-mounds are conical or elliptical in form, and vary in size from the small tumulus, whose outline can scarcely be traced, to barrows quite twenty feet high, and a hundred feet or more in diameter at the base.

The practice of entombing the dead in artificial tumuli was abandoned by the Southern Indians very shortly after the advent of the European, and there are good reasons for believing that the custom had fallen into disuse prior to that time. The summits and flanks of many large mounds which were never constructed for burial-purposes, contain, only a few feet below the surface, the skeletons of modern Indians. Natural elevations and river-bluffs are frequently filled with graves when there is nothing externally to distinguish them as ancient places of sepulture. It would seem from some of the earliest accounts we possess, that in the sixteenth century and among the Florida tribes only kings and high-priests were honored with mound-tombs.

From the absence of burial-mounds in many localities which we know must have been thickly settled and occupied for many centuries by the red race, we are led to the conclusion that the construction of sepulchral tumuli was limited, and that the common dead —undistinguished by such laborious sepulture—were returned to the bosom of mother earth with frail monuments marking the places of their final repose.

Even where we possess no historic knowledge of the preliminary funeral customs, or of the peoples by whom they were observed, it is curious to note the circumstance that contiguous barrows, similar in outward appearance, when opened, reveal different modes of interment. As wave after wave breaks upon the beach of the great ocean and then is dissipated into the evanescent foam or returns to the main to be seen and heard no more, each leaving, however, upon the strand its own sea-shells to tell that the tide was once there, so during the flight of the lapsed centuries have various tribes swept over the same locality, occupying it in turn, and, when departing, abandoning to those who came after, manifest proofs of their temporary dominion, and of the rites observed by them in the inhumation of their dead.

Within the historic period, the Choctaws maintained the custom of erecting mounds over their dead—the bodies being reserved in bark and cane coffins and deposited in a bone-house until they had accumulated sufficiently to warrant the labor of a general interment. In the early narratives we note a singular absence of all personal observation of sepulchral mound-building, and since our acquaintance with the manners of the Southern Indians the erection of tumuli above the dead was seldom attempted by them. Instead of concealing the corpses in the womb of the laboriously-constructed earth and shell mounds, they deposited their dead in cane baskets—having first enveloped them in shawls and mats of native manufacture—and laid them away in caves and crevices in the rocks, hid them in hollow trees, exposed them upon scaffolds, covered them with logs and stones, submerged them in rivers and lakes, and buried them in graves carefully lined with bark and poles. Of the funeral rites observed by the Southern Indians since the European colonization of this region, we will be advised by the following references.

Among the Natchez the dead were either inhumed or placed in tombs. These tombs were located within or very near their temples. They rested upon four forked sticks, fixed fast in the ground, and were raised some three feet above the earth. About eight feet long, and a foot and a half wide, they were prepared for the reception of a single corpse. After the body was placed upon it, a basket-work of twigs was woven around and covered with mud, an opening being left at the head through which food was presented to the deceased. When the flesh had all rotted away, the bones were taken out, placed in a box made of canes and then deposited in the temple. The common dead were mourned and lamented for a period of three days. Those who fell in battle were honored with a more protracted and grievous lamentation.

The *demise* of a Sun was followed by putting to death large numbers of his subjects, both male and female, that he might not appear unattended in the spirit-world.

In 1725 the *Stung Serpent*, who was the brother of the *Great Sun*, died. M. Le Page du Pratz was present on the occasion, and furnishes the following description of what then occurred: "We entered the hut of the deceased and found him on his bed of state, dressed in his finest cloaths, his face painted with vermilion, shod as if for a journey, with his feather-crown on his head. To his bed were fastened his arms, which consisted of a double-barreled gun, a pistol, a bow, a quiver full of arrows, and a tomahawk. Round his bed were placed all the calumets of peace he had received during his life, and on a pole, planted in the ground near it, hung a chain of forty-six rings of cane, painted red, to express the number of enemies he had slain. All his domesticks were round him, and they presented victuals to him at the usual hours, as if he were alive. The company in his hut were composed of his favourite wife, of a second wife, which he kept in another village and visited when his favourite was with child, of his chancellor, his physician, his chief domestic, his pipe-bearer, and some old women, who were all to be strangled at his interment. . . . Soon after, the natives begun the dance of death, and prepared for the funeral of the *Stung Serpent.* Orders were given to put none to death on that occasion, but those who were in the hut of the deceased. A child, however, had been already strangled by its father and mother, which ransomed their lives upon the death of the *Great Sun*, and raised them from the rank of *Stinkards* to that of *Nobles.* Those who were appointed to die were conducted twice a day, and placed in two rows before the temple, where they acted over the scene of their death, each accompanied by eight of their own relations who were to be their executioners, and by that office exempted themselves from dying upon the death of any of the suns, and likewise raised themselves to the dignity of men of rank. . . . On the day of the interment, the wife of the deceased made a very moving speech to the *French* who were present, recommending her children—to whom she also addressed herself—to their friendship, and advising a perpetual union between the two nations. Soon after, the master of the ceremonies appeared in a red-feathered crown, which half encircled his head, having a red staff in his hand in the form of a cross, at the end of which hung a garland of black feathers. All the upper part of his body was painted red, excepting his arms, and from his girdle to his knees hung a fringe of feathers, the rows of which were alternately white and red. When he came before the hut of the deceased, he saluted him with a great *hoo*, and then began the cry of death, in which he was followed by the whole people. Immediately after, the *Stung Serpent* was brought out on his bed of state, and was placed on a litter, which six of the guardians of the temple bore on their shoulders. The procession then began, the master of the ceremonies walking first, and after him the oldest warrior, holding in one hand the pole with the rings of canes, and in the other the pipe of war—a mark of the dignity of the deceased. Next followed the corpse, after which came those who were to die at the interment. The whole procession went three times round the hut of the deceased, and then those who carried the corpse proceeded in a circular kind of march, every turn intersecting the former, until they came to the temple. At every turn, the dead child was thrown by its parents before the bearers of the corpse, that they might walk over it; and when the corpse was placed in the temple' the victims were immediately strangled. The *Stung Serpent* and his two wives were buried in the same grave within the temple; the other victims were intered in different parts, and after the ceremony they burnt, according to custom, the hut of the deceased." [1]

[1] Du Pratz' "History of Louisiana," vol. ii., p. 216. London, 1763.

The Virginia kings, after death, were disposed of in the following manner: The body was slit in the back, and through the opening thus made the flesh was removed—the sinews being left so as to preserve the attachments of the various joints. The bones were then dried, the skin being prevented from shrinking by an application of oil or grease. Subsequently they were carefully disposed in proper order in the skin, the vacuities caused by the removal of the flesh being nicely filled with fine white sand, so as to restore the body to its natural size and appearance. Thus prepared, the corpse was laid upon a shelf, raised above the floor, in the building erected for the preservation of the corpses of their kings and rulers. This shelf was overspread with mats. The flesh removed during this rude process of embalming, having been exposed upon hurdles to the sun and thoroughly dried, was sewed up in a basket and set at the feet of the body. In this house of the dead was set up a Quioccos or idol, as a guard or sacred watcher over the remains. A priest remained in constant attendance night and day, whose office it was to keep every thing in order.[1]

The common people were buried in the earth in ordinary graves.

Among the Carolina tribes, the burial of the dead was accompanied with special ceremonies—the expense and formality attendant upon the funeral, according with the rank of the deceased. The corpse was first placed in a cane hurdle and deposited in an out-house, made for the purpose, where it was suffered to remain for a day and a night, guarded and mourned over by

[1] Hariot's "Virginia," plate xxii. Francoforti ad Mœnum, 1590. "History and Present State of Virginia" (Beverly). Book iii., chap. viii., p. 47. London, 1705. "A True Relation of Virginia" (Smith), p. 43. Boston, 1866.

the nearest relatives, with dishevelled hair. Those who are to officiate at the funeral, go into the town, and, from the backs of the first young men they meet, strip such blankets and match-coats as they deem suitable for their purpose. In these the dead body is wrapped, and then covered with two or three mats made of rushes or cane. The coffin is made of woven reeds, or hollow canes tied fast at both ends. When every thing is prepared for the interment, the corpse is carried from the house in which it has been lying, into the orchard of peach-trees, and is there deposited in another hurdle. Seated upon mats, are there congregated the family and tribe of the deceased, and invited guests. The medicine-man or conjurer, having enjoined silence, then pronounces a funeral oration, during which he recounts the exploits of the deceased, his valor, skill, love of country, property, and influence, alludes to the void caused by his death, and counsels those who remain to supply his place by following in his footsteps, pictures the happiness he will encounter in the world of spirits to which he has gone, and concludes his address by an allusion to the prominent traditions of his tribe. He is followed by other speakers. "At last," says Mr. Lawson,[1] "the Corpse is brought away from that Hurdle to the Grave by four young Men, attended by the Relations, the King, old Men, and all the Nation. When they come to the Sepulcre, which is about six Foot deep and eight Foot long, having at each end (that is, at the Head and Foot), a Light-Wood or Pitch-Pine Fork driven close down the sides of the Grave, firmly into the Ground; (these two Forks are to contain a Ridge-Pole, as you shall understand presently) before they lay the Corps

[1] "History of Carolina," etc., p. 181. London, 1714.

into the Grave, they cover the bottom two or three times over with the Bark of Trees, then they let down the Corps (with two Belts that the *Indians* carry their Burdens withal) very leisurely, upon the said Barks; then they lay over a Pole of the same Wood in the two Forks, and having a great many Pieces of Pitch-Pine Logs, about two Foot and a half long, they stick them in the sides of the Grave down each End, and near the Top thereof, where the other Ends lie on the Ridge-Pole, so that they are declining like the Roof of a House. These being very thick-plac'd they cover them [many times double] with Bark; then they throw the Earth thereon, that came out of the Grave, and beat it down very firm; by this Means the dead Body lies in a Vault, nothing touching him. . . .

"Now, when the Flesh is rotted and moulder'd from the Bone, they take up the Carcass and clean the Bones, and joint them together; afterwards, they dress them up in pure white dress'd Deer-skins, and lay them amongst their Grandees and Kings in the *Quiogozon*, which is their Royal Tomb or Burial-Place of their Kings and War-Captains. This is a very large magnificent Cabin [according to their Building] which is rais'd at the Publick Charge of the Nation, and maintain'd in a great deal of Form and Neatness. About seven foot high, is a Floor or Loft made, on which lie all their Princes and Great Men that have died for several hundred Years, all attir'd in the Dress I before told you of. No Person is to have his Bones lie here, and to be thus dress'd, unless he gives a round Sum of their Money to the Rulers for Admittance. If they remove never so far, to live in a Foreign Country, they never fail to take all these dead Bones along with them, though the Tediousness of their short daily

Marches keeps them never so long on their Journey. They reverence and adore this *Quiogozon* with all the Veneration and Respect that is possible for such a People to discharge, and had rather lose all, than have any Violence or Injury offer'd thereto. These Savages differ some small matter in their Burials; some burying right upwards and otherwise. . . . Yet they all agree in their Mourning, which is to appear every Night, at the Sepulcre, and howl and weep in a very dismal manner, having their faces dawb'd over with Light-wood Soot [which is the same as Lamp-black] and Bear's Oil. This renders them as black as it is possible to make themselves, so that theirs very much resemble the Faces of Executed Men boil'd in Tar. If the dead Person was a Grandee, to carry on the Funeral Ceremonies they hire People to cry and lament over the dead Man. Of this sort there are several that practise it for a Livelihood, and are very expert at Shedding abundance of Tears, and howling like Wolves, and so discharging their Office with abundance of Hypocrisy and Art. The women are never accompanied with these Ceremonies after Death; and to what World they allot that Sex, I never understood, unless, to wait on their dead Husbands; but they have more Wit than some of the Eastern Nations, who sacrifice themselves to accompany their Husbands into the next World. It is the dead Man's Relations by Blood, as his Uncles, Brothers, Sisters, Cousins, Sons, and Daughters, that mourn in good earnest, the Wives thinking their Duty is discharg'd, and that they are become free when their Husband is dead; so, as fast as they can, look out for another to supply his Place."

The ceremonies attendant upon the sepulture of

the Choctaw dead are thus described by Captain Bernard Romans:[1] "As soon as the deceased is departed a stage is erected and the corpse laid on it and covered with a bear-skin; if he be a man of note it is decorated and the poles painted red with vermillion and bear's oil; if a child, it is put upon stakes set across: at this stage the relations come and weep, asking many questions of the corpse, such as, Why he left them? Did not his wife serve him well? Was he not contented with his children? Had he not corn enough? Did not his land produce sufficient of every thing? Was he afraid of his enemies? etc., and this accompanied by loud howlings; the women will be there constantly, and sometimes, with the corrupted air and heat of the sun, faint so as to oblige the by-standers to carry them home; the men will also come and mourn in the same manner, but in the night or at other unseasonable times when they are least likely to be discovered.

"The stage is fenced round with poles, it remains thus a certain time, but not a fixed space, this is sometimes extended to three or four months, but seldom more than half that time. A certain set of venerable old Gentlemen who wear very long nails as a distinguishing badge on the thumb, fore and middle finger of each hand, constantly travel through the nation [when i was there i was told there were but five of this respectable order] that one of them may acquaint those concerned of the expiration of this period, which is according to their own fancy; the day being come the friends and relations assemble near the stage, a fire is made, and the respectable operator, after the body is

[1] "A Concise Natural History of East and West Florida," etc., pp. 89, 90. New York, 1775.

taken down, with his nails tears the remaining flesh off the bones and throws it with the entrails into the fire, where it is consumed; then he scrapes the bones and burns the scrapings likewise; the head, being painted red with vermillion, is, with the rest of the bones put into a neatly made chest (which, for a chief, is also made red), and deposited in the loft of a hut built for that purpose, and called bone-house; each town has one of these; after remaining here one year or thereabouts, if he be a man of any note, they take the chest down, and in an assembly of relations and friends they weep once more over him, refresh the colour of the head, paint the box red, and then deposit him to lasting oblivion.

"An enemy, and one who commits suicide, is buried under the earth as one to be directly forgotten and unworthy the above ceremonial obsequies and mourning."

Mr. Bartram's account is substantially the same, save that he intimates there is a general inhumation so soon as the bone-house becomes full of coffins. Then the respective coffins are borne by the nearest relatives of the deceased to the place of interment, where they are all piled one upon another in the form of a pyramid, and the conical hill of earth heaped above. The funeral ceremonies are concluded with the solemnization of a festival called the *feast of the dead.*[1]

The Muscogulges buried their dead in the earth—a deep pit, about four feet square, being dug under the cabin and couch occupied by the deceased. This grave was carefully lined with cypress-bark, and in it the corpse placed in a sitting posture. Such articles of

[1] *See* Bartram's "Travels," etc., p. 514. London, 1792. Compare Adair's "History of the American Indians," pp. 183, 184. London, 1775.

property as he valued most, were deposited with him.[1] Among the Alibamons—who also buried their dead in a sitting posture—to the suicide was denied the rite of sepulture. He was regarded as a coward, and his body was thrown into a river.[2]

The funeral customs of the Chicasaws[3] did not differ materially from those of the Muscogulges. They interred the dead as soon as the breath left the body, and beneath the couch on which the deceased expired.

Lieutenant Timberlake[4] intimates that the Cherokees, living upon the banks of the Tennessee, seldom buried their dead, but threw them into the river. Mr. Adair's observations were entirely different. He asserts[5] that when any member of this nation died away from home—if his companions were not closely pursued—the corpse was placed on a scaffold, covered with notched logs, to protect it from wild beasts and birds. When they imagined that the flesh had been consumed and the bones become dry, they returned to the spot, enveloped the skeleton in white deer-skins, brought it home, and, having mourned over it, buried it with the usual solemnities. Piles of stones were heaped up to commemorate the spots where fell their distinguished warriors, and to these rude monuments each passer-by added a stone in token of his appreciation of the valor and brave deeds of the deceased.

When a Cherokee died at home, his corpse was at once washed and anointed, brought out of his lodge and placed in a sitting posture on the skins of wild

[1] Bartram's "Travels," etc., p. 513. London, 1792. Romans' "Florida," p. 98. New York, 1775.

[2] Bossu's "Travels through Louisiana," vol. i., pp. 257, 258. London, 1771.

[3] Romans' "Florida," p. 71.

[4] "Memoirs," etc., p. 67. London, 1765.

[5] "History of the American Indians," p. 180. London, 1775.

beasts, supported by all his articles of property disposed around him, and with his face turned westward, as though looking into the door of the winter-house. A eulogium was then pronounced; and, when the period allotted for mourning had elapsed, the body carried three times around the house, in which it was to be interred, those officiating stopping for half a minute at the completion of each circuit. The religious man of the family of the deceased, who walked in front, chanted the funeral-song, in the chorus of which the procession joined.

Mr. Adair was present when a chief was buried. It would appear that he was interred beneath the floor of a winter-house. The preliminary funeral rites having been performed in the manner just indicated, "they laid," says our observer, "the corpse in his tomb in a sitting posture, with his face towards the east, his head anointed with bear's oil and his face painted red, but not streaked with black, because that is a constant emblem of war and death; he was drest in his finest apparel, having his gun and pouch and trusty hiccory bow, with a young panther's skin full of arrows, alongside of him, and every other useful thing he had been possessed of, that, when he rises again, they may serve him in that tract of land which pleased him best before he went to take his long sleep. His tomb was firm and clean inside. They covered it with thick logs, so as to bear several tiers of cypress bark, and such a quantity of clay, as would confine the putrid smell, and be on a level with the rest of the floor. They often sleep over those tombs, which, with the loud wailing of the women at the dusk of the evening, and dawn of the day, on benches close by the tombs, must awake the memory of their relations very often; and if they were killed by an enemy, it helps to irritate and set on such revengeful tempers, to retaliate blood for blood."

Juan Ortiz—sole survivor, among the Florida tribes, of the expedition of Panphilo de Narvaez, and for twelve long years condemned to slavery in the "Land of Flowers"—was, by his captors, compelled to stand guard at the temple in which the Indian dead reposed. Upon peril of his life he was forced to watch, lest the wild beasts should come by night and steal away the bodies. The story of his good fortune in delivering from the jaws of a predatory wolf the corpse of an Indian boy, is familiar to the readers of the narratives of De Soto's expedition.

The general respect paid by the natives to their dead, the care exhibited in the proper solemnization of their funeral rites, the private and public exhibitions of sorrow, the expressed belief in the existence of a spirit-world, the effort to furnish the deceased with such articles as would prove most serviceable upon the long journey, and in new and pleasant fields, the jealousy with which they watched over and defended the places of sepulture, and the earnestness and honor with which they perpetuated the memories of the great when they no longer walked among the living, declare that these primitive peoples—how barbarous soever they, in other respects, might have been—held no "light thoughts from objects of mortality," drew no "provocatives of mirth from anatomies," and showed no jugglers' tricks with skeletons. Their corpses were never knaved out of their graves to have their skulls made into drinking-bowls, or their bones turned into pipes. In nothing was the character of the Southern Indian worthy of greater commendation than in his veneration for the reputation and the tomb of his deceased leader, in the solicitude with which he laid his relative and friend to rest beneath the shadows of his native forests and within sight of his own village, and in the vigilance with which he insured the undisturbed repose of the dead of family and tribe.

Truthfully might the returning Indian, as he muses over the deserted and mutilated burial-place of his fathers, exclaim:

> "This bank, in which the dead were laid,
> Was sacred when its soil was ours;
> . . . . .
>
> "But now the wheat is green and high,
> On clods that hid the warrior's breast,
> And scattered in the furrows lie
> The weapons of his rest;
> And there, in the loose sand, is thrown
> Of his large arm the mouldering bone.
>
> "Ah! little thought the strong and brave
> Who bore their lifeless chieftain forth,
> Or the young wife, that weeping gave
> Her first-born to the earth,
> That the pale race, who waste us now,
> Among their bones should guide the plough."

CHAPTER V.

General Observations on Mound-Building.—Bartram's Account of the Georgia Tumuli.—Absence of Megalithic Monuments and Animal-shaped Mounds.—Distribution of the Ancient Population.—Few Sepulchral Mounds erected since the Advent of Europeans.—Antiquity of the Tumuli.

WHAT Sir Thomas Browne[1] quaintly styles "the restless inquietude for the diuturnity of our memories," an ambitious desire to wrest from oblivion the names and graves of such as were famed for feats of arms or remarkable for some individual excellence, an appreciation of the fact that in the tomb of the dead hero lived recollections which, while they dignified the past, also inspired hope in the present and proved a powerful incentive to future action, and that inclination (so natural to the human heart in all ages) to render the most affectionate and honorable sepulture to the departed, have united in causing the erection of some of the oldest and most prominent artificial monuments extant upon the earth's surface. Urnal interments, burnt relics and earth-mounds, inasmuch as they "lie not in fear of worms," endure when personal and even national memories have perished. In some of them rest the surest and earliest physical proofs of the antiquity of man. Amid the depths of forests,

[1] "Hydriotaphia."

where every thing like a history or even a tradition of the peoples who once dwelt beneath their shadows, is, to us of the present day, emphatically "in the urn," the curiosity of subsequent ages has, in ancient graves and sepulchral tumuli, caught a glimpse of many things appertaining to a forgotten past, learned lessons of the general pyre, the last valediction, the funeral customs, the religious rites and the domestic economy of nameless nations whose former existence could otherwise have been scarcely more than conjectured.

In periods the most remote, the earth-mound seems to have suggested itself as the most natural and enduring method of perpetuating the memory and of designating the last resting-place of the illustrious dead. The mound at Aconithus, erected over Artachies—the superintendent of the canal at Athos—remains, to this day, a memorial of Persian usage, a public recognition of the ability of that engineer, so famous in his generation, and a proof of the fidelity of Herodotus as an historian. Those mighty tumuli which tower along the banks of the Borysthenes are the tombs of Scythian kings. The neighborhood of the Gygæan Lake, near Sardis, in Asia Minor, is rendered remarkable by the presence of circular mounds, among which, perhaps, the most recent is that "prince of tumuli," the tomb of Alyattes, King of Lydia, which for nearly twenty-five hundred years has braved the changing seasons.

Allusions to such structures are not infrequent among the ancient poets. Thus Orestes, when addressing the manes of the murdered Agamemnon, says:

"If but some Lycian spear 'neath Ilium's walls
Had lowly laid thee,
A mighty name in the Atridan halls
Thou wouldst have made thee.

> Then hadst thou pitched thy fortunes like a star
> To son and daughter shining from afar!
> Beyond the wide-waved sea the *high-heaped mound*
> Had told forever
> Thy feats of battle, and with glory crowned
> Thy high endeavor."

The ceremonies attendant upon the burial of Patroclus are thus commemorated in the "Iliad:"

> "The Greeks obey. Where yet the embers glow
> Wide o'er the pile the sable wine they throw,
> And deep subsides the ashy heap below.
> Next the white bones his sad companions place,
> With tears collected, in the golden vase.
> The sacred relics to the tent they bore;
> The urn a vale of linen covered o'er.
> That done, they bid the sepulchre aspire,
> And cast the deep foundations round the pyre.
> High in the midst they heap the *swelling bed*
> *Of rising earth*, memorial of the dead."

Tydeus and Lycus were buried under earthen barrows, and Alexander the Great caused a tumulus to be heaped above his friend Hephæstion at a cost of twelve hundred talents. So ancient are some of these earth-mounds that they were old and mysterious in the days of Homer. Even in more polished ages, and in seasons of extreme opulence, the memory of the mound-tomb was not forgotten. Its rude earth dome was seen surmounting a circular arrangement of exquisite porticos, columns, and decorated walls, facing nearly every degree of the circle, and resplendent in all the carving and polish which the most beautiful marble could receive.[1]

Apart from monuments which we know to have been erected within the historic period, scattered over

[1] *See* Smyth's "Antiquity of Intellectual Man," pp. 102, 103. Edinburgh, 1868.

the plains, peopling the valleys, and crowning the hills of Europe, Asia, Africa, America, and the islands of the ocean, we find ancient tumuli—abundant and silent witnesses of the early constructive labors of nameless tribes and nations.

More than three hundred years ago, artificial tumuli within the present geographical limits of Georgia attracted the notice of the Spanish adventurers and early voyagers. These physical traces of a population apparently older and more patient of labor than that which they found in possession of the soil, while they excited the wonder and curiosity of the colonists, do not appear to have enlisted any careful inquiry, or to have received a minute examination. The most august of them were dismissed with little more than a bare mention of their existence, and, even where descriptions were attempted, they were either so meagre in their outlines as to be almost valueless for the purposes of definite information, or so exaggerated as to savor more of romance than of reality.

At a remove from those who could verify their observations by personal examination and careful inspection—filled with vague conjectures touching manners and matters entirely novel in their character—in a region wild, remote, and abounding with strange scenes, unusual features and but partially-comprehended traditions—with imaginations often excited to the last degree—influenced by extravagant rumors—sometimes investing an occurrence, a suggestion, or an object, with an air of importance far beyond its deserts, and again treating with entire neglect or disdainful words things which were really worthy of specific mention and historic commemoration, the early narrators compel the candid reader to receive their relations *cum grano salis.*

Since the date of their observations, and even of Mr. Bartram's visit, the winds and rains of many seasons have sadly changed the appearance of these earth-mounds. Worn away by the elements, marred by the ploughshare, and torn asunder by the curious, many of them have been despoiled of their original proportions. The branches of the forest-trees which once overshadowed them are, in not a few instances, no longer outstretched for their preservation, and some have been wholly crushed out of existence by the tread of a statelier civilization.

Making, however, due allowance for such changes, after a somewhat extended and careful survey of these monuments, we cannot resist the impression that the early descriptions are frequently not only over-wrought, but unnatural. What would now be regarded as an ordinary conical mound has, on more than one occasion, been represented as possessing physical peculiarities of an unusual and remarkable character.

Garcilasso mentions the existence of large artificial tumuli with precipitous sides, flat on the top, and located in rich valleys, near the banks of beautiful streams, and says that they were erected for the purpose of sustaining the houses of chiefs and their families. Wooden stairways made by cutting out inclined planes fifteen or twenty feet wide, flanked on the sides with posts and with poles laid horizontally across the earthen steps, afforded the means of ascending to their tops. At the foot of these mounds a square was marked out, around which were built the dwellings of the principal men of the tribe. Outside appeared the wigwams of the common people. A disposition to place the residence of the chief in a commanding position—thereby elevating the cacique above his subjects—and a desire to contribute to his personal security are assigned as motives for the expenditure of so much labor.

Various are the allusions made by that intelligent and interesting traveller, Mr. William Bartram, to the presence of ancient tumuli within the limits of Georgia. Some of his descriptions are evidently exaggerated, but they are the most minute which have been preserved for our information. From them we select the following.

Above the town of Wrightsboro and overlooking the low grounds of the north branch of Little River, he saw "very magnificent monuments of the power and industry of the ancient inhabitants of these lands. . . . I observed," he writes, "a stupendous conical pyramid, or artificial mount of earth, vast tetragon terraces, and a large sunken area, of a cubical form, encompassed with banks of earth; and certain traces of a larger Indian town, the work of a powerful nation, whose period of grandeur perhaps long preceded the discovery of this continent."[1]

At Silver Bluff, on the Savannah River, the surface of the ground was rendered remarkable by "various monuments and vestiges of the residence of the ancients; as Indian conical mounts, terraces, areas, etc., as well as remains or traces of fortresses of regular formation."[2]

Near Fort James, which was located not far from the confluence of the Broad and Savannah Rivers, the surgeon of the garrison drew the attention of Mr. Bartram to some Indian monuments "worthy of every

[1] "Travels," etc., p. 37. London, 1792.
[2] Ibid., p. 313.

traveller's notice. . . . These wonderful labours of the ancients stand in a level plain, very near the bank of the river, now twenty or thirty yards from it. They consist of conical mounts of earth, and four square terraces, etc. The great mount is in the form of a cone, about forty or fifty feet high, and the circumference of its base two or three hundred yards, entirely composed of the loamy rich earth of the low-grounds; the top or apex is flat: a spiral path or track leading from the ground up to the top is still visible, where now grows a large, beautiful spreading Red Cedar (Juniperus Americana); there appear four niches, excavated out of the sides of this hill, at different heights from the base, fronting the four cardinal points; these niches or sentry boxes are entered into from the winding path, and seem to have been meant for resting-places or look-outs. The circumjacent level grounds are cleared and planted with Indian Corn at present; and I think the proprietor of these lands, who accompanied us to this place, said that the mount itself yielded above one hundred bushels in one season: the land hereabouts is indeed exceedingly fertile and productive."[1]

Having suggested that these tumuli were intended to serve as "look-out towers," having commented upon the fact that such public works would have required the united labor and attention of a whole nation—circumstanced as the Indians then were—to have constructed one of them almost in an age, and after describing several smaller mounds "round the great one, with some very large tetragon terraces on each side, near one hundred yards in length," with surfaces elevated four, six, eight, and ten feet above the ground, our author concludes by hazarding the conjecture that these arti-

[1] "Travels," etc., pp. 322, 323. London, 1792.

ficial elevations were designed as "retreats and refuges" from the swelling tide of the river during seasons of sudden inundations.

The mounds on the east bank of the Ocmulgee River, near Macon, did not escape the observation of Mr. Bartram. Even the lonely mounds along the Alatamaha attracted his attention.

The council-house of the Cherokee town of Cowe, he tells us, was a large rotunda capable of accomodating several hundred people. It stood "on the top of an ancient artificial mount of earth, of about twenty feet perpendicular," and—the rotunda itself being rather more than thirty feet high—the whole fabric possessed an elevation of about sixty feet. "It is proper to observe," he continues, "that this mount on which the rotunda stands, is of a much ancienter date than the building, and perhaps was raised for another purpose. The Cherokees themselves are as ignorant as we are, by what people or for what purpose these artificial hills were raised; they have various stories concerning them, the best of which amount to no more than mere conjecture, and leave us entirely in the dark; but they have a tradition common with the other nations of Indians, that they found them in much the same condition as they now appear, when their forefathers arrived from the West and possessed themselves of the country, after vanquishing the nations of red men who then inhabited it, who themselves found these mounts when they took possession of the country, the former possessors delivering the same story concerning them: perhaps they were designed and appropriated by the people who constructed them, to some religious purpose as great altars and temples."[1]

[1] "Travels," etc., pp. 365, 366. London, 1792.

During the progress of this investigation it will be perceived that mound-building—which seems to have been falling into disuse among the Southern Indians prior to the dawn of the historic period—was entirely abandoned very shortly after intercourse was established between the Europeans and the red-men. We will observe, moreover, that these ancient tumuli were, by later tribes, subjected to secondary uses, so that in not a few instances the summits and flanks of large temple-mounds originally designed for religious objects —such as the worship of the sun—were, by the Creeks and Cherokees, converted into stockade-forts, used as elevations for council-lodges and the residences of their chiefs, or devoted to the purposes of sepulture. This can scarcely be wondered at when we remember that many of the nomadic tribes who peopled this region were unstable in their seats, engaged in ever-recurring and annihilating wars, and constantly yielding to the conquest of more powerful neighbors who, expelling them from some coveted hunting-ground or fishing-resort, possessed themselves of the desired domain, caring little for the frail memories which clustered about the name and monuments of the vanquished. In an age entirely devoid of letters, it is not surprising that with the lapse of time the victors should have preserved not even a distinct tradition of the conquered. It will be remembered that the North American Indian was generally quite reticent as to his people and their old customs, and frequently denied to the stranger a knowledge of matters which he did not desire either to discuss or to reveal. When we reflect upon the careless and uncertain manner in which the annals of these peoples were perpetuated, it is not improbable that in the course of centuries all definite accounts of the builders of these artificial elevations and the history of their construction should have faded from the recollection even of the descendants of those by whom they were erected.

In one of his addresses to the pupils of the Royal Academy, Sir Joshua Reynolds remarked that when the ignorant inhabitants of the East were questioned concerning the stately ruins which filled their land—melancholy monuments of former grandeur and long-lost science—their universal response was, "They were built by magicians." Finding a vast gulf between its own powers and works indicative of skill and great labor, the untaught and inert mind of the savage dismisses the contemplation of their origin and primal uses either with an avowal of utter ignorance on the subject or by referring their creation to the agency of some supernatural influence. It is proper, therefore, to receive with caution the traditions delivered by the modern Indians with regard to the erection and history of the more august tumuli which dignify the valleys and tower along the banks of some of the principal rivers in Georgia. With the exception of stone graves, rock-piles, and walls loosely constructed of stones, laid one upon the other, there is, in this State, a remarkable absence of megalithic monuments, such as dolmens, menhirs, and avenues, which abound in so many portions of the Old World. We search in vain for animal-shaped mounds; and yet Georgia, in almost every section, teems with vestiges of an ancient population now wholly extinct within her borders. Stone tumuli and rudely-constructed rock-walls rear their heads even upon the summit of lofty Yonah. The spurs of the Blue Ridge give frequent evidence of inhumations whose mouldering heaps have for generations defied the annihilating influences of the tempest. The beautiful valleys of Nacoochee, of the Etowah, the Oostenaula, the Chattahoochee, and other streams, are rendered remarkable by the presence of tumuli of unusual size. Upon the banks of the Savannah, by the waters of the Ogeechee, and within the swamps of the Alatamaha, are found surprising monuments of ancient industry and devotion. Even throughout the lonely pine-barren region similar remains exist wherever a truant stream or moss-clad swamp infuses new vigor into the forest growth, and affords friendly cover for game. The coast and the low-lying islands are literally studded with tumuli beneath which the unnumbered and nameless dead of centuries repose.

As the presence of these mounds may be regarded as indicating the particular localities most thickly peopled by the aborigines in years long since reckoned with an unrecorded past, we are able to state, in general terms, that the tendency of this early population was toward the rivers and deep swamps, the rich valleys and the sea-coast. The physical inducements which impelled nomadic tribes to give a preference to such seats are obvious. Seldom are earth-mounds found at a considerable remove from water-courses. Water and game were the chief attractions in the choice of a settlement. Rich alluvial lands, whose fertility would make amends for the rude cultivation bestowed upon them, were often selected as the sites of their villages. In those early days the rivers abounded with fish, and the deep swamps were replete with terrapins, alligators, deer, and other game. In the depths of these swamps, beneath the shadows of moss-covered trees and by the sides of the sluggish lagoons, large mounds are not infrequent. It is upon the islands, however, and along the headlands of the coast, that they appear in greatest numbers.

Take, for example, that group of more than forty mounds upon the Colonel's Island, in Liberty County, located in the vicinity of a large spring, which for unnumbered years has been sending forth its copious and refreshing waters. Besides the regular sepulchral tumuli composed of sand, the adjacent fields are literally hoary with shell-mounds and the *débris* of long-continued encampments. Extended oyster-beds, neighboring creeks abounding with crabs, shrimp, and salt-water fish of every variety native to the coast, woods in former years well stocked with game, the natural advantages of a high, dry bluff sheltered from north-easterly gales, and this never-failing supply of fresh water, without doubt rendered this a very attractive spot to the Indian. His settlement here was permanent and extensive. Most of the tumuli in this neighborhood are sepulchral in their character. Such is the distinguishing peculiarity of nearly all the coast mounds.

The ancient tumuli still extant within the geographical limits of Georgia are frequently associated in groups, and at other times exist as isolated monuments erected upon or near localities possessing some natural advantages for observation, defence, or for the facile procurement of food. In form they are circular, elliptical, quadrangular, and polygonal. Some are flat on the top, resembling truncated pyramids and truncated cones. The prevailing type, however, is that of the conical earth-mound. There is every variety in size, from the large temple-mound on the Etowah—more than sixty-five feet high, and with a summit diameter of over two hundred feet—to the small sepulchral tumulus whose existence can scarcely be recognized. Many are almost level with the ground, and decomposing human bones, mingled with fragments of pottery, lie exposed upon the surface. Constructed of loose mould, clay, and sand, they are liable to constant diminution in size, and eventually to total obliteration. The consequence is, they are all more or less reduced, and we may readily believe that many of the smaller ones and those of oldest dates have entirely disappeared.

Aside from the careful and laborious preparation of their Chunky-Yards,[1] the construction of elevated foundations for their rotundas, and the erection of occasional and small tumuli above some deceased persons of note, it would appear that the Georgia tribes had well nigh abandoned the custom of mound-building prior to the advent of the Europeans. In Plate XL. of the "Brevis Narratio"[2] we have a spirited representation of the ceremonies observed by the Florida Indians upon the occasion of the sepulture of their kings and priests. Located in the vicinity of the village appears a small conical mound surmounted by the shell drinking-cup of the deceased, and surrounded by a row of arrows stuck in the ground. Gathered in a circle about this sepulchral tumulus the bereaved members of the tribe, upon bended knees, are bewailing the death of him in whose honor this grave-mound had been heaped up.

Bartram[3] commemorates the fact that in his day the Choctaws covered the pyramid of coffins, taken

[1] *See* Bartram's "Creek and Cherokee Indians." "Transactions of the American Ethnological Society," vol. iii., part 1, p. 52.

[2] Francoforti ad Mœnum, De Bry. Anno 1591.

[3] "Travels," etc., pp. 514, 515. London, 1792.

from the bone-house, with earth, thus raising "a conical hill or mount."

Tomo-chi-chi pointed out to General Oglethorpe a large conical mound near Savannah, in which he said the Yamacraw chief was interred, who had, many years before, entertained a great white man with a red beard, who entered the Savannah River in a large vessel, and in his barge came up to Yamacraw bluff.[1]

Within the range of my personal observation, glass beads, silver ornaments, hawk-bells, metallic kettles, and occasionally a rusty gun or rifle-barrel, have been found in earth mounds; but they evidently belonged to secondary interments, the graves in which they were located being either on the top or sides of the tumuli, and but a few feet deep.

Only in one instance has the writer discovered any article of European manufacture interred with the dead in whose honor the mound was erected. Upon opening a small mound on the coast, a few miles below Savannah, an earthen pot, several arrow-heads, a stone celt, and a portion of an old-fashioned sword, were seen in immediate association with the decayed bones of a human skeleton. This tumulus was conical in form, seven feet high, and about twenty feet in diameter at the base. It contained a single skeleton, and that lay, with the articles enumerated, at the bottom and on a level with the plain. The oak handle, most of the guard, and about seven inches of the blade of the weapon still remained. The rest had perished from rust. Strange to say, the oak had more effectually than the metal resisted the "gnawing tooth of time." This mound had never, prior to this occa-

[1] "History of the Province of Georgia," etc., by John Gerar William De Brahm, p. 38. Wormsloe, 1849.

sion, been opened, or in any manner disturbed, except by the winds and rains of the changing seasons. The interment was primary, and the articles were lodged with the dead before this mound-tomb was heaped above him.

It may be confidently asserted, therefore, that burial-mounds were erected by the Southern Indians within the historic period; but it is not clear that the modern tribes had aught to do with the construction of those larger tumuli, in form resembling truncated pyramids and truncated cones, sometimes terraced, frequently surrounded by a ditch or embankment, and intended for purposes other than those of sepulture.

Whatever may have been the antecedent usages of the natives with respect to the erection of sepulchral tumuli, it is quite certain that their use was discontinued very shortly after the arrival of the colonists. Then, instead of being carefully disposed in the womb of the laboriously-constructed mound, the dead were exposed upon hastily-prepared scaffolds, hidden away in ledges of rocks, buried beneath the floors of their lodges, concealed in hollow trees, submerged in ponds, lakes and rivers, or interred in the forests with but ephemeral *indicia* to mark their last resting-places. When used at all by the later tribes, these ancient tumuli seem to have been employed as convenient localities for what we may call secondary interments.

It is safe to assert that most of the mounds antedate the historic period. Compared with each other they differ materially in age. This is not to be wondered at, when we remember that the occupancy of this region by the red race, if we credit their traditions and properly interpret the monuments which they have left behind them, must have lasted for many generations. Some of these tumuli are not less than eight centuries old, while at least one, as we have already intimated, was thrown up after the European had visited the New World. In the absence of all definite information, the antiquity of these tumuli may be readily inferred from their location, internal evidence, and from the growth of the forest-trees which overshadow them. One of the noblest specimens of the live-oak we have ever seen grew upon the summit, and with its majestic arms threw a protecting influence above and around the entire mound; the dead, nameless here for evermore; his tomb a rude heap of native earth in the solitude of the wild-wood he once loved so well; his companions gone, his memory forgotten, and this pride of the forest seemingly a guardian of the consecrated spot, with its deep foliage affording an inviting retreat wherein the pleasant birds of spring might warble their morning and evening songs, its sturdy roots preserving the symmetry of the grave, its overarching branches defending its yielding form from the ruthless influences of the tempest. Attired in its garb of sober green, with its drapery of sombre moss swaying slowly and solemnly in the ambient air, it appeared an aged mourner watching over the dead of the children of the forest.[1]

If to the time probably consumed in the actual construction of some of the largest tumuli, we add the period intervening between their completion and abandonment—the length of which, although entirely a matter of conjecture, could assuredly have been by no means inconsiderable—and then note the fact that,

[1] This live-oak was nearly ten feet in diameter, and we know that it is a tree of slow growth.

when first observed by the whites, they were deserted and overgrown with forest-trees apparently as large as any which composed the surrounding forests—not forgetting the further circumstance, that the Indians who were domiciled here could impart to the inquiring European not even a tradition of the time when or of the peoples by whom they were built—in endeavoring to ascertain their age, the mind is irresistibly led back to a remote date.

That the peoples who once possessed the hydrographical basin of the Mississippi, and, departing, left behind them all along the banks of the Father of Waters, in the valleys of the Ohio, the Scioto and elsewhere, striking monuments of their labors, superstitions, and combined industry, at some remote period occupied at least some of the fertile valleys of Cherokee, Middle and Western Georgia, is not improbable. The location and physical peculiarities of some tumuli and enclosures, the character of the remains found in and near them, the presence of stone idols and metallic ornaments, and the traditions of modern Indians—who regarded them with commingled ignorance and wonder—unite in claiming for them not only a marked antiquity, but also a striking resemblance to the monuments of the Mississippi Valley. When compared with mounds which we know to be the product of the labor of the ancestors of the present Indians, characteristic differences are observed, for which we are sometimes at a loss satisfactorily to account.

While it may be regarded as a matter of speculation whether the builders of the terraced mounds and enclosed works within the confines of Georgia were the actual progenitors of the Indians who occupied this country when it was first visited by the European, and while we may not be able fully to explain how it came to pass that the later tribes were more nomadic in their habits, less patient of labor, and so neglectful of many of the customs which seemingly obtained among the peoples whose combined industry erected these enduring monuments—in the light of the Spanish narratives, after a careful consideration of the relics themselves, and in view of all the facts which have thus far been disclosed, both by personal observation and the investigation of others, while freely admitting that the modern Indians, from various causes, had ceased to engage in the erection of works in whose completion, with the indifferent implements at command, so much tedious physical effort was involved, we nevertheless see no good reason for supposing that these more prominent tumuli and enclosures may not have been constructed in the olden time by peoples akin to and in the main by no means further advanced in semi-civilization than the red-men native here at the dawn of the historic period. In a word, we do not concur in the opinion, so often expressed, that the mound-builders were a race distinct from and superior in art, government, and religion, to the Southern Indians of the fifteenth and sixteenth centuries.

CHAPTER VI.

Mounds on the Etowah River.—Temple for Sun-worship.—Stone Images.—Fish-preserves.—Tumuli in the Valley of Little Shoulder-bone Creek.—Circular Earth-work on the Head-waters of the Ogeechee.—Stone Tumulus near Sparta.—Mounds on the Savannah River.—Meeting between the Cacica of the Savannah and De Soto.

PASSING from these general observations, we proceed to consider the physical peculiarities of some of the most interesting and prominent groups of ancient mounds and enclosures within the present geographical limits of Georgia.

The first we shall notice are located upon the right bank of the Etowah River, on the plantation of Colonel Lewis Tumlin, a few miles from Cartersville, in Bartow County. Viewed as a whole, this group is the most remarkable within the confines of the State. These mounds are situated in the midst of a beautiful and fertile valley. They occupy a central position in an area of some fifty acres, bounded on the south and east by the Etowah River, and on the north and west by a large ditch or artificial canal, which at its lower end communicates directly with the river. This moat (G G, Plate I.) at present varies in depth from five to twenty-five feet, and in width from twenty to seventy-five feet. No parapets or earth-walls appear upon its edges. Along its line are two reservoirs (D D), of

Plate 1.

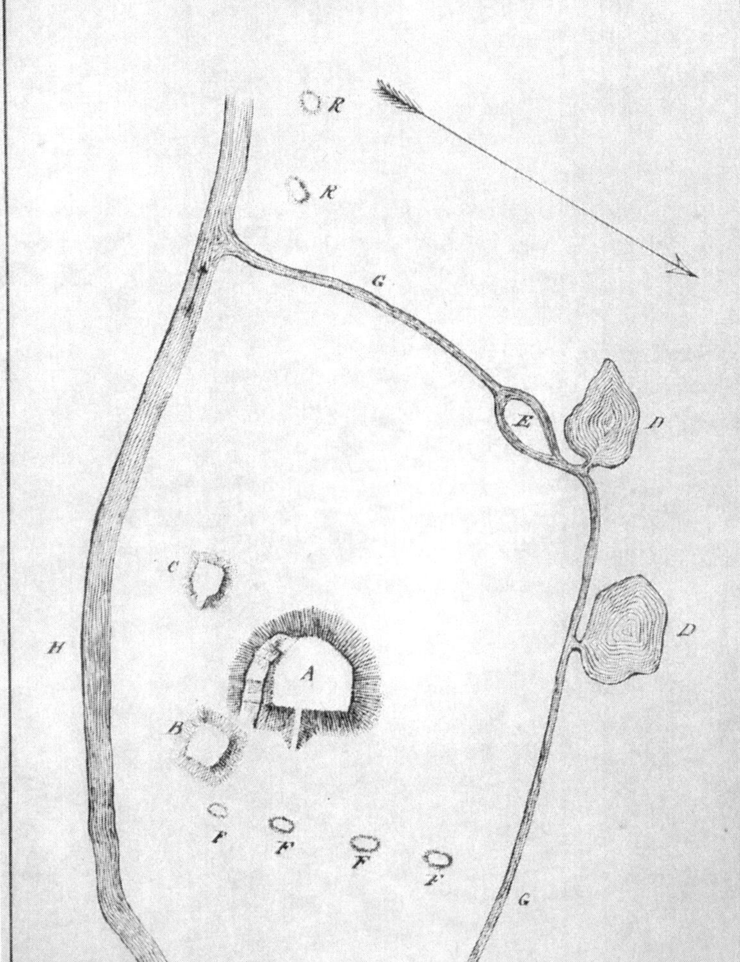

AM. PHOTO-LITHOGRAPHIC CO. N.Y. (OSBORNES PROCESS.)

about an acre each, possessing an average depth of not less than twenty feet, and its upper end expands into an artificial pond (P), elliptical in form, and somewhat deeper than the excavations mentioned.

Within the enclosure formed by this moat and the river are seven mounds. Three of them are preëminent in size, the one designated in the accompanying plan (Plate I) by the letter A, far surpassing the others both in its proportions and in the degree of interest which attaches to it.

To the eye of the observer, as it rests for the first time upon its towering form, it seems a monument of the past ages, venerable in its antiquity, solemn, silent, and yet not voiceless, a remarkable exhibition of the power and industry of a former race. With its erection the modern hunter tribes, so far as our information extends, had naught to do. Composed of earth, simple, yet impressive in form, it seems calculated for an almost endless duration. The soil, gravel, and smaller stones taken from the moat and the reservoirs were expended in the construction of these tumuli. The surface of the ground, for a considerable distance around the northern bases, was then removed and placed upon their summits. Viewed from the north, the valley dips toward the mounds, so that they appear to lift themselves from out a basin.

The central tumulus rises about sixty-five feet above the level of the valley. It is entirely artificial, consisting wholly of the earth taken from the moat and the excavations, in connection with the soil collected around its base. It has received no assistance whatever from any natural hill or elevation.

In general outline it may be regarded as quadrangular, if we disregard a slight angle to the south. That taken into account, its form is pentagonal, with summit admeasurements as follows: length of northern side, one hundred and fifty feet; length of eastern side, one hundred and sixty feet; length of southeastern side, one hundred feet; length of southern side, ninety feet, and length of western side, one hundred feet. Measured east and west, its longest apex diameter is two hundred and twenty-five feet; measured north and south, it falls a little short—being about two hundred and twenty feet. On its summit, this tumulus is nearly level. Shorn of the luxuriant vegetation and tall forest-trees which at one time crowned it on every side, the outlines of this mound stand in bold relief. Its angles are still sharply defined. The established approach to the top is from the east. Its ascent was accomplished through the intervention of terraces, rising one above the other—inclined planes leading from the one to the other.[1] These terraces are sixty-five feet in width, and extend from the mound toward the southeast. Near the eastern angle, a pathway leads to the top; but it does not appear to have been intended for very general use. May it not have been designed for the priesthood alone, while, assembled upon the broad terraces, the worshippers gave solemn heed to the religious ceremonies performed upon the eastern summit of this ancient temple?

East of this large central mound—and so near that their flanks meet and mingle—stands a smaller mound about thirty-five feet high, originally quadrangular, now nearly circular in form, and with a summit diameter of one hundred feet. From its western slope is an easy and immediate communication with the terraces of

[1] These inclined planes have been considerably worn away by the elements, so that this main approach reminds the observer of a broad, winding ramp.

the central tumulus. This mound is designated in the accompanying plate by the letter B. Two hundred and fifty feet in a westerly direction from this mound, and distant some sixty feet in a southerly direction from the central mound, is the third (C) and last of this immediate group. Pentagonal in form, it possesses an altitude of twenty-three feet. It is uniformly level at the top, and its apex diameters, measured at right angles, were, respectively, ninety-two and sixty-eight feet.

East of this group, and within the enclosure, is a chain of four sepulchral mounds (F F F F) ovoidal in shape. Little individual interest attaches to them. Nothing, aside from their location in the vicinity of these larger tumuli and their being within the area formed by the canal and the river, distinguishes them from numerous earth-mounds scattered here and there throughout the length and breadth of the Etowah and Oostenaula Valleys.

The artificial elevation E, lying northwest of the central group, is remarkable for its superficial area, and is completely surrounded by the moat which, at that point, divides with a view to its enclosure. The slope of the sides of these tumuli is just such as would be assumed by gradual accretions of earth successively deposited in small quantities from above.

The summits of these mounds, and the circumjacent valley for miles, have been completely denuded of the original growth which overspread them in rich profusion. The consequence is, these remarkable remains can be readily and carefully noted.

We marvel at the amount of labor expended in their construction, and conjecture that they are either the product of the combined energies of a population by no means inconsiderable, or else the representatives of the successive industry of perhaps several generations. Of one fact we may be persuaded, that there was not, in the eighteenth century, a single Indian tribe in this vicinity possessing either the disposition or the means of subsistence sufficient to enable it to apply the unproductive labor necessary for the erection of such works. Nor were the Cherokees in such a social or political status as would have empowered their chiefs to have compelled such an expenditure of the physical energies of their nations. Nomadic tribes, relying upon the bow and arrow for subsistence, and changing their seats under the influences of want and inclination, are loath to assume the erection of such huge earth-works. We have the positive testimony of the Cherokees, that they had not even a tradition of the race by whom these tumuli had been reared. During the period of our acquaintance with them idol-worship did not exist among the Cherokees; and yet within this enclosure three stone idols have been found, and numerous terra-cotta images fashioned after the similitude of man, beast, and bird. Of these stone idols it may be remarked, in passing, that two were cut from a dark sandstone, were respectively twelve and fifteen inches in height, and represented the male human figure in a sitting posture—the knees drawn up almost upon a level with the chin, the hands resting upon either knee. The third, and the most carefully-sculptured Indian idol the writer has ever seen, was a female figure made of a dark talcose slate. As, in a subsequent chapter, our attention will be specially directed to a somewhat careful examination of these and kindred antique images, and also to an inquiry into the nature and extent of idol-worship as practised by the Southern Indians at a remote period, a more extended notice of these interesting relics is here pretermitted.

Outliving the generations during which they were fashioned and perhaps invested with supernatural powers, and surviving the incoming and the outgoing of subsequent nomadic tribes, these stone images preserve the peculiar forms and expressions which were in that age of shadows traced by the hand of semi-civilized art upon the shapeless stone, and declare the former existence of peoples whose names are unknown, whose origin is the subject of mere conjecture, and whose history and customs are perpetuated simply by a few scattered remains which, in the deluge of time, like floating plants have escaped the general shipwreck.

Unique specimens of idol-pipes, stone plates, large shell ornaments, and other relics not common among the Cherokees, confirm the impression that these tumuli were not the results of the labor of the modern Indians. The large trees which grew upon these mounds when they were first visited by the early settlers, and their utterly abandoned condition at the period of our primal acquaintance with them, add forcible testimony in behalf of their decided antiquity. The great age of these structures is further demonstrated by the character of the works themselves, which are not the hastily-erected monuments of migrating bands, but the ruins of temples, areas, and burial-places, carefully considered, of massive dimensions, and indicating the consecutive, combined, and extensive labor of a considerable population permanently established.

The eastern angle of the central mound is very prominent, and the upper surface in that direction is more elevated. Just here have been found traces of hearths or altars, giving ample token of the continued presence of fire and perhaps of sacrifice. The terraces lie toward the east, and there is that about this tumulus which induces the belief that it was erected for religious purposes, and that upon its eastern summit religious rites were performed and oblations offered to the great divinity, the sun. The broad terraces and the adjacent dependent tumuli afforded space for the assembling of worshippers at the appointed hour, when, from the elevated eastern summit of the large tumulus, the eye of the officiating priest caught the earliest rays of the rising sun, as, lifting his face from out the shadows of the distant hills, he smiled upon this beautiful valley.

In the true relation of the vicissitudes which attended the Governor Don Hernando de Soto and some nobles of Portugal in the discovery of the province of Florida,[1] we are informed by the Gentleman of Elvas, that "on Wednesday, the nineteenth day of June, the Governor entered Pacaha, and took quarters in the town where the Cacique was accustomed to reside. It was enclosed, and very large. In the towers and the palisade were many loopholes. There was much dry maize, and the new was in great quantity throughout the fields. At the distance of half a league to a league off, were large towns, all of them surrounded with stockades. Where the Governor stayed was a great lake near to the enclosure; and the water entered a ditch that well-nigh went round the town. From the River Grande to the lake was a canal, through which the fish came into it, and where the Chief kept them for his

[1] Buckingham Smith's translation, pp. 112, 113. Bradford Club Series, No. 5. New York, 1866.

eating and pastime. With nets that were found in the place, as many were taken as need required; and however much might be the casting, there was never any lack of them. . . . The Cacique of Casqui many times sent large presents of fish, shawls, and skins."

While the earth removed in the construction of the ditch and excavations was primarily employed in the erection of the tumuli within the enclosure, while they may in one sense be regarded as the sources of the mounds, and while their sizes and depths were, to a certain extent, regulated by the supply of material requisite for the completion of the projected truncated pyramid—which we suppose to have been a temple—and its dependent mounds, we are of opinion that, during the progress of the entire work, direct reference was had to the final use of these excavations and of this canal as fish-preserves, whence the priests, caciques, and noted personages of the nation, who probably dwelt within the enclosure formed by the moat and the river, could at all seasons derive an abundant supply of fish. The canal leading from the artificial pond in which it takes its rise, communicates directly with both reservoirs, and, after passing them, empties into the Etowah. Through this canal fishes could have been readily introduced from the river into all three of these artificial lakes, and there propagated. Cane or wooden wears—in such common use among the Southern Indians during the sixteenth century—would have prevented all escape, and thus these reservoirs would have answered the purposes of FISH-PRESERVES. Such we believe them to have been.

In the retired valley of Little Shoulder-Bone Creek, about nine miles from the village of Sparta, in Hancock County, may be seen another group of ancient tumuli,[1] not unlike those we have just examined. Of the date of their construction, and of the peoples by whom they were erected, the Creeks and Cherokees professed utter ignorance. To the oft-repeated inquiry who were the authors of these monuments and when were they built, the uniform response of the red-men was, "We know not; our fathers found them here when they first possessed the land."

From all these mounds the original forest-growth has been removed, and we are therefore denied the information which would be derived from an examination of the cortical layers of the venerable trees which formerly grew upon and overshadowed them after their abandonment by those to whose labors their existence was due. Here and there upon their summits still exist mouldering stumps and roots, affording ample proof of the vigor and proportions of that growth which the industry of a later race has carefully removed.

Approaching this series of tumuli from the west, the first which engages our attention (designated in the accompanying sketch by the letter G), in general outline nearly resembles a truncated cone; being slightly ovoidal, and with summit-diameters, measured east and west, and north and south, of, respectively, fifty-two and forty-two feet. Its base-diameter, running east and west, is one hundred and forty feet. Measured at right angles, it falls a little short of this. Its present altitude is sixteen feet.

One hundred and fifty yards east of this mound is the largest tumulus of the group (C). It is a truncated, pentagonal pyramid, its base-diameters, measured north and south, and east and west, being respec-

[1] Plate II.

Plate II.

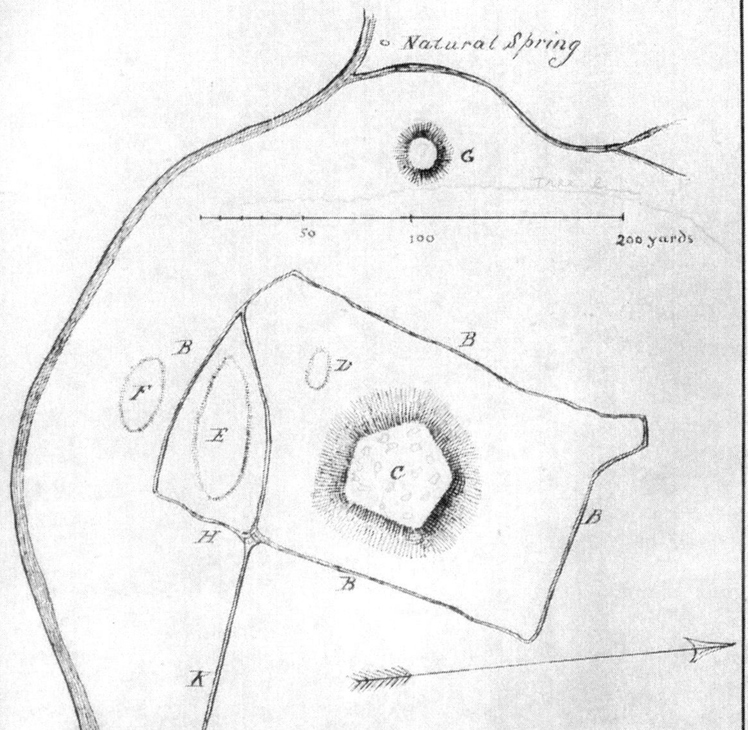

AM PHOTO-LITHOGRAPHIC CO N.Y. (OSBORNE'S PROCESS.)

tively one hundred and eighty and one hundred and eighty-four feet. Its summit-diameters, ascertained in the same directions, are respectively eighty and eighty-eight feet. This mound is forty feet high.

By a reference to its profile (L), it will be perceived that it is higher toward the east. The approach to the summit was from the east, and the eastern third of the superior surface was not only elevated above the rest, but was also made scrupulously level. Here, a little below the surface, have been found traces of a hearth composed of baked clay or rude brick. Charred fragments of wood and other indications attest the former continued existence of fires upon this spot.

Considerable excavations have been made in the eastern slope. Composed, as it is, of the alluvial soil of the valley, the planters of the neighboring hills (entirely ignoring the claims of this ancient monument to preservation and respect—we had almost added veneration—at the hands of a utilitarian age), in by-gone years frequently resorted to it as a convenient source of fertilization for their impoverished lands.

This tumulus, so august in its proportions, has in its construction derived no aid from any natural hill or elevation. It stands apart, and in the midst of a level valley. The slope of the sides is just such as would be assumed by the gradual accumulation of loose earth deposited from above.

It is not improbable that the Indians used the summit and sides of this tumulus for the purposes of sepulture. Skeletons have been found near the surface, in a degree of preservation and possessing certain *indicia* which forbid the belief that their inhumation was coeval with the construction of the mound.

The tumuli D, E, and F, appear to have been designed and used exclusively as burial-mounds. For so many years have they been traversed by the ploughshare, and wasted by the winds and rains, that they have doubtless lost much of their original proportions. Their surfaces are covered with fragments of human bones, and pottery, beads, arrow and spear heads, stone implements, stone ornaments, pipes, clay images, etc., etc.

The mounds C, D, and E, are isolated by a moat or ditch, indicated by the letters B B. The total area thus enclosed is between four and five acres. An additional ditch separates the mound E from the other two; and, at the point H, are traces of an excavation or reservoir, from which a third ditch (K) leads to an adjacent small creek or stream emptying into Little Shoulder-Bone Creek. The earth taken from these moats or ditches, and removed in digging the reservoir, was expended in the erection of the tumuli. There are no indications of embankments along their edges. All trace of this moat will soon disappear, and marked changes have already occurred within the recollection of the older inhabitants.

Within the enclosure, stone idols—similar in appearance to those found in the valley of the Etowah—and clay images, resembling the human form in distorted shape and feature, and fashioned after the similitude of beasts and birds, have been gathered.

The fact has been distinctly attested by early travellers, that the Indians of this region never worshipped idols. We have the further testimony that they not only never manufactured these symbols of pagan worship, but emphatically disclaimed all knowledge of the people by whom they were made. Who, then, were these mound-builders, and who the artificers that chiselled these rude stone images which did not fall down from Jupiter?

Every indication suggests and encourages the belief that this locality was, for a long period of time, densely populated. The surface of the ground, not only within the enclosure, but up and down the valley for a considerable distance, is replete with various relics. They lie also, in considerable quantities, commingled with human bones, in the sepulchral mounds. Few and unsatisfactory are the memories which they suggest. Feeble *indicia* of general customs, they do little else than furnish physical proofs of the former existence of nameless peoples who, living without letters, have left behind them no legacies to history.

The surface of the enclosure—saving the presence of the mounds—is very level, and from it have been carefully removed all stones, bowlders, and fragments of rock, with which other portions of the valley and the adjoining hill-sides abound.

On Plunkett Creek, about three-quarters of a mile distant, is a mound twelve feet high, with a summit-diameter of forty feet and a base-diameter of one hundred and twenty-five feet. It is conical in shape, and its principal elevation is toward the east. Unlike the other tumuli in this valley, the present mound is mainly composed of fragments of rocks and stones; and, apart from this fact, possesses no distinguishing peculiarity. Its profile is shown in Fig. 2, Plate II.

Intermediate between this mound and the group which we have been considering, is an enclosed work, parallelogrammic in outline, containing an acre and a quarter. The ditch surrounding it is some four feet wide, and between three and four feet deep. (*See* Fig. 3, Plate II.)

Upon the head-waters of the Great Ogeechee River, five miles from Sparta, is an earth-work, circular in form, with a gate or opening terminating at the creek. The embankment is still nearly three feet high, and upon it are growing trees as large and, to all appearances, as old as any in the surrounding forest. (*See* Fig. 4, Plate II.)

The belief is current in the neighborhood, that this work was an intrenched camp of De Soto, but there is no satisfactory foundation for this impression.

Located upon a high, rugged ridge, three miles from Sparta, and in a direction opposite to that which led us to the so-called "Spanish Fort," are the remains of a stone tumulus originally fifteen feet high, and twelve feet in diameter at its base, nearly resembling a sugar-loaf in form. It was composed exclusively of fragments of rocks, carefully piled one above the other. A few years since a planter, moved by curiosity, undertook the removal of this mound. The labor was but partially accomplished, and the only result attained was the almost total demolition of this unique little tumulus. (*See* Fig. 5, Plate II.)

Tradition designates "Silver Bluff," or its vicinity, as the site of the ancient village of Cutifachiqui. There, if we rightly interpret the geography of the Fidalgo of Elvas, dwelt an Indian queen, young and attractive, who with royal hospitality welcomed to her capital and the freedom of her nation the adventurous De Soto and his daring companions, lone wandering and yet not lost amid the unbroken forests and howling wildernesses of a vast region hitherto untrodden by the white man. The historian of the expedition dwells at length and with evident satisfaction upon the reception extended by this Indian queen to the knightly Ferdinand. Learning from three captives that a woman held the sovereignty of this country, the General sent forward special messengers to her with offers of friendship. Her response of welcome was returned by her sister in person. Shortly afterward the queen appeared in a stately canoe, with an awning in the poop supported by a lance. She sat upon two cushions, and was accompanied by a number of Indian women—her attendants and maids of honor. Many escorting canoes followed. Invested with all the pomp and dignity which the limited resources of her age and race could throw around her, she crossed the Savannah River and approached the bank where the Spanish Cavalier waited to receive her. Responding with ease, grace, and fervor, to his handsome address, she landed and conferred upon him many presents—among them a pearl necklace, the beads of which are particularly mentioned as of great value and remarkable size. The next day the expedition crossed the Savannah River in canoes and on rafts, and found rest, food, and refreshment, in the wigwams and beneath the wide-spreading mulberry-trees of the chosen town of the cacica.

Upon the eve of his departure, De Soto arrested the queen and forced her to accompany him on his forward march to Chiaha. For seven long days was she compelled to travel on foot through a wretched country, and it was not until the eighth day that she succeeded in making her escape. During this unwilling journey with the Spaniards she is said to have carried a casket made of reeds, containing pearls of great value. These she preserved, and so apt did she prove in concealing herself within the shadows of her native forests, that she completely eluded the pursuit of the

Spaniards, who were most desirous of retaining her as a hostage for their safe conduct through the territories of the neighboring cassiques who rendered homage to her.[1] The narrative leaves her in the wilds of an unknown forest returning to her people and chosen abode; and it may be that one of the rude earth-mounds which tower along its banks, designates the last resting-place of the beautiful, the hospitable, the ill-treated queen of the Savannah.

No storied urn or monumental bust, no epitaph deeply graven on enduring marble, no sepulchral column, perpetuates her memory or her greatness; and yet certain tumuli, sternly wrestling with all-subduing time, lonely and voiceless in this generation, even now repeat the story of the Indian queen, whose cordial welcome of and generous hospitality to the adventurous, travel-worn stranger, were requited by unkindness, ingratitude, and dishonor.

In 1776, Mr. Bartram states that there were in this vicinity what he is pleased to denominate Indian conical mounts, terraces, and areas, and also the remains or traces of fortresses which were supposed to be ancient camps of the Spaniards, who formerly fixed themselves at this place in the hope of finding silver.[2]

Four years afterward, to the local history of this region another chapter was added, whose incidents, authentic in their character, furnish a bright illustration of those partisan adventures and patriotic exploits which not unfrequently signalized the conduct of the Southern campaign in the days of the good and great General Greene.

[1] Roberts' "Florida," pp. 47, 48. London, 1763. "Narratives of the Career of Hernando de Soto," translated by Buckingham Smith, p. 62., *et seq.* New York, 1866.

[2] "Travels," etc., p. 313. London, 1792.

The annual royal present to the Indians, consisting of powder, ball, small-arms, liquor, salt, blankets, and other articles of which the impoverished Continentals stood most sadly in need, was, in May, 1780, on deposit at Fort Galphin, about twelve miles below Augusta, on the north side of the Savannah River, awaiting distribution. Colonel Brown's force at Augusta had been reduced by the detail of two companies of infantry, detached to guard this present. They were at that time stationed in the Stockade Fort at this point. Made aware of this fact through the vigilance of his scouts, carefully concealing his movement, and leaving his artillery and the tired of his battalion behind under command of Eaton, Lieutenant-Colonel Lee determined to press forward at once and secure these much-coveted supplies for the American camp. Mounting a detachment of infantry behind his dragoons, by forced marches and without the knowledge of the enemy, on the 21st of May, 1780, he halted his panting squadrons beneath the pines which skirted the field in which Fort Galphin was located. The day was excessively sultry, and men and animals were so oppressed by heat and overcome by thirst, that his little column was for the time incapable of further exertion.

After a short rest, Colonel Lee directed his dismounted militia to make, unobserved, the circuit of the fort, and to attack it from a point opposite to that which he then occupied. This strategy was invoked under the impression that the garrison would be drawn from the fort in the pursuit of these few militiamen, and thus its capture, by a rapid assault under his immediate supervision, insured beyond a question. As was expected, so soon as the militia *débouched* from the woods, the garrison flew to arms, and, rushing from the fort, pursued the militia, who, at first resisting feebly, quickly retired—their retreat being covered by some cavalry previously disposed for that purpose. At this juncture a rapid advance under Captain Rudolph was ordered, and the assaulting column easily gained possession of the fort.

In the language of the author of the "Memoirs of the War in the Southern Department," "the garrison, with the valuable deposit in its safe keeping, gave a rich reward for our toils and sufferings."[1]

An old brick house still stands which witnessed the prowess of the gallant cavalry colonel and his brave troopers on that sultry May morning.

But it is not of this old brick house with its Revolutionary memories, nor of the bright blade of the Virginia chieftain, that we speak. It is not our purpose to pursue the track of the Spanish expedition, or to recount the traditions of the locality. Our object is simply to chronicle the existence and perpetuate the recollection of the prominent physical peculiarities of a marked group of ancient tumuli resting upon the left bank of the Savannah River, some twelve or fifteen miles by water below the city of Augusta. Thirty-five years ago this group numbered six mounds, but the restless river, with recurring freshets, encroaching steadily upon the Carolina shore, has already rolled its turbid waters over two of them, while other two have so far yielded to the levelling influences of the ploughshare as to be almost entirely obliterated. Consequently but two remain, and they only in major part, one-third of each having been washed away by the current; and the day is probably not far distant when tradition only will

[1] Vol. ii., p. 89, *et seq.* Philadelphia, 1812.

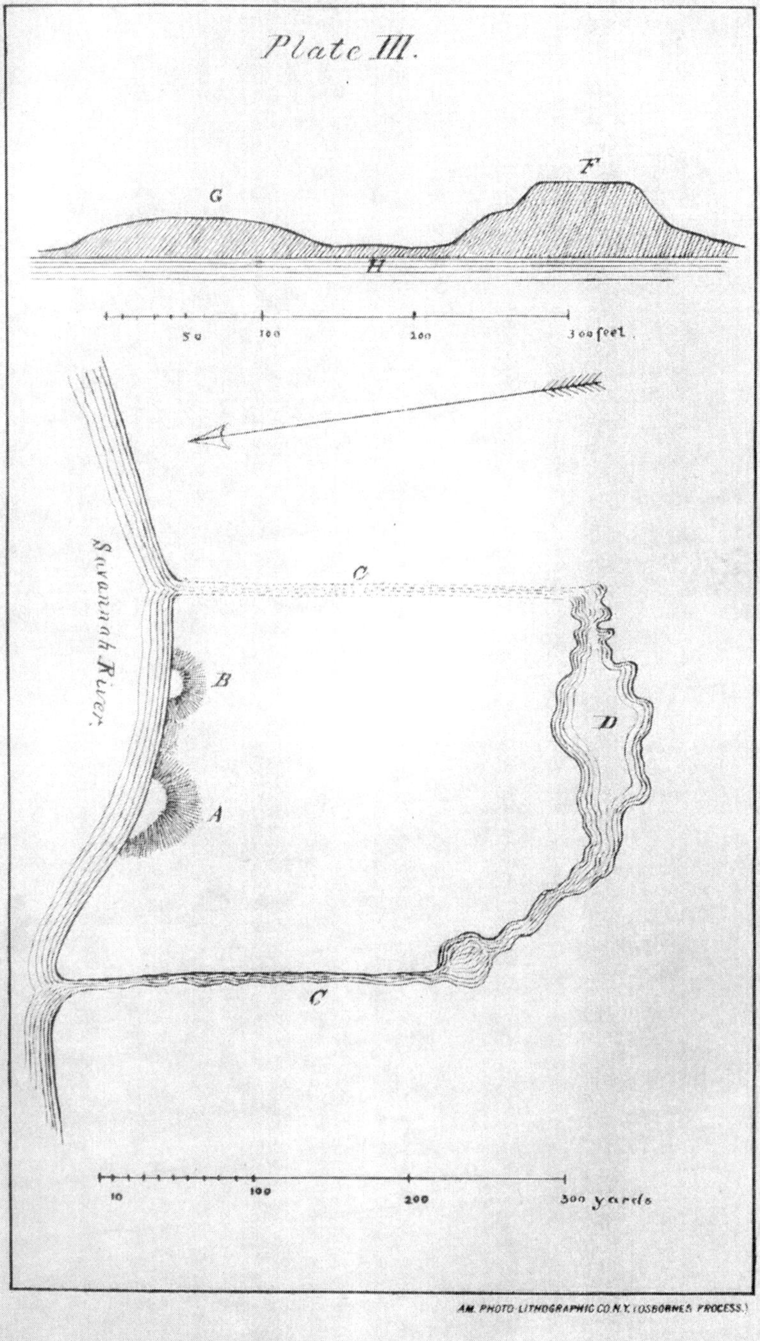

AM. PHOTO-LITHOGRAPHIC CO. N.Y. (OSBORNES PROCESS.)

designate the spot once memorable in the annals of a former race as the site of monuments of unusual size and interest.

These tumuli are located on Mason's Plantation, upon the very edge of the Savannah River, and in the midst of the wide, deep swamp, which here on either bank stretches away for miles, exhibiting one uniform, level, alluvial surface. What was once a mighty forest, grand and impenetrable in its majestic trees and tangled brakes, is now a rich cornfield whose harvests have for many years with a yield of a hundred-fold rewarded the toil of the intelligent husbandman. The surrounding space being thus denuded of its original growth, the tumuli loom up in uninterrupted proportions, while from the river, which has wellnigh cut them in twain, the observer enjoys a most favorable opportunity, as presented by their perpendicular fronts, for closely examining their physical composition. Freshets have performed what it would have required long days of toil to have accomplished, and even then the work would not have been done half so well. It is sad to realize, however, that these encroachments which at present bring hidden things to view, and enable the examiner to pursue his investigations with facility, are dooming the objects themselves to early and absolute annihilation. Some forest-trees, chiefly beech and locust, still crown the summits and flanks of these fragmentary mounds trembling upon the brink of the remorseless river.

The largest tumulus, designated in the accompanying sketch by the letter A (Plate III.), rises thirty-seven feet above the plain, and forty-seven above the water-line as it existed at the date of this visit. Measured east and west, its summit diameter was fifty-eight feet, while, in consequence of the encroachment of the river, when measured in a northerly and southerly direction, it fell a little short of thirty-eight feet. Its base-diameter, ascertained in an easterly and westwardly direction, was one hundred and eighty-five feet. Although its outlines have been somewhat marred by the whirling eddies of the river, as its swelling waters, in the spring of the year gathering marvellous volume and impetus, have again and again swept by, inundating the entire swamp-region, this tumulus may be truthfully described as a truncated cone—its sides sloping gently and evenly, and its apex surface level. If terraces ever existed, they are no longer apparent. The western flank of this mound was extended for a distance some twenty yards or more beyond the point where it would otherwise have terminated, respect being had to the configuration of the eastern and southern slopes. About two feet below the present surface of this extension is a continuous layer of charcoal, baked earth, ashes, broken pottery, shells, and bones. This layer is about twelve inches thick. So far as our examination extended—and it was but partial—the admixture of human bones was very slight—the bones, of which there were vast numbers, consisting of those of animals and birds native to this region. One is at a loss to explain the existence of this stratum of charcoal, ashes, shells, fragmentary pottery and bones, unless upon the hypothesis that it comprises the *débris* of a long-seated encampment or permanent abode of the aborigines upon this little bluff. This stratum can be traced along the water-front of the mound, as though it existed prior to its construction. The superincumbent mass of earth seems to have been heaped above it. Where it penetrates the tumulus, it is wellnigh coincident with a prolongation of what was at the time the surface of the surrounding swamp.

The mound itself is composed of the alluvium of the adjacent field, which is a micaceous clay, richly impregnated with vegetable mould. No traces of inhumation could be perceived, and the composition of the tumulus was homogeneous as far as ascertained.

It is earnestly hoped that some one will carefully note from time to time the encroachments of the river, as in all likelihood the central portions of this mound will soon be laid bare, and then, its contents, if any, will be fully disclosed. Thus will an opportunity be afforded for a most satisfactory examination.

One hundred and twenty-five feet due east of this large tumulus, is the smaller mound designated by the letter B. Its appearance, general outline and composition, are so nearly analogous to those of the larger mound, that a specific description is scarcely necessary. It may be remarked, however, that, possessing a base-diameter of one hundred and fourteen feet, it rises fifteen feet above the surface of the ground and twenty-five feet above the level of the river.[1]

It will be perceived by a reference to the accompanying sketch (Plate III.), that these tumuli were, in days long since numbered with an unrecorded past, isolated by a moat (C C), whose traces are still quite observable. The enclosed space—the river forming the northern boundary—contains a conjectured area of about eight acres. Commencing at the river, eastwardly of the smaller mound and distant from its flank some thirty yards, this ditch extends in a southerly direction until it merges into what now seems to

[1] For profiles of these tumuli, *see* letters F and G, Plate III. The water-line is represented by H.

be a natural lagoon (D). Following this in a westwardly course, it finally leaves it, and thence runs almost due north to the river into which it empties at a remove of about eighty yards from the western flank of the larger tumulus. Here the communication with the river is still perfect, but the upper mouth of this moat is now dry. It varies in width from twenty to forty feet, and is in some parts wider still.[1]

In all probability the earth removed in the construction of this canal was devoted to the erection of these tumuli; and there are here and there in their vicinity physical evidences of the fact that the surrounding soil contributed to their further elevation. Terra-cotta vases, pots and pans, arrow and spear heads, stone articles of use and ornament, mortars, pipes, and bone and shell beads, are found in the adjacent fields, but there lives not a tradition of the time when, and of the tribes by whom, these tumuli were built. Lonely, storm-beaten, freshet-torn, they stand nameless and without a history in this generation—silent, yet convincing illustrations of the ephemeral character of the nomadic races which for centuries peopled this entire region, and, departing, left behind them neither letters nor monuments of art—nothing save these rude earth-mounds and occasional relics to give assurance of their former existence.

In the twilight of what by-gone and unrecorded century were these tumuli built? Whence came, and who the peoples that lifted them from out the bosom of our common mother? Served they as friendly refuge in seasons of freshet and of storm? Were sacred fires ever kindled upon your summits and within this consecrated area? Within your hidden depths do the

[1] This also may have been a fish-preserve.

brave and honored of your generation sleep that sleep which knows no waking until the final trump shall summon alike the civilized and the savage to the last award? Or are ye simple watch-towers, deserted of your sentinels—forts, abandoned of your defenders? We question, but there are no voices of the past in the ambient air. We search among these tombs, but they bear no epitaphs. The sacred fires, if ever kindled, were turned into ashes long ago, and naught but darkness is here. We gaze upon these monuments, but they are inscriptionless, and the Savannah rolling its swollen waters about them will soon sweep even these mute earth-mounds out of existence. For a few short moments this tawny-hued river will grow more turbid with the dissolving mass of native clay, and then, borne away upon its bosom, and settling darkly in the depths of this swiftly-moving stream, nothing will evermore be seen of these august witnesses of the memorable meeting between the Spanish Adventurer and the Cacica of the Savannah.

CHAPTER VII.

Tumuli on the Ocmulgee River, opposite Macon.—Brown's Mount.—Mound on Messier's Plantation, in Early County.

Of the mounds on the left bank of the Ocmulgee River, opposite the city of Macon, the largest and most noteworthy (A, Plate IV.), lying farthest down the river, is located upon the summit of a natural hill, and occupies a commanding position. The earth of which it is composed was gathered in the valley and conveyed to the top of the hill so as, in the end, to increase its elevation by some forty-five or fifty feet. The summit diameters of this tumulus, measured north and south, and east and west, are respectively one hundred and eighty and two hundred feet. On the west is an artificial plateau, still about eight feet high, seventy-two feet long and ninety-three feet wide. On the north and east are three spurs or elevated approaches, over which, as paths, the laborers, during the construction of the mound, carried their burdens of sand and clay in cane baskets, and, by means of which, when the tumulus was completed, ascent to its summit was rendered more facile. It is not improbable that this was a temple-mound, used by priests and devotees in their established worship of the sun.

Plate IV.

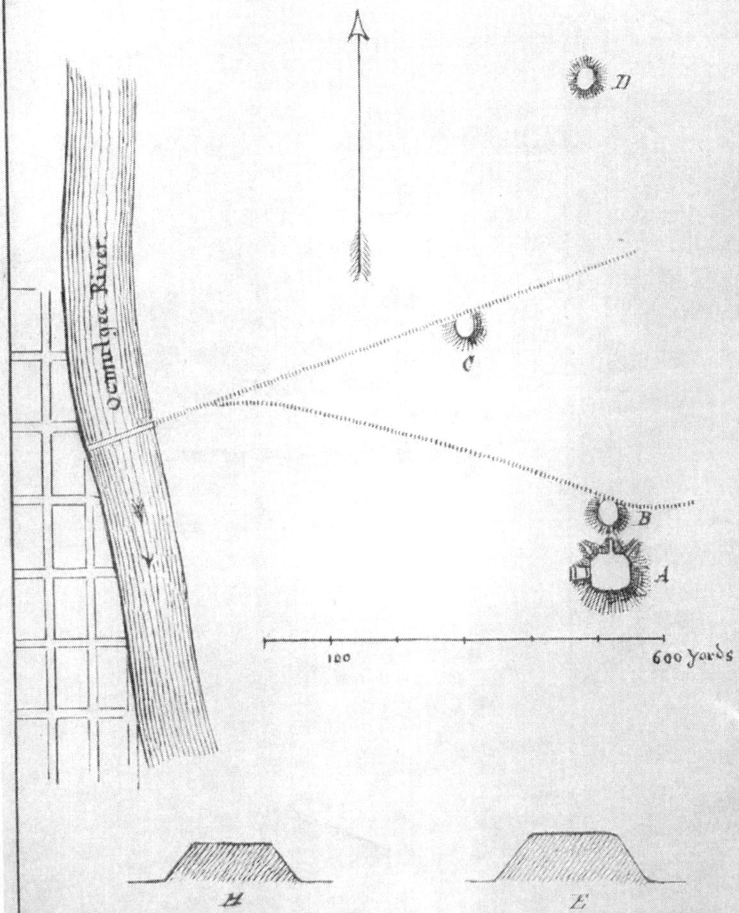

AM. PHOTO-LITHOGRAPHIC CO. N.Y. (OSBORNE'S PROCESS.)

One hundred feet north of this tumulus is a second mound (B) about ten feet high, elliptical in shape, with a summit-diameter, measured in the direction of the major axis, of one hundred and twenty-eight feet. Northwest of this mound and distant between three and four hundred yards, is the third of the group (C), its outlines marred by the elements, and its northern slope carried away by the excavation for the new track of the Central Railway. It is still about forty feet high and is conical in form—its mean summit-diameter being about eighty-two feet. On its top is the decayed stump of a tree, more than five feet thick.

About four hundred yards in a northeasterly direction is the last tumulus of this series (D). In general characteristics it closely resembles the mound last mentioned. These mounds are all flat, and may be described as truncated cones, with the exception of the temple-mound, which assimilates the form of an octagonal, truncated pyramid. The temple-mound was erected for religious purposes; the others were heaped up, probably, in honor of the dead. In their vicinity the fields are filled with sherds, shells of the pearl-bearing unio, and fragments of articles of ancient domestic economy. Upon the acclivity east of the central mound are the manifest remains of an aboriginal settlement. Here, in excavating for the new track of the Central Railway, the workmen a short time since unearthed, a few feet below the surface, several skeletons, in connection with which were found beads of shell and porcelain, a part of a discoidal stone, several arrow and spear points, two stone celts, a clay pipe, an earthen pot, and other matters of a primitive character fashioned for use or ornament.

This excavation for the line of the railway necessitated the removal of a considerable portion of the northern side of the central mound. In the conduct of this work, the laborers, while cutting through the slope of the mound, and at a depth of perhaps three feet below the superior surface, exhumed several skulls, regular in outline and possessing the ordinary characteristics of American crania. Associated with these skeletons were stone implements—the handiwork of the red race—and Venetian beads and copper hawk-bells acquired through commercial intercourse with the early traders and voyagers. The fact was patent that at least some of these inhumations had occurred subsequent to the period of primal contact between the European and the Indian.

Passing below these interments—which were evidently secondary in their character—and arriving at the bottom of the mound, a skull was obtained which differed most essentially from those we have described as belonging to a later inhumation. It was vastly older than those of the secondary interments, and had been artificially distorted to such an extent that the cerebellum was quite obliterated, while the front portion of the skull had not only been flattened but irregularly compressed, so as to cause an undue elevation and divergence to the left.

For the purposes of comparison we have (in Plate IV.–A) figured two skulls, the first (1) being that of a modern Indian buried upon the side of the mound only a few feet below the surface; the other, the cranium of the primitive man in whose honor the tumulus was constructed. Of this latter skull we have both a front and side view (Figs. 2 and 3, Plate IV.–A).

Among the relics found in the vicinity of this old, artificially-compressed skull, was a total absence of

Plate IV-A

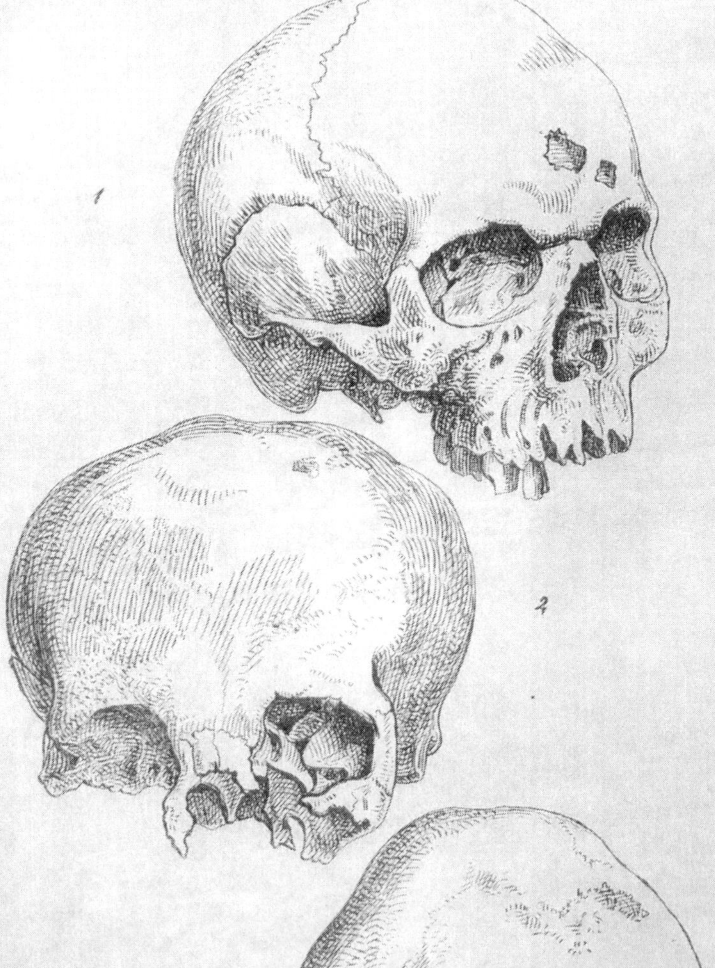

AM. PHOTO-LITHOGRAPHIC CO. N.Y. (OSBORNES PROCESS.)

European ornaments. Here we have an interesting demonstration of the fact that these ancient tumuli were, in turn, used by tribes who perhaps had no knowledge the one of the other. The flattened and distorted skull belongs to the mound-building people to whose industry the erection of these tumuli is to be referred. It was in perpetuation and in honor of such primal sepulture that this mound was heaped up. In the course of time these sepulchral and temple structures, abandoned of their owners, passed into the hands of other and later red races, who buried their dead upon the superior surface and along the slopes of these ancient tumuli, having at the time, perchance, no personal acquaintance with, and frequently not even a distinct tradition of, the peoples to whose exertions these evidences of early constructive skill were attributable.

In the absence of letters and of recorded memories most easily does one wave of human life sweep over another, obliterating all former recollections save such as are lodged in the womb of mounds, or preserved in the generous bosom of mother earth:

> "The very generations of the dead
> Are swept away, and tomb inherits tomb,
> Until the memory of an age is fled,
> And, buried, sinks beneath its offspring's doom." [1]

The Creeks did not claim that these tumuli were erected by them. They declared that they were here when their ancestors first possessed themselves of the region. Who these flat-head mound-builders were, is matter for conjecture. It may be that they were a colony of the Natchez, journeying hither from their old habitat on the banks of the Mississippi. Certain

[1] "Don Juan," canto iv., cii.

it is, that these tumuli antedate the traditions of the Creeks who were native here at the period of the English colonization.

Below these mounds—in the valley-lands of the Ocmulgee, upon Lamar's plantation—are several large tumuli. The presence of these mounds, and the numerous relics scattered throughout the length and breadth of the valley for miles, afford ample testimony that this rich alluvial soil was once the seat of a numerous and, perhaps, permanent population. The *débris* of frequent encampments along the bluffs of the river prove that the aborigines, during the lapsed centuries, congregated here in numbers for fishing and hunting; and old clearings in the valley give evidence that they supported themselves in part by the cultivation of maize.

The many unio-shells overlying the surface of the fields and intermingled with the refuse piles of former encampments, corroborate the fidelity of the Spanish narratives and furnish present physical assurance that the natives of this region carefully collected these shells that the animals which they contained might serve as food, and their valves, so iridescent with pearly nacre, afford material for the manufacture of beads, gorgets, and other ornaments. From them, also, were pearls obtained, which the Indians perforated with heated copper spindles that they might be strung and worn as necklaces, armlets, anklets, and about the shoulders and waist.

The presence of gorgets, made of marine shells, and numerous columns of the *strombus gigas*, some in an imperfect condition, and others entirely finished and perforated longitudinally so that they could be used as pendants, attest the commerce which existed between the coast Indians and those occupying the interior.

"BROWN'S MOUNT," situated on the line between Bibb and Twiggs Counties, from its summit affords a fine view of the city of Macon, while, from its western exposure, which is very precipitous, the eye ranges all over the Ocmulgee Basin and across the country far away to the valley of the Flint River.

Following the natural conformation of the summit boundaries, and at some points retired a distance of twenty yards or more from the edge of the hill, are the remains of an old wall—constructed of bowlders of rock, and earth—which encircled and fortified the entire top of the mount. About sixty acres, I am informed, are thus enclosed. Attendant upon the wall are traces of both an outside and an inside ditch, the former being originally about ten feet wide and four feet deep, and the latter some three feet wide and between two and three feet deep. The earth removed in the construction of these ditches was used, in conjunction with the stone-bowlders, in building this wall. Within the recollection of persons still living, this wall was four feet high, and between four and five feet in thickness. It will be perceived that the height of the wall was practically increased by the depth of the interior ditch; so that the defenders standing in the ditch would be completely protected from the shafts of their assailants.

The defensive abilities of this circumvallation were augmented by elevated platforms and lunettes constructed all along the line at intervals of about thirty yards. The interior dimensions of these lunettes may be expressed by ten feet in front and eight feet in depth. By this arrangement, at close intervals, the defenders were thrown in advance of the line; and, elevated upon platforms, were enabled not only to deliver a powerful direct fire, but also with their arrows and spears to enfilade the main line, thereby securing a double advantage in case of attack, and affording material aid to those who were defending the wall or curtains connecting these advanced works.

In some places the wall has become well-nigh obliterated; at other points it is still quite distinct, and its entire circuit, as well as the outlines of the lunettes, can be traced all along the crest of the hill. Upon the wall, trees are growing more than three feet in diameter. This was, without doubt, the work of the red-men, and in ancient times constituted a fortified retreat. Similar structures exist within the limits of Georgia and in many portions of the United States. It will be remembered that, in the absence of any speedier mode of transmitting intelligence, the Indians signalled by means of fires kindled upon prominent points. Through their intervention the approach of danger was heralded, and the lurid warning quickly repeated until the members of the tribe, through all their abodes, were rapidly put upon the alert. Such is the location of Brown's Mount, and so abrupt and commanding its exposure on the west, that signal-fires kindled there could be readily seen and interpreted even by the primitive dwellers upon the banks of Flint River. From the side which looks toward Macon kindred warnings—cloudy pillars of smoke by day and bright flames by night—would quickly summon the warriors of the Upper Ocmulgee, and put those, who there inhabited, upon notice. Doubtless, during the forgotten past, this fortified hill answered important military uses in the conduct of the ever-recurring strifes which existed among the red-men.

The impression, entertained by some, that this circumvallation was the work of De Soto and his followers, is erroneous.

Within the enclosure are the traces of two small earth-mounds, and near the northeastern side is a pond or basin, elliptical in form, covering about a quarter of an acre. Of late years it has been drained, and at the time of my visit it contained no water. The statement was made that this was an artificial basin and that its bottom had been plastered with clay at some remote period, so as the more effectually to retain the rain-water which would, from time to time, accumulate in it. I had no means at command for making an examination, and testing the truth of this assertion. The pond was overgrown with trees, and filled with decayed leaves and loam. To all appearances, it seemed a natural reservoir, although it may be that the natives originally made this excavation with a view to supplying themselves with water in the event of a siege. The natural supply of this fluid, upon ordinary occasions, was probably derived from four springs issuing from the northern, eastern, southern, and western faces of the hill—in each instance, within not much more than fifty yards of the wall. Indications still exist tending to establish the fact that the paths leading to at least some of these springs were protected by stone walls or partially-covered ways. The summit of this hill is well adapted to cultivation, and, in one locality, I observed a circular depression, about forty feet in diameter, which suggested the belief that it might be the former site of one of those semi-sunken public granaries in use among the Southern Indians, of which the early historians have given us substantial descriptions.

In the first volume of Pickett's "History of Alabama"[1] may be found a sketch, and also a description of a group of mounds on the plantation of Mr. Messier, in Early County, Georgia. Both have been reproduced without variation, or subsequent verification, in White's "Historical Collections of Georgia."[2] The unusual, haycock appearance of these tumuli and the prim, sharply-defined circumvallation have always seemed extravagant, and encouraged the belief that the plan and accompanying explanation had been carelessly prepared, and were in the main erroneous. Impressed with this conviction, and being unable to make a personal examination of the locality, the author requested Major James Audley Maxwell—a well-known and skilful civil engineer—to visit the spot and favor him with an accurate survey of such ancient earth-works as were now to be seen. This he has kindly done, and to him are we indebted for the following plan and description conveying a correct idea of the present condition of these interesting evidences of early constructive skill. It will be readily noted how widely the impressions of an intelligent engineer differ from the notions of a casual observer.

The Messier Mound—so called because situated on the plantation of Mr. Messier, of Early County—is located about twelve miles east of the Chattahoochee River, and from the summit of a hill looks down upon the narrow valley of the Little Colomokee Creek. Crowning the natural hill with an artificial elevation of fifty-five feet, from its top is afforded a commanding view of the surrounding country. In the vicinity of this tumulus and stretching away to the west, are seen the culti-

[1] Page 168. Charleston, 1851.

[2] Page 425. New York, 1854.

vated fields of Mr. Messier, while on the east, north, and south, are the swamps of Colomokee and its tributaries, beautiful in the luxuriant and variegated foliage native to this semi-tropical region. The most facile approach to the mound is from the west, access from any other quarter being rendered difficult by natural obstacles not easily overcome. The Messier mound is not one of a group, but stands apart, prominent in size and marked in its physical peculiarities. Other tumuli exist in the vicinity, one of them near enough to appear on the scale of the accompanying map; but none of these smaller mounds differ in any essential respect from the numerous hemispherical heaps of earth erected as burial-places by the Indians who formerly inhabited Southwestern Georgia and Southeastern Alabama. Tradition, speaking through the mouths of the descendants of early European settlers, declares that the modern Indians lived here in large numbers, and that, while claiming the smaller mounds as the last resting-places of their noted dead, they regarded the great mound with commingled wonder, ignorance, and superstition. This traditional testimony is confirmed by the presence of numerous arrow and spear heads, fragments of pottery, pipes, and other relics of the skill and industry of the red race. Whether viewed near by or from a distance, the large tumulus seems but a huge mass of foliage—the outlines of this earthwork being concealed by leafy terraces of huge trees covering the sides and growing along the slopes from base to summit. The top of the mound is a level plane, and was long since denuded of all vegetation for the purpose of cultivation. Beneath the trees a tangled undergrowth of vines, bushes, and briers, in inextricable confusion, forms an inviting retreat for the rabbit and the rattlesnake. It is only at some risk, and with indefatigable industry that the exact form of this huge earthwork can be determined. While it is not singular that cursory observers should have formed erroneous impressions on this point, it is remarkable and worthy of condemnation that the results of such careless examinations should have been publicly heralded as conveying proper impressions of this interesting monument.

The form of this mound is that of the frustum of a four-sided pyramid; the top surface a level plane—a rectangular parallelogram—the north and south sides being each sixty-six feet in length, and the east and west sides each one hundred and fifty-six feet long. The base-plane is not precisely level, but declines somewhat from the north toward the south, so that the vertical height of the mound at the northeast and northwest corners is fifty-three feet, while the vertical height at the southeast and southwest corners is fifty-seven feet. The northern boundary of the base of this pyramid is one hundred and eighty-eight feet long—the southern boundary about one hundred and ninety-eight feet, while the eastern and western boundaries are each three hundred and twenty-four feet. The slope of the east, west, and south sides is about one and a quarter to one—or steeper than the natural slope of earth—while the north side slopes rather more than one and a half to one, which is about the natural slope of the earth of which this mound is composed. The foregoing description, in connection with the map and profiles (*see* Plate V.), cannot fail to convey an accurate conception of the shape of this mound. It must be remembered, however, that no earthwork can be said to conform precisely to any mathematical figure. The angles are

Plate V.

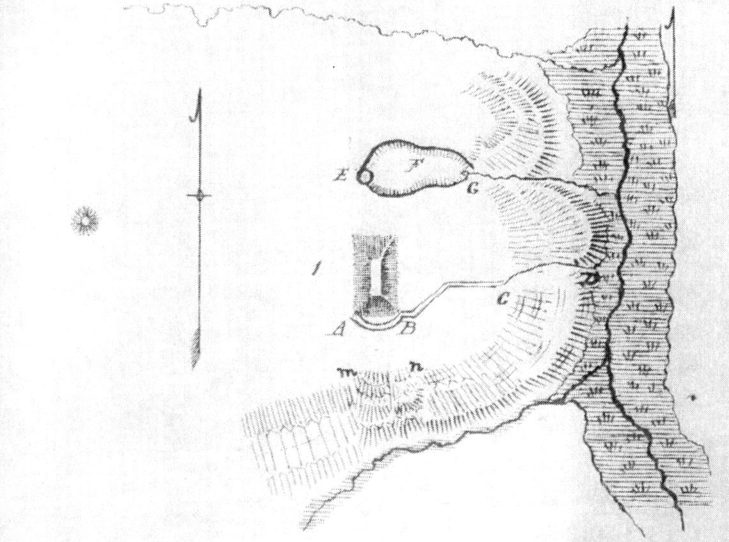

MAP SHOWING THE MESSIER MOUND.

200 — 600 yards

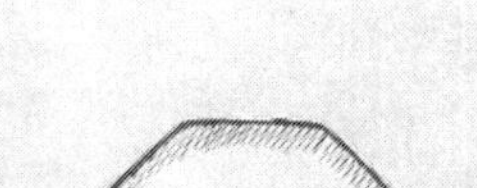

2

PROFILE THRO CENTRE ON EAST & WEST LINE

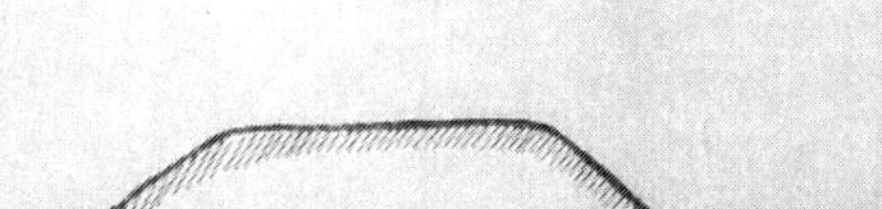

3

PROFILE THRO CENTRE ON NORTH & SOUTH LINE SHOWING MOAT

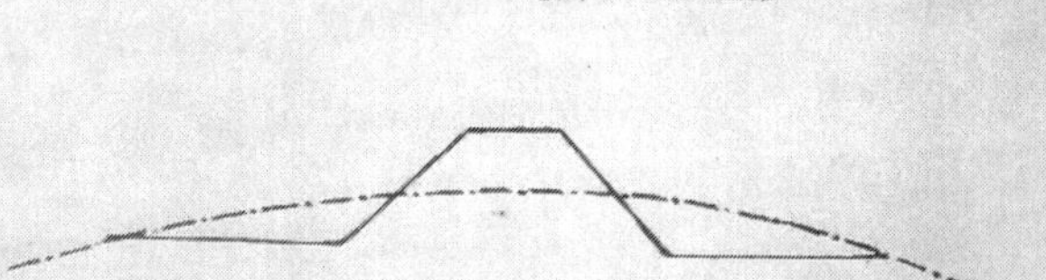

4

40 — 120 feet.

TO ILLUSTRATE A MODE OF CONSTRUCTION

AM. PHOTO-LITHOGRAPHIC CO.N.Y. (OSBORNES PROCESS.)

always more or less rounded, and the slopes and surfaces to a greater or less degree convex or concave. The form of this mound agrees as accurately with the description given as does that of any modern earthwork with the shape prescribed by the civil engineer. The slopes are even more perfect than those of railway embankments. The fact that they are steeper than the natural slope must be explained upon the hypothesis of superior construction—as by the thorough packing of the earth in successive, thin layers. The greatest departure from mathematical conformity to the pyramid occurs at the angles, which are rounded by curves of from five to fifteen feet in length. This may have been the result of design rather than the effect of time. Along the northeastern and northwestern angles the ascent to the top may most conveniently be made, but there are no indications of any special provision for this purpose. There are no terraces. The space contained between the south side of the mound and the moat—easily recognized upon the map by its resemblance, in form, to the segment of a circle—is not a terrace. However important the use to which this space may have been dedicated, it possesses no dignified elevation, but apparently occupies the same level with the original surface upon which the mound was erected. It is said that long ago a cavernous opening in the southern slope of the mound was visible opposite the centre of this segment-like space, but there is now no indication that such an opening ever existed.

This tumulus contains about seventy-five thousand cubic yards of earth, and would weigh from ninety thousand to one hundred thousand tons. By means of modern appliances its erection could be compassed at a cost of some fifty thousand dollars, provided the earth was taken from the excavations from which the ancient mound-builders obtained it. The industrious labor of one thousand savages, properly applied for the space of one year, would have accomplished the work with the aid of baskets or even earthen-ware pots for the transfer of the earth. These figures may or may not engender disappointment. We naturally incline to the marvellous, and if the reader expresses surprise, let him compare the result with the scanty means then at command—the effect with the apparently meagre cause.

We turn now to the surroundings of this huge tumulus. On the west lies a level plain well suited for the wigwams and streets of an Indian village—for play-grounds and fields both for manly exercise and the cultivation of maize. On the remaining sides the ground descends toward the neighboring streams, but there is no abrupt declivity from the immediate edge of the mound. For a distance of two hundred feet on the south, four hundred on the east, and seven hundred on the north, the natural plain is interrupted only by artificial excavations. These are A B the moat, B C D the ditch, and E F G the pit, from all of which earth was taken and used in the construction of the mound.

From B to C the ditch is remarkably regular in form, and will average twelve feet in depth, ten feet in width at the bottom, and thirty feet in width at the top. At the point C this ditch, as described, ceases abruptly, and here commences a small ditch only two feet deep—apparently a natural channel worn by descending rain-water—deepening and widening until it reaches the edge of the swamp at D. From B to C this ditch is clearly artificial: from C to D it is seemingly not so. We should not positively conclude, however, that this ditch did not originally extend to the creek. From C to D a large ditch would naturally, with the lapse of time, become smaller in consequence of the constant accumulation of sand and clay brought down by the water. From B to C on the contrary, the ditch would receive no water except such as fell into its open mouth, and would preserve its outlines. No indications remain suggesting that this ditch was formerly a covered way.

The moat—so called for want of a better name—is simply a prolongation of the ditch from B to A in the form shown in the accompanying sketch (Plate V.). From B to A it becomes uniformly wider and shallower. At B, it is ten feet deep; at A two feet deep; and, half-way between those points, its depth does not exceed six feet. It is not probable that its original form and depth have materially changed. The slopes are so gradual that midway between the points A and B a buggy and horse can be driven across. There is nothing remarkable about the segment-shaped space lying between the moat and the mound except its regularity of outline.

The ditch and moat furnished earth sufficient to raise the mound to an altitude of only one foot. The rest of the material used in its construction was taken from the great pit E F G, which, although not accurately measured, seemed just large enough to have furnished the required quantity. Its area is about two acres, and its average depth twenty-five feet, with easy slopes on the side nearest the mound. At the point E, however, the descent is perpendicular, and here an immense circular well, sixty feet in diameter and forty feet deep, may still be seen, clearly defined in all its parts. The bottom of this well is fifteen feet below the bottom of the pit, so that when the water in the well rises above the level of the bottom of the pit it flows off through the pit toward the point G, where this artificial excavation connects with a natural gorge in which rises and flows a small stream of never-failing water. The original head of this gorge was at G, and the location of the pit was doubtless selected with a view to draining off, through this natural channel, the water which would necessarily accumulate in the pit during the process of its construction and materially retard the prosecution of the work. For this purpose the excavation was commenced at G, and progressed toward E, the water passing off in a direction opposite to that in which the labor proceeded.

It is said that there formerly existed, and still remain in the vicinity, lines of earthwork a mile in length, but the writer could find no one able to point them out. Consequently he has not attempted to locate them on the map. South of the mound, at and from *m* to *n*, along the steep slope of the hill, the surface of the ground has been washed into numerous gullies in which may be found many fragments of human bones. These are exposed after every heavy rain, but they are so old and in such a decayed condition that they soon crumble into dust. The probability is that the side of the hill in this direction was extensively used for the purposes of sepulture. Some years ago a well was dug from the top of the mound, passing along its centre, to the depth of fifty feet. This investigation was not undertaken in the interest of science, but with the hope of finding precious metals and valuable stones. Disappointed in their expectations, the workmen subsequently closed this opening; and from them no useful information has been gathered touching the contents and stratification of the tumulus.

Arrow and spear heads, stone axes, fragments of quartz—not native to this region—and numerous sherds of earthen vessels, variously and fancifully ornamented, lie scattered upon the surface of the ground, and are turned up by the ploughshare in every direction.

Before the writer visited this mound he had formed a theory with regard to the method of its construction, which a careful examination compelled him to reject. Had he enjoyed the honor of serving as engineer-in-chief to his Majesty the King of the Mound-builders, he would have suggested the selection of a hill like that represented by the heavy broken line in Fig. 4, Plate V. The earth taken from the dotted areas on either side, and placed so as to form the truncated pyramid indicated by the continuous line, would have produced a mound as large as the Messier mound, at an expenditure of only one-tenth the labor. The Messier mound has received, however, no assistance whatever from any such device. It is entirely artificial, and the suggestion is named in this connection simply because it may turn out, upon the examination of other large tumuli, that they may have been built after this fashion.

White-oaks—some of them more than nine feet in circumference—are growing upon the sides of this mound. Their annual rings were not counted, nor is it known how many generations of forest-trees may have lived and died upon this tumulus, each giving its tribute of soil to the surface, since the date of its abandonment by those who compassed its erection. If any superior stratum of baked earth, or any traces of sacrificial altars once existed upon the summit, they are not now exposed to view.[1]

In the opinion of the writer, the Messier mound was erected not for defensive purposes, but as a temple for the solemnization of religious rites—probably for the worship of the sun. The erection of earth-walls in the vicinity was designed to facilitate the security and defence of a locality upon which so much labor had been expended by these primitive peoples. These are incidental, however, and subordinate to the primal object, which was the construction of this huge mound-temple. As a defensive work this tumulus is well located, although its position is much inferior to many others which might be suggested in the neighborhood.

It appears probable that in ancient times there existed an underground communication between the well E and the mound. That well contains water now, and in all likelihood has never been dry.

Evidently these ditches and excavations were originally the sources whence was procured earth required for the erection of the mound. To what secondary uses they may subsequently have been dedicated must remain a matter of conjecture. In the religious festivals of these primitive peoples ablutions subserved an

[1] In the description of this mound furnished by Dr. Charles A. Woodruff to Mr. Pickett, more than twenty years ago, and published by him in his history of Alabama, hearth-stones are mentioned on the summit, with fragments of charred wood about them. These may have been indicative of sacrificial uses, or they may have been simply the places where the Creeks in later years kindled their signal-fires or cooked their daily food. The forest-trees then growing upon the mound were stated by Dr. Woodruff to be from four to five hundred years old. Of the earth-wall enclosing the mound, Major Maxwell found no trace. "The arched passage, three hundred yards in length, leading from the large mound to the creek, and probably intended to procure water for religious purposes," spoken of by Dr. Woodruff, was probably nothing more than the segment-shaped moat and ditch described by Major Maxwell.

important part, and the convenient presence of water was deemed essential. What precise significance may have been attached to its conveyance, in a particular way, to the neighborhood of the temple-mound is now unknown. In the event of an attack, a liberal supply of this indispensable fluid was absolutely necessary; and it may be that in the location of the large reservoir and of the moat, respect was had to this contingency likely to occur at any moment in view of the predatory habits of many of the tribes which, at that remote period, migrating hither and thither, sought to dispossess present owners of chosen seats which pleased their rude fancies or seemed most prodigal of those stores upon which they mainly depended for subsistence. We conclude with one other suggestion, and it is this, that the large excavation and the semicircular moat may have been used as *fish-preserves.* We have already noted the fact that the Southern Indians, in the olden time, were in the habit of breeding fishes in artificial ponds, capturing them with nets of their own manufacture as occasion required.

We might multiply examples, for they exist in various localities, but enough has, we trust, already been said, to convey a correct impression of the distinguishing characteristics of the ancient tumuli belonging to the class to which our attention has been directed.

Upon even a cursory examination of these groups of mounds with their attendant ditches, earth-walls, and fish-preserves, it is difficult to resist the impression that they are the remains of peoples more patient of labor and in some respects superior to the nomadic tribes which, within the memory of the whites, clung around and devoted to secondary uses these long-deserted monuments. There is not a considerable stream within the limits of Georgia in whose valleys tumuli of this sort are not to be found. They appear in Florida, and are very frequent in Alabama, where truncated pyramids are even more abundant. Tennessee, South Carolina, Mississippi, and Louisiana, are dotted with interesting monuments of this class. The occupation of this entire region by these mound-building peoples was by no means inconsiderable. It is in fertile valleys and upon the alluvial river-flats, whose soil afforded ample scope for agricultural pursuits, that these tumuli are mainly seen. Why the older Indian tribes should have erected monuments so much more substantial and imposing than those which were constructed by the modern Indians, it is difficult to answer. The Cherokees and Creeks did not, in many things, equal the aborigines of the sixteenth century as described by the historians of the expeditions. Whence the cause of this evident decadence in industry, craft, and power? Can it be that the burdens imposed, the desolations wrought, and the diseases introduced among the natives by the Spaniards, contributed to this demoralization? Time was, if we may fairly judge from the appearance and manifest uses of some of these more august tumuli and their attendant relics, when those who built and cared for them held a position at least somewhat in advance of the later Indian tribes. Forming permanent settlements, they devoted themselves to agricultural pursuits, erected temples, fortified localities, worshipped the sun, possessed idols, wrought largely in stone, fashioned ornaments of foreign shells, and occasionally of gold, used copper implements, and were not entirely improvident of the future. Such was the fertility of the localities most thickly peopled by them, so pleasant the climate, and so abundant the supply of game, that these ancient settlers were in great measure relieved from that stern struggle which, among nomadic tribes and under more inhospitable skies, constitutes the great battle with Nature for life. With but few temptations to wander, except as their numbers increased, they seemingly devoted much attention to establishing their temples, protecting their settlements, and confirming their chosen seats. And yet they were not exempt from the vicissitudes which have befallen greater and more civilized nations—reverses born of the cupidity and cruelty of strangers, losses and positive destruction encountered at the hands of despoiling barbarians. It may be that they were compelled to abandon their valley-homes in consequence of the incursions of more warlike peoples.

Certain it is that the inroads of the Spaniards violently shocked this primitive population, imparting new ideas, interrupting established customs, overturning acknowledged government, impoverishing whole districts, engendering a sense of insecurity until that time unknown, causing marked changes, and entailing losses and demoralizations perhaps far more potent than we are inclined, at first thought, to believe.

CHAPTER VIII.

Chunky-Yards.—Elevated Spaces.—Mounds of Observation and Retreat.—Tumuli on Woolfolk's Plantation.—Sepulchral Tumuli.—Chieftain-Mounds.—Custom of burying Personal Property with the Dead.—Savannah owes a Monument to Tomo-chi-chi.—Family or Tribal Mounds.—Cremation.

RESPONDING to certain inquiries (propounded in all likelihood by Dr. B. S. Barton) touching his personal observation of the customs, government, and antiquities of the Creek and Cherokee Indians, Mr. William Bartram furnished the following plan and description of the CHUNKY-YARDS (*see* p. 179).

"The *Chunky-Yard* of the Creeks, so called by the traders, is a cubi-form area (A) generally in the centre of the town—the Public Square (located upon the square eminence C) and the Rotunda or great winter Council-House (situated upon the mound B, nine or ten feet high) standing at the two opposite corners. It is generally very extensive, especially in the large, old towns, is exactly level, and sunk two, sometimes three feet below the banks or terraces (b b b b) surrounding it, which are sometimes two, one above and behind the other, and are formed of earth cast out of the area at the time of its formation; these banks or terraces serve the purposes of seats for the spectators. In the centre of the yard there is a low circular mount or eminence (c), in the centre of which stands erect the *chunky-pole*, which is a high obelisk, or four-square pillar declining upwards to an obtuse point, in shape and proportion much resembling the ancient Egyptian obelisk. This is of

Fig. 2.

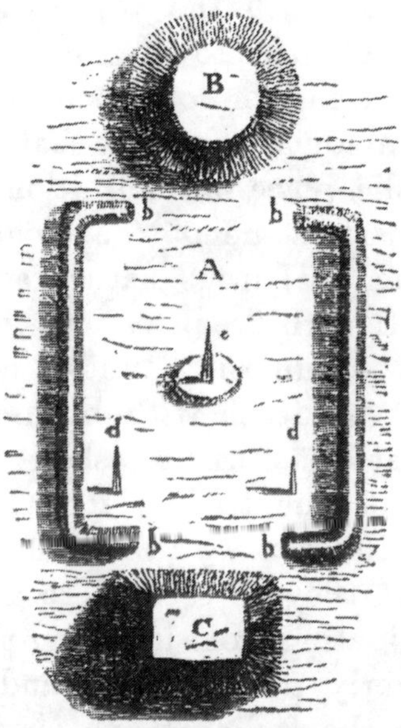

wood—the heart or inward resinous part of the sound pine-tree—and is very durable; it is generally from thirty to forty feet high, and to the top of this is fastened some object to shoot at with bows and arrows, the rifle, etc., at certain times appointed. Near each corner of the lower and further end of the yard stands erect a less pillar, or pole (d d), about twelve feet high: these are called the *slave-posts*, because to them are bound the captives condemned to be burnt, and these posts are usually decorated with the scalps of their slain enemies: the scalps, with the hair on them, and strained on a little hoop, usually five or six inches in width, are suspended by a string six or seven inches in length round about the top of the pole, where they remain as long as they last. I have seen some that have been there so long as to lose all the hair, and the skin remaining white as parchment or paper. The pole is usually crowned with the white dry skull of an enemy. In some of these towns I have counted six or eight scalps fluttering on one pole in these yards. Thus it appears evidently enough that this area is designed for a public place of exhibition of shows and games, and formerly some of the scenes were of the most tragical and barbarous nature, as torturing the miserable captives with fire in various ways, as causing or forcing them to run the gauntlet naked, chunked and beat almost to death with burning chunks and fire-brands, and at last burnt to ashes.

"I inquired of the traders for what reason this area was called the *chunky-yard;* they were in general, ignorant, yet they all seemed to agree in a lame story of its originating from its being the place where the Indians formerly put to death and tortured their captives, or from the Indian name for it, which bears such a signification.

"The Indians do not now (1773–1789) torture their captives after that cruel manner as formerly; but there are some old traders who have been present at the burning of captives.

"I observed no chunky-yards, chunky-pole, or slave-posts, in use in any of the Cherokee towns; and when I have mentioned in my journal chunky-yards in the Cherokee country, it must be understood that I have seen the remains or vestiges of them in the ancient ruins of towns; for in the present Cherokee towns that I visited, though there were the ancient mounts and signs of the yard adjoining, yet the yard was either built upon or turned into a garden-spot, or the like.

"Indeed, I am convinced that the chunky-yards now or lately in use among the Creeks are of very ancient date—not the formation of the present Indians. But in most towns they are cleaned out and kept in repair, being swept very clean every day, and the poles kept up and decorated in the manner I have mentioned." [1]

The physical traces of these chunky-yards are still extant in various portions of the State of Georgia. In the southwestern part of the State the forms of these tumuli and enclosed areas, and their relative positions in association with the outlines of the general settlement, are in some instances quite observable. There are also spaces, parallelogramic in shape, elevated from two to four feet above the surface of the ground, uniformly level at the top and free from irregularities, which apparently were designed as play-grounds. Some of these were rendered hard by an admixture of clay and would have afforded excellent opportunity for rolling the discoidal stones which contributed so largely to the amusement and gaming proclivities not only of the Southern, but also of many of the other North American Indians. We will have occasion, in a subsequent part of this work, to notice more particularly the use of these discoidal stones.

In order to facilitate the rapid communication of intelligence, upon an emergency, the Southern Indians erected conical earth-mounds upon commanding

[1] Transactions of the American Ethnological Society, vol. iii., part 1, pp. 34–36, 51, 52. New York, 1853.

points, such as the tops of hills, or elevated river-bluffs. Fires kindled upon their summits could be readily recognized and interpreted. The signals thus given were repeated from the tops of kindred mounds within convenient distances; and so, in the absence of the warning bugle-note, the sound of drum, the booming of cannon, and the passage of the electric spark, within a short period an entire tribe could be put upon the alert. These MOUNDS OF OBSERVATION are recognized by their peculiar situations, and from the further fact that they contain nothing other than the traces of the fires once kindled upon them now underlying the roots of overshadowing trees.

Striking examples of this class of mounds may be seen on Woolfolk's plantation, on the Chattahoochee River a few miles below Columbus, and at other points along the line of that river. Some years since, one of the largest was used to construct a heavy dam, and nothing was found in it save a shell drinking-cup and bits of charcoal. These tumuli are located with direct reference to the facile transmission of signals along the reaches in the river, and are so disposed that fires kindled upon their summits may be readily seen from a distance, and repeated. Situated in the river-swamp—which is liable to annual overflow—they served as safe retreats for the natives during freshets. On various occasions have the field-hands and plantation-animals sought refuge upon the summit of the large truncated mound which stands just in rear of the negro quarters on this valuable place. Many tumuli of a like character might be mentioned, but these will serve as examples.

It was the remark of Ulloa, "If we have seen one American, we may be said to have seen all, their color and make are so nearly alike." So might we affirm, in a general way, of the SEPULCHRAL MONUMENTS of the Georgia tribes. Although assimilated by many ob vious resemblances, for the purposes of our present description, they may be considered as resolving themselves into one or the other of the following classes.

Tumuli containing a single skeleton, or at most two or three skeletons, we designate CHIEFTAIN-MOUNDS. The erection of such tumuli by the Florida Indians in honor of their deceased caciques and priests, is mentioned in the "Brevis Narratio."[1] Such mounds, varying in height from five to twenty-five feet, are found in many localities, and usually occupy prominent positions in the vicinity of the spot which constituted the village-site. They are for the most part conical in form, and the human bones which they contain do not indicate the action of fire. Not infrequently the dead was interred in a sitting posture.

Such was the case in a large mound carefully opened by the writer upon the Colonel's Island. The corpse had evidently been placed upon the ground and held in position while the loose sand was heaped around and above. In the neighborhood of the feet and hands were numerous bone and shell-beads which, at the time of the inhumation, encircled the wrists, arms and ankles. Near the skeleton lay three stone axes, several spear and arrow heads, two pipes of rather unusual size—one of clay and the other of steatite—and a terra-cotta bowl, the property of the deceased at the period of his death.

In another mound the body had first been seated in the centre of the spot to be surmounted by the tumulus, and there, with his possessions deposited by his

[1] Plate xl. Francoforti ad Mœnum. De Bry, anno 1591.

side, was securely encased in a covering of tenacious red clay, six or eight inches in thickness, and oven-shaped. In this manner—the clay becoming dry and hard—the sitting posture was maintained while the earth-tomb was heaped above.

Sometimes a stout light-wood post was first driven into the ground, and the dead, seated with their backs to the post, were securely lashed to it by means of thongs or grape-vines. Two instances of this sort have been brought to our knowledge. In one mound a single skeleton was found at the foot of the post. In the other the remains of three skeletons appeared, back to back, the post being in the centre.

Captain Bossu[1] informs us that the Alibamons buried their dead in a sitting posture, stating, in justification of the custom, that man being upright, should have his head turned toward heaven, which was to be his habitation. "They give to them," he continues, "a calumet and some tobacco to smoke, that they may make peace with the inhabitants of the other world. If the corpse be of a warrior, he is buried with his arms, which are a musket, some powder and bullets, a quiver full of arrows, a bow, and a hatchet, or club; and besides these a mirror and some vermilion, with which they may dress themselves in the other world."

Upright burials are said, by Surveyor-General Lawson,[2] to have been practised by the Carolina Indians.

In preparing their dead for sepulture, the Muscogulges placed the corpses in a sitting posture, depositing with them such articles of property as were held of greatest value.[3] In celebrating the funeral rites of

[1] "Travels through Louisiana," etc., vol. i., p. 257. London, 1771.

[2] "History of Carolina," etc., p. 182. London, 1714.

[3] Bartram's "Travels," etc., p. 513. London, 1792.

a chieftain, the Cherokees seated the corpse in the tomb with the face turned toward the east, the head anointed with bear's oil, and the countenance painted red. He was attired in his finest apparel, "having his gun and pouch, and trusty hiccory bow, with a young panther's skin, full of arrows, alongside of him, and every other useful thing he had been possessed of."[1]

The practice of depositing in the grave all articles which the deceased deemed most valuable, obtained among all the Southern tribes. It has been truthfully remarked that "in all ages when the disengaged activity of man ever carries a keen and military edge with it, and his great employment is necessarily war and the chase, the weapons of both would naturally be deposited with the dead."

The ancient Germans contributed to the funeral pile the arms and the horse of the deceased. Among the more civilized Grecians expensive vases, mirrors, and ornaments were lodged in the tombs of the departed. The grave has often proved the receptacle of treasure, and the storehouse of all that was most valuable among the possessions of the deceased. The souls of the Scythian kings and the Peruvian Incas were, by costly immolations, richly furnished forth with companions, the most select, for the otherwise lonely journey. Even the sepulchre of David was made the thesaurus of more than three thousand talents.[2] In a strange land this custom was not neglected by the Indian. During the visit of Tomo-chi-chi to England, in 1734, one of his companions died in London, of the small-pox. Previous to interment in

[1] Adair's "History of the American Indians," p. 182. London, 1775.
[2] Squier's "Antiquities of New York," p. 114. Buffalo, 1851.

the church-yard of St. John's, Westminster, the body was sewn up in a blanket and bound between two boards. The clothes of the deceased, with a quantity of glass beads, some pieces of silver, and other articles of personal property, were thrown into the grave and buried with him.

The Spaniards under De Soto obtained large quantities of pearls by rifling the tombs, and pillaging the temples in which dead Indian chiefs were lying in state. The later graves which the Cherokees have left in Northern Georgia assure us of the fact that this custom of depositing with the dead all articles of value, the property of the deceased, was observed long after the establishment of commercial intercourse between the Indians and the Europeans. We are also advised that these deposits were held sacred, and that among these tribes the graves of the departed, no matter how rich in coveted treasure they might have been, were never rifled.

It is to the graves of the common dead and the tumuli erected in honor of departed chieftains, priests, and distinguished warriors, that we are largely indebted for many of the most interesting and perfect relics which grace our collections, and acquaint us with the condition of the arts among these primitive peoples.

Returning from this digression, we may assert that these chieftain-mounds, when once completed, were never reopened for the reception of other bodies. The fact that, as a general rule, only a single skeleton is found in these mounds, and the further circumstance of their prominent size and location, very properly, we think, designate them as the last resting-places of the chiefs or distinguished personages of the tribe. Upon this supposition we are enabled the more readily to understand the secret of their superior proportions. They may be regarded as the offering of the tribe or community—each member with ready hand assisting in erecting over the deceased leader a mound which, while it perpetuated the name and deeds of the honored dead and remained a monument of tribal respect and gratitude, begat also a pleasing satisfaction in the breast of all who had aided in its construction. Each of these silent, wasted mounds had its legends transmitted from sire to son, its heroic memories which brought the warm blood of conscious pride to the cheek alike of warrior and maiden; but they have all perished with those whose delight it was to perpetuate them.

These chieftain or priest mounds may be considered as individual in their character, the result of one impulse, the consummation of a general labor prosecuted without intermission to completion. When we affirm that when once finished they were never reopened to admit the sepulture of parties other than those in whose honor they were erected, we take no note of those secondary interments, frequently occurring upon the tops and sides, which were probably made by later peoples, strangers to the original and distinctive memories of these tumuli.

Composed of sand, clay, mould, and sometimes of shells, the slope of their sides is such as would be assumed by the gradual accumulation of loose material piled from above. Often pits and sunken spaces in the immediate neighborhood indicate the localities whence was obtained the earth expended in their construction.

These primitive peoples were at one time careful in the erection of marked tumuli above deceased kings and priests. With inferior means at command, they perpetuated by physical signs the memories of the places where they slept with far greater zeal than did the Europeans the graves of the greatest of the red-men who had proved themselves invaluable allies, and through whose influence an infant colony was preserved, in the midst of a howling wilderness, from cruel attack and absolute massacre.

Near Yamacraw bluff—a spot rendered memorable by the landing of General Oglethorpe, the founder of the colony of Georgia—Tomo-chi-chi, Mico of the Yamacraws, extended the open hand of welcome to the distinguished stranger, and took upon himself vows of friendship which he never ceased to observe until he bowed his hoary head in death not far from the ancient pines beneath whose hospitable shade the governor first pitched his tent. In the presence of the colonists, few, feeble and filled with doubts and apprehensions—before his followers brave and jealous of their moss-clad forests, in a manner at once expressive of genuine hospitality and redolent of that imagination so characteristic of his race, he presented General Oglethorpe with a buffalo-skin adorned with the head and feathers of an eagle. "The eagle," said he, "is an emblem of speed, and the buffalo of strength. The English are as swift as the bird and as powerful as the beast, since like the former they flew over the seas to the uttermost parts of the earth, and like the latter are so strong that nothing can withstand them." Wisely divining in this small band the seeds of a great nation whose superior intelligence and resources were destined to exercise a controlling influence over his people, he added; "The features of the eagle are soft and signify love; the buffalo-skin is warm and denotes protection; therefore I hope the English will love and protect the little families of the sons of the forest."

Firm in his friendship, even unto the end, at the advanced age of ninety-seven he breathed his last; and, dying, desired that his body might be interred among his friends, the English, in Savannah. This request was complied with, and he was buried with military honors in Percival Square.[1]

It may appropriately be asked, Where is his monument? Over this mico, the white men—those whom he counselled, assisted, and saved, and their descendants—have reared not even a simple mound-tomb. To them did he confide the solemnization of his funeral rites and the perpetuation of his last resting-place, and they have paid no tribute to the memory of his grave. Of such neglect, think we, would not they have been guilty whose primal wrath against the early colonists was, through the persuasions and influence of this aged mico, turned into friendship.

To herself and the recollections of her infant days, to the expressed wishes of General Oglethorpe who purposed the erection of a suitable shaft in honor of this departed king, as an honest acknowledgment of the debt for which she stands bound to her first and best friend among the red-men, does Savannah owe a fitting monument to the brave, the generous, the noble-hearted Indian chief, the venerable Tomo-chi-chi.

Tumuli filled with numerous skeletons may be regarded as FAMILY OR TRIBAL MOUNDS. The Indians of Southern Georgia frequently burnt their dead.

[1] C. C. Jones, Jr. "Historical Sketch of Tomo-chi-chi," pp. 120–127. Albany, N. Y., 1868.

"Plan of the City of Savannah and its Fortification, by John Gerar William De Brahm," p. 36 of "History of the Province of Georgia," etc. Wormsloe, 1849.

This custom, however, was not universal, and it obtained to a very limited extent among the tribes resident in the middle and upper portions of the State. The practice of reserving the skeletons until they had multiplied sufficiently to warrant a general cremation or inhumation seems to have been adopted.

It was no easy task for the aborigines to erect a tumulus. Hence, saving the construction of grave-mounds in honor of distinguished personages, the labor of sepulchral mound-building was postponed until the accumulations of the bone-house claimed the attention of an entire community. Adair says that the bones of those who died away from home or were slain in battle were carefully preserved and, at some convenient season, brought back and interred in a solemn manner. To be deprived of the customary rites of sepulture was a calamity which an Indian could not contemplate with indifference.

Funeral rites the Romans called *justa*, the Greeks *δίκαια*, thereby intimating the inviolable obligation which Nature imposed upon the living to perform the obsequies of the dead. As among these civilized nations the belief existed that the souls of the departed could not be admitted into the Elysian fields unless suitable funeral rites had been duly solemnized, in like manner did the red-men cherish the faith that a becoming observance of their rude obsequies was essential to the entrance of their spirits into the hunting-grounds of the blest. Here we have an explanation of the reason why they so carefully, in that remote period, collected the skeletons of their dead and laid them to rest in the burial-places of their kindred.

Bartram noticed among the Choctaws the following funeral custom: "As soon as a person is dead, they erect a scaffold eighteen or twenty feet high, in a grove adjacent to the town, where they lay the corpse, lightly covered with a mantle. Here it is suffered to remain, visited and protected by the friends and relations, until the flesh becomes putrid, so as easily to part from the bones; then undertakers, who make it their business, carefully strip the flesh from the bones, wash and cleanse them, and, when dry and purified by the air, having provided a curiously-wrought chest or coffin, fabricated of bones and splints, they place all the bones therein. It is then deposited in the bone-house—a building erected for that purpose in every town. When this house is full, a general, solemn funeral takes place. The nearest kindred or friends of the deceased, on a day appointed, repair to the bone-house, take up the respective coffins, and, following one another in the order of seniority—the nearest relations and connexions attending their respective corpse, and the multitude following after them—all, as one family, with united voice of alternate Allelujah and lamentation, slowly proceed to the place of general interment, where they place the coffins in order, forming a pyramid; and lastly cover all over with earth, which raises a conical hill or mount."[1]

These observations of Mr. Bartram are fully corroborated by the statements of Captain Bossu,[2] Mr. Adair,[3] and others.

Upon the islands and headlands along the coast, the skeletons, with a requisite amount of wood, were first placed in a pile upon the ground. Fire was then applied, and, above the smouldering remains carelessly

[1] "Travels through North and South Carolina, Georgia," etc., pp. 514, 515. London, 1792.

[2] "Travels through Louisiana," etc., vol. i., pp. 298, 299. London, 1771.

[3] "History of the American Indians," pp. 183, *et seq.* London, 1775.

heaped together, a mound of earth was erected. The charred bones and partially-consumed fragments of wood are seldom seen until we have reached the level of the plain upon which the tumulus stands. With rare exceptions, tribal mounds of this description contain but a single stratum of bones, showing that when the cremation was ended and the tumulus finished, it was never reopened. As may well be expected, the bones in these mounds are disposed without order. Being at best but fragmentary in their character, they are intermingled with ashes, charred pieces of wood, broken pottery, cracked pipes, and other relics sadly impaired by the action of fire. The fires kindled in solemnization of these funeral customs were so intense as in some instances to crack the stone celts deposited with the dead. Shell ornaments entirely disappear, and the ordinary clay-pipes are generally broken to pieces.

La Hontan states that the natives dwelling upon the banks of the Mississippi burnt their dead, "reserving the bodies" until they had accumulated sufficiently to warrant the general burning, which was performed out of the villages and in certain places set apart for that purpose. Du Pratz,[1] on the contrary, asserts positively that "none of the nations of Louisiana were acquainted with the custom of burning their dead." In the opinion of Mr. Haywood,[2] some of the Tennessee mounds afford ample evidence of cremation.

As we have already intimated, tumuli declaring unmistakably the fact that the skeletons which they cover were burnt prior to the inhumation, are exceptional in their character; and, so far as our observation extends, are chiefly confined to the coast-region of the State.

[1] "History of Louisiana," vol. ii., p. 213. London, 1763.

[2] "Natural and Aboriginal History of Tennessee," p. 138. Nashville, 1823.

Why this custom should have obtained in some instances, and not in others, we are unable to explain.

Mr. Jefferson[1] examined, with considerable care, a barrow on the low grounds of the Rivanna, about two miles above its principal fork, opposite some hills on which there had been an Indian town. It proved to be a repository of the dead, and he conjectured that it contained not less than a thousand skeletons. In this mound the bones lay in strata, separated by intervening spaces of earth, the skeletons of the different strata indicating the fact that they had lain for unequal periods in the ground—those nearest the surface being least decayed. The first collection of bones had been deposited on the ground and covered with stones and earth. A second had been laid on this, and covered in like manner. Other depositions were added from time to time, until the tumulus was completed.

Mounds have been opened by the writer, in various portions of Georgia, whose construction was compassed in a similar manner. Generally, however, these sepulchral tumuli contain but a single stratum of bones, and these laid upon the surface of the earth. The skeletons were deposited in a horizontal position, and were often piled one upon the other in such numbers, that the layer of bones, despite the weight of the superincumbent mass of earth, was sometimes a foot or more in thickness. In building these mounds the adjacent earth was used; and it would appear from numerous fragments of pottery, and from large mussel and conch-shells intermingled with the soil constituting the tumuli, that the sand and clay were first scooped up by means of these shells, and then transported in terra-cotta vessels, many of which were broken during the operation.

[1] "Notes on Virginia," query xi.

These sherds and shells have no connection with the relics deposited with the dead. Mr. Haywood [1] suggests, from personal observation, that similar means were employed in the erection of some of the burial-mounds of Tennessee. Baskets made of split cane and rushes were, doubtless, freely engaged in the conveyance of sand and other materials for the construction of these tumuli.

It is unnecessary to mention the particular locations of tumuli of this class, because they are still to be seen in nearly every part of the State. In form they are circular or elliptical, varying in height from two to twenty feet, and in diameter from twenty to one hundred and fifty feet. In cultivated fields many have been so sadly worn away by the ploughshare and the action of the elements, that they are nearly level with the ground—fragments of bones and scattered relics lying exposed upon the surface.

[1] "Natural and Aboriginal History of Tennessee," pp. 138, 139. Nashville, 1823.

CHAPTER IX.

Shell-Mounds.—Tumulus on Stalling's Island.—Shell-Heaps and their Contents.—Rock-Piles.—Indian Affection for the Graves of their Departed.—Ancient Burial-Ground on the Coast.—Rock-Walls, Embankments, and Defensive Enclosures.—Stone Mountain.—Fortified Towns of the Southern Indians.

We turn now to the Shell-Mounds. It is not an exaggeration to say that some of the islands and localities bordering upon the salt-water are hoary with these tumuli. Many are burial-mounds, while vast numbers of them are little more than the refuse-piles accumulated, during the lapse of years, about the Indian settlements. Those of the latter sort—composed of oyster, clam, mussel, and conch shells, the bones of deer, raccoons, buffalo, sea-turtles, large birds, and fishes, intermingled with fragments of pottery and the *débris* of the encampments—remind us of those heaps to which the Danish archæologists have given the name of kjökkenmöddings. Shell-mounds formed the common graves of the Indians occupying the coast. They abound upon all the sea-islands, and are thickly congregated upon the outer bluffs and along the banks of salt-water streams. The admixture of shells imparted a permanency to many small mounds which, otherwise, would long since have been entirely obliterated. Most of them contain more than one skeleton; the bones being generally disposed in a horizontal position. In a few instances the dead were inhumed in a sitting posture. Only occasionally do the human bones found in these tumuli indicate the action of fire.

It is well known that the Lower Creeks subsisted, to a large extent, upon oysters and fishes. Bringing oysters, conchs and clams from their natural and exhaustless beds in the adjacent creeks and marshes, they carried them to their villages and ate them. As a necessary consequence, there occurred a rapid accumulation of shells which were carelessly thrown into heaps near the doors of their lodges. It was just as easy to use these shells in erecting mounds over the dead as to cover the skeletons with sand. That such a disposition was frequently made of such refuse shells admits of no question. When we open these mounds it is not an unusual occurrence to find, intermingled with the shells and sand overlying the skeletons, the bones of large fishes, deer, and other wild animals, birds and sometimes dogs, accompanied by broken pieces of pottery, arrow-heads, flint knives, stone axes, and charred wood. The drift-shells—collected by the action of the tides into ridges so common along the coast—were also employed in the construction of these tumuli. Some are composed entirely of shells. Others are made chiefly of sand, with a layer of shells, varying from six inches to three feet in thickness, overlying the whole. Others, again, appear to have been formed by the careless admixture of shells and sand, just as either material at the moment chanced to be most convenient. Others, still, consist of alternate layers of human bones, sand, and shells.

A sepulchral shell-mound is rarely seen above

thirteen feet in height. Most of them do not rise more than three or four feet above the plain. In form they are elliptical and circular, with base-diameters varying from ten to forty feet. As a rule, the human bones and articles deposited in them are in a better state of preservation than those found in the ordinary earth-mounds on the main. The dry sand of the coast and the shell-covering afforded no mean defence against the disintegrating influences of time and the elements. So numerous are they in some localities on the sea-islands, that they mar the fertility of the cotton-fields. Multitudes of them have been entirely levelled by continued ploughing, and nothing but scattered shells mark the spots where they formerly stood. These tumuli afford physical proof of the general and long-continued occupancy of the coast-region by the red-men. A delightful climate, frequent springs of fresh water, mild airs in winter and cool sea-breezes in summer, fish and game in abundance, magnificent forests, and a variety of indigenous fruits, rendered this portion of the State very attractive to these improvident nomads. Appreciating these advantages, they availed themselves of them, and formed settlements in this section apparently more numerous and abiding than was their custom elsewhere.

The existence of these shell-mounds is not exclusively confined to the coast. Take, for example, that remarkable tumulus located upon Stalling's Island, in the Savannah River, more than two hundred miles from its mouth. Elliptical in shape, with a diameter, measured in the direction of its major axis, of nearly three hundred feet, and a minor diameter of one hundred and twenty feet, and with an average elevation of more than fifteen feet, this mound has been formed, to a large extent, of the mussel, clam, and snail shells of this fresh-water stream. The layers of these shells are eight or ten inches in thickness, with intervening strata of sand. Human bones lie in strata. It is a huge necropolis, and contains, at a moderate calculation, hundreds of skeletons. It could not have been the work of a year or of a generation. It is the accumulation of successive and long-continued inhumations. There is something solemnly impressive in the thought that by common consent this quiet, retired, isolated, beautiful spot should have been consecrated exclusively to the purposes of sepulture. The absence of grave-mounds in its vicinity, the unusual dimensions of this tumulus, the numerous skeletons entombed within its bosom, all attest the fact that this mound must have been used as the general cemetery of the tribes once occupying the adjacent hills and valleys.

Removed from the noise and confusion of the villages, and yet so near that the bright rays of the fires nightly kindled upon either bank revealed the outlines of this island of the dead—lying not in the path trod by the hunter—away from the conflicting voices of the council-lodge and the wild delights of the place of feasting and dancing, and yet just where the eye of affection could ever turn and rest upon its hallowed form, this tumulus has stood for centuries and still stands, a convincing proof of that respect paid to their dead, and of that care bestowed upon their sepulture, which characterized the primitive peoples of these Southern forests.

Who will recall the associations which cluster about this silent and yet not voiceless tomb; who enumerate the vicissitudes which have occurred since the first canoes, with measured dip and attendant train of mourners, landed here their precious burdens? Whose memory will recount the names, numbers, and deeds of those who have been here interred—who can tell the day when the first sleeper was laid to rest, and the first shell, bright from the bosom of the Savannah, was placed upon the new-made grave?

The hand of the conqueror has been heavily laid upon the descendants of those who here builded this memorial of their sorrows. Even the remembrance of their former existence is fading from the recollection of those who have supplanted them in the dominion over forest, hill, and river; and yet decay—more kind than they—leaves untouched this striking monument of their affection for the dead. The forest-trees with sturdy roots encircle this mound—their overarching branches shielding its outlines from the annihilating influences of the storm. The murmuring voices of the stream, which so often charmed the living ear, still bring joy and gladness as in days of yore, and the song-birds still warble sweetly their morning and evening lays above these nameless dead. All else is hushed save the whispers of the wind among the forest-branches, the startled note of the solitary water-fowl, frightened from its retreat among the reeds by the passing boat, and the soothing ripple of the river. The warrior—his stout heart turned to clay, his spear-heads scattered, his stone axe lying unused near his skeleton hand; the chieftain—his council-fires dead, his heroic deeds unsung, his memory forgotten; the medicine-man—his healing arts entombed, his charms crumbled into dust, his potent herbs ungathered in the tangled brake; young man and maiden upon whose plighted troth even the cold moon beamed kindly; the care-worn mother, her toilsome journey ended—the tender infant—all rest in one common grave, and here they will remain until the last trump shall summon both civilized and savage before the judgment-seat of Him who is mightier than them all.[1]

Professor Jeffries Wyman[2] has furnished an interesting account of the FRESH-WATER SHELL-HEAPS on the St. John's River in East Florida. The distribution of such heaps is very general. They are found upon the banks of most of the fresh-water rivers of Georgia. The largest which the writer has examined are located upon the Savannah River, in Columbia County, near the confluence of the Great Kiokee Creek. Artificial in their character, they may in general terms be described as the *débris* of the long-continued encampments of the natives upon the river-bluffs, while engaged in hunting and fishing. They are frequently several hundred feet in length, and from two to five feet or more in height. Fresh-water mussels formed an important article of food with the Indians, and were extensively gathered both for this purpose, and for the pearls which they contained. Their shells enter largely into the composition of these heaps. Intermixed with them are seen numerous fragments of pottery, stone axes, chisels, crushing-stones, awls, mortars, net-sinkers, arrow and spear points, flint knives, shell beads, soapstone ornaments, pipes, and the bones of deer, buffalo, alligators, turtles, raccoons, of smaller animals, and of birds and fishes. Many of the larger bones are split longitudinally, as though the Indians, before discarding them, had extracted the marrow.

[1] *See* "Monumental Remains of Georgia," by Charles C. Jones, Jr. Part I., p. 18, *et seq.* Savannah, 1861.

[2] "An Account of the Fresh-Water Shell-Heaps of the St. John's River," etc., reprinted from the *American Naturalist*. Salem, Mass., 1868.

This was done by the ancient inhabitants of Southern France, and by other primitive peoples, who, not content with devouring the flesh of the animals which they killed, split, or pounded the bones and sucked out the animal juices contained in them.[1]

The size of these refuse-piles affords striking proof of the long-continued occupancy of these bluffs by the Indians, and their contents advise us both of the food eaten, and the articles and implements used by these ancient peoples. Vast quantities of net-sinkers and spear and arrow points were manufactured here—the surface of the heaps being at some points covered with thousands of chips and partially-formed implements. When we come to consider the use of nets, and the different modes of fishing adopted by the Southern Indians, we will have occasion to refer to these fresh-water shell-heaps. Refuse-piles of a kindred character have been observed all along the Atlantic coast from the Bay of Fundy to Cape Sable, and also upon the Gulf coast. Such are extant in numbers upon the Georgia coast, indicating the favorite localities where the Indians congregated and subsisted upon oysters, clams, conchs, fishes, and animals and birds native to the region. The particular spots occupied by individual lodges or huts are sometimes thus perpetuated. In such instances we find the circular, depressed space formerly covered by the wigwam, surrounded by a ridge or embankment of oyster-shells. These refuse-piles can be readily distinguished from the sepulchral shell-mounds.

In order to designate the grave of a remarkable warrior, who had fallen in battle, and whose body

[1] Sir John Lubbock's "Prehistoric Times," second edition, p. 317. London, 1869.

could not at the time be brought home by his companions, the Cherokees and other nations inhabiting hilly regions were wont to cover the body of the slain with stones collected on the spot. Every passer-by contributed his stone to the pile, until it rose into a marked and permanent memorial of the dead. "In the woods," says Adair,[1] "we often see innumerable heaps of small stones in those places, where, according to tradition, some of their distinguished people were either killed or buried, till the bones could be gathered: there they add *Pelion* to *Ossa*, still increasing each heap, as a lasting monument and honour to them, and an incentive to great actions."

At a point where a decisive battle had been fought between the Carolinians, under General Middleton, and the Cherokees, in which many of the latter had been killed, and the survivors compelled to abandon their settlements in the low countries and betake themselves for safety to inaccessible retreats in the mountains, Bartram[2] observed "vast heaps of stones," indicating the graves of the red warriors who had perished during the conflict. Dr. Brickell[3] affirms the existence of monuments of this sort among the Carolina Indians.

In various parts of middle and Cherokee Georgia these STONE-PILES have attracted our notice. They consist simply of fragments of rock and loose bowlders collected from the beds of adjacent streams, or picked up on the surface of the ground, and piled one upon the other until the structure attained an altitude of from three to twelve feet. It is intimated by some of the

[1] "History of the American Indians," p. 184. London, 1775.

[2] "Travels through North and South Carolina, Georgia," etc., p. 346. London, 1792.

[3] "Natural History of North Carolina," p. 380. Dublin, 1737.

early travellers that these tumuli were temporary in their nature, and were designed merely as a protection to the bones of the dead, until they could be collected and carried home for interment in the burial-grounds of the tribe or community of which the deceased were members.

Within the historic period some of the North-Georgia tribes, imitating the custom of the Europeans, dug graves in the earth three or four feet deep, lining the bottom and sides with poles and bark. The corpse, enveloped in a blanket, was then carefully laid in this rude coffin, a cover of bark and poles being placed above, so as to protect it from contact with the restored earth. After the grave was filled, stones were added to give shape and permanency to the place of sepulture. The custom of depositing with the dead all articles of use and ornament was scrupulously observed. Various are the articles of European manufacture which have been obtained from these later graves.

Frequently the body was hidden away in some fissure of the rocks, or in the hollow of a tree—the entrance, in each instance, being securely closed.

They often interred beneath the floor of the cabin, and then burnt the hut of the deceased over his head, consuming such personal property as was not lodged in the grave, and thus obliterating all traces of the inhumation.

At other times, apparently to avoid the trouble of sepulture, the dead bodies were thrown into some neighboring river.[1]

Intercourse with swindling European traders caused the Indians to neglect those laborious rites of sepulture which at an earlier period were religiously ob-

[1] "Memoirs of Lieutenant Timberlake," p. 67. London, 1765.

served. In this respect, as in almost every other, they became indifferent and demoralized; and yet up to the period of their removal from the State, they cherished an abiding attachment for the graves of their kindred and chiefs. The idea of abandoning them was perhaps the most difficult they could be induced practically to entertain. "Why," asks the Viscount de Chateaubriand,[1] "are the savages of America, among all the nations of the earth, those who pay the greatest veneration for the dead? In national calamities the first thing they think of is to save the treasures of the tomb; they recognize no legal property but where the remains of ancestors have been interred. When the Indians have pleaded their right of possession, they have always employed this argument, which, in their opinion, was irrefragable: 'Shall we say to the bones of our fathers—Rise and follow us to a strange land?' Finding that this argument was disregarded, what course did they pursue? They carried along with them the bones which could not follow.

"The motives of this attachment to sacred relics may easily be discovered. Civilized nations have monuments of literature and the arts for memorials of their country; they have cities, palaces, towers, columns, obelisks; they have the furrows of the plough in the fields cultivated by them; their names are engraven in brass and marble; their actions are recorded in their chronicles.

"The savages have none of these things; their names are not inscribed on the trees of their forests; their huts, built in a few hours, perish in a few moments; the wooden spade with which they till the soil has but just skimmed its surface without being

[1] "Travels in America and Italy," vol. i., p. 215. London, 1828.

capable of turning up a furrow; their traditional songs are vanishing with the last memory which retains, with the last voice which repeats them. For the tribes of the New World there is, therefore, but a single monument—the grave. Take from the savages the bones of their fathers, and you take from them their history, their laws, and their very gods; you rob these people in future times of the proof of their existence, and of that of their nothingness."

But a short time since we stood in the midst of an ancient and extensive Indian burial-ground on one of the low-lying islands which fringe the Georgia coast. Earth and shell mounds were thickly congregated on every hand. A bold spring issuing from a sandy bluff—adjacent salt-water streams and wide-spread marshes filled with oysters, crabs, and fishes, and neighboring forests once abounding with game—rendered this, in the olden time, a spot highly attractive to the red-men. The solemnity of death and of desolation—so far at least as this entombed race was concerned—rested upon every thing. Even the traditions of the locality were forgotten, and the grand old live-oaks which knew these sleepers during their waking hours whispered no legends of their customs, their wars, their loves, their lives, or their deaths. Their feeble "footprints on the sands of time" had been obliterated by the tread of a statelier civilization, and there were none to care for their graves. The same sun was sinking to his rest. The breath of the myrtle and the orange still perfumed the ambient air. Kindred waves washed the bermuda-covered shore and dashed their spray, as in former days, against the roots of the vine-clad cedars. Eagles of the same bold flight soared majestically in the tranquil heavens, and contiguous woods were vocal with the notes of birds native here for centuries. The same blue sky, the same soft sea-breezes, the same generous mother earth, kindred forests and flowers, the same loves and voices of Nature, but all else how changed! The living Indian frequented no more his favorite groves. Autumnal leaves long ago covered the last trace of his rude hut. His watch-fires were dead. His council-lodge years ago mouldered into utter decay. His village was converted into a cotton-field, and the ploughboy trampled upon and furrowed mound-tombs hallowed by unrecorded memories of chiefs, warriors, priests, medicine-men, and the nameless dead of tribe and family. Never more will weeping mother with trembling hand fashion the funeral-vase. The sorrowing circle will never again assemble around the sepulchral fires, nor stalwart arms above the ashes of the dead heap the grave-mound. Beaten upon by the rains and wasted by the winds, there will soon be scarce a vestige of these tumuli. Few, if any, will gather up and deposit in some secure resting-place these neglected bones as they whiten in the sun and crumble into dust amid the fields of the present owners of the soil.

"Mors sola fatetur
Quantula sint hominum corpuscula."

The world, waxing old, forgets the names, palaces, pyramids, and sky-searching towers even of those who once held mighty sway over vast domains; and, in the wreck of ages whole nations, living and dying without letters, are remedilessly engulfed in the great ocean of oblivion.

As we mused amid these silent, storm-beaten graves, the mournful strains of the Coplas of Manrique entered with peculiar pathos into our saddened thoughts.

> "Our lives are rivers gliding free
> To that unfathomed, boundless sea—
> The silent grave.
> Thither all earthly pomp and boast
> Roll, to be swallowed up and lost
> In one dark wave.
> Thither the mighty torrents stray,
> Thither the brook pursues its way,
> And tinkling rill.
> There all are equal. Side by side,
> The poor man and the son of pride
> Lie calm and still."

We conclude this account of the more prominent traces of early constructive skill by an allusion to the existence of ROCK-WALLS, EMBANKMENTS OF EARTH, AND ENCLOSURES which were designed, we think, principally for defensive purposes. The circumvallation by means of which the top of "Brown's mound" was fortified has already been mentioned and described.

About half-way up Stone Mountain, in De Kalb County, where the acclivity becomes very marked as one ascends the western slope, on both sides of the usual pathway are the remains of a rock-wall which was originally intended for the protection of the upper portion of the mountain. This wall is still in some places two feet high, and is composed of fragments of rock, all capable of manual amotion, piled one upon the other. At either end this wall extended to the precipitous sides of the mountain where—its defensive presence being no longer necessary—access to the summit was either altogether denied or rendered so difficult and perilous as to preclude the possibility of any thing like a combined attack. Where the approach to the upper part of the mountain was most facile, and where, by common consent, a path or trail seems to have been established, an opening occurs in the wall. This opening or gate-way was effectually commanded by a ledge of rocks a little higher up the mountain and directly in front of the gap, constituting a formidable natural breastwork from which, in all security, the defenders could have launched their arrows and spears against an enemy seeking to force a passage along this, the most practicable route up the mountain. In anticipation of an attack, this opening could have been rapidly closed, and thus the entire defensive line effectually established. Below this circumvallation are numerous fragments of rock which, originally forming a part of the wall, have, in the course of time, become detached and entirely separated from it.

This huge pile of granite, towering in naked grandeur far above the adjacent valleys, was a favorite resort of the Indians during the summer months. In many places upon the summit of Stone Mountain may still be seen the indications of this former occupancy.

Similar rock-walls exist upon Mount Yonah, and guard the summits of other solitary peaks within the confines of Georgia. From their number and location it would appear that these fortified mountain-tops constituted the retreats of the natives when sore pressed in the plains. Protracted sieges were then unknown, and in the nature of things impossible. Hence, pursuit was speedily abandoned when the advance was interrupted by formidable barriers of this description.

Nor were these rock-defences confined exclusively to the mountains. They sometimes appear in the valleys, and are circular, quadrangular, or irregular in shape according to the physical conformation of the locality for the protection of which they were erected.

We note also embankments of earth from two to four feet high and from three to five feet in width, generally circular in form and sometimes semilunar in shape—in the latter case the horns extending to and resting upon some stream. Within such enclosures are embraced areas varying in size from two to twenty acres, and it is suggested that, in many instances, these parapets formed the foundations in which were securely embedded the lower ends of the stockades with which the Southern Indians were wont to fortify their principal towns. Less nomadic in their habits than the Northern and Western tribes, and bestowing no little attention upon the cultivation of maize, the southern nations rendered permanent their seats and protected their homes against the incursions of wandering bands who from time to time sought to dispossess them of their cleared fields, their fish-preserves, and their substantial granaries.

In plate xxx. of the Brevis Narratio,[1] De Bry furnishes us with a spirited sketch of a walled town built by the Florida Indians. The following is a translation of the accompanying text: "The Indians build their towns in this wise. Having made choice of a spot near a running stream, they level it off as evenly as they can. They next draw a furrow of the size of the intended town, in the form of a circle, in which they plant large round stakes, twice the height of a man, and set closely together. At the place where the entrance is to be, the circle is somewhat drawn in

[1] Francoforti ad Mœnum, anno 1591.

after the fashion of a snail-shell, making the opening so narrow as not to admit more than two at a time. The bed of the stream is also turned into this entrance. At the head of the entrance a small round building is usually erected: within the passage is placed another. Each of them is pierced with slits and holes for observation, and is handsomely finished off after the manner of the country. In these guard-houses are placed those sentinels who can scent the trails of enemies at a great distance. As soon as their sense of smelling tells them that some are near, they hasten out, and, having found them, raise an alarm. The inhabitants, on hearing the shouting, immediately fly to the defense of the town, armed with bows, arrows, and clubs.

"In the middle of the town stands the king's palace, sunk somewhat below the level of the ground, on account of the heat of the sun. Around it are ranged the houses of the nobles, all slightly covered with palm[1] branches; for they make use of them only during nine months of the year, passing, as we have said, the other three months in the woods. When they return, they take to their houses again; unless, indeed, they have been burned down in the mean time by their enemies, in which case they build themselves new ones of similar materials. Such is the magnificence of Indian palaces."

In plate xix. of the "Admiranda Narratio," we have a plan of the town of Pomeiooc, and are informed that while the villages of the Virginia Indians were also defended by stockades, the poles inserted in the ground were smaller and less strong than those used by the Florida tribes. Both the Gentleman of Elvas and

[1] Palmetto.

Hernandez de Biedma allude to the existence of stockaded forts defended by the natives.[1]

Du Pratz,[2] speaking of the Louisiana Indians, says: "When a nation is too weak to defend itself in the field, they endeavor to protect themselves by a fort. This fort is built circularly of two rows of large logs of wood, the logs of the inner row being opposite to the joining of the logs of the outer row. These logs are about fifteen feet long, five feet of which are sunk in the ground. The outer logs are about two feet thick, and the inner about half as much. At every forty paces along the wall a circular tower jets out; and at the entrance of the fort, which is always next to the river, the two ends of the wall pass beyond each other and leave a side opening. In the middle of the fort stands a tree with its branches lopt off within six or eight inches of the trunk, and this serves for a watch tower. Round this tree are some huts for the protection of the women and children from random arrows; but notwithstanding all these precautions for defence, if the besieged are but hindered from coming out to water, they are soon obliged to surrender."

The town of Mauilla, where De Soto's army encountered such determined resistance and loss at the hands of the Alibamons, was strongly fortified by piles driven in the ground "with timbers athwart, rammed with long straw and earth between the hollow spaces," so that the work, in the language of Herrera, "looked like a wall smoothed with a trowel." At intervals of eighty paces were towers in which eight men could

[1] "Narratives of the Career of Hernando de Soto," translated by Buckingham Smith. No. V. Bradford Club Series, pp. 99, 100, 248. New York, 1866.

[2] "History of Louisiana," etc., vol. ii., p. 251, *et seq.* London, 1763.

fight. These were loop-holed, and the town was entered by means of two gates.

It is probable that most of the earth-walls or parapets in the valleys, with traces of an exterior ditch and sometimes of an interior trench also, indicate simply the locations of the palisades planted for the protection of ancient towns. The upright position and defensive power of these posts, inserted in the ground, would have been materially strengthened by a bank of earth thrown up on both sides of the stockade; and nothing would be more natural than the presence of ditches or trenches, both within and without, whence material was obtained for this purpose. In these enclosures the position of the gate-ways is often quite distinct.

CHAPTER X.

Stone Graves in Nacoochee Valley and elsewhere.—Copper Implements and the Use of that Metal among the Southern Indians.—Cane-Matting.—Shell Drinking-Cups.—Shell Pins.—Age of Stone Graves.—Evidence of Commerce among the Aborigines.

In the upper part of Nacoochee Valley, and near its western extremity, is a prominent earth-mound. Located not far from the Chattahoochee River, and rising some twenty feet or more above the surface of the surrounding valley, it has long constituted a marked feature in this beautiful region. For many years its slopes and summit have been cultivated, and, within the recollection of the older inhabitants, this tumulus has lost much of its original dimensions. Elliptical in shape, it has a flat top, declining somewhat toward the southwest. Measured in a northeasterly and southwesterly direction, at right angles, its base-diameters are, respectively, one hundred and ninety, and one hundred and fifty feet; while its apex-diameters, ascertained in the same directions, do not fall short of ninety and sixty feet. It is entirely artificial, and appears to be wholly composed of the earth gathered from the neighborhood of its base. There are no terraces, the sides sloping gradually from the summit. Tradition has preserved no memories of the people by whom it was erected, and its treasures, if any, are still concealed within its own bosom.

In June, 1870, Capt. J. H. Nichols, while ploughing in the vicinity of this tumulus, discovered, several inches below the surface of the field, a number of large stone slabs. They were lying at a remove of about thirty feet from the western slope of the mound. At a loss to account satisfactorily for their presence in this locality, and his curiosity being excited, he set about removing them. During the progress of the investigation, he unearthed three stone graves, quite near each other, but not disposed in a uniform direction. These graves were parallelogrammic in shape, being seven feet long, three feet wide, and a little more than two feet and a half deep. They were all filled with earth, and the surface of the field above them was somewhat elevated beyond the level of the surrounding valley. The sides consisted of rough slabs of slate, between two and three feet long, and about two feet wide, set up on end. The bottom of the central grave was paved with oval bowlders which had evidently been obtained from the bed of the Chattahoochee. But one of the three—and that the central grave—was covered. For the covering, or lid, flat slabs of stone rather more than three feet in length had been employed; so that when they rested upon the upright sides and ends of the grave, the enclosure of this vault or rude sarcophagus was complete.

In this central grave a male skeleton, measuring more than six feet, lay extended at full length. Each of the other two graves contained the bones of more than one skeleton lying in disorder, and carelessly piled in without any regard to regularity. It was obvious that these bones were in a detached condition when they were placed in these enclosures. It seemed impossible from them to construct distinct and complete skeletons. When removed from the graves and exposed to the air, most of them crumbled. Further investigation will probably develop the existence of other stone graves of similar construction in this vicinity.

So far as we are informed, these are the first ancient stone graves which have been observed within the geographical limits of Georgia. We have already seen that shell and earth mounds abound along the coast. The valleys of the Savannah, the Chattahoochee, the Etowah, the Oostenaula, the Alatamaha, and of other rivers, are rendered remarkable by the presence of tumuli august in their proportions. Even the lonely pine-barren region is not wholly wanting in these proofs of the former occupancy of the red race. In Cherokee Georgia heaps of stones designate the last resting-places of the Indians, while a cleft in the rock, a hollow tree, or a small mound often formed a hiding-place for the dead. In other portions of the State regular inhumations occurred with but slight external marks to commemorate the places of sepulture. Although it was confidently believed that the stone-grave makers of the Tennessee and Cumberland Valleys might have crossed the mountains which intervened and possessed themselves of the pleasant valleys of Georgia, the fact that they had actually done so, and, in accordance with their established custom, deposited their dead in rude sarcophagi in these localities, was never fully established until by the recent investigations of Capt. Nichols.

Bartram[1] observed in the environs of Keowe, "on the bases of the rocky hills immediately ascending from the low grounds near the river bank, a great number of very singular antiquities, the work of the ancients." They were between four and five feet in length, two feet high, three feet wide, and constructed of four flat stones—two set on edge forming the sides, a third closing one end, and a large flat stone placed horizontally on the top of these three completing the enclosure—the other end being left open. He could not determine whether they were ovens, sacrificial altars, or sepulchres, and all inquiries failed to elicit any definite information with regard to their uses, both from the Indians and the trader who accompanied him. These structures were upon the surface of the ground and varied in their dimensions.

To Mr. Haywood[2] we are indebted for early notices of the existence of stone graves in Tennessee, at not a great remove from the boundary-line of Georgia. Professor Troost found them in the Cumberland Valley, and described them "as rude fabrics composed of rough flat stones (mostly a kind of slaty limestone, or slaty sandstone, both abundant in our State). Such flat stone was laid on the ground in an excavation made for the purpose; upon it were put (edgewise) two similar stones of about the same length as the former, and two small ones were put at both extremities so as to form an oblong cavity, lined with stones, of the size of a man; the place for the head and feet had the same dimensions. When a coffin was to be constructed next to it, one of the side-stones

[1] "Travels," etc., p. 370. London, 1792.

[2] "Natural and Aboriginal History of Tennessee," pp. 123, 201–207. Nashville, 1823.

served for both, and consequently they lay in straight rows, in one layer only. I never found one above the other."[1]

On the banks of the Merameg, about fifteen miles above the confluence of that river with the Mississippi, Mr. Say in 1819 observed numerous stone graves. They did not rise above the general surface of the ground, but their presence was readily ascertained by the projecting vertical stones which enclosed them. The sides of the graves were neatly constructed of long flat stones vertically implanted and adapted to each other, edge to edge, so as to form continuous walls. Their coverings consisted of flat stones placed horizontally above them. These graves varied in length from three to six feet. They were filled with earth, and the bones which they contained appeared to have been deposited after they had been separated from the flesh, and from each other, in accordance with a custom which obtains among some Indian tribes even to the present day. In some of these vaults rude pottery was found. It had been represented that these graves contained the skeletons of a diminutive race of men, but a careful examination of their contents proved conclusively the utter falsity of the statement. Near the city of St. Louis more graves of this description were observed. Mr. Say expresses the opinion that these sepulchral chambers are more modern than the tumuli which abound in this region.[2]

In the State of Missouri, between the river Aux Vaix and the Saline, on the farm of a Mr. Bogy, are

[1] Transactions American Ethnological Society, vol. i., p. 359.

[2] "Account of an Expedition from Pittsburgh to the Rocky Mountains," etc., compiled from the Notes of Major Long, etc., vol. i., pp. 55–57. London, 1823.

many small elevations, evidently artificial, with trees from fourteen to eighteen inches in diameter growing upon them. They contain graves, the outlines of which are formed of sharp stones standing on edge and sloping inward at the bottom.[1]

In May, 1843, Dr. A. Wislizenus visited and examined quite a number of stone graves in the neighborhood of Prairie du Rocher, Randolph County, Illinois, three miles east of the Mississippi River, and not far from old Fort Chartres.

His description is as follows: in general construction they were coffin like—their side-walls, top, and bottom, being formed by flat limestones joined together without cement. The size of the grave was adapted to that of the person to be buried in it, varying in length from one and a half to seven feet, in width from one foot to eighteen inches, and in depth from one foot to a foot and a half. The top layer of stones was seldom deeper than half a foot below the ground. Although located near each other, no order was observed in the position and direction of these graves.[2]

To Professor Charles Rau I am indebted for the following memoranda of his researches among the stone graves of Illinois:

Indian cemeteries are of frequent occurrence in the "American Bottom," which extends along the bank of the Mississippi, in the State of Illinois, and is bounded toward the east by the picturesque "Bluffs"—an extended range of elevations indicating the former left bank of the "Father of Waters." These cemeteries are usually found on the brow of a hill, in accordance

[1] *See* Bulletin American Ethnological Society, vol. i., pp. 49, 50.
[2] *See* Transactions St. Louis Academy of Science, vol. i., pp. 66, 67.

with the custom of the Indians to select elevated places for burying their dead. The graves consist of rough limestone slabs, loosely put together at right angles, so as to form a kind of stone coffin enclosing the corpse on all sides. The bottom, sides, and cover, are all formed of stone slabs. Rectangular in shape, these graves vary in length according to the size of the occupant. Their average depth is about three feet—the top stones being covered with earth. The side-slabs protruding a few inches above the ground indicate the single graves. These are often arranged in rows contiguous to each other, but are sometimes distributed without any view to regularity. You may see, for instance, at the same burial-place, six or seven graves in a row, and a few others joining them in a quite unsymmetrical way. No fixed rule prevailed in the location of these graves with reference to the cardinal points. Professor Rau examined a group of seven or eight situated on a high eminence of the Bluff, a mile northeast of the conical rock formation known as the "Sugar Loaf," near the town of Columbia, in Monroe County, Illinois. One of these graves was nearly quadrangular in shape, measuring between five and six feet each way. After removing the covering he found a skeleton in a rather decayed state, lying flat on the bottom stones, with the arms not extended along the side of the body, but stretched out at right angles with it. Hence the unusual width of the grave. The skeleton was that of a medium-sized individual; skull not very large, and the teeth, although much worn, in excellent condition. Not only the grave but also the skull, and even the hollows of the bones were filled with earth. No trace of any manufacture appeared in this grave.

In another cemetery similar to that just alluded to, but containing more graves, situated on the spur of the Bluffs, five miles south of Columbia, decayed human bones were seen embedded without order in various portions of the earth which filled one of the graves. Fragments of a skull were found quite distant from each other. From the thinness of the fragments and their curvature, it was conjectured that the remains were those of a child perhaps ten or twelve years old. Nothing of artificial origin was discovered in this grave. Obviously it had never been disturbed, for the ground within the stone enclosure was very hard and traversed by roots as large as a man's arm. In this instance the bones must have been interred after the flesh had been removed. It is a fact well remembered by many persons in this neighborhood that the Indians who inhabited this region during the early part of the present century (probably Kickapoos) buried their dead in stone coffins. Dr. Shoemaker, who resided on a farm near the town of Columbia, in 1861, showed Professor Rau, in one of his fields, the empty stone grave of an Indian who had been killed by one of his own tribe, and there interred within the recollection of some of the old farmers of Monroe County. The skeleton, which had been exhumed a few years previously, was in a good state of preservation, and Dr. Shoemaker used the skull in imparting practical instruction to a medical student then in his office.

Other small cemeteries of a like character were observed by Professor Rau in the neighborhood of "Sulphur Springs," in Jefferson County, Missouri. In them several food-vases were found.

By far the most extensive investigations, however,

are those recently conducted by Professor Joseph Jones, M. D., in the Cumberland Valley and in various other localities in the State of Tennessee.

Most of the stone graves, examined by Dr. Jones, were parallelogrammic in form. Some of them were coffin-shaped, others were square; and, in one instance, in the centre of a mound, he observed a hexagonal stone grave, with parallelogrammic stone graves radiating on all sides from it. Some graves were only ten inches long, and five inches wide. These contained the bones of infants. The largest he saw were about eight feet long, and two feet and a half wide. Intermediately, were graves of all sizes. Their depths varied from ten inches to a foot and a half. As a rule the larger graves contained but a single skeleton. In the square graves it was not unusual to find portions of more than one skeleton: for example, two skulls were not infrequent. The flesh had evidently been removed from the bones before they were placed in these receptacles. On more than one occasion he noticed the bones of the toe inserted in the nasal openings of the skull. The body was never enclosed in a sitting posture. The square graves appeared to be the common receptacles for the collected bones of the dead. In the centre of the sarcophagus the skull was often located, and the long bones of the skeleton were arranged around it. In many instances no order was observed in the collocation of the bones. Dr. Jones saw acres of stone graves in several of the valleys of Tennessee.

Near Brentwood, twelve miles from Nashville, he opened a mound which was composed entirely of stone graves, located one above the other, to the height of four tiers in the centre. Those lowest in order were uniformly square graves. Just above them were long and square graves, while the two upper tiers consisted of graves between six and seven feet in length, and about a foot and a half wide. The top stones of the highest graves were so arranged as to form a continuous stony covering for the entire mound. This tumulus, which was but an aggregation of individual graves, was seventy-five feet in diameter, and between six and seven feet high. It was covered with a layer of earth, several inches thick. This unique mound was located near the centre of an enclosure, some ten acres in extent, surrounded by an earth-wall, three feet high, at the date of his visit.

The valleys of the Cumberland, the Harpeth, Duck, and Stone Rivers, teem with the sepulchres and monuments of the stone-grave makers.

From these graves Dr. Jones obtained numerous stone and clay images, marine shells, stone implements, arrow and spear heads, a stone sword, agricultural implements, various ornaments of stone, clay, and shell, pots, vases of curious devices, and copper crosses. This collection possesses rare value for the student of American archæology. It is very rich in crania.

Upon some of the bones taken from these graves the ravages of syphilis were unmistakable. From various indications which were satisfactory to his own mind, Dr. Jones was convinced that inhumations had occurred in these rude vaults since the period of primal contact between the Europeans and the red race.

It is perhaps not unlikely that the Chaouanons constructed many of these Tennessee graves, and, crossing the mountains which intervened, peopled Nacoochee

Valley and other portions of Georgia. The Shawnees, Shawanoes, Utchees, and Sauvanogees or Savannahs, at some remote period may have acknowledged allegiance to this race—a people from which sprang some of the noblest specimens of the red-men of whom we have any knowledge. The Utchees claimed to be autochthons, and always contended that they were the original proprietors of the soil. It is not too much to expect that future investigations will confirm the conjecture that stone graves will be found in the valleys of the Chattahoochee, the Etowah, the Oostenaula, the Coosa, and perhaps the Savannah.

The custom of reserving the bodies until they had accumulated sufficiently to warrant something like a general inhumation, and the practice of turning over the corpses to certain persons, who answered in a rude way to the calling of undertakers, that they might strip the flesh from the bones and enclose the latter in bark coffins until the set time of burial occurred, obtained, as we have already intimated, among more than one of the North American tribes.[1]

An examination of the stone graves of Nacoochee Valley inclines us to the belief that to the prevalence of some such custom as this are the two graves indebted for the remains of several dead enclosed within them. The lack of order in the disposition of the bones, and the careless commingling of various portions of several skeletons, are evident, while in the central grave the corpse was carefully laid at full length upon the stone flooring. As we proceed we will perceive additional reasons for conjecturing that

[1] "Travels of William Bartram," p. 514. London, 1792. "Travels of J. Carver," p. 402. London, 1778.

this grave formed the receptacle of some chief or warrior of note. He was an old man of great stature. The few teeth remaining in the lower jaw were much worn, and the alveolar processes had been greatly absorbed. Unfortunately, the skull was in such a decayed condition that it could not be preserved.

It is a fact worthy of note that stone graves, not unlike those which we have been considering, have been found in England, Scotland, Germany, France, and in other portions of the world. They are the simplest forms of tombs; and, because of their durability and the facility with which they could be constructed, very naturally commended themselves to the use of such as were jealous of the bones of their dead. In a word, they may be described as sepulchral chambers or stone chests—either rectangular or approaching polygonal forms, in consequence of the rough and misshapen character of the materials employed—roofed with blocks of Nature's own hewing.

As we have remarked, each of these graves contained human remains. In the central grave was the skeleton of an old man more than six feet high. This corpse had been carefully deposited upon the floor of the vault, at full length, the arms lying paralled with the body. In the other two graves the bones had been disposed without any regard to regularity. Portions of several skeletons were found in each, and it was evident that they had been inhumed in utter disregard of every thing savoring of order. None of these graves had been disturbed previous to this examination. Although located in a cleared field, which had been cultivated for a number of years, the ploughshare had never before touched the stone covering which sheltered them.

Plate VI.

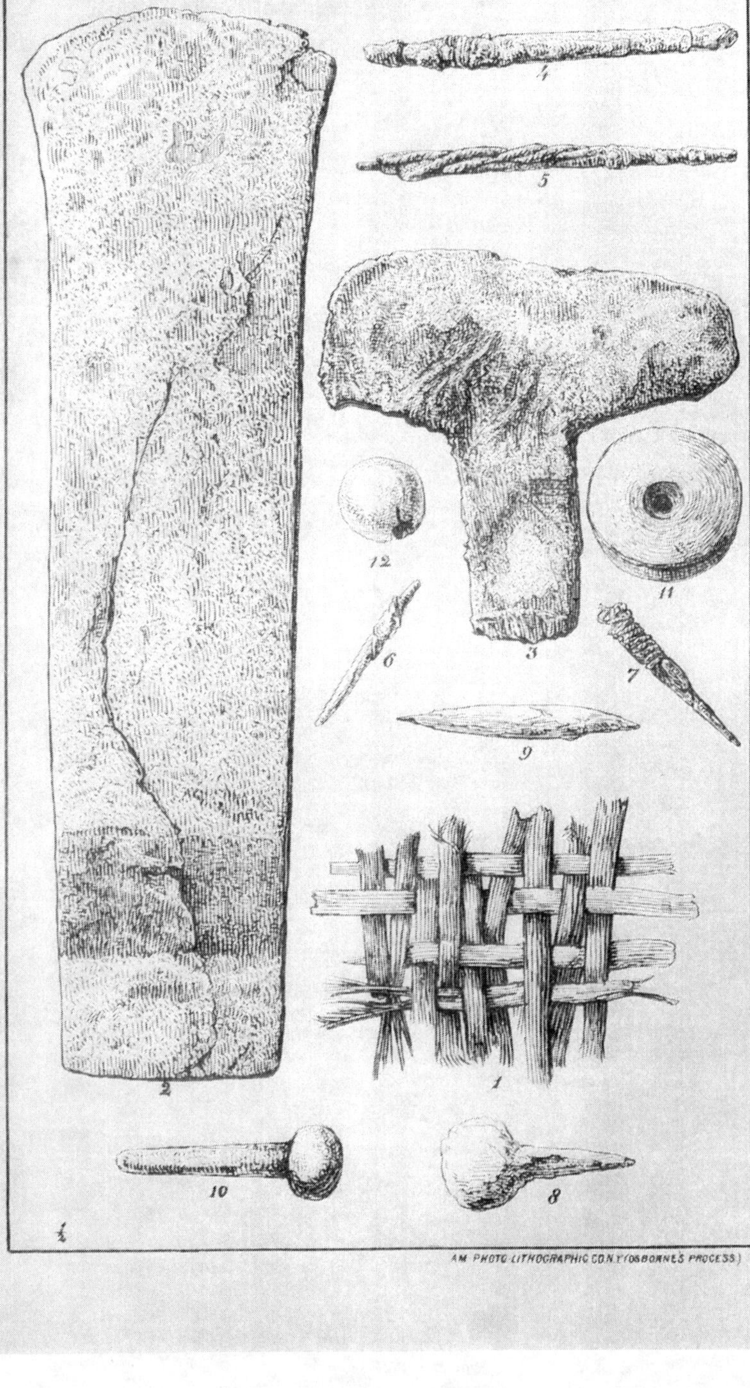

AM. PHOTO-LITHOGRAPHIC CO.N.Y. (OSBORNE'S PROCESS.)

The most remarkable object found in the central or chieftain grave, was a COPPER IMPLEMENT. It lay near the shoulder of the skeleton, and beneath it was a piece of cane-matting, probably the remnant of the sheath or basket which enclosed it when first deposited in the grave of its owner. The only portion of the matting or basket-work in condition to be removed and preserved was that part which was immediately underneath and in contact with the implement. It was discolored by the oxide of copper, which exerted a conservative influence. This *sheath* or *matting*[1] consisted of thin layers of split cane, about the quarter of an inch in width, interwoven at right angles with each other. The cane had been prepared for the purpose, by being split into strips of uniform width. From these the softer, inner portions had been removed, so that only the thin, hard, outer surface remained. Those at all familiar with this reed will readily remember how very firm and almost indestructible by ordinary exposure its tough integument is. The use of this material by the Cherokees in the manufacture of baskets and other articles of ornament and domestic value, was continued until a late period. Adair says: "They make the handsomest clothes-baskets I ever saw, considering their materials. They divide large swamp-canes into long, thin, narrow splinters, which they dye of several colours, and manage the workmanship so well, that both the inside and outside are covered with a beautiful variety of pleasing figures."[2] Traces still exist, indicating that the strips of cane composing the piece of matting we are now

[1] *See* Fig. 1, Plate VI.
[2] "History of the American Indians," p. 424. London, 1775.

considering were originally dyed, some of them black, and others yellow. The moisture of the earth, the deposit of the oxide of copper, and the gnawing tooth of Time have sadly interfered with the primal coloring. This is probably nothing more than the fragment of a cane-basket—then in general use among the Indians—which was deposited in the grave at the time of the inhumation. Possibly the copper axe and other articles of the deceased were then placed in it.

The *copper implement*,[1] which is an object of unusual interest, is nearly ten inches in length, two inches and three quarters wide at the cutting edge, and two inches wide at the upper or helve end. The cutting edge is arching, while the other end, except at the corners, is square. It possesses an almost uniform thickness of a little less than the tenth of an inch, and weighs nine and three-quarter ounces avoirdupois.

An inch and a quarter from the upper end, and extending diagonally across the implement, is a smooth, worn space on each side, about an inch and a quarter in width, showing where and how this axe was inserted in its handle. We can determine the precise angle of inclination which the axe sustained to the handle. The abrasion caused by the handle is very distinct. This implement is made of pure copper, and the lamination is clearly discernible. That it had been used, is evidenced both by the abrasion caused by the handle, and also by the fact that the cutting edge is somewhat split and broken—the implement being otherwise perfect. So thin, however, is this axe, it seems scarcely probable that it could have been applied to

[1] *See* Fig. 2, Plate VI.

any general practical uses. The material of which it is made being pure, native copper, if subjected to violent contact with any hard substance, would necessarily bend and prove comparatively valueless. We think it was carried as a badge of distinction and treasured as a valuable ornament or possession, and not employed as a weapon of war or used for incisive purposes. Manufactured of native copper, it was beaten into its present form without the intervention of heat. In its construction the workman regarded his material as a sort of malleable stone, dealing with it as such, and not as a metal capable, under the influences of heat, of being readily hammered into the desired shape. The surface of this axe is considerably oxidated, except where it was surrounded by the handle, which would indicate not only that it was attached to the handle at the time of its inhumation, but also that the handle must have consisted of some hard substance, which lasted for a long period subsequent to the inhumation and thus protected the inserted portion of the implement from those influences which operated to oxidate the exposed surface. The handle had worn that portion of the axe which it enclosed quite smooth; and this fact, while evincing no inconsiderable use, tended to render such part least liable to decomposition or oxidation. No trace of the handle remained in the grave. Clavigero says the Mexicans had copper axes, with which they cut trees, and that they were inserted in an eye of the handle. In a similar way was this axe attached; lashings of deer-sinews, bark, or buck-skin being used to keep it securely fastened.[1]

[1] *See* "Ancient Monuments of the Mississippi Valley," p. 198, Fig. 83.

It will be remarked that the peculiar features of this Nacoochee axe are its length, it unusual thinness, and the existence of a clearly-defined space on each side, showing not only that it was inserted in the eye or split of a handle, but also the precise point and angle at which it was so enclosed and held in position. Compared with the Chillicothe axe,[1] the Long-Island axe, and others which might be mentioned, it will readily be perceived how materially the present axe differs from them all both in shape and weight. So far as our knowledge extends, this specimen is unique in more than one particular.[2]

Copper implements are rarely found in Georgia. The present is the finest specimen, which, after no mean search, has rewarded our investigations. Native copper exists in portions of Cherokee Georgia, Tennessee, North Carolina, and Alabama, but it is generally found in combination with sulphur, and not in a malleable form. We are not aware of any locality, among those enumerated, whence the Indians could have secured that metal in either quantity or purity sufficient to have enabled them to have manufactured this implement.

If we may credit the accounts of the early voyagers and adventurers, the tribes of this region, at the times when the Europeans first visited them, were possessed of but little copper.

Sir Walter Raleigh's companions observed copper ornaments in the hands of some of the Indians of the coast. Of the many mounds, however, which the writer has carefully opened and examined along the

[1] Transactions American Ethnological Society, vol. ii., p. 174.

[2] Similar implements are said to have been taken from a grave-mound in Mississippi, but they have not passed under the writer's observation.

coasts of South Carolina, Georgia, and Florida, not one contained a single copper implement or ornament of native manufacture.

In the narrative of the first attempt of the French, under Captain John Ribault, in 1562, to colonize the newly-discovered country of Florida, mention is made of the fact that the natives spoke of mines of copper in the mountains of Appalatcy.[1] It has never, we believe, been satisfactorily ascertained whether this reference was to particles of gold or copper; and the stream of gold[2] said to be issuing from the foot of the mountains had in all likelihood no surer physical existence than the fountain of perpetual youth, conjectured, longed for, eagerly sought, but undiscovered amid the everglades of the "Land of Flowers." The Fidalgo of Elvas alludes to the circumstance that the Indians informed the Governor De Soto of the existence, at Chisca, of a foundery of gold and copper, but makes specific mention of no copper implements in the possession of the natives, except some chopping-knives at Cutifachiqui, which were thought to have a mixture of gold in them.[3]

Cabeça de Vaca says: "Among the articles that were given to us, Andres Dorantes received a bell of copper, thick and large, figured with a face, which they (the Indians) had shown, greatly prizing it. They told him that they had gotten it from others, their neighbors; and we asking them whence they had obtained it, they said that it had been brought from the direction of the north, where there was much copper, and that it was highly esteemed. We concluded

[1] French's "Historical Collections, Louisiana and Florida," p. 170. New series.

[2] Ibid., p. 288. New series.

[3] "Narratives of the Career of Hernando De Soto," etc., translated by Buckingham Smith. New York, 1866.

that whencesoever it came, there was a foundry and that work was done in hollow form."

At a subsequent period, upon showing this bell to other Indians, their response was, "in the place whence that had come there were many plates of the same material, and that it was a thing they greatly esteemed." [1]

But one other allusion is made to copper, in this narrative, and it is this; when in the prairie country of Texas, Cabeça de Vaca saw a copper article, which had been fashioned by the natives in the form of a "hawk-bill."

In the Portuguese narrative the Indians are said to have obtained pearls from the beds of the interior rivers, which they pierced with heated copper spindles and strung around their necks, arms, and ankles.

At each of the three gates of the Temple of Talomeco, three miles distant from the town of Cutifachiqui, were stationed gigantic wooden statues, variously armed with clubs, maces, canoe-paddles, *copper hatchets*, drawn bows, and long pikes. These implements were ornamented with rings of pearls and *bands of copper*. [2]

On the bank of the Mississippi River, Hennepin was courteously received by an Indian chief, clothed in a "kind of white gown," which women had spun of the bark of trees. Before him two male attendants carried a "*thin plate of copper* as shining as gold." [3]

Hariot, Captain John Smith, and others, allude

[1] "Narrative of Alvar Nuñez Cabeça de Vaca," translated by Buckingham Smith, p. 92. Washington, 1851.

[2] Garcilasso de la Vega, pp. 274, 282.

[3] Hennepin's "New Discovery," etc., p. 156. London, 1698.

to the presence of "diuerse small plates of copper," in the possession of the Virginia Indians; and De Bry has figured ornaments of the same metal worn by the natives of Florida.

Without multiplying these references, it may, we think, be confidently asserted that while the early writers note the presence of copper implements and ornaments among the Indians of this region, their narratives prove that such were comparatively rare and highly prized by the natives. It is not shown that they were manufactured here, and we very much doubt whether there was in the Southern States (or within the geographical limits at present embraced by them) a natural vein or deposit of copper, accessible to the Indians, of sufficient size and purity to have afforded them the material necessary for the fashioning of such an implement as that now before us. Our impression is, that the metal of which the Nacoochee axe is formed was obtained from the shores of Lake Superior, and that probably the implement itself was there made.

The art of melting copper was neither understood nor practised by the natives. Of the method of working it while in a heated state, the primitive artist appeared to be entirely ignorant. Regarding this metal simply as a sort of malleable stone, he contented himself with obtaining pieces of suitable size from the ground or from natural blocks or veins, and hammering them into the desired shapes.

The Lake-Superior region furnished the Indians with most if not all the copper they used. The interesting researches of Mr. Whittlesey [1] and others have shown how extensive were those ancient mining

[1] "Ancient Mining on the Shores of Lake Superior."—Smithsonian Contributions to Knowledge. April, 1863.

operations along the shores of that lake. The methods and implements employed for detaching pieces of this metal from their natural masses, and hammering them into various shapes, have also been carefully noted and described. Messrs. Squier and Davis,[1] Professor Wilson,[2] and others, concur in the opinion that the copper used by the Indians in the preparation of these cold-wrought implements and ornaments was obtained chiefly, if not entirely, from the ancient mines of Lake Superior.

This copper axe from the shores of Lake Superior in the stone grave of an Indian in the beautiful valley of Nacoochee is surely an interesting proof of the commerce which existed among the tribes of North America. In this connection we would refer to another ornamental copper axe and to some copper rods or spindles found in an ancient grave in the Etowah Valley. It will be remarked how closely this implement (Plate VI., Fig. 3) resembles the Oxaca axe figured by Du Paix. Like the thin axe from the stone grave in Nacoochee Valley it is of native copper, laminated in its structure, and was hammered into its present shape without the intervention of fire. This axe, also, is thin, and could not well have been used for incisive purposes.

The design of the small copper rods, of which Figures 4, 5, 6, and 7, Plate VI., are illustrations, it is difficult to conjecture. It has occurred to us that they may be the spindles alluded to by the historians of De Soto's expedition, with which, when heated, the natives were wont to perforate pearls so that they could be strung and worn as beads.

[1] "Ancient Monuments of the Mississippi Valley," p. 203.
[2] "Prehistoric Man," p. 174.

Copper pendants for the ear have been found in several of the valleys of Upper Georgia. They were small, thin, pear-shaped ornaments, perforated in the upper end to facilitate the suspension. The surfaces of these pendants were frequently ornamented with incised lines, apparently traced with a flint flake.

Two fine specimens of the *Cassis flammea* were taken from these graves—one of them from the central sarcophagus. They were nearly ten inches in length and about seven inches in diameter. From them, both the interior whorls and columellas had been removed, so that they answered the purpose of drinking-cups or receptacles of some sort. Dr. Troost saw in Tennessee one of these shells with an idol inside of it—an opening having been made for its reception. This image was in a kneeling posture, with its hands clasped in front.[1] Dr Drake found in some ancient tumuli near Cincinnati, large marine shells of the sort we are now considering. They had been cut longitudinally so as to form very convenient drinking-cups.[2] Professor Jones informs me that conchs of this description were seen by him not infrequently in the stone graves of the Cumberland Valley. The presence of marine shells in graves of a similar character, in other localities, has been noted by more than one observer. These conchs were brought from the Southern Atlantic coast, or from the shores of the Gulf of Mexico. Here we have another illustration of the commerce which must have obtained among the tribes of this country.

A soapstone ornament and several shell pins were obtained from the central grave. Of the shell pins or

[1] Transactions American Ethnological Society, vol. i., p. 361.

[2] Long's "Expedition to the Rocky Mountains," etc., vol. i., pp. 57, 58. London, 1823.

ornaments there are two varieties, both of which are correctly represented in the accompanying plate. The first (Fig. 8, Plate VI.) is like a large-headed wrought-nail. The other (Fig. 9, Plate VI.) is pointed at both ends. The surface of each is much decomposed, color, dead white, and the feel, limy. The third relic (Fig. 10, Plate VI.) is made of soapstone, and has received as careful a polish as that material will permit.

The precise uses to which these implements or ornaments may have been put can only be conjectured. That the form is not accidental is established by the coinciding shape of the soapstone specimen, and by the fact that several specimens of both varieties of the shell pins were found in the central grave. Similar relics have recently been taken from Brake-bill mound in Tennessee, and from a mound on the Chattahoochee River below Columbus. We will allude again to these articles in our chapter upon shell ornaments.

The soapstone ornament is a little less than two inches long. Its head is rather more than half an inch in diameter.

The shell pins with heads are, on an average, about an inch and three-quarters in length. The mean diameter of their heads is three-quarters of an inch. They all terminate in a sharp point. Those without heads are fully two inches in length, swelling in the centre to three-tenths of an inch in diameter, and tapering to a point at either end. These shell ornaments were manufactured probably from the thicker portions and columns of sea-conchs or marine shells.

Cabeça de Vaca declares that the thicker portions of large marine shells, and of sea-conchs, were carried by the natives who occupied the coast-regions of the

Gulf of Mexico, into the interior, and were there exchanged for skins and other articles. In some such way, in all likelihood, was the material obtained from which these shell pins were fashioned.

The perforated stone[1] in its shape and size is not unlike the spindle-whorls found at Meilen and elsewhere in Europe.[2] Whether it was indeed used for a similar purpose, or merely worn as an ornament, or with what specific intent fashioned, we cannot state with certainty. We incline to the belief that it was probably suspended as an ornament.

An imperforate discoidal stone, a grooved axe, badly worn, a beautifully-polished wedge-shaped axe or stone celt, a chisel of greenstone, a fragment of a soapstone pipe, and a large stone bead (Fig. 12, Plate VI.) complete the catalogue of relics taken from these graves.

In the vicinity were ploughed up Venetian beads, fifty-five in number, varying in shape and color, some of them being red, others blue, others white (of which variety some have a blue wreath, inlaid, encircling them), others green, with crimson and yellow horizontal stripes upon them, and others black. The material of which they are all made is either glass or porcelain.

In the ancient town of Cutifachiqui, De Soto[3] found a dirk and beads which belonged to Europeans who, the Indians said, had many years before sailed into the port distant two days' journey from this point.

Biedma[4] narrates that De Soto, while at this In-

[1] Fig. 11, Plate VI.

[2] *See* Keller's "Lake Dwellings of Switzerland," Plate III., Fig. 13.

[3] "Relation of the Knight of Elvas," p. 64 (Buckingham Smith's translation).

[4] "Relation," etc., p. 240 (Buckingham Smith's translation).

dian village, caused a mosque to be opened in which were interred the chief personages of the country. In it were found pearls, two wooden axes of Castilian make, *a rosary of jet beads*, and some false pearls, such as were brought from Spain for the purpose of traffic with the natives. It was conjectured that these European articles had been obtained by the Indians from the followers of the Licentiate Ayllon.

Rosaries[1] of glass beads, with crosses and hatchets of Vizcayan make, were discovered in unrolling the bodies of some dead Indians entombed (if we correctly interpret the geography of the expedition) on the bank of the Savannah River. This occurred in 1540, while the army of De Soto was enjoying the hospitalities of the queen who ruled over the tribes of this region.

When speaking of the beads manufactured by the natives, the early historians enumerate such as were made of pearls, shells, sea-snails, stone, clay, and bone. From Indian mounds on the Georgia coast the writer has taken glass and porcelain beads, which proves that the custom of mound-building, or at least of interring the dead in mounds already constructed, existed at a period subsequent to the early intercourse between the Indians and the Europeans. In an oval mound about six miles, by water, above Lake Monroe, in Florida, Dr. Brinton saw numerous small blue and large white glass beads, which he regarded as inhumed at the time of the formation of the tumulus.[2]

We know that the Spaniards brought quantities of European beads with them, with which to conciliate the natives, and that the missionaries who accompanied

[1] Fontaneda, p. 45 (Buckingham Smith's translation).

[2] "Notes on the Floridian Peninsula," p. 170.

their expeditions were not wanting in an abundant supply of rosaries. Nothing was more common, or, according to the report of the times, more conducive to the spread of Christianity in these benighted wilds, than the general dissemination of rosaries and wooden crosses. The acceptance at the hands of the priests, by the Indian, of such a gift, was too often chronicled as an instance of conversion.

Beads were also distributed by the early navigators at various points along the coast. The discoverers of the Mississippi dispersed them freely among the tribes then peopling the banks of the "Father of Waters," and the wanderings of the pioneers of the west are still verified by the presence of these coarse ornaments. After having grossly violated the hospitalities of the Queen of the Savannah, De Soto moved with his command along the line of the Savannah River to its head-waters. Thence turning to the south-west, before reaching the confluence of the Etowah and the Oostenaula Rivers, in his journeyings through Cherokee Georgia, it is probable that he passed either directly through or very near Nacoochee Valley.[1]

Certain it is that, during the sixteenth century, ample opportunity would have been afforded to a prominent chief of this valley to have possessed himself of such beads as those which we are now examining.

No trace of iron, bronze, or steel, existed in these graves. The presence of the copper axe and stone implements furnishes good ground for believing that their owner had enjoyed no opportunity for exchang-

[1] Map compiled by J. C. Brevoort, in Buckingham Smith's translation of the "Narratives of the Career of Hernando de Soto." No. 5, Bradford Club Series, New York, 1866.

ing his rude weapons and ornaments for the more serviceable tools which, at an early period, were freely offered by the colonists. This fact, and the total absence of the old Venetian beads found in the neighborhood, and undoubtedly once the property of the Indians, enable us, with considerable confidence, to assign to these graves an antiquity of not less than three hundred and thirty years. Probably they are much older. This peculiar mode of sepulture, we have already seen, was adopted by the Indians, in some instances, within historic times.

The existence of extensive trade relations among the aborigines is beautifully verified by the contents of these graves. Here, concentrated in the ownership of a single individual, we see a basket or mat made of a reed not native to the valley—stone implements, laboriously manufactured of materials brought from a distance—a cassis and shell ornaments from the Atlantic Ocean, or the Gulf of Mexico, and a copper axe from the shores of Lake Superior.

Upon the rock-walls which fence in this beautiful valley, are engraven no memories of the tribes who in the olden time committed to the protection of these rude sepulchres the bodies of their dead.

A people without letters, they have passed away, leaving not even an inscription upon their tombs.

Nevertheless, from out the void of forgotten centuries, from the womb of these nameless sarcophagi, come these implements and ornaments to tell us at least somewhat of the manners and customs of those who are gone—to remind us of the careful consideration they bestowed upon the last resting-places of their departed—of their belief in a future state—of the progress they had made in the rudiments of art—of the position they occupied in the scale of semi-civilization —and to assure us that among the red nomads of these primitive wilds the advantages of an interchange of values with distant nations were neither wholly unknown nor entirely neglected.

Thus these relics become in very deed the

> "Registers, the chronicles of the age
> They were made in, and speak the truth of history
> Better than a hundred of your printed
> Communications." [1]

[1] Shakerly's "Marmyon's Antiquary."

CHAPTER XI.

Arrow and Spear Heads.—Use of the Bow.—Skill in Archery.—Manufacture and General Distribution of Arrow and Spear Points.—Various Forms of these Implements.—Stone Dagger.—Flint Sword.

Of all the various stone implements evidencing the handiwork of primitive man, by far the most numerous, and perhaps not the least interesting, are the arrow and spear heads. So general is the distribution of these instruments of war and of venery, not only throughout the length and breadth of vast continents, but also in the habitable islands of the ocean, it would really appear as though in every quarter of the globe, at some time or other, man existed in such a state of rude development that his principal hope of food and defence resided in the constant use of these rough weapons. So closely do these implements resemble each other, both in material and form of construction, whether found in Danish shell-mounds or British barrows, exhumed from the peat-bogs of Ireland, or wrested from the diluvial matrix of France, brought to light from out the darkness of long-forgotten caves, or fished up from the pile-dwellings of Robenhausen, gathered amid the forests of Africa, or upon the steppes of Asia, rescued from the *débris* of a New-Zealand encampment, or delivered from the womb of an American tumulus, that even the practised eye is often at a loss to discover physical peculiarities which can sufficiently distinguish them the one from the other. Chronologically considered, the stone periods which they represent may be separated by hundreds and perhaps thousands of years. Nearly synonymous as these relics appear, it by no means follows that they are necessarily synchronous. The tendency of present investigations is to the conclusion that in America the stone age reached its richest and fullest development, and that the arrowmakers of the Western Hemisphere were surpassed by none in the selection of their materials and in the skill displayed in fashioning them into forms of use and symmetry.

Within the geographical limits of Georgia spear and arrow points of unusual beauty and excellence are found in sepulchral tumuli, in shell-heaps, in relic-beds, and in greater or fewer numbers upon the surface of the ground. New specimens are, each year, unearthed by the ploughshare and washed from their hiding-places by the summer showers. Most frequently are they seen in the rich valleys, along the banks of rivers, and upon the islands and headlands of the coast. Their presence in quantities indicates the chosen seats of the aborigines. Even in pine-barren regions, where the soil is poor, vegetation thin, and streams and swamps are infrequent—localities at best but sparsely populated by the Indians—we are assured of the fact that over these uninviting districts the natives wandered in pursuit of game, and here and there lost an arrow-point carried away by a wounded animal or bird, broken from its shaft by contact with some tree, or accidentally dropped from the hunter's quiver. Occasional specimens are turned up in ditching the rice-fields, showing that even amid the deep, dank recesses of the primeval cypress-forests the Indians pursued the deer, the bear, the wild-turkey and other game. It is in the rich valleys of Middle and Upper Georgia, and along the coast, that these relics occur most frequently. Ready supply of oysters, clams, fresh-water mussels, fish, and game, mainly determined the natives in the selection of their permanent habitations. Add to this the presence of a good natural spring, and you will readily find abundant proof of former occupancy by the red race. There can be no doubt but that the manufacture of these flint implements was carried on at various points on the headlands and islands of the coast. In the refuse-piles, numerous spear and arrow points may be gathered, some completely and others only partially formed. Chips, flakes, and cores mark the spots where the primitive arrow-maker plied his trade, and this at a considerable remove from localities whence the materials for the construction of these implements could have been obtained.

The writer has observed upon the margin of more than one swamp in Southern Georgia the clearly-defined traces of open-air workshops for the manufacture of flint implements. Let one instance suffice: On Arcadia plantation, in Liberty County, near the edge of Midway swamp, is a little knoll whose top is littered with flakes, chips, and arrow and spear points in various stages of completion. Some had evidently been discarded during the process of manufacture, upon the discovery of an unexpected defect in the material; while others, failing to yield the desired fracture, had been thrown aside as involving too great an expenditure of labor. Fine nuclei of flint and quartz lay half embedded in the soil. These had been brought from a distance. They could not have been obtained within a hundred miles of this locality, and, in all likelihood were procured at a remove much greater than that which we have named. The spear and arrow heads of the coast are remarkable for the beauty of the material from which they were made, and for the skill displayed in their construction.

Particular attention was paid to the selection of the more attractive and bright-colored varieties of flint, jasper, and quartz. Many of these arrow and spear heads are beautiful, and may be justly regarded as marvels of skill in flint-chipping. Some are serrated, and almost every known form finds here its type. We have seen that at least some of these implements were here manufactured from nuclei, brought from a distance. It is probable, however, that most of them were obtained in a manufactured state from other localities. It is said that, among the Indians of Cherokee Georgia, in ancient times, were men who devoted their attention to the manufacture of spear and arrow heads, and other stone implements. As from time to time they accumulated a supply, they would leave their mountain-homes and visit the seaboard and intermediate regions for the purpose of exchanging these implements for shells and various articles not readily obtainable in the localities where they resided. These were usually old men, or persons who mingled not in the excitements of war and the chase. To them, while engaged in these commercial pursuits, free passage was at all times granted. Their avocation was deemed honorable, and they themselves were welcomed wherever they appeared. If such was the case, we have here an interesting proof both of the trade relations existing among the aboriginal tribes and of the marked recognition, by an uncivilized race, of the claims of the manufacturer.[1] In the symmetry and beauty of these coast implements, we perceive the good sense and precaution exhibited by the primitive merchantman in selecting such arrow and spear points as would most surely commend themselves to the taste of his customers, and secure for him the most liberal returns of the articles highly esteemed among his own people.

In the relic-beds and shell-heaps along the banks of fresh-water streams—marking the localities where the Indians resorted for fishing—many rudely formed slate and graywacke arrow and spear points are found. There, the material being abundant and easily worked, no special care seems to have been bestowed upon the manufacture of these implements. Jasper and milky quartz were also freely used. From some of these relic-beds thousands of these arrow and spear heads have been obtained, and in every stage of development, from the rough stone just beginning to be worked, to the finished implement. In the valleys of Upper Georgia our search has been rewarded by exquisite specimens made of pellucid crystals, violet and smoky quartz, chalcedony, jasper, and flint. Party-colored materials were evidently held in special esteem, and so neatly are many of them chipped that the skilled lapidary of the present day might find his powers taxed to rival the workmanship here displayed.

Absolutely dependent as the Indians were upon the use of the bow and arrow and the spear for subsistence and protection, nomadic in their habits, and

[1] "Indian Remains in Southern Georgia," by Charles C. Jones, Jr., p. 19. Savannah, 1859.

constantly engaged in hunting or intertribal contentions,[1] we are not surprised at the general distribution, all over the face of the country, of these their simplest and most common implements. Their bows—long since unstrung—have crumbled into dust. Arrow-shaft and spear-handle are seen no more, but these nuclei, flint-chips, and skilfully-formed stone points—indestructible by time—fortunately still remain for our study and information.

According to the relation of Cabeça de Vaca, the Indians were all archers, being admirable in their proportions, spare, and of great activity and strength. Their bows were as thick as a man's arm, eleven or twelve palms in length, and capable of projecting arrows for a distance of two hundred paces, with such precision as to miss nothing. Detailing a skirmish which occurred between the Spaniards and the natives, he says the latter fought from behind trees, covering themselves so that the Christians could not get sight of them. He affirms that they "drove their arrows with such effect that they wounded many men and horses." Even the "good armor" of the Spaniards did not avail for their protection against these missiles. Some of the soldiers swore "that they had seen two red-oaks, each the thickness of the lower part of the leg, pierced through from side to side by arrows. . . . This," continues the historian, "is not so much to be wondered at, considering the power and skill with which the Indians are able to project them. I myself saw an

[1] Wilson, writing in 1682, asserts that the Carolina tribes were so constantly engaged in wars "one town or village against another," that the Indian population suffered "no increase of People"—several nations having been "in a manner quite extirpated by Wars amongst themselves since the *English* settled at *Ashly* River." "Account of the Province of Carolina," p. 15. London, 1682.

arrow that had entered the butt of an elm to the depth of a span."

On another occasion the same author states that upon an examination of the corpses of the Spaniards who had fallen in battle, their bodies were found to have been traversed from side to side by arrows; and although some of the dead soldiers were clad in good armor, it did not afford adequate protection or security against the nice and powerful archery of the Indians. An instance is given where an arrow, shot by an Indian, pierced through the saddle and housings and penetrated one-third of its length into the body of of a Spaniard's horse. The bows were made of wood and remained unbent until needed for battle or the chase. The strings were formed of deer-sinews, strips of deer-skins, or the twisted gut of animals. Hard canes and wood were used for arrows.[1]

The Fidalgo of Elvas describes the Indians as being exceedingly ready with their weapons, and "so warlike and nimble that they have no fear of foot-soldiers; for if these charge them they flee, and when they turn their backs they are presently upon them. They avoid nothing more easily than the flight of an arrow. They never remain quiet, but are continually running, traversing from place to place, so that neither cross-bow nor arquebuse can be aimed at them. Before a Christian can make a single shot with either, an Indian will discharge three or four arrows: and he seldom misses of his object. When the arrow meets with no armor, it pierces as deeply as the shaft from a cross-bow. Their bows are very perfect; the arrows are made of certain canes, like reeds, very heavy and

[1] *See* "Relation of Alvar Nuñez Cabeça de Vaca," translated from the Spanish by Buckingham Smith, pp. 39, 40, 48, *et seq.* New York, 1871.

so stiff that one of them, when sharpened, will pass through a target. Some are pointed with the bone of a fish, sharp, and like a chisel, others with some stone like a point of diamond; of such the greater number, when they strike upon armor, break at the place the parts are put together; those of cane split and will enter a shirt of mail, doing more injury than when armed (i. e., with chips of hard stone).[1]

"The Indians," continues the same narrator, "never lack meat. With arrows they get abundance of deer, turkeys, conies, and other wild animals, being very skillful in killing game."

While the army of De Soto was quartered in the province of Cofachiqui, Añasco was dispatched by the governor to secure the attendance of the mother of the princess of this country, who was represented to be in the possession of a large quantity of most valuable pearls. As a guide he took with him a youthful warrior, brave and handsome, and a near relative of the princess. Having proceeded nearly three leagues, Añasco and his comrades halted for their mid-day meal. While they were reposing beneath the shade of some wide-spreading trees, the Indian guide, who had become very moody and thoughtful, quietly took off his quiver, and, placing it before him, drew out the arrows slowly, one by one. They were admirable for the skill and elegance with which they were formed. Their shafts were reeds. Some were tipped with bucks'-horns, wrought with four corners, like a diamond; some were pointed with the bones of fishes, curiously fashioned; others with barbs of the palm

[1] "True Relation, etc., etc., given by a Fidalgo of Elvas," translated by Buckingham Smith, pp. 26, 27. New York, 1866. Compare "Letter of Hernando de Soto," etc., etc., translated by Buckingham Smith, p. 56. Washington, 1854.

and other hard woods; and some were three-pronged. They were feathered in a triangular manner to render their flight of greater accuracy. The Spaniards could not sufficiently admire their beauty; they took them up, and passed them from hand to hand, examining and praising their workmanship and extolling the skill of their owner. The youthful Indian continued thoughtfully emptying his quiver until, almost at the last, he drew forth an arrow with a point of flint, long and sharp and shaped like a dagger; then, casting around a glance, and seeing the Spaniards engaged in admiring his darts, he suddenly plunged the weapon in his throat and fell dead on the spot.

Unwilling to betray the place of concealment of his mother, and fearing to incur the displeasure of his queen by disobedience of her mandate, he gave himself willingly to death.[1]

The Chevalier Tonti,[2] alluding to the force with which their arrows were projected by the natives, says: "That which is wonderful in this, is the havock which the Shot sent by the Savages makes; for, besides the exactness and swiftness of the Stroke, the force of it is very surprizing, and so much the rather, because it is nothing else but a Stone, or a Bone, or sometimes a piece of very hard Wood pointed and fastned to the end of an Arrow with some Fishes-glue, that causes this terrible effect. When the Savages go to War, they poison the Point or extremity of their Dart so that if that remains in the Body Death follows of necessity; the only Remedy in this case is to draw out the Arrow through the other side of the Wound, if it goes quite

[1] Irving's "Conquest of Florida," chapter xlvii., pp. 225, 226. New York, 1851.

[2] "An Account of Monsieur de La Salle's Last Expedition and Discoveries in North America," p. 71. London, 1698.

through; or, if not, to make an aperture on the other side, and so to draw it through; after which they know by instinct certain Herbs the application of which both draws out the Venom and Cures them."

In Laudonnière's introduction to his history of Jean Ribault's first voyage to Florida,[1] we are told that the Indians had no weapons other than bows and arrows. The bow-string was made "of the gut of the stag, or of a stag's skin which they know how to dress as well as any man in France, and with as different sorts of colors. They head their arrows with the teeth of fishes, and stone which they work very finely and handsomely."

The following interesting account is taken from the "History of the Bucaniers of America:"[2] "On the ninth day after our arrival, our women slaves being busied in ordinary employments of washing of dishes, sewing, drawing water out of wells which we had made on the shore, and the like, one of them who had seen a troop of Indians towards the woods, cried out Indians, Indians! We ran presently to our arms and their relief, but coming to the wood we found no person there, but two of our women slaves killed upon the place with arrows: in their bodies we saw so many arrows sticking, as if they had been fixed there with particular care, for otherwise we know that one of them was sufficient to kill any man. These arrows were all of a rare shape, being eight feet long, and as thick as a man's thumb; at one end was a hook of wood, tied to the body of the arrow with a string, at the other end was a case or box like the case of a pair of tweezers, in

[1] "Historical Collections of Louisiana and Florida," by B. F. French. New Series, pp. 170, 171. New York, 1869.

[2] Vol. i., pp. 212, 213, fifth edition. London, 1771.

which we found little pebbles or stones; the color was very red, very shining, as if they had been locked up, all which we believed were the arms of their leaders. These arrows were all made without instruments of iron; for whatever the Indians make, they harden first artificially with fire, and then polish them with flints."

To Thomas Ash we are indebted for the following description of the Carolina Indians, as he saw them in 1682:[1] "The natives of the country are from time immemorial *ab Origine Indians*, of a deep Chestnut colour, their Hair black and streight, tied various ways, sometimes oyl'd and painted, stuck through with Feathers for Ornament or Gallantry; their Eyes black and sparkling, little or no Hair on their Chins, well limb'd and featured, painting their Faces with different Figures of a red or sanguine Colour, whether for Beauty or to render themselves formidable to their Enemies, I could not learn. They are excellent Hunters; their Weapons, the Bow and Arrow, made of a Read, pointed with sharp Stones or Fish-Bones; their Cloathing, Skins of the Bear and Deer, the Skin drest after their Country Fashion."

Discussing the "handicrafts" of the Virginia Indians, Beverly writes: "Before I finish my account of the Indians it will not be amiss to inform you that when the English went first among them, they had no sort of Iron or Steel Instruments; but their Knives were either Sharpen'd Reeds or Shells, and their Axes sharp Stones bound to the end of a Stick and glued in with Turpentine. By the help of these they made their Bows of the Locust Tree, an excessive hard Wood when it is dry, but much more easily cut when it is green, of which they always took the advantage. They

[1] "Carolina; or a Description of the Present State of that Country," etc., published by T. A., Gent., pp. 34, 35. London, 1682.

made their Arrows of Reeds or small Wands, which needed no other cutting but in the length, being otherwise ready for Notching, Feathering, and Heading. They fledged their Arrows with Turkey Feathers, which they fastned with Glue made of the Velvet Horns of a Deer, but it has not that quality it's said to have, of holding against all Weathers; they arm'd the Heads with a white transparent Stone, like that of Mexico mention'd by Peter Martyr, of which they have many Rocks; they also headed them with the Spurs of the Wild Turkey Cock."[1]

Adair testifies to the accuracy with which the Cherokee Indians, in his day, used their bows and arrows and threw their feathered darts. Speaking of these peoples, he declares: "They make perhaps the finest bows and the smoothest barbed arrows of all mankind. On the point of them is fixed either a scooped point of buck-horn, or turkey-cock spurs, pieces of brass, or flint stone. The latter sort our forefathers used, which our witty grandmothers call elf-stones, and now rub the cows with, that are so unlucky as to be shot by night fairies. One of those flint arrow-points is reckoned a very extraordinary blessing in a whole neighborhood of old women, both for the former cure, as well as a preservative against every kind of bewitching charm."[2]

As early as 1761 the Cherokees seem to have abandoned the use of stone arrow-heads, and in their stead to have substituted points of metal. Lieutenant Henry Timberlake, from his personal observations, furnishes us with their method, then in vogue, of pointing arrows: "Cutting a bit of thin brass, copper, bone, or scales of

[1] "History and Present State of Virginia," book iii., p. 60. London, 1705.
[2] "History of the American Indians," p. 425. London, 1775.

a particular fish, into a point with two beards, or some into an acute triangle, they split a little of their arrow, which is generally of reeds; into this they put the point, winding some deer's sinew round the arrow, and through a little hole they make in the head; then they moisten the sinew with their spittle, which, when dry, remains fast glewed, nor ever untwists. Their bows are of several sorts of wood, dipped in bear's oil, and seasoned before the fire, and a twisted bear's gut for the string."[1]

Spear-heads were fastened to wooden handles, eight or ten feet in length, and were hurled as javelins. At close quarters they were employed to ward off blows, and to deliver thrusts, without quitting the hand. Among the Carolina Indians Lawson observed in 1701 long arrows headed with pieces of glass, which they had broken from bottles. "They had shaped them neatly, like the head of a dart, but which way they did it I cant tell."[2] It is not improbable that this historian mistook the material of which these arrow-points were made. The resemblance between some varieties of quartz, or obsidian and glass, is so close, than an error may thus have occurred in the observation. We know that the Indians of California sometimes make arrow-heads from old glass bottles, and Captain Cook states that the New-Zealanders found means to drill a hole, with jasper, through a piece of glass which he had given them, so that it might be suspended as an ornament from the neck. It may be, therefore, that the remark of Mr. Lawson is entirely correct.

Without multiplying these historical references, it

[1] "Memoirs of Lieutenant Henry Timberlake," pp. 61, 62. London, 1765.
[2] Lawson's "History of Carolina." Reprint, p. 99. Raleigh, 1860.

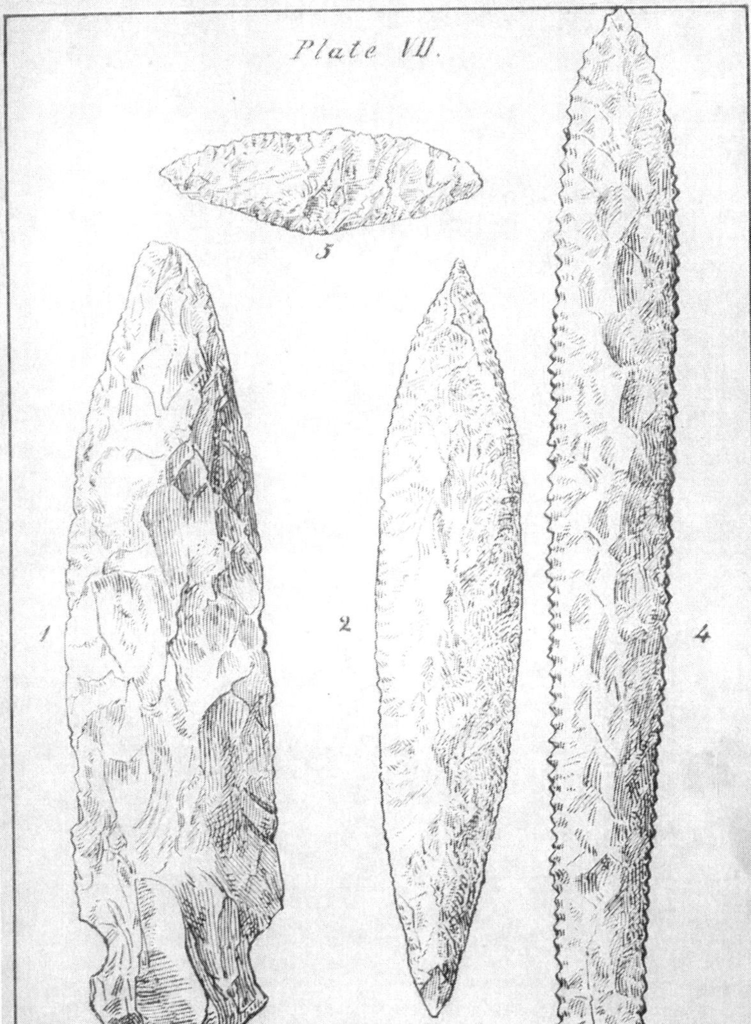

AM. PHOTO-LITHOGRAPHIC CO. N.Y. (OSBORNE'S PROCESS.)

is evident that, at the period of our earliest acquaintance with the Southern Indians, the bow and arrow were in general use, constituting, in the hands of the natives, an indispensable, effective, and deadly weapon. Appreciating the vast numbers of arrow and spear heads which, during the lapse of many centuries, must have been manufactured and expended by these peoples in hunting, fishing, in their games and in frequent wars, we are prepared fully to understand why these flint implements are found in such quantities, and why they should form the most common proof of the former occupancy of the soil by the red-men.

The largest spear or lance head we have seen within the geographical limits of Georgia, was obtained in a grave-mound which stood upon the point of land formed by the confluence of the Etowah and Oostenaula Rivers. It is nearly fourteen inches in length, and three inches and a quarter in width—weighing two pounds and two ounces, avoirdupois. (*See* Fig. 1, Plate VII.) It is perfect, with the exception of the point which was broken off at the time this implement was taken from the mound. No spear-head of such magnitude, so far as my knowledge extends, has been found within the limits of the Southern States. It is made of flint, and the conchoidal fractures caused in removing the flakes are clearly defined. The tumulus from which this spear-head was obtained was circular in shape, about twelve feet high, and with a base-diameter of fifty feet. It contained numerous skeletons, and afforded a rich yield of various and interesting relics. Sharing the fate which has overtaken so many of these aboriginal monuments, but little now remains to mark the spot once rendered so attractive by the presence of this beautiful tumulus. The grand forest-trees which formerly grew upon and threw their protecting shadows about it—trees which, in all likelihood, sheltered De Soto and his companions, as resting upon the verdant banks of the Etowah they were hospitably entertained by the Cacique of Ichiaha—have all been cut down, and the earth and clay composing the mound carted away to assist in levelling the streets of the city of Rome, and aid in the construction of a landing-place for a ferry-boat.

The second spear-head (Fig. 2, Plate VII.), pointed at both ends, and regularly chipped, was found in the valley of the Chattahoochee, a few miles below the city of Columbus. It is twelve inches and a half in length, two inches and four-tenths wide, and weighs ten and three-quarter ounces. It was probably hafted in a bone, horn, or wooden socket at the end of the shaft. The similarity between this implement and that figured by Messrs. Squier and Davis, on page 211, of the "Ancient Monuments of the Mississippi Valley," is remarkable. I refer to No. 3 in Fig. 99. It may be that this formidable implement was used as a dagger.

The beautiful spear-heads represented by Nos. 1 and 2, Plate VIII., were taken from a chieftain mound near Darien, in McIntosh County. The remaining figures in this plate illustrate the prevailing types of these implements, as they are to this day found in tumuli, ploughed up in the fields, gathered from relic-beds, or picked up on the sites of ancient villages and open-air workshops.

It will be perceived that among the arrow-heads figured in the accompanying plate,[1] are all the varieties enumerated by Sir W. R. Wilde, viz., the *triangular*,

[1] Figs. 1 to 41 inclusive, Plate IX.

Plate VIII.

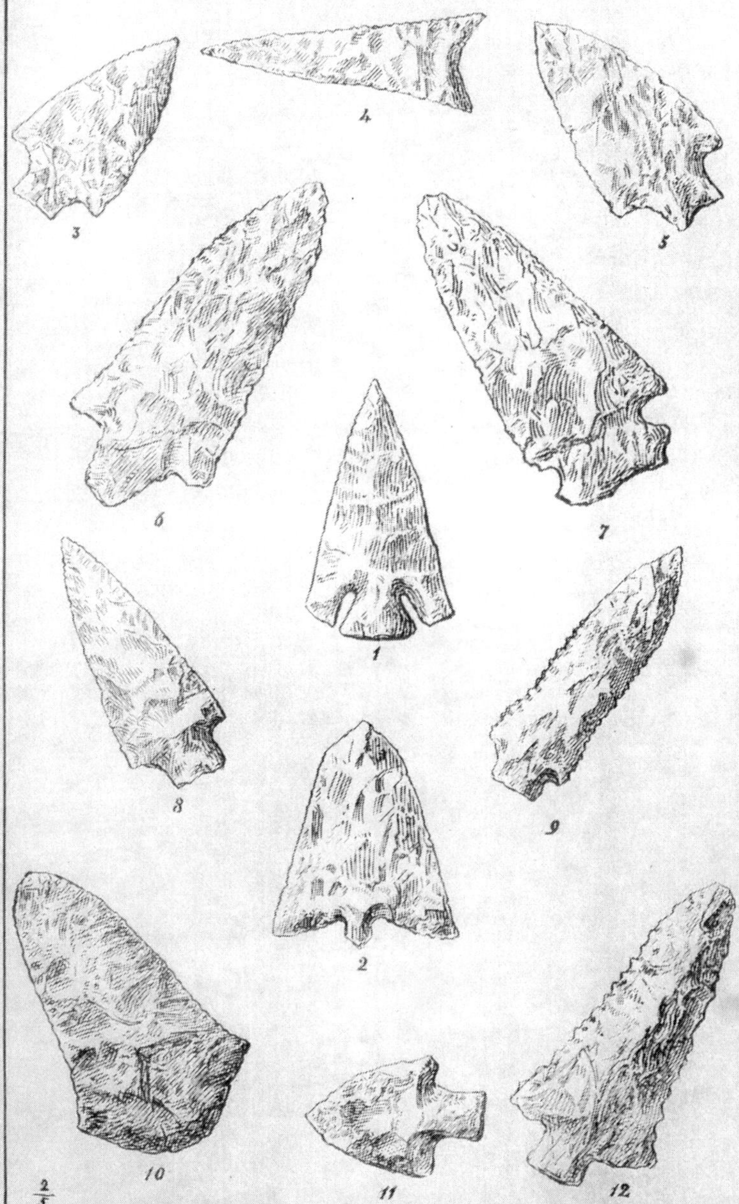

2/5

AM PHOTO-LITHOGRAPHIC CO. N.Y. (OSBORNE'S PROCESS.)

the *indented*, the *stemmed*, with a tang or projection for insertion into the shaft—the *barbed* and the *leaf-shaped.* Nor does this catalogue embrace them all. The modifications of the one idea of arming the point of the reed or wooden arrow with a piece of chipped flint are numerous. From a collection of more than two thousand, we have selected these as presenting those forms in general use. The shark's tooth may have suggested the shape of the indented arrow-point, and the serration of the edges. Fossil-shark's teeth are found in various parts of Georgia and Carolina. Their existence was known to the aborigines, who sometimes perforated and wore them as ornaments about their necks. The writer has taken them from the earth-mounds on the coast.

Some of these arrow-points (Fig. 40, Plate IX.) are flat, with their edges bevelled in opposite directions. The object of this arrangement was to cause the arrow, in its flight, to take a rotary motion, thereby increasing the violence of the wound when the barb had entered the flesh. The same effect was accomplished by using the half twist in feathering the shaft. By means of such mountings the flight of the arrow was rendered more steady.

The use, by the Indians, of the hard canes, so common in the Southern swamps, as arrow-stems, seems to be substantiated by the spike-shaped flint tips of which No. 32, Plate IX., may be regarded as typical. These could readily have been inserted in the hollow of the reed, cut for that purpose at such a remove from the joint nearest the butt of the arrow, that the inserted end of the spike, closely fitting, would rest against and be held in position by it. Often has the writer adopted this method of spiking his arrows, during his youthful days, and with flint tips precisely like those under consideration, gathered from the shell-mounds and picked up in the old Indian fields on the Colonel's Island.

The taste displayed in the selection of choice and beautiful material, and the skill exhibited in the manufacture of these spear and arrow heads are often surprising and excite our admiration. Pellucid crystals, smoky quartz, chalcedony, carnelian, jasper of variegated coloring, flint, and other hard stones, were chipped with a regularity and delicacy truly astonishing. Especially does our wonder grow when we remember that these results were accomplished without the aid of metallic tools. Perfectly-formed arrow-points exist in the writer's cabinet, less than half an inch in length.[1]

Bossu says that, among the Chactaws, the children exercised themselves in shooting with a bow and arrow for prizes. "He that shoots best gets the prize of praise from an old man, who calls him an apprentice warrior; thus they are formed by emulation, without corporal punishment; they are very expert in shooting with an instrument made of reeds, about seven feet long, into which they put a little arrow, feathered with the wool of a thistle, and, in aiming at an object, they blow into the tube, and often hit the aim, and frequently kill little birds with it."[2]

Captain Romans, in speaking of the same Indians, writes: "The young savages also use a very strait cane,

[1] Lieutenant Timberlake, in his memoirs (p. 45), mentions the circumstance that the Cherokee children at eight and ten years of age were very expert at killing birds and small game, with a sarbacan or hollow cane through which they blew a small dart, and with such precision that they rarely missed of striking "the larger sort of prey" in the eye. These small arrow-points, to which allusion has been made, were probably chipped for children's arrows.

[2] "Travels through Louisiana," vol. i., p. 306. London, 1771.

Plate IX.

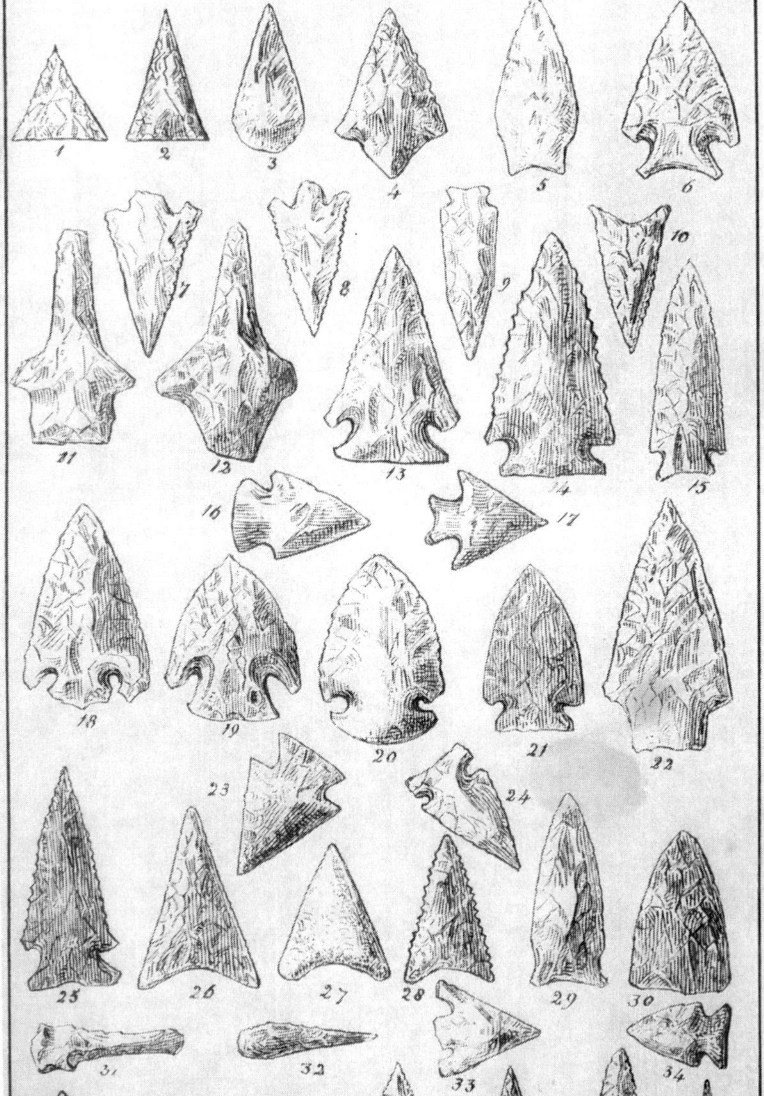

AM. PHOTO-LITHOGRAPHIC CO. N.Y. (OSBORNE'S PROCESS.)

eight or nine feet long, cleared of its inward divisions of the joints; in this they put a small *arrow*, whose one end is covered one-third of the whole length with cotton, or something similar to it; this they hold nearest their mouth, and blow it so expertly as seldom to miss a mark fifteen or twenty yards off, and that so violently as to kill squirrels and birds therewith."[1]

Between this miniature arrow-tip and the large flint spear-head, measuring nearly fourteen inches, these implements are seen of every intermediate length, and of various colors—red, blue, yellow, white, black and brown predominating. The arrow and spear points of the Southern Indians, as a general rule, are more beautiful than those manufactured by tribes who inhabited northern latitudes. The abundance of birds and small game in the swamps and deep forests of this semi-tropical region invited the use of flint implements of a delicate character.

If not inserted in the end of a hard cane, the arrow-point was attached to a reed or wooden shaft (a slit or notch having been made for its reception) by means of moistened threads of deer-sinews, glue, or small strips of buckskin. The moistened fibres of deer-sinews were generally used. These filled all inequalities, both in the stone tip and in the butt of the arrow, were very tenacious, and when dry compassed the juncture quite securely. Hickory, locust, white-oak, ash and red-cedar are said to have been the favorite woods employed by the Indians in the manufacture of their bows. These they seasoned thoroughly by artificial heat, and frequently anointed with bear's grease to render them flexible and keep them from

[1] "Concise Natural History of East and West Florida," etc. New York, 1775.

cracking or breaking. The customary shape of the bow was that of a single curve, strengthened in the middle. Usually plain, these bows were sometimes ornamented, their ends terminating in tips of bone or stag's horn.

De Bry[1] has favored us with several representations of the bows, arrows, and quivers of the Florida Indians.

His general description is conveyed in the following words: . . . "strenui tamen & pugnaces, nec alia habent, præter arcum & sagittas, arma. Arcus nervum ex cervino intestino aut corio adeo concinne parare norunt, ut Galli melius non possint, & variis coloribus inficiunt; pro mucrone sagittarum sunt piscium dentes & lapides affabre adaptati. Adolescentes cursu, sagittarum missione & pilæ ludo exercentur. . . . Venatione & piscatione magnopere delectantur."[2]

Of the weapons of the Virginia Indians he says: "Eorum arma ad nocendum sunt duntaxat arcus ex corylo, & sagittæ ex arundine, deinde stipites lignei plani, duorum cubitorum longitudine;" and furnishes us in plate iii., as well as elsewhere, with the form of the bow, arrow, and quiver.[3]

Reserve arrows were carried in a rude quiver, made of deer, fawn, or cougar skin, suspended from the left shoulder, and hanging just behind the right hip where most convenient access could be had. Often these arrows were not feathered, the weight of the stone tip being of itself sufficient to preserve regularity

[1] "Brevis Narratio," etc., plates xiii., xiv., xix., xxv., xxvii., xxxi., xxxiii., *et seq.* Francoforti ad Mœnum. Anno 1791.

[2] Idem. Secunda Pars, p. 3.

[3] "Admiranda Narratio," etc., p. 25, plates iii., xxiii., Francoforti ad Mœnum. Anno 1590.

of flight. The rapidity and precision with which the Indians discharged their arrows, when occasion required, are emphatically testified to by the Spaniards, who in those early days, because of their cruelties, incurred the enmity of the natives.

In the battle of Mauilla there fell, of the armor-clad Christians, two hundred. Of the living, one hundred and fifty received seven hundred wounds from the Indian arrows. Here is proof most emphatic of how valiantly and successfully the red-men could handle their rude weapons, in the face of mailed warriors, in defence of home and country. Testimony is not wanting substantiating the efficiency and force with which the arrow is projected by modern Indians. The history of the early conflicts of the colonists is filled with examples of the deadly effects of such ancient artillery, and the Dakota chief Wah-na-tah is said, on one occasion, to have discharged his arrow with so much vigor that it entirely traversed the body of a female buffalo and killed her calf on the other side.[1]

It only remains for us to consider the method adopted by the natives in the manufacture of these flint implements. So far as my knowledge extends, the use of iron was entirely unknown among the primitive peoples of this region. Copper implements there were, of limited variety, but these occur very rarely, and are too soft for contact with stone. We are consequently compelled to the belief that the Indians fashioned these spear and arrow heads by chipping them with implements of stone. It may be that the serrated edges, and perhaps some of the more delicate arrow-heads, were formed with the aid of instruments

[1] Schoolcraft's "Archives of Aboriginal Knowledge," vol. iv., pp. 95, 96. Philadelphia, 1860.

of bone, ivory, or horn, as in the case of those manufactured by the western Esquimaux tribes, as described by Admiral Sir E. Belcher.[1] This, however, is scarcely probable, although Captain John Smith, in his sixth voyage, speaking of the Virginia Indians, says: "His arrow-head he quickly maketh with a little bone which he ever weareth at his bracept, of a splint of a stone or glasse, in the form of a heart, and these they glew to the end of their arrowes. With the sinews of deer and the tops of deer's horns boiled to a jelly they make a glue which will not dissolve in cold water."

We are of opinion that the Southern Indians flaked their flint implements by percussion and not by pressure. The latter method might answer with obsidian, but it would prove an endless and futile process if quartz, chert, jasper, and flint are the materials used in the manufacture.

Schoolcraft thus describes the mode observed by North American Indians in the preparation of flint arrow and spear heads: "The skill displayed in this art, as it is exhibited by the tribes of the entire continent, has excited admiration. The material employed is generally some form of horn-stone, sometimes passing into flint. This mineral is often called chert by the English mineralogists. No specimens have, however, been observed where the substance is gun-flint. The horn-stone is less hard than common quartz, and can readily be broken by contact with the latter. Experience has taught the Indian that some varieties of horn-stone are less easily and regularly fractured than others, and that the tendency to a conchoidal fracture is to be relied on in the softer varieties. It

[1] *See* Stevens' "Flint Chips," p. 80, *et seq.* London, 1870. Compare Evans' "Ancient Stone Implements, etc., of Great Britain," pp. 37, 38. London, 1872.

has also shown him that the weathered or surface fragments are harder and less manageable than those quarried from the rocks or mountains. To break them he seats himself on the ground, and holds the lump on one of his thighs, interposing some hard substance below it. When the blow is given, there is a sufficient yielding in the piece to be fractured, not to endanger its being shivered into fragments. Many are, however, lost. After the lump has been broken transversely, it requires great skill and patience to chip the edges. Such is the art required in this business, both in selecting and fracturing the stones, that it is found to be the employment of particular men, generally old men who are laid aside from hunting, to make arrow and spear heads."[1]

Catlin, in his "Last Rambles amongst the Indians," speaking of arrow-making among the Apaches, says: "Every tribe has its *factory* in which these arrow-heads are made, and in those only certain adepts are able or allowed to make them for the use of the tribe. Erratic bowlders of flint are collected (and sometimes brought an immense distance) and broken with a sort of sledge-hammer, made of a rounded pebble of horn-stone set in a twisted withe holding the stone and forming a handle. The flint, at the indiscriminate blows of the sledge, is broken into a hundred pieces, and such flakes selected as from the angles of their fracture and thickness will answer as the basis of an arrow-head.

"The master-workman, seated on the ground, lays one of these flakes on the palm of his left hand, holding it firmly down with two or more fingers of the same hand, and with his right hand, between the

[1] "Archives of Aboriginal Knowledge," vol. iii., p. 467. Philadelphia, 1860.

thumb and two forefingers, places his chisel (or punch) on the point that is to be broken off; and a coöperator (a striker) sitting in front of him, with a mallet of very hard wood, strikes the chisel (or punch) on the upper end, flaking the flint off on the under side, below each projecting point that is struck. The flint is then turned and chipped in the same manner from the opposite side, and so turned and chipped until the required shape and dimensions are obtained—all the fractures being made on the palm of the hand.

"In selecting a flake for the arrow-head, a nice judgment must be used, or the attempt will fail; a flake with two opposite parallel, or nearly parallel planes, is found, and of the thickness required for the centre of the arrow-point. The first chipping reaches near to the centre of these planes, but without quite breaking it away, and each chipping is shorter and shorter until the shape and the edge of the arrow-head are formed.

"The yielding elasticity of the palm of the hand enables the chip to come off without breaking the body of the flint, which would be the case if they were broken on a hard substance. These people have no metallic instruments to work with, and the instrument (punch) which they use, I was told, was a piece of bone; but on examining it, I found it to be a substance much harder, made of the tooth (incisor) of the sperm-whale, which cetaceans are often stranded on the coast of the Pacific. This punch is about six or seven inches in length, and one inch in diameter, with one rounded side, and two plane sides, therefore presenting one acute and two obtuse angles to suit the points to be broken. This operation is very curious, both the holder and the striker singing, and the strokes of the mallet given exactly in time with the music, and with a sharp and *rebounding* blow, in which, the Indians tell us, is the great *medicine* (or mystery) of the operation."[1]

Commenting upon this description, Mr. Stevens observes: "What Catlin has said with reference to a *rebounding* blow, is perfectly true; it is impossible to flake flint with a dull, heavy, smashing blow; it is the measured and rebounding blow—a shock rather than a blow—which, given with judgment, enables the material to take its own line of cleavage, and produces what is so well known as the conchoidal fracture. It is the presence of this conchoidal fracture, resulting from human skill, that distinguishes the mere splinter of flint from the flint-flake."[2]

Lieutenant Beckwith, in 1854, saw a Pah-Utah Indian, seated on the ground, make from a fragment of quartz, with a piece of round bone, one end of which was semispherical with a small crease in it (as if worn by a thread) the sixteenth of an inch deep, an arrow-head which was very sharp and piercing, and in all respects similar to those in general use among the Indians of that region. He says: "The skill and rapidity with which it was made, without a blow, but by simply breaking the sharp edges with the creased bone, by the strength of his hands—for the crease merely served to prevent the instrument from slipping, affording no leverage—were remarkable."[3]

In 1860, Hon. Caleb Lyon communicated to the American Ethnological Society an account of the manufacture of arrow-heads of flint, glass, obsidian, and other materials, by the Shasta Indians of California: "The Shasta Indian seated himself on the floor,

[1] Catlin, "Last Rambles amongst the Indians," chapter v., p. 187, *et seq.*

[2] "Flint Chips," pp. 83, 84. London, 1870.

[3] "Report of Explorations for a Route for the Pacific Railroad," 1854, p. 43.

and, placing the stone anvil upon his knee, which was of compact talcose slate, with one blow of his agate chisel he separated the obsidian pebble into two parts, then giving another blow to the fractured side, he split off a slab a fourth of an inch in thickness. Holding the piece against the anvil with the thumb and finger of his left hand, he commenced a series of continuous blows, every one of which chipped off fragments of the brittle substance. It gradually assumed the required shape. After finishing the base of the arrow-head (the whole being only little over an inch in length), he began striking gentler blows, every one of which I expected would break it into pieces. Yet, such was their adroit application, his skill and dexterity, that in little over an hour he produced a perfect obsidian arrow-head. I then requested him to carve me one from the remains of a broken porter-bottle, which (after two failures), he succeeded in doing. He gave as a reason for his ill-success, he did not understand the grain of the glass. No sculptor ever handled a chisel with greater precision, or more carefully measured the weight and effect of every blow, than this ingenious Indian; for, even among them, arrow-making is a distinct trade or profession, which many attempt, but in which few attain excellence. He understood the capacity of the material he wrought, and, before striking the first blow, by surveying the pebble, he could judge of its availability as well as the seulptor judges of the perfection of a block of Parian. In a moment, all that I had read upon this subject, written by learned and speculative antiquarians, of the hardening of copper for the working of flint axes, spears, chisels, and arrow-heads, vanished before the simplest mechanical process. I felt that the world had been better served had they driven the pen less and the plough more."[1]

In view of these positive observations, it is fair to presume that the method adopted by the modern Indians in the manufacture of their common flint arrow and spear heads was but the perpetuation of a mode which existed among the red-men prior to historic times. It is the writer's impression that the flint implements found in Georgia and the Southern States were made by percussion—hammers of wood and stone, and stone chisels being used in removing the flakes.

In conclusion, it may not be uninteresting to analyze for a moment the prevailing types of these arrow and spear points. The primary, rudimentary, or simplest shape is that of either an isosceles or equilateral triangle (Figs. 1 and 2, Plate IX.).

How various soever the forms may be, upon examination they will be found to be modifications of this idea. Thus, if the lower corners of the triangular arrow-point are rounded, we have the leaf-shaped implement (Fig. 3, Plate IX.).

Still preserving the triangular form, and merely cutting a notch on each side to facilitate its attachment to the shaft, we obtain the very common variety indicated in Figs. 9, 15, and 21, Plate IX.

Hollowing out the base of the triangle gives us the indented or shark's-tooth form (Figs. 10, 26, 27, and 28, Plate IX.).

Add the notch on each side, and we see the beautiful implement to this day manufactured by the California Indians, so skilfully, out of obsidian (Fig. 41, Plate IX.).

[1] "Bulletin of the American Ethnological Society," vol. i., p. 39. New York, 1860–'61.

The spike-shaped arrow-point (Figs. 31, 32, Plate IX.), found among the refuse-piles marking the spots where the Southern Indians congregated for the purposes of hunting and fishing, is but another modification of the same triangular idea, to facilitate its insertion in the hollow of the hard cane.

Various are the modifications of the base of the triangle, designed either to form a tang or projection for sinking into the shaft, or to facilitate its attachment to the arrow-stem.

Another form not infrequent in Georgia, and quite common in Tennessee, in which the apex of the triangle and the base have both been rounded, is seen in Fig. 20, Plate IX.

To these may be added the arrow-point with a bifurcated tang (Fig. 36, Plate IX.).

We ought to mention also the *chisel-ended*, the *one-barbed* or *single-winged*, and the *repointed* arrow-heads. We are inclined, however, to regard the numerous specimens of these sorts which have passed under our observation (and of which we have many in our collection) as examples rather of misfortune than of original design. They may be rated as abnormal types, and reckoned as unwilling deviations, on the part of the manufacturer, from the symmetrical forms he desired to attain. Accident in manufacture, and the effort to remodel the implement after it had been broken, gave rise to most of these unusual varieties. They show how carefully these primitive peoples economized their stone weapons, reforming them after they had been seriously impaired, and using them even when they scarcely answered the accurate purposes for which they were designed. Under the general term *wasters*, we might enumerate many partially-formed, defective, and misshapen arrow and spear points with which the relic-beds and open-air workshops, located upon the banks of many Southern streams, abound.

It is hardly proper, however, to pursue this attempt at classification any further. Were we to note all the varieties which suggest themselves, we would be led into a multiplicity of illustrations which would do little more than represent the individual skill and fancies of the respective workmen, the various casualties to which these implements had been subjected during the process of manufacture and subsequent use, and the modifications of form consequent thereupon.

Fashioned all after the same general idea, there is, nevertheless, in the many beautiful varieties which we encounter, in the delicacy and regularity with which these flint implements have been chipped into forms of ornament and use, much to engage our attention and elevate our conception of the skill of these primitive arrow-makers.

Before dismissing the further consideration of these implements of war, venery, and piscary, we would refer to two unusual relics, one found in a grave-mound near the Warrior River, in Alabama, and the other taken by Professor Joseph Jones from a stone grave in Tennessee.

Tho former (Fig. 3, Plate VII.) is a *flint dagger*, well chipped, and seven inches and a half in length. If our information be correct, this is the first relic of this description which has been brought to light within the territorial limits once occupied by the Southern tribes. In regularity of outline, and excellence of manufacture, it is not inferior to the Danish daggers—the handle being more completely formed than that of any of the three figured by Sir

John Lubbock on page 97 of his "Pre-historic Times." The situs of this implement, and the age of the tumulus from which it was taken, forbid the idea that it could have been modelled after the fashion of a modern dagger. It should be referred to the invention and skill of the ancient peoples who erected the mound and filled the region with specimens of their proficiency in flint-chipping.

The latter (Fig. 4, Plate VII.), Professor Jones calls a *stone sword.* This interesting relic was found by Dr. Jones in an hexagonal stone grave, forming the centre of a burial-mound, located within an ancient earthwork enclosing thirteen tumuli on the bank of the Big Harpeth River, near Franklin, Tennessee. A little less than twenty-two inches in length, this flint implement is an inch and three quarters broad at its widest part, and is serrated on both edges. It is carefully chipped on either side from the edge toward the central portion, where it is an inch thick. Strong and serviceable was this weapon. Hafted in horn or wood, it could have been used as a sword; or, attached to the end of a shaft, it would have constituted a formidable spear. In either case, if properly handled, it would have proved an effective and dangerous weapon. After all, we cannot positively affirm that this serrated implement was not intended to subserve the uses of a saw. In all likelihood, however, it was fashioned to answer the purposes of a lance-head, sword, or dagger.

Fig. 5 of Plate VII. is a typical form of the stone daggers manufactured by the ancient peoples of this semi-tropical region. Made of flint, it closely resembles some varieties of spear-points and cutting implements.

CHAPTER XII.

Grooved Axes.—Hand and Wedge-shaped Axes or Celts.—Perforated and Ornamental or Ceremonial Axes.—Chisels.—Gouges.—Scrapers.—Flint Knives.—Awls, or Borers.—Leaf-shaped Implements.—Smoothing-Stones.—Drift-Implements.

IGNORANT of the uses of iron—that most valuable of all metals—the Southern Indians in their agricultural, mechanical, and warlike pursuits, were driven to great shifts to supply the deficiency. In this attempt stone, wood, bone, shell, and copper to a limited extent, were employed. Implements formed of these materials answered in a rude way the various wants of these primitive peoples, the same tool being often applied to different uses as the necessities of the case and the poverty of the owner demanded. Of all the ancient incisive implements characteristic of the North American tribes, none is more marked or more generally distributed than the STONE AXE. With the exception of arrow and spear points, there is, in the various illustrations furnished by De Bry, a singular absence of every thing like stone weapons and tools. War-clubs, cane knives, hoes made of fish-bones, and wooden paddles are distinctly portrayed, but not a single stone axe is figured. In plate xxvii. (conviviorum apparatus) of the "Brevis Narratio," lying upon the ground near the large pot upon the fire, is a stout implement like a bill, with a handle probably two feet in length. Head, point, and handle are all of the same material, and evidently of wood. The axe figured in the hands of a native in the act of killing Peter Gambie in a boat, is certainly metallic, and of European manufacture.[1]

If we relied upon these illustrations for information, they would lead us to believe that stone implements were infrequent among the Indians of Virginia and Florida. Other investigations, the testimony of tumuli and of cultivated fields, and the contents of numerous relic-beds assure us, however, that such was not the fact. Various authorities might be cited concurring in the statement that the manufacture and use of stone axes by the North American Indians were very general. From the many which suggest themselves, we select the following that the historical evidence on this subject may be fairly presented:

"Instead of Hatchets and Knives," says Father Hennepin,[2] "they (the Indians) make use of sharp Stones which they fasten in a cleft piece of Wood with Leather Thongs."

By Loskiel[3] we are informed that "their hatchets were wedges, made of hard stones, six or eight inches long, sharpened at the edge, and fastened to a wooden handle. They were not used to fell trees, but only to peel them, or to kill their enemies."

In commenting upon the "handicrafts" of the Virginia Indians, Beverly[4] writes:

[1] "Brevis Narratio," etc., plate xlii. Francoforti ad Mœnum, De Bry. Anno 1591.

[2] "Continuation of the New Discovery," etc., p. 103. London, 1698.

[3] "History of the Mission of the United Brethren," etc., p. 54. London, 1794.

[4] "History and Present State of Virginia," book iii., p. 60. London, 1705.

"Before I finish my account of the *Indians* it will not be amiss to inform you that when the *English* went first among them they had no sort of Iron or Steel Instruments; but their Knives were either Sharpen'd Reeds or Shells, and their Axes sharp Stones bound to the end of a Stick, and glued in with Turpentine. By the help of these they made their Bows of the Locust Tree, an excessive hard Wood when it is dry, but much more easily cut when it is green, of which they always took the advantage."

To Lafitau[1] we are indebted for the following interesting account: "Stone axes have been in use in America from time immemorial. They are made of a kind of very hard and tough stone, and it requires much labor to make them fit for use. They are prepared by the process of grinding on a sandstone and finally assume, at the sacrifice of much time and labor, nearly the shape of our axes, or of a wedge for splitting wood. The life of a savage is often insufficient for accomplishing the work, and hence such an implement, however rude and imperfect it may be, is considered a precious heirloom for the children. When the stone is finished the difficulty of providing it with a handle arises. They select a young tree, of which they make a handle, without cutting it. They split one end and insert the stone. The tree grows, tightens around it, and encloses it so firmly that it hardly can be torn out."

This method of hafting a stone axe was also practised by the Louisiana and Alabama Indians who, according to Captain Bossu,[2] chose a young tree in

[1] "Mœurs des Sauvages Amériquains," vol. i., p. 110. Paris, 1724 (Prof. Rau's translation).

[2] "Travels through the Part of North America formerly called Louisiana," etc., vol. i., p. 223. London, 1771.

which—having made an incision with a flint or pebble as sharp as a razor—they inserted "a stone cut in the form of a hatchet." As the tree grew up, it encased the stone which by that means became inseparable from it. Afterward they cut off the tree at the proper length, so as to have a handle to the axe of convenient form. The same writer intimates that lance-heads and darts were fastened to their shafts in a similar manner. Du Pratz[1] describes the axes of the Louisiana Indians as made of a dark-gray stone of fine grain. "Whether these stones," says he, "were naturally flat or were ground on other hard stones, such as the sand-stone found in Louisiana, certain it is they succeeded in making axes. These stone axes are an inch or more thick at the head, and half an inch in thickness for three-quarters of their length. The edge is bevelled (*formé en biseau*) but not cutting, and may be four inches wide, while the head is only three inches in width. This head is provided with a cavity—deep enough to admit a finger—in order to facilitate the fastening of the blade in the split end of the handle; and this end is, moreover, firmly bound, to prevent further splitting. But there is another inconvenience. In using these axes it was not possible to cut wood, but merely to bruise it; and therefore they always hacked the trees close to the ground in order that the fire which they kindled here might consume more readily the fibres of the wood bruised by the axe. Finally, by dint of labor and patience they succeeded in felling the tree. This labor requires much time; and formerly, therefore, they were much more occupied than at present, being now provided with axes which we trade to them."

[1] "Histoire de la Louisiane," vol. i., p. 166. Paris, 1785.

Writing with special reference to the Cherokee Indians, Adair[1] advises us that they "formerly had stone axes, which in form commonly resembled a smith's chisel. Each weighed from one to two or three pounds weight. They were made of a flinty kind of stone: I have seen several which chanced to escape being buried with their owners, and were carefully preserved by the old people as respectable remains of antiquity. They twisted two or three tough hiccory slips, of about two feet long, round the notched head of the axe; and by means of this simple and obvious invention they deadened the trees by cutting through the bark, and burned them, when they either fell by decay or became thoroughly dry. With these trees they always kept up their annual holy fire; and they reckon it unlawful, and productive of many temporal evils, to extinguish even the culinary fire with water. . . . By the aforesaid difficult method of deadening the trees, and clearing the woods, the contented natives got convenient fields in process of time."

It may be fairly stated that greenstone or diorite was the favorite material used by the Southern Indians in the manufacture of their axes. Tough and durable in its character, this stone best answered the purposes for which implements of the sort we are now considering were designed. Comparatively few were made of flint. Rarely does a chipped axe occur—by far the greater number being ground or rubbed into the desired shape through the tedious process of attrition with some other stone.

With a view to a more definite description, the stone axes of the Southern Indians may be classified thus:

[1] "History of the American Indians," etc., p. 405. London, 1775.

I. Grooved Axes.—These are frequently met with in the sepulchral tumuli, upon the sites of old villages, in relic-beds, and in cultivated fields. In former times they were in very general use. It may be remarked, in passing, that this type, while not unknown, was certainly unusual among the ancient peoples of Europe. In the ninety-six plates which illustrate the "Lake Dwellings of Switzerland, and other parts of Europe, by Dr. Ferdinand Keller,"[1] we seek in vain for an axe of this description. There is a remarkable absence of implements of this kind among the many and interesting relics so intelligently discussed and presented by Mr. Evans in his recent admirable work upon "The Ancient Stone Implements, Weapons, and Ornaments of Great Britain." But two are figured by Mr. Nilsson[2]—one of diorite found in the ground, near Gaddaröd, in the parish of Hörröd, and the other of hornblend, taken from a bog near Lund. He appears somewhat at a loss how to classify them, and inclines to the opinion that they were "wedges with which to split wood." Here, however, no doubt exists in the mind of the observer. The largest grooved axe found within the geographical limits of Georgia, which has passed under the personal observation of the writer, weighs nearly ten pounds, is ten inches and a quarter in length, six inches wide, and two inches and a half thick. The groove is an inch and a half wide, and nearly half an inch in depth. The elevated ridges on each side of the groove are three quarters of an inch wide. In the formation of this groove or transverse furrow, as well as in imparting shape to this implement,

[1] London, 1866.

[2] "Primitive Inhabitants of Scandinavia," plate viii., figs. 166, 167. London, 1868.

Plate X.

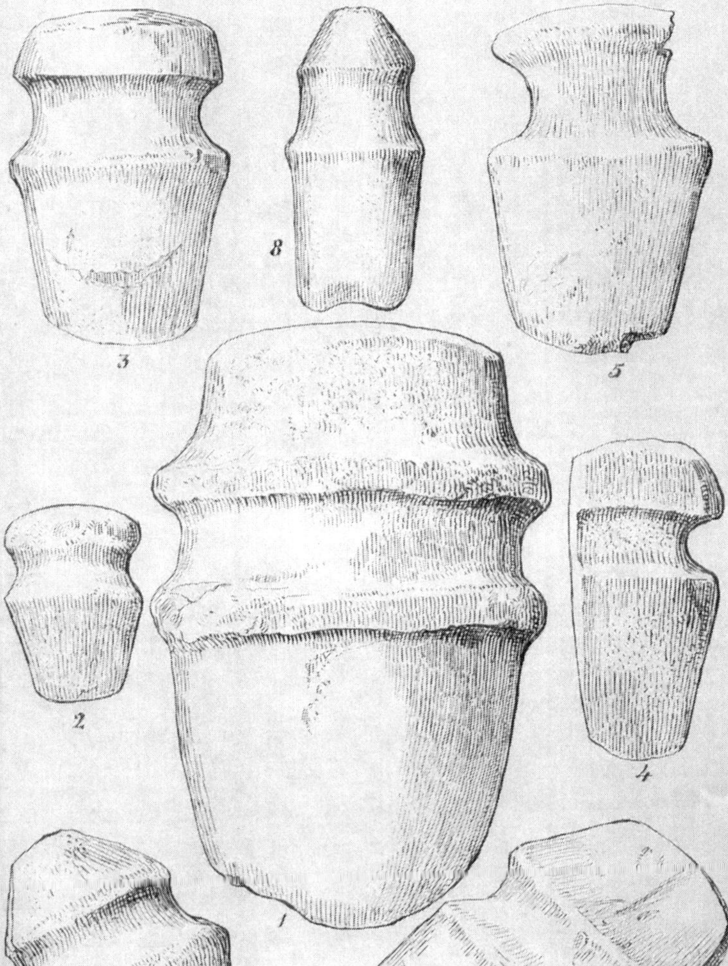

AM. PHOTO-LITHOGRAPHIC CO. N.Y. (OSBORNE'S PROCESS.)

a pointed flint was used to peck away the portions of the stone sought to be removed. Traces of this process are clearly perceptible, although after it was completed the axe was polished with no little care. This specimen is represented by Fig. 1, Plate X., and was taken from a tumulus located at the confluence of the Etowah and the Oostenaula Rivers.

Between this axe and the small but well-formed specimen represented in Fig. 2, Plate X., weighing only half a pound, the writer has in his collection more than fifty grooved axes, taken from mounds and relic-beds, and picked up in the fields within the present limits of Georgia. Although of different shapes and weights they belong to the same class. A few typical forms are represented in the accompanying plate. (*See* Figs. 3, 4, 5, 6 and 7, Plate X.)

Of axes of this description it may be affirmed that their weights vary from half a pound to nine pounds. Occasionally they will turn the scale even at seventeen pounds. In length they differ from three to twelve or fourteen inches, and in width from two and a half to nine inches. The average width of the groove is about an inch and a quarter; its depth from a quarter to half an inch. The presence of the transverse furrow indicates the manner in which these axes were hafted. If not inserted in the growing tree and there allowed to remain until the wood had closed tightly around the groove, a strong withe, following the groove, was bent around the axe, and the ends brought together beneath, where they were firmly lashed by means of deer-sinews or thongs of buckskin. In order to make the implement more secure in the handle, thus formed, it will be observed that in many instances the lower or inner side of the axe was carefully squared or slightly hollowed out so as to permit the insertion of a tightening wedge. (*See* Figs. 4, 6, and 7, Plate X.) In most cases the groove is near the head of the axe; occasionally, however, this tranverse furrow runs across the central portion, thus affording an opportunity for a double edge. Specimens of this latter variety, so far as our observation extends, are carelessly made, and of soft material. They could have been used for little else than offensive purposes.

We have already been assured by the testimony of early observers that grooved axes were extensively engaged in deadening forest-trees, so as to clear certain tracts of land for cultivation. They were also employed in removing the bark and bruising the outer fibres near the roots of the trees so that the fires kindled around them might the more readily eat into the trunks and insure their early fall. It is well known that the Indians of this region, in their mechanical operations, upon every practicable occasion invoked the agency of fire. By its assistance the tree selected for the future canoe was felled, then burnt off at the required length, and finally shaped and hollowed out. In plate xii. (*Linterium conficiendorum ratio*) of the "Admiranda Narratio,"[1] we have a lively representation of the entire operation. It is more than probable that during the progress of such labors these implements, with suitable handles, proved very serviceable in removing the charred surface from time to time so as to afford fresh fuel for the flame.

An examination of the heads of these axes acquaints us with the circumstance that many of them are bruised and splintered, which indicates that they were used

[1] Francoforti ad Mœnum. De Bry, anno 1590.

either as clubs or as wedges for splitting wood. In the latter case—the edge being placed and by means of the handle held in position—the axe was driven into the wood by blows struck upon its head with a stone or wooden maul.[1]

These heads are sometimes rounded, again flat, and at other times wellnigh pointed.

We incline to the belief that the smaller and medium-sized specimens were tomahawks or battle-axes. Cleverly hafted and at close quarters they would, in stalwart hands, constitute a formidable offensive weapon, whether the blow be delivered from the edge or the head.

Many of these axes are badly worn, thus showing the long-continued use to which they were subjected, and advising us of the fact that their edges were time and again reground or sharpened. So often have some of them been sharpened, that nearly the entire blade has been worn away. The edge was renewed by rubbing it upon a whetstone. Several of these whetstones are in the writer's collection, deeply furrowed and hollowed by the sharpening of these implements. The edges of these axes were sharpened evenly on both sides.[2]

Near akin to the grooved axe is the stone adze, of which Fig. 8, Plate X., may be taken as a fair example. Implements of this sort are rare, and were fashioned in the same manner and of similar material employed in the manufacture of the grooved axes which we have been considering. The specimen before us is made of a tough diorite, is five inches and a quarter in length,

[1] *See* Nilsson's "Stone Age," third edition, p. 68. London, 1868.

[2] For forms of such axes found in other portions of the United States, *see* "Ancient Monuments of the Mississippi Valley," p. 217. "Archæologia Americana," vol. i., p. 233, *et seq.*

two inches wide, and an inch and a quarter in thickness. It has been subjected to considerable use, the cutting edge being chipped and worn, while the lower portion of the flat surface retains the polish derived from long-continued service.

This adze may have been hafted to a wooden handle, forming with the implement an angle more or less acute at the pleasure of the workman, one end being bent and adjusted to the flat surface opposite the groove, where it was retained in proper position by deer-skin thongs or ligaments of some sort; or, a flexible branch or withe may have been wound round the groove and the two ends bound together so as tightly to embrace the blade after the fashion generally observed in mounting the ordinary grooved axe. The bent handle, we think, was probably adopted.

II. HAND AND WEDGE-SHAPED AXES, OR STONE CELTS.[1]—In the accompanying Plate XI. are figured six varieties of this class. As in the case of the grooved axes, so with those we propose now to consider, greenstone or diorite was the material usually selected for their manufacture. A few chipped flint axes have been found. The largest specimen represented weighs three pounds and a half, is ten inches and a half in length, and three inches and a half broad at the cutting edge. Its symmetry of proportion is admirable. Some of these axes are nearly cylindrical, and resemble very closely the variety called by Mr. Nilsson the cross-axe with edge ground on both sides. Others have the broad sides somewhat convex, and the narrow sides flat. Some have blunt heads and are fan-shaped, widening very much at the cutting end.

[1] Compare Evans' "Ancient Stone Implements, etc., of Great Britain," chap. vi. London, 1872.

Plate XI.

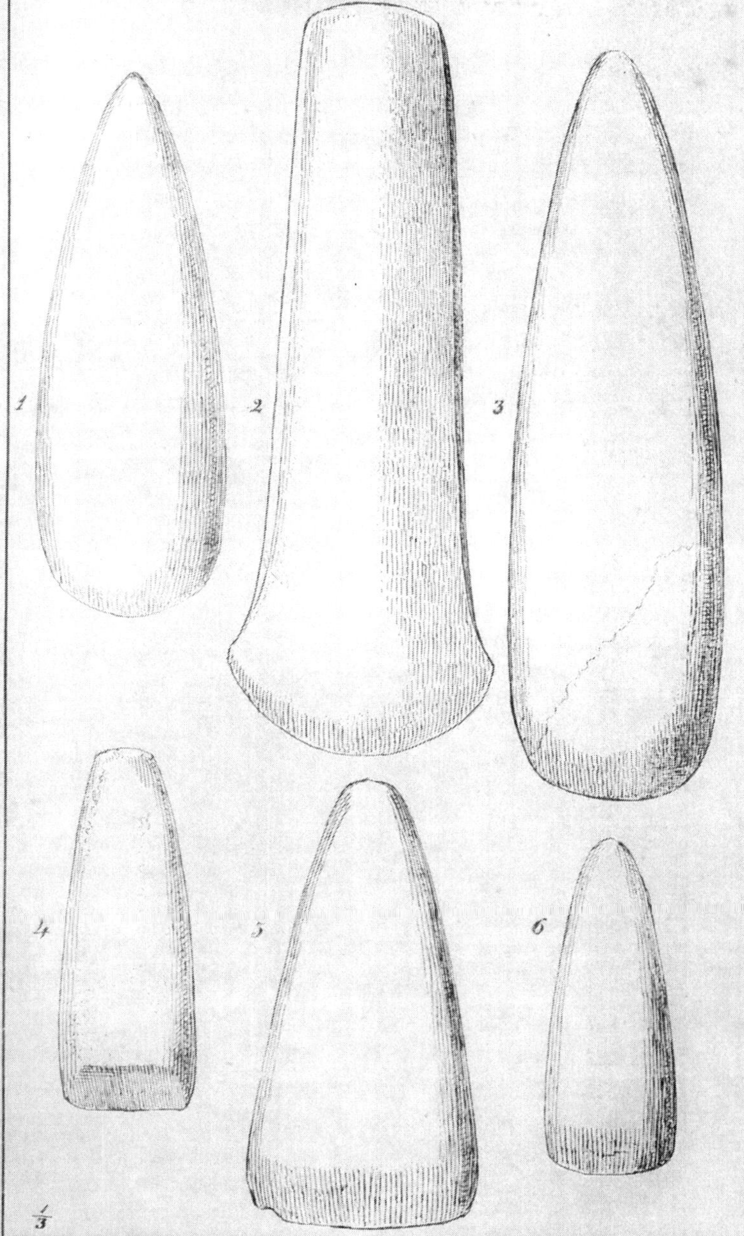

AM. PHOTO-LITHOGRAPHIC CO. N.Y. (OSBORNE'S PROCESS.)

Others still, terminate in a sharp point at the upper end, as though the intention was with it to loosen or break up the material worked upon, and then, with the cutting end, to remove the particles and smooth the surface. Such a tool would have been very convenient in many instances. Particularly valuable would it have proved for dressing the interior of a wooden canoe hollowed out by fire. Within the old oak canoe, unearthed in 1780, at St. Enoch's croft, and near the prow, lay a beautifully-finished stone axe very similar to the pointed celt we have figured in the accompanying plate. It was doubtless one of the simple implements with which this primitive Clyde boat had been fashioned.[1] A like tool was equally effective in giving shape to the cypress canoes which in ancient times navigated the yellow waters of the Savannah and the Alatamaha. These wedge-shaped axes or celts differ in length from three inches to a foot; are, at the cutting end, from two to four inches broad, and in weight vary from half a pound to five pounds and upward. The heads are rounded, square, flattened, or pointed. The cutting edge is square, rounded, or semicircular. In all cases, so far as our observation extends, the edge has been ground from both sides. Occurring frequently in many portions of the Southern States, it is certain that their use was very general among the Indians. The larger and longer varieties were probably managed by hand, and were not hafted. Those of smaller size may have been inserted in wooden, bone, or horn handles, although even these were entirely capable of manual use without such aid. The absence of a groove and the elongated form are the distinguishing peculiarities of this class.

[1] Wilson's "Prehistoric Man," p. 104. London, 1865.

These implements are much better adapted to incisive purposes than the grooved axes. Their edges show continued use, and frequent sharpening. Sometimes their heads afford evidence of the fact that they had been struck with a stone or club and thus driven after the fashion of a wedge; but usually, and especially in the case of the longer and larger varieties, the weight of the implement and the strength of the arm sufficed for the accomplishment of the prescribed labor. All of them were first chipped or pecked into shape, and then rendered smooth by the tedious process of attrition. It is very difficult satisfactorily to discriminate between some varieties of these wedge-shaped axes and some forms of stone chisels. So meagre was the supply of tools in the possession of the Indians, and to such various uses were the same implements often and necessarily applied, that it is almost impossible to subject them to a rigid classification.

Professor Joseph Jones discovered in a sepulchral mound on the bank of the Cumberland River, opposite the city of Nashville, Tennessee, an axe of this class with *a stone handle*. The entire implement was cut out of a solid piece of greenstone (*see* Plate XII.). The handle is thirteen inches and a half in length, an inch and a half wide, and about an inch thick. At the lower end is a hole for the suspension and convenient transportation of the weapon when not in actual use. The axe is about six inches long, two inches and a quarter wide at the cutting edge, and an inch and a half broad at the other end. It is three-quarters of an inch thick, and in general appearance resembles many of the stone celts at one time in such common use among the Southern Indians. This relic possesses special interest and value, and may be regarded as per-

Plate XII.

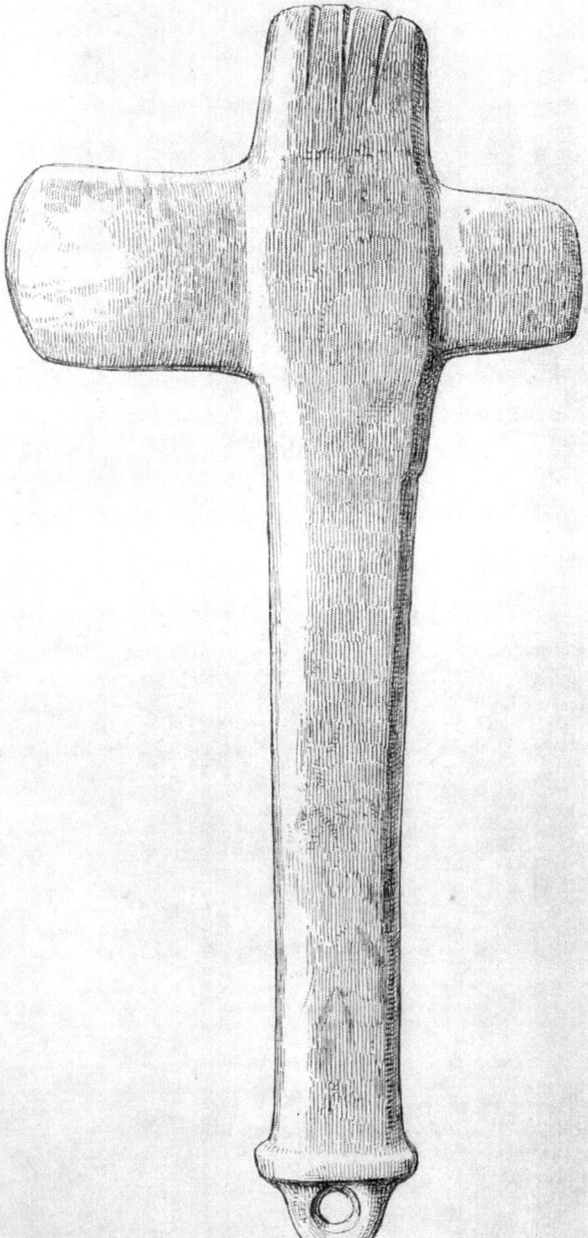

$\frac{1}{2}$

AM. PHOTO-LITHOGRAPHIC CO. N.Y. (OSBORNES PROCESS.)

petuating the manner in which axes of this class were frequently hafted for domestic and perhaps warlike purposes.

An implement precisely similar in material and construction was taken from a grave-mound in York District, South Carolina, about ten years ago. Relics of this description are very rare, and were fashioned at the expense of much time and labor. Both of them were carefully polished in every part. We accept them, not only as curious mementos of a shadowy past, but as enduring proofs of the peculiar mode in which implements of this class were mounted and carried by these primitive peoples.

It would really appear that the ancient workman, as though mindful of the curiosity which would exist in the minds of coming generations touching the customs and manufactures of an age without letters or established traditions, designed by this permanent legacy to remove all doubt, and bequeath an imperishable token for the information of those who should come after.

The thin copper axes found in Nacoochee Valley and in a few other localities, are to be referred to the present class. They were inserted in a split handle, and were rather objects of distinction and ornament than serviceable implements. Having, however, in another chapter commented upon these interesting relics at some length, we need here do no more than mention their existence.

III. Perforated Axes or Hatchets.[1]—It is a noteworthy circumstance that these implements were generally shaped prior to their perforation. It might

[1] Compare Evans' "Ancient Stone Implements, etc., of Great Britain," chap. viii. London, 1872.

very well be supposed that the workman, anxious to detect any concealed defect in the material which in the end might render useless his entire labor, would have at least blocked out his axe before he entered upon the tedious process of drilling; but that he should not only have fully shaped, but in some instances even polished the weapon before he commenced drilling the hole for its handle, appears singular. Such, nevertheless, is the fact. As we write, the physical proofs are before us. Of several specimens now on the desk, one is entirely finished and polished, but lacks the handle-hole. A second (Fig. 1, Plate XIII.), pecked into the desired shape, but not yet ground, indicates on the nether side the commencement of the drilling process. Upon a careful examination of a third, it will be perceived that the drill-hole has been completed only one-half the required distance. A core or nipple, nearly a quarter of an inch in length, appears at the bottom (Fig. 2, Plate XIII.), clearly showing that a hollow reed, aided by sharp sand and water, was the instrument by means of which the perforation was compassed.

Many of these ornamental axes are pick-shaped and made of soft material, such as slate. They vary in length from three to seven inches. The perforations are made longitudinally through the centre—the points being rounded but not brought to a cutting edge. Fig. 3, Plate XIII., may be taken as a typical representation.

The blades are scarcely more than three-eighths of an inch in thickness; and, in addition to the handle-hole, appears a lateral perforation as though for the suspension of the axe. The entire length is rather more than six inches, and the width of the blades an inch and a half. Axes of this shape occur frequently

Plate XIII.

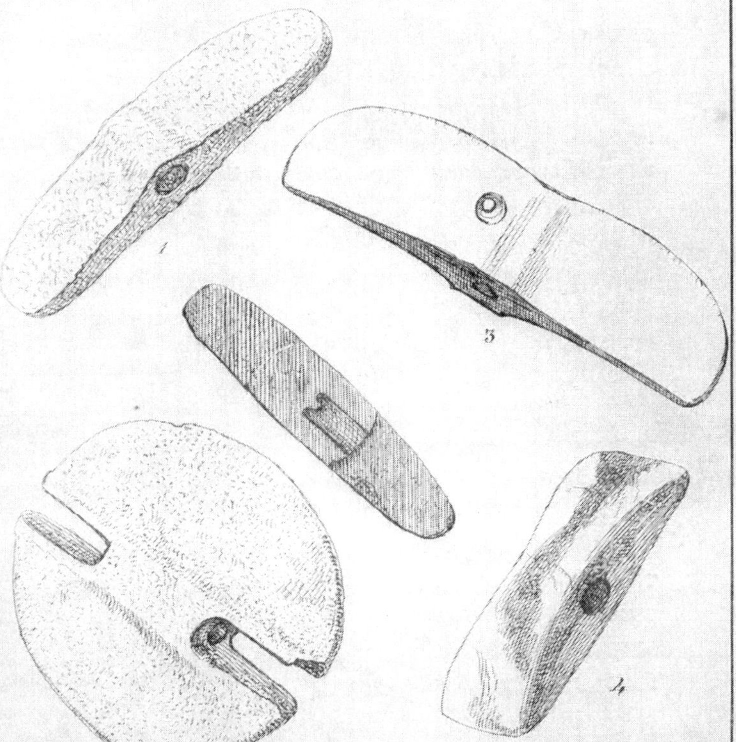

AM. PHOTO-LITHOGRAPHIC CO. N.Y. (OSBORNE'S PROCESS)

in the relic-beds along the banks of the rivers where the natives congregated for fishing and hunting. Most of them are broken. Their edges are not sharp. Fashioned principally of a talcose slate, they were utterly unfit for service and must be regarded as ornamental or ceremonial axes. They vary in size and form, most of them being less than six inches in length and very light. Steatite was also used in the manufacture of these relics.[1] In a grave-mound in Louisiana, three beautiful specimens of this variety of ornamental or ceremonial hatchets were found several years since. They were made of a ferruginous quartz. Where the two blades united, these implements were reënforced and perforated. There was also a lateral perforation in each blade, at the distance of about three-quarters of an inch from the central perforation. These relics were marvels of symmetry, and polished in the highest degree. Their edges indicated no wear. Evidently these implements, upon whose construction such great care and labor had been bestowed, were not intended for incisive purposes but were designed as ornaments or badges of distinction, or for ceremonial uses.

Fig. 4, Plate XIII., closely resembles what Mr. Nilsson[2] would call an "Amazon, or two-edged axe." A similarly-shaped implement is represented in the "Sword of Tiberius." Zenophon mentions it in his "Anabasis," and Horace in one of his Odes speaks of *Amazonia securis.*[3] The specimen before us, made of a tough, close-grained diorite, beautifully polished, is four inches long, an inch and three-eighths in diameter where it is perforated, and an inch and three-

[1] *See* "Ancient Monuments of the Mississippi Valley," pp. 218, 219. Washington, 1848.

[2] "Stone Age," p. 71, plate viii., fig. 173. London, 1868.

[3] "Carminum," liber iv., 4. 20.

quarters wide at the edges. The handle-hole is four-tenths of an inch in diameter. This axe is stout and strong, but it will be observed that while the implement itself is capable of withstanding the shock consequent upon the delivery of a substantial blow, so small is the perforation that no handle, other than one of metal, could prove at all lasting or serviceable. We incline to the belief that this also was an ornamental or ceremonial axe—intended for display, and not for actual use.

We notice only one other variety (Fig. 5, Plate XIII.), made of syenite, weighing one pound eleven ounces, four inches and a half in length, two inches and three-quarters in width, and an inch and three-quarters thick in the middle. The edges of this stout weapon are slightly convex, and five-eighths of an inch thick, the sides of the blades gradually approaching each other from the middle toward the ends. The perforation for the handle is an inch and a quarter in depth, and rather more than half an inch in diameter. The implement appears to be finished, although it may be questioned whether the maker did not intend, if uninterrupted in his labor, to continue his drilling until the axe was entirely perforated. The bottom of the aperture is concave, showing that a solid drill was used. Circular striæ are observable the entire depth of the hole.

After a careful examination of a large number of these perforated axes, we are under the impression that most of them were carried as matters of ceremony, ornament, or distinction; and it may be that the American war-chief suspended from his belt one of these delicate implements, and regarded it with emotions near akin to those which possessed the breast of the Scandinavian warrior as he cherished and displayed his *victory-stone.*

The use of these stone axes was abandoned very shortly after intercourse was established betwen the red-men and the white traders. Even in Adair's time such implements were rarely to be seen, and those which had escaped interment with their former owners were carefully preserved by the old people and regarded as "respectable remains of antiquity." [1]

It was the lamentation of the old chieftain at Mucclasse, that the white man had not sooner come among the children of the forest to teach them the use of letters, and furnish them with the iron hatchet, the knife, the hoe, and the gun.

Eagerly did the Indians bargain for metallic implements; and the European manufacturers, pandering to the savage taste, fashioned the axes and hatchets intended for the American market, of those peculiar and often complex types with which the red-men of the last two centuries have been, in the popular esteem, so inseparably associated. "The warlike arms used by the Cherokees," says Lieutenant Timberlake [2] (writing in 1761), "are guns, bows and arrows, darts, scalping-knives, and tommahawkes, which are hatchets; the hammer-part of which being made hollow, and a small hole running from thence along the shank, terminated by a small brass-tube for the mouth, makes a compleat pipe. There are various ways of making these, according to the country or fancy of the purchaser, being all made by the Europeans; some have a long spear at top, and some different conveniencies on each side. This is one of their most useful pieces of field-furniture,

[1] "History of the American Indians," p. 405. London, 1775.
[2] "Memoirs," etc., pp. 51, 52. London, 1765.

serving all the offices of hatchet, pipe and sword; neither are the Indians less expert at throwing it than using it near, but will kill at a considerable distance."

CHISELS.—So uncertain is the boundary-line which separates the wedge-shaped axe or stone celt from the chisel, that we are often at a loss to determine the class to which certain specimens should properly be assigned. The truth is, remembering the poverty of their owners and the various expedients to which they were necessarily compelled to resort in conducting their mechanical operations, we cannot seriously err when we say that some tools were used indiscriminately as wedges, hand-axes, and chisels. Of the true character and design of some of them, however, we may speak with at least some degree of confidence.

Numbers 1, 2, 3, and 4, Plate XIV., may be regarded as typical specimens of the ordinary chisels. They are all made of greenstone, carefully polished. Numbers 2 and 4 were, in all likelihood, hafted in sockets of wood, stag's-horn, or bone, in like manner as those, of not dissimilar shape, which have been found in the curious and most interesting lake-dwellings of Switzerland and other parts of Europe. Others wanted handles, and their heads give ample evidence of the fact that they were driven by means of a small wooden or stone maul. These implements are generally thin, varying in length from two and a half to eight inches, and in width from one to three inches. They are ground from both sides, to form the cutting edge. In various relic-beds and shell-heaps which I have examined (e. g., those on the banks of the Savannah River, especially in Columbia and Richmond Counties, and on the islands and headlands along the coast), I

Plate XIV.

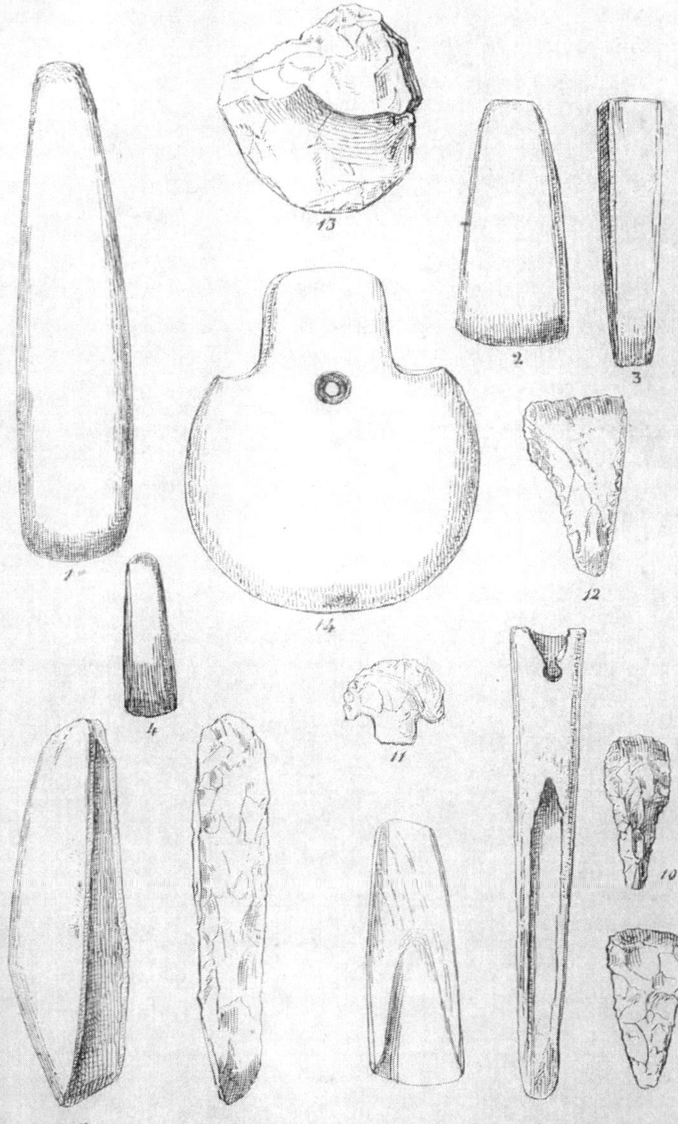

1/3

AM. PHOTO-LITHOGRAPHIC CO. N.Y. (OSBORNES PROCESS)

have found the larger bones of the deer, the bear, and the buffalo, fractured longitudinally and split open. The caves of France and Spain afford proof that the bones of animals were there split and crushed by the primitive peoples in order to extract marrow from them. The Laplanders, the Esquimaux, the Australians and other savage nations have been doing the same thing[1] within the historic period; and it is not improbable that in splitting bones for this purpose, these chisels were in part used by the Southern Indians. Some of these implements are square, with flat sides; others are cylindrical, with the sides somewhat convex; others still, being quite thin, are brought to a cutting edge, both at the end, and for a considerable distance on either side. Those made of flint were first chipped and then ground. The greenstone specimens are carefully polished in every part.

The GOUGE differs from the chisel in that it is usually larger and stronger, and by having one side of the lower end scooped out and the other rounded, so as to present a curvilinear edge. I have seen no relics of the Southern Indians resembling the delicate flint hollow chisels described by Mr. Nilsson and other European archæologists. Numbers 5, 6, and 7, Plate XIV., represent the prevailing types. They are generally from four to nine inches in length, and from one to four inches wide. The principal labor in their construction was expended upon the lower end and in forming a symmetrical edge. Where the implement was grasped with the hand or hafted, less care was bestowed upon its polish. The upper end almost always has been splintered or broken to a greater or less extent by blows. Some of the smaller specimens may

[1] Sir John Lubblock, "Pre-historic Times," pp. 311, 316, 428. London, 1869.

have been hafted, but the larger were evidently intended for hand-use. Some of these tools were fashioned with a protuberance or elevation on the back—distant from the cutting edge about a third the length of the implement—by means of which a considerable leverage was gained by simply inserting the lower end in the material to be removed and then pressing downward with the upper end or handle. (*See* Fig. 5, Plate XIV.) Diorite was the chief stone from which these gouges were made. Comparatively few specimens occur, and they do not seem to have passed into very general use among the Southern tribes, or at least such of them as inhabited the region to which our attention has been chiefly directed.

Bone-gouges are more frequently met with. They are made of the leg-bones of deer and buffaloes (Fig. 8, Plate XIV.).

SCRAPERS.—The spoon-shaped scraper of France and Switzerland is more pronounced in form and purpose than any implement of like character it has been my good fortune to find among the relics of the Southern tribes.[1] With them, however, scrapers were extensively used, but commonly in the shape of substantial flint flakes, struck off by a single blow, and with the wider end chipped to a square or rounded cutting edge. We see also leaf-shaped or triangular implements, thick in the middle—their edges chipped until they were sharp—which were capable of serving the double use of knife and scraper.

The Esquimaux scraper figured by Sir John Lubbock, on page 93 of his "Pre-historic Times," is the counterpart of more than one specimen found in the

[1] Compare also the scrapers figured by Mr. Evans, in his elaborate work upon the "Ancient Stone Implements, etc., of Great Britain," chapter xiii. London, 1872.

shell-heaps on the banks of the Savannah River. For the removal of hair from hides, and in sundry ways, such tools would have proved very serviceable to the primitive workmen. Shell scrapers were also employed.

Sometimes when a stout arrow or spear head had lost its point, it was repaired and subjected to a secondary use which entitled it to be classed among scrapers. Fig. 11, Plate XIV., is an illustration of this. At the point of fracture it has been nicely chipped to a cutting edge. In the present instance this edge is semicircular, but the writer has several in his collection whose cutting edges are square. This scraper is an inch and a quarter wide, and was made of a beautiful variegated jasper. Professor Rau has an implement of this sort, which shows most clearly on its edge the polish caused by the continued use to which it had been subjected.

By far the most elaborate scraper I have seen in this region, is that represented by Fig. 14, Plate XIV. It consists of a close-grained dark diorite, and was taken from a burial-mound in the Etowah Valley. An implement precisely similar in shape, and somewhat larger, was unearthed in the same valley, in 1870, near the confluence of the Etowah and Oostenaula Rivers. The specimen before us is five inches and a quarter in length, four inches and a half in width, and half an inch thick.

The perforation is nearly half an inch in diameter, and was compassed by drilling from both sides. The cutting edge extends from one shoulder all the way round to the other. The handle is flat and its sides are square. At the nether portion the edge has been much worn by continual use. The entire implement is well polished.

An implement of similar shape has been represented and classed by Messrs. Squier and Davis among ornamental axes.[1] With due deference to the opinion of those gentlemen, we feel constrained to differ from them in this suggestion. Had this been an ornamental axe, suspended for the purposes of display, there would have been no marked abrasion of the edge. As it is, the proofs of long-continued use are evident all along the lower portion of the edge and for fully two-thirds of the way up, on either hand, toward the shoulders. We incline to the belief that it was a scraper, and that the hole drilled through the lower part of the handle was intended to admit the insertion of a buckskin thong by means of which the implement, when grasped, could have been fastened around the wrist or the back of the hand, and thus the steady and forcible use of the tool greatly facilitated. Thus employed it would have proved of great value in dressing skins and for different purposes to which a large scraper could have been applied. Figs. 9, 10, 12, and 13, Plate XIV., represent other forms of scrapers manufactured by the primitive peoples of this region.

FLINT KNIVES.—Closely allied to the scraper, and of such construction that they might very readily have been used both as knives and scrapers, are numerous leaf-shaped implements of which Figs. 1, 3, 6, 8, and 9, Plate XV., may be regarded as typical. These are thin, being chipped from the middle toward the sides where they are brought, all around, to a cutting edge. They vary in length from one to six inches, and in width from half an inch to three inches and a half. Some of them terminate in points so acute that they resemble piercers.

[1] "Ancient Monuments of the Mississippi Valley," page 218, Fig. 114, No. 6. Washington, 1848.

Plate XV.

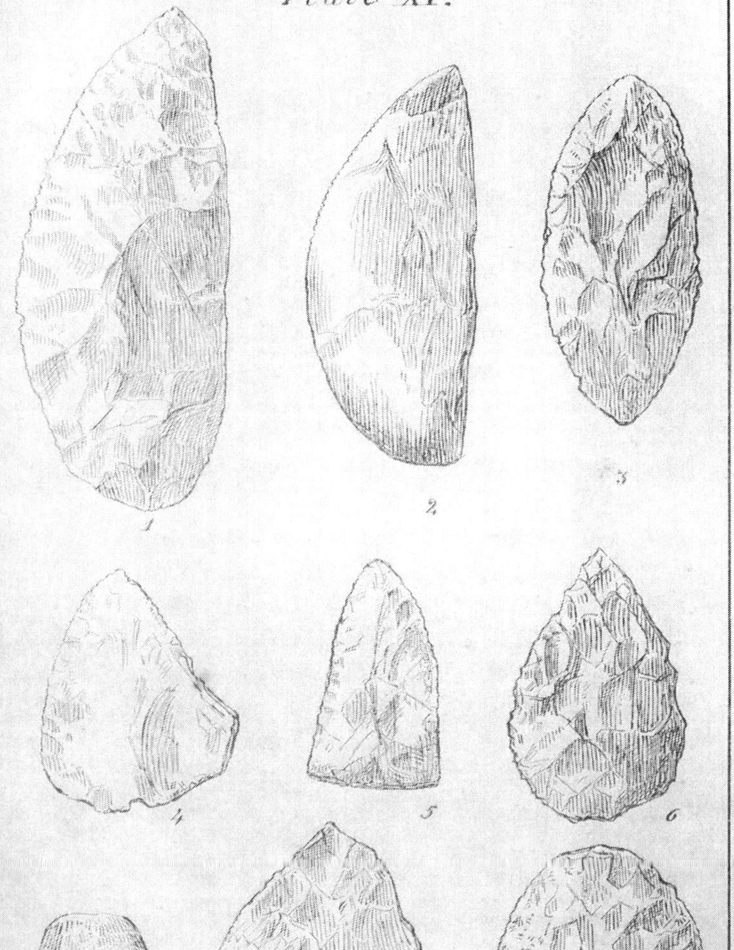

AM. PHOTO-LITHOGRAPHIC CO N.Y. (OSBORNES PROCESS)

Although the forms of flint knives in use among the primitive peoples of this region are various and often exceedingly rude, numbers 1 to 9, Plate XV., may be considered the prevailing types.[1] The great anxiety of the Indian was to obtain a cutting edge. This secured, he often expended but little labor upon the rest of the implement. Consequently, we meet with many semilunar knives whose backs are thick and square and carelessly chipped. Such were designed to be held in the hand. The backs of others are thin, and these were probably hafted in longitudinal handles of bone or wood. Other knives are almost razor-shaped; and others still—elongated in form and with a square cutting edge—required, for convenient use, that the upper end should be inserted in a handle. Some of the larger leaf-shaped implements are so much elongated that it is difficult satisfactorily to determine whether they were intended as spear-heads or as incisive tools. In plate xv. of the "Brevis Narratio," De Bry furnishes a frightful illustration of the enormities perpetrated upon the bodies of their slain enemies by the Florida Indians by means of arrows, clubs, and cane knives (*arundinis fragmentis*), but he nowhere, so far as we now remember, figures a single flint implement which could be called a knife.

Awls, or Borers.—We are informed in the early Spanish narratives that the Southern Indians, with heated copper spindles, perforated pearls so that they might be strung and worn as ornaments. That this was not the only kind of piercing implement fashioned by the natives, is evidenced by the presence of flint awls or borers, four forms of which are here figured

[1] Compare Evans' "Ancient Stone Monuments, etc., of Great Britain," chapter xv. London, 1872.

(*see* Figs. 2, 3, 4, and 5, Plate XVI.). Number 5 may have answered the double purpose of awl and scraper.[1] The point, as well as the square edge at the opposite end, exhibits that peculiar polish which is born only of prolonged use and attrition.

Ordinary piercing implements were also formed from bone, and of these number 1, Plate XVI., is an excellent example. It is made of a deer's tibia, and is seven inches and a half in length. The scars left upon its surface by the flint implement employed in shaping and polishing it, are still very perceptible. Sharp-pointed fish-bones were also extensively used, and these are often found in the shell-heaps and relic-beds both on the coast and along the banks of fresh-water rivers. Flint saws are not infrequent.

Before concluding this brief notice of the cutting and piercing implements of the Southern Indians, it is proper to notice a class of tools—similar in general features to the ordinary hand-axes—made sometimes of slate, at other times of a hornblendic stone, again of diorite, and rarely of flint, whose edges are blunt and rounded, or square. They were, to all appearances, designed as smoothing or polishing stones (*see* Figs. 6, 7, and 8, Plate XVI.), and may have been used in dressing skins. Their edges are all worn very smooth from constant attrition. The implement represented in Fig. 9, Plate XVI., typifies a large class, examples of which abound in the relic-beds on the Savannah River. Their use is not well ascertained, but their flat surfaces are very smooth as though they had been constantly employed in rubbing. There are

[1] The similarity between this implement and that figured by Mr. Evans on page 289 of his "Ancient Stone Implements, etc., of Great Britain" (London, 1872), is very striking.

Plate XVI.

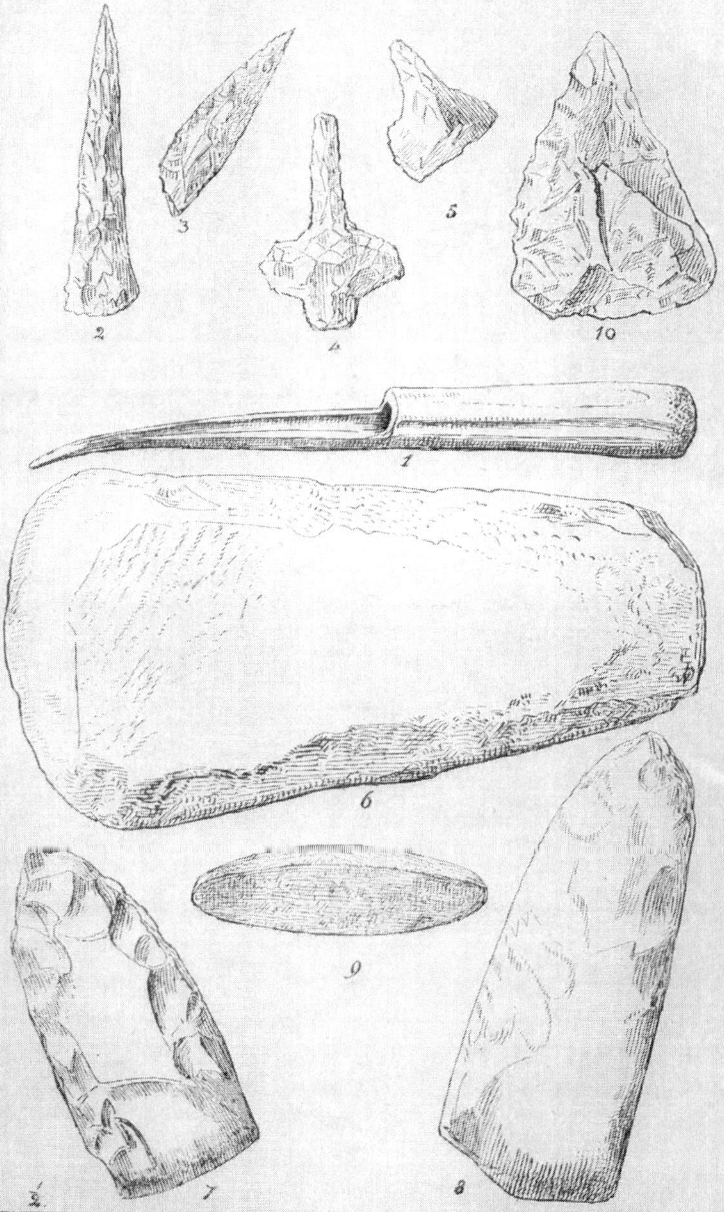

AM. PHOTO-LITHOGRAPHIC CO. N.Y. (OSBORNES PROCESS)

also stout triangular-shaped flint articles, which may be regarded as primitive axes, as unfinished spear-heads, or as scrapers. This matter of classification is, to a considerable extent, arbitrary; and while in most instances we have no hesitancy in determining the uses and characters of various relics, we not infrequently encounter specimens concerning whose specific employment and accurate archæological arrangement any thing more than a suggestion appears unjustifiable.

The implements we have been examining, were obtained from mounds, shell-heaps and relic-beds, gathered upon the sites of ancient villages and fishing-resorts, or ploughed up in cultivated fields. Before bringing the present chapter to a close, we desire to allude to some rudely-chipped, triangular-shaped implements found in Nacoochee Valley under circumstances which seemingly assign to them a very remote antiquity. In material, manner of construction, and in general appearance, so nearly do they resemble some of the rough, so-called flint hatchets belonging to the drift type, as described by M. Boucher de Perthes, that they might very readily be mistaken the one for the other.

Through this valley flows the Chattahoochee. The region being auriferous, the attention of the early settlers was soon attracted to an examination of the bed of this stream. Particles of gold were found intermixed with the sand and pebbles which lay at the bottom. In order to facilitate mining operations, canals were cut, sometimes deflecting the current from its channel, and at other times branching off from the river so as to unearth the precious metal which had gravitated out of sight. These sections passed through the soil and the underlying drift composed of sand, gravel, and bowlders, and reached down to the hard slate-rock below. During one of these excavations, at a depth of some nine feet below the surface, intermingled with the gravel and bowlders of the drift and just above the rocky substratum upon which the deposit rested, were found three flint implements, similar in shape, one of which is here figured (Fig. 10, Plate XVI.). It is three inches and a quarter in length, and two inches and an eighth in width. It is said that articles of a like character have been discovered in the drift along the line of Duke's Creek, but they have not passed under the writer's observation. In this drift, so far as my knowledge extends, no human bones have as yet been found. Prominent earth-mounds, stone graves, and frequent relics attest the fact that this valley was for a long period thickly populated by the red race. These indications of a former occupancy are chiefly confined, however, to the surface, or its vicinity. When the white men possessed themselves of this beautiful region, these mounds were covered with trees, to all appearances as vigorous and as old as those which composed the adjacent forests. Indian inhumations outside of the tumuli are shallow. Spear and arrow heads, stone mortars, pipes, beads, discoidal stones, axes, and various relics indicating use and ornament, are confined to the mounds, graves, and the surface of the valley. Such do not obtain in the drift. I am not in possession of data sufficient to warrant the expression of an opinion touching the age of Nacoochee Valley as at present constituted. That it has undergone no material change for centuries, is demonstrated by the presence of these large earth-mounds and the big forest-trees which grew upon them after they were neglected or abandoned by those who erected them.

The Chattahoochee has been pursuing its present course through this charming valley for lo! these many, many years, and there are no indications of any violent and sudden mutations which would have modified the period requisite for the gradual formation of the soil and surface of this valley. That the implements in question were brought down with and deposited in the drift when as yet there was little or no vegetable life in the valley, seems highly probable. How many centuries have looked down upon the gradual accumulation of the soil which now overlies the drift, none can answer; but of one thing we may rest satisfied, that these specimens of the rude labor of prehistoric man may well claim high antiquity. They are as emphatically drift inplements as any which have appeared in the diluvial matrix of France. Thus, in Nacoochee, while the Neolithic age is richly represented, the Palæolithic period is not entirely wanting in its characteristic types.

If we are ignorant of the time when the Chattahoochee first sought a highway to the Gulf—if we know not the age of the artificial tumuli which still grace its banks—if we are uncertain when the red nomads who in fear and wonder carried the burdens of the adventurous De Soto as he conducted his followers through primeval forests and by the side of this softly moving stream, first became dwellers here—how shall we answer when questioned as to the age in which these rude drift implements were fashioned and used by the primitive peoples?

CHAPTER XIII.

Agriculture and Agricultural Implements.—Ceremony of the Busk.—Cultivation of Maize.—Mortars and Pestles.—Crushing-Stones.—Nut-Stones.—Use of Walnut and Hickory-nut Oil.

ALTHOUGH in the mythology of the red-men of the South the beneficent Ceres, who first taught mortals how to turn the soil with a plough,[1] received no individual deification, they were not insensible of her benignant influences, ever present in the genial warmth of bright skies, engendering fertility in the soft earth and causing to spring up beneath their feet a beautiful plant whose fruit proved in very deed a "staff of life." By nothing was the gradual development of the semi-civilization of the Muscogulges, the Creeks, the Choctaws, the Cherokees, and other Indian tribes more clearly indicated than by their general and regular cultivation of the maize, an American plant, whose value—recognized by these aborigines for many antecedent centuries and extensively appreciated at the dawn of the historic period—has ever since received ready acknowledgment wherever introduced to the notice of civilized man. Regarded as a direct gift from the Author of Life to his red children, it was highly

[1] "Publii Virgilii Maronis Georgica," lib. i., v. 146. Londoni, apud A. Dulau & Co., 1800.

prized and held in peculiar esteem. To make light of, or waste either the grain, or the cob from which it was taken, was never permitted. Certain ceremonies were observed in the spring when it was planted; and of all their rites the Busk—celebrated just before they garnered the ripe ears from the fields—was, perhaps, the most solemn and imposing. Of the American Indians the Southern nations were the most civilized and the least nomadic in their habits. Enjoying a mild climate, and possessing fruitful and well-watered valleys, they located permanent seats, were provident of the future, and surrounded themselves with more of the comforts and conveniences of life than appertained to the Northern and Western hunter tribes. Attached to the soil, often building considerable towns fortified by palisades, and composed of huts and houses substantial after their kind, and furnished with mats, benches, and various aptly-made domestic utensils, they lifted themselves at least somewhat above that rude, beggarly, and precarious existence which so painfully characterized the condition of so many of the aborigines inhabiting other portions of this country, oppressed by greater penury and contending against the rigors of more tempestuous seasons.

The territory over which cultivation by the natives extended, is bounded on the east by the Atlantic, on the south by the Gulf of Mexico, on the west, generally by the Mississippi, or perhaps more properly by the prairies, and on the north by the nature of the climate.[1] The population of those regions in which the soil was cultivated, was more permanent and numerous than that of localities where the individuals relied

[1] *See* Mr. Gallatin's "Synopsis of the Indian Tribes," "Archæologia Americana," vol. ii., p. 149.

for their subsistence upon the natural products of the earth and the waters. It was also less barbarous. The most cursory examination of the early accounts will advise us of the fact that maize was extensively cultivated by, and formed a standard article of food among the Southern Indians. The English at Jamestown were, at times, almost wholly sustained by the liberality of the natives; and Captain John Smith, in recounting the friendship of Pocahontas, mentions the circumstance that she in person accompanied from the Indian fields the "conductas" of grain which relieved the wants of the colonists. Both Cabeça de Vaca[1] and Captain Ribault[2] found it growing freely in Florida. From Tampa Bay, De Soto addressed a letter to the Justice and Board of Magistrates in Santiago de Cuba, informing them that Baltazar de Gallegos, whom, with eighty lancers and a hundred foot-soldiers, he sent to reconnoitre the country, had seen "fields of maize, beans, and pumpkins, with other fruits and provisions, in such quantity as would suffice to subsist a very large army without its knowing a want."[3] On one occasion his army marched for two leagues through continuous fields of corn. During the progress of the expedition the Spanish soldiers subsisted almost exclusively upon food furnished by the natives. The maize, stored in granaries and standing in cultivated fields, furnished bread for the troops, while the blades of the corn proved excellent forage for the horses.

While passing through the pine-barren regions, where the soil was poor and the population scant, bitterly did the Christians complain of the hardships

[1] "Relation," etc., translated by Buckingham Smith, p. 35. New York, 1871.

[2] "The Whole and True Discoverye of Terra Florida." London, 1563.

[3] "Narratives of the Career of Hernando de Soto," translated by Buckingham Smith, p. 285. New York, 1866.

there encountered. Often were they sorely pressed to escape starvation. Ample fields and houses filled with corn were frequently met farther on, and there heavy were the contributions levied, and numerous the captives made who were compelled, even in chains, to accompany the conquerors and bear weighty burdens of maize and mortars in which to prepare it for cooking. It would appear from the early narratives that the principal towns and maize-fields of the natives were located in rich valleys where a generous soil yielded with least labor the most remunerative harvest. While beans, pumpkins, dried plums, grapes, persimmons, mulberries, nuts, and other spontaneous products of the earth, were freely used, it is quite certain that the Southern Indians relied chiefly upon their crops of corn. Upon its cultivation general and systematic attention was bestowed. In a former chapter we have seen that the grooved axe was extensively employed in girdling trees so as to deprive them of life, and thus, in the end, cause the forest-growth to disappear from the spots which had been selected for cultivation. Indian fields in which not even the trace of a stump or root could be perceived were frequently observed by the first European settlers. For the location of such fields the richest spots adjacent to the villages were selected. These were planted in common—no fences,[1] in the olden time, indicating the bounds of individual labor, or private storehouses the fruits of personal toil. The soil was the property of all—and each, sharing in the general toil, participated in the common harvest. "About their houses," says Captain Ribault, "they labor and till the ground, sowing their fields with a grain called *Mahis*, whereof

[1] *See* Brickell's "Natural History of North Carolina," p. 344. Dublin, 1737.

they make their meal, and in their gardens they plant beans, gourds, cucumbers, citrons, peas, and many other fruits and roots unknown to us. Their spades and mattocks be made of wood, so well and fitly as is possible, which they make with certain stones, oyster-shells and muscles, wherewith also they make their bows and small lances, and cut and polish all sorts of wood that they employ about their buildings and necessary use."[1]

The Gentleman of Elvas[2] intimates that each Indian had his own field which he planted and harvested for his individual account. The natural fruits, he continues, were common for all. In some parts of the territory traversed by Cabeça de Vaca[3] three crops of maize and beans were raised during the year. A Natchez chief, among other things, offered M. Le Page Du Pratz[4] twenty barrels of maize in exchange for a sun-glass.

We are informed by Adair[5] that while the gardens contiguous to the houses were fenced in, the large fields were, in this regard, quite unprotected. In plate xxi. of the "Brevis Narratio," six Indians are seen busily engaged in preparing the ground and in planting corn. No fences or enclosures of any sort are represented. It would appear from the explanatory note[6]

[1] "The Whole and True Discoverye of Terra Florida." London, 1563.

[2] "Narratives of the Career of Hernando de Soto," translated by Buckingham Smith, p. 201. New York, 1866.

[3] "Relation," etc., translated by Buckingham Smith, p. 172. New York, 1871.

[4] "History of Louisiana," vol. ii., p. 183. London, 1763.

[5] "History of the American Indians," p. 406. London, 1775.

[6] "Diligenter colunt terram Indi, eam ob causam ligones è piscium ossibus parare norunt viri, quibus manubria lignea aptantes, terram fodiunt satis facilè, nam mollior est: ea deinde probè confracta & æquata, feminæ fabas & milium sive Mayzum serunt, præeuntibus nonnullis, quæ defixo in terram baculo foramina faciunt, in quæ fabæ & milij grana inijciantur. Facta semente, agros relinquunt," etc.

that the Indians diligently cultivated the soil, using for this purpose fish-bones attached to wooden handles. With these agricultural implements the men broke up and made even the surface of the ground. Following after them came the women who, with the aid of sticks, made holes in the newly-prepared and soft earth, into which beans and grains of corn, carried for that purpose in small baskets, were dropped. The planting being over, the seed was left to fructify—but little attention being bestowed upon the growing crop.[1]

No specimens of these bone agricultural implements or of the wooden spades and mattocks[2] mentioned by Captain Ribault have passed under our observation. These, as well as the scapulas of the deer and the buffalo, which were used for a similar purpose, have crumbled into dust. Occasionally, however, we meet with stone hoes, of which Fig. 1, Plate XVII., may be regarded as typical. This relic is made of greenstone. It is five inches and a quarter in length, and nearly two inches and three-quarters in width. For a distance of more than two inches and a half from the edge it exhibits on both sides that delicate polish which is engendered only by constant attrition and long-continued use. The groove afforded the means of lashing it securely to a handle whose end was doubtless bent for that purpose, so that the blade should remain at right angles to it. It will be observed that this implement is slightly curved, and has very much the appearance of the half of a grooved axe split in twain longitudinally. It is, nevertheless,

[1] Compare "A Briefe and True Report of the New-found Land of Virginia," etc., "made in English by Thomas Hariot," etc., pp. 14, 15. Francoforti ad Mœnum. De Bry, anno 1590.

[2] *See* also Brickell's "Natural History of North Carolina," p. 326. Dublin, 1737. Bossu's "Travels through Louisiana," etc., vol. i., p. 224. London, 1771. Loskiel's "History," etc., p. 68. London, 1794.

a complete and well-formed hoe. Remembering the shallow manner in which the natives cultivated the soil, we can readily believe that it would have abundantly answered the purpose for which we suppose it to have been designed. Fig. 2, Plate XVII., represents a spade made of greenstone which was found by Prof. Joseph Jones in a Tennessee grave-mound. Were the handle shorter, it might be classed as a scraper or smoothing-stone. This implement is beautifully polished. Its entire length is seventeen inches and a quarter, the handle—which is round and tapering—being fourteen inches and a quarter long, and the blade three inches long and nearly as wide. The blade, both on its sides and bottom, was brought to an edge. We suppose this to have been an agricultural tool.

Large and roughly-chipped, leaf-shaped flint implements, of which Figs. 3, 4, and 5, Plate XVII., may be taken as types, are found in considerable numbers. These, we think, should be properly classed among primitive agricultural tools. None of them, however, so far as my observation extends, are as well formed or clearly marked as the notched implements from East St. Louis, so well described by Prof. Rau in the Smithsonian Report for 1868.[1]

After favoring us with an account of the manner in which the Louisiana Indians constructed their huts, Du Pratz[2] says: "Near all their habitations they have fields of maiz and of another nourishing grain called *Choupichoul*, which grows without culture. For dressing their fields, they invented houghs which are formed in the shape of an L, having the lower part flat and sharp; and to take the husk from their corn they made

[1] P. 401, *et seq.*

[2] "History of Louisiana," etc., vol. ii., p. 225. London, 1763.

Plate XVII.

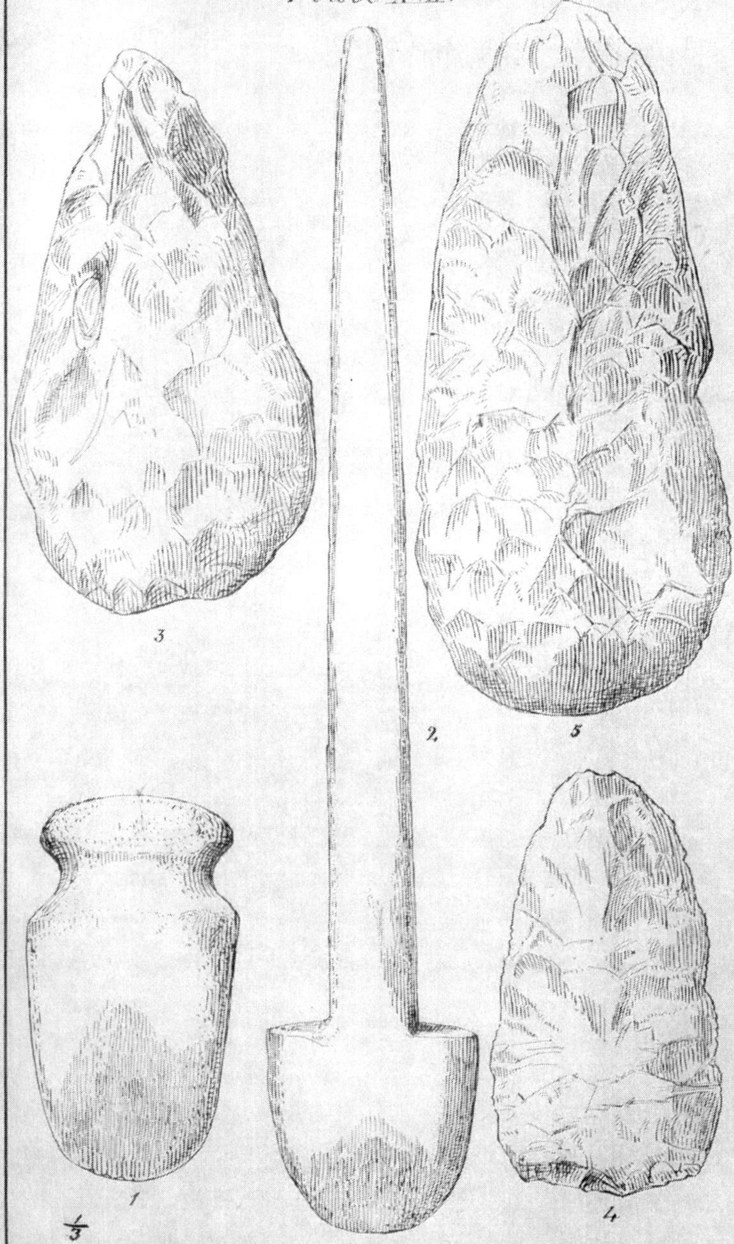

AM. PHOTO-LITHOGRAPHIC CO. N.Y. (OSBORNE'S PROCESS.)

large wooden mortars, by hollowing the trunks of trees with fire."

The corn having attained its maturity, and being ready for harvest, a day was named by the mico for the celebration of the annual festival known among the Creeks as Boos-ke-tau. In Cussetuh, eight days were spent in conducting the prescribed ceremonies, while in towns of lesser importance four days sufficed for the observance of this memorable season of purification, thanksgiving, and rejoicing.

On the morning of the first day,[1] the warriors clean the yard of the square and sprinkle it with white sand. The a-cee, or decoction of the cassine yupon, is made. The fire-maker kindles the fire, as early as he can, by friction. Four logs, each as long as a man can cover by extending his two arms, are cut and brought by the warriors and placed in the centre of the square, end to end, thus forming a cross. The outer ends indicate the cardinal points. In the centre of the cross the new fire is made. These four logs are burnt out during the first four days.

The Pin-e-bun-gau (turkey-dance) is danced by the women of the turkey tribe, and while they are dancing the possau is brewed. This is a powerful emetic. From twelve o'clock to the middle of the afternoon the possau is drunk. After this four men and four women dance the Toc-co-yule-gau (tadpole). From evening until daylight E-ne-hou-bun-gau (the dance of the people second in command) is danced by the men.

About ten o'clock, the second day, the women dance Its-ho-bun-gau (the gun-dance). After twelve, the men go to the new fire, take some of the ashes, rub

[1] "Sketch of the Creek Country by Colonel Benjamin Hawkins." Collection of the Georgia Historical Society, vol. iii., part 1, p. 75. Savannah, 1848.

them on the chin, neck, and belly, jump head-foremost into the river, and then return into the square. The women having prepared the new corn for the feast, the men take some of it and rub it between their hands and then on their faces and breasts, and then they feast.

During the third day the men sit in the square.

Early in the morning of the fourth day the women get the new fire, clean out their hearths, sprinkle them with sand, and kindle their fires. The men finish burning out the first four logs, and then rubbing themselves with the ashes on their chins, necks, and bellies, go into the water. This day salt is eaten, and they dance Obungauchapco (the long dance).

The fifth day four new logs are brought and placed in the same position as on the first. They drink also a-cee, the strong decoction of the cassine yupon.

During the sixth day they remain in the square.

The seventh day is passed in like manner.

On the eighth day they get two large pots and their physic-plants, to wit: Mic-co-ho-yon-e-juh, Toloh, A-che-nau, Cup-pau-pos-cau, Chu-lis-sau, Tuck-thlau-lus-te, Tote-cul-hil-lis-so-wau, Chofeinsuck-cau-fuck-au, Cho-fe-mus-see, Hil-lis-hut-ke, To-te-cuh-chooc-his-see, Welau-nuh, Oak-chon-utch-co, and Co-hal-le-wau-gee. These are all put into the pots and beaten up with water. The chemists (E-lic-chul-gee, called by the traders physic-makers) blow into the decoction through a small reed, and then the men drink it and rub it over their joints until the afternoon. They then collect old corn-cobs and pine-burs, and, placing them in a pot, burn them to ashes. Four virgins who have never had their menses bring ashes from their houses, and, having put them into the pot, stir all together. The men take white clay, and mix it with water in two pans. A pan of this clay and one of ashes are carried to the cabin of the mico. Two pans similarly filled are taken to the cabin of the warriors. With the clay and ashes they rub themselves. Two men, appointed to that office, bring flowers of tobacco of a small kind (Itch-au-chu-le-puc-pug-gee) or, as the name imports, the old man's tobacco, which was prepared on the first day, and putting it in a pan on the mico's cabin, give a little of it to all who are present.

The mico and councillors then go four times around the fire, and every time they face the east throw some of the flowers into the fire. They then go and stand to the west. The same ceremony is repeated by the warriors.

A cane is stuck up at the cabin of the mico, with two white feathers in its end. A member of the Fish tribe (Thlot-lo-ul-gee) takes it just as the sun goes down and moves off toward the river, all following him. When half-way to the river, he gives the death-whoop. This he repeats four times between the square and the water's edge. Here, they all locate themselves as close together as they can stand. The cane is stuck up at the water's edge, and they all put a grain of the old man's tobacco on their heads and in each ear. At a given signal, four times repeated, they throw some of this tobacco into the river, and every man upon a like signal plunges into the stream and picks up four stones from the bottom. With these they cross themselves four times on the breast, each time throwing a stone into the river and giving the death-whoop. They then wash themselves, take up the cane with the feathers, return and stick it up in the square, and visit through the town. At night they dance O-bun-gau-Haujo (the mad dance), and this finishes the ceremony. This happy institution of the Boos-ke-tuh [1] restores man to himself, his family, and to his nation. It is a general amnesty which not only absolves the Indians from all crimes, murder excepted, but seems to bury guilt itself in oblivion. In ancient times this festival was celebrated at the appearance of the first new moon during which the corn became fully eared. Subsequently, however, it was regulated by the season of the harvest.[2] From the time consumed and the formalities observed in its solemnization, it is manifest how important and sacred this Feast of the Busk was in the estimation of the agricultural tribes of the South. The ingathering of the matured maize-crop was preceded by an extinguishment of former fires and the kindling of one consecrated new flame, which was to prove the parent of light and heat for the coming year. This was the season of physical and moral purification, of general forgiveness, universal amnesty and united thanksgiving. Then was the blotted chapter of the old year closed and sealed, and a new, clean page opened in the life of every one. No wonder that these primitive peoples held this maize in special honor and watched its growth with emotions other than and superior to those which would have been suggested, had they regarded it

[1] For other accounts of the solemnization of this festival, *see* Du Pratz' "History of Louisiana," vol. ii., p. 189, *et seq.;* Schoolcraft's "Archives of Aboriginal Knowledge," vol. v., p. 267, *et seq.;* Adair's "History of the American Indians," p. 99, *et seq.;* Bartram's "Indians of the South," part 1, of vol. iii. of the Transactions of the American Ethnological Society. Bartram's "Travels through North and South Carolina, Georgia," etc., etc., p. 507, *et seq.;* Brickell's "Natural History of North Carolina," p. 326.

For the ceremony and preparation of the Black-Drink, *see* Schoolcraft's "Archives of Aboriginal Knowledge," vol. v., p. 266, *et seq.;* "Brevis Narratio," plate xxix.

[2] Adair's "History of the American Indians," etc., p. 99. London, 1775.

simply as an ordinary plant and a common article of food.

This festival over, immediate attention was directed to harvesting the crop. Bartram[1] says that the whole town then assembled, and every man carried to his own granary the fruits of his labor from the part of the general plantation allotted to him in the spring. This share of the harvest became his individual property. Previous, however, to their carrying off their crops from the field, he continues, "there is a large crib or granary, erected in the plantation, which is called the king's crib; and to this each family carries and deposits a certain quantity according to his ability or inclination, or none at all if he so chooses: this in appearance seems a tribute or revenue to the Mico; but, in fact, is designed for another purpose, i. e., that of a public treasury supplied by a few and voluntary contributions, and to which every citizen has the right of free and equal access when his own private stores are consumed; to serve as a surplus to fly to for succour; to assist neighbouring towns, whose crops may have failed; accommodate strangers or travellers; afford provisions or supplies when they go forth on hostile expeditions; and for all other exigencies of the state; and this treasure is at the disposal of the king or Mico."

It is probable that this harvest-labor formerly devolved to a large extent upon the women. In plate xxiii. of the "Brevis Narratio," women, and men of that bestial class improperly styled in the early narratives *Hermaphrodites*, are busily engaged in the transportation of baskets filled with fruits. The preceding plate exhibits to us a storehouse—located on the low bank of

[1] "Travels," etc., p. 510. London, 1792.

a stream—toward which several canoes filled with fruits and corn are tending. These granaries or storehouses among the Florida Indians were built of stones and earth, and covered with palmetto-leaves and clay. For their erection some cool spot was selected where protection was afforded against the violent rays of the sun. Such storehouses served as depositories not only for maize, fruits, nuts, and roots, but also for dried fishes, alligators, dogs, deer, and other jerked meats. These were first exposed upon a scaffolding,[1] made of poles, beneath which a fire was kindled and kept burning until the meat, thoroughly smoked and dried, was thus preserved from early decomposition.

These hoards of corn, meat, and fruits, are frequently mentioned in the early narratives. In the language of the "Gentleman of Elvas,"[2] "four leagues before coming to Chiaha fifteen men met the Governor—bearing loads of maize—with word from the cacique that he waited for him, having twenty barbacoas full." Garcilasso de la Vega[3] states that one of De Soto's officers found in one house five hundred measures of ground maize, besides a large quantity in the grain. Lawson[4] says that the cabins intended for granaries[5] were made without windows.

The maize thus constituting a chief source of subsistence among the Southern Indians, it is interesting to note the method generally adopted by them in preparing it for cooking. The Fidalgo of Elvas makes the broad assertion that the bread which is eaten

[1] Plate xxiv., "Brevis Narratio."

[2] "Narratives of the Career of Hernando de Soto," translated by Buckingham Smith, p. 69. New York, 1866.

[3] "Conquête de la Floride," vol. i., p. 250. Leyden, 1731.

[4] "History of Carolina," p. 290. Reprint. Raleigh, 1866.

[5] *See* also Brickell's "Natural History of North Carolina," p. 327. Dublin, 1737. Loskiel's "History," etc., p. 68. London, 1794.

throughout Florida is made of maize; and, at Apalachen, Cabeça de Vaca observed numerous mortars for cracking this grain. In plate xxviii. of the "Brevis Narratio" (*conviviorum apparatus*), a flat, round stone mortar, set upon the ground, is represented among other articles. A native, on bended knee, with a short, stout pestle in his hand, is in the act of grinding something for the feast. The intimation is, however, that he is at present simply bruising[1] some fragrant herbs to serve as a seasoning for the food which is boiling in the great clay pot. Among the North and South Carolina Indians "the savage men never beat their corn to make bread, but that is the women's work, especially the girls, of whom you shall see four beating with long, great pestils in a narrow wooden mortar; and every one keeps her stroke so exactly, that 'tis worthy of admiration."[2]

"Their common food," says Captain Bernard Romans,[3] "is the zea or Indian corn, of which they make meal and boil it; they also parch it and then pound it; thus taking it on their journey they mix it with cold water, and will travel a great way without any other food; . . . they have also a way of drying and pounding their corn before it comes to maturity; this they call *boota copassa* (i. e., cold flour); this in small quantities thrown into cold water boils and swells as much as common meal boiled over a fire; it is hearty food, and being sweet, they are fond of it," etc.

To Adair[4] are we indebted for the following account of the mortars in which the women beat the

[1] "Alter aromata cibis inspergenda in plano aliquo lapide atterit."

[2] Lawson's "History of Carolina," p. 336. Raleigh, reprint, 1860.

[3] "Concise Natural History of East and West Florida," etc., p. 68. New York, 1775.

[4] "History of the American Indians," etc., p. 416. London, 1775.

flinty corn until all the husks were carefully taken off, and the cracked grains—well sifted and fanned—neatly prepared for boiling in large earthen pots: "The Indians always used mortars instead of mills, and they had them, with almost every other convenience, when we first opened a trade with them; they cautiously burned a large log to a proper level and length, placed fire a-top, and wet mortar round it, in order to give the utensil a proper form; and when the fire was extinguished, or occasion required, they chopped the inside with their stone-instruments, patiently continuing the slow process till they finished the machine to the intended purpose."

Of this maize, the same writer informs us, the Indians of Upper Georgia and the adjacent region possessed three varieties: the first was small, matured in two months, and was called by the English "six weeks' corn;" the second was yellow and flinty, and known among the natives as "hommony-corn;" while the third, which was largest and yielded a white, soft grain, was called "bread-corn." "In July, when the chestnuts and corn are green and full-grown, they half-boil the former and take off the rind; and having sliced the milky, swelled, long rows of the latter, the women pound it in a large wooden mortar, which is wide at the mouth and gradually narrows to the bottom; then they knead both together; wrap them up in green corn-blades of various sizes, about an inch thick, and boil them well, as they do every kind of seethed food. This sort of bread is very tempting to the taste, and reckoned most delicious to their strong palates. They have another sort of boiled bread, which is mixed with beans or potatoes; they put on the soft corn till it begins to boil, and pound it sufficiently fine. . . .

When the flour is stirred and dried by the heat of the sun or fire, they sift it with sieves of different sizes curiously made of the coarser or finer cane splinters. The thin cakes mixt with bear's oil were formerly baked on thin broad stones placed over a fire, or on broad earthen bottoms fit for such a use. . . . When they intend to bake great loaves they make a strong, blazing fire, with short, dry, split wood on the hearth. When it is burnt down to coals they carefully take them off to each side and sweep away the remaining ashes; then they put their well-kneaded broad loaf, first steeped in hot water, over the hearth, and an earthen bason above it, with the coals and embers atop. This method of baking is as clean and efficacious as could possibly be done in any oven; when they take it off they wash the loaf with warm water, and it soon becomes firm and very white. It is likewise very wholesome and well-tasted to any except the vitiated palate of an Epicure."

While it is well ascertained that wooden mortars and pestles were in general use among the Indians[1] at the period of our first acquaintance with them, and furnished a ready method for husking and pounding their maize, it is equally certain that at some remote time mortars, pestles, and crushing implements, made of stone, were not uncommon. Dr. Dickeson and other explorers have found them in the tumuli of Alabama, Mississippi, Louisiana, and Texas. They have been taken from the mounds of South Carolina and Florida. From a single relic-bed on the right bank of the Savannah River, a few miles above Augusta, I obtained, at

[1] *See* Du Pratz' "History of Louisiana," vol. xi., p. 225. London, 1763. Loskiel's "History," etc., p. 67. London, 1794. Schoolcraft's "Archives of Aboriginal Knowledge," vol. iii., Plate 28, Fig. C.

one time, thirteen stone mortars made of flat bowlders taken from the bed of the stream and hollowed out on both sides to the depth of two or three inches. (*See* Figs. 1 and 2, Plate XVIII.) The average diameter of these shallow, basin-like excavations was rather more than nine inches. No labor had been expended in shaping the stones. The natives took them as they found them, and simply formed the cavities. Placed upon the ground or held in the lap, with the assistance of the ordinary disk-shaped crushing-stones — large numbers of which were seen in the vicinity—the green corn could have been mashed, the parched corn pounded, or the husks beaten from the ripe grains. This rude variety is frequently met with in many portions of the State. Belonging to the same class, except that it has been hollowed out only on one side, is the mortar represented in Fig. 3, Plate XVIII.

The bowl is scarely more than an inch in depth, and about five inches in diameter. By far the most symmetrical and carefully-fashioned mortar I have seen was ploughed up in a field in Liberty County, some ten miles from the sea-coast. Made of a yellow, ferruginous quartz, with a flat bottom and circular walls gradually expanding as they rose, its general shape was that of an inverted, truncated cone. Entirely artificial, the exterior was well polished. About ten inches high, eight inches in diameter at the top, and seven inches at the bottom, the interior had been excavated to the depth of nearly eight inches. At the top the walls were about three-quarters of an inch thick, and increased in thickness as they descended. No material exists in this section of the State from which such a utensil could have been manufactured. The probability is, that it was made at a considerable re-

Plate XVIII.

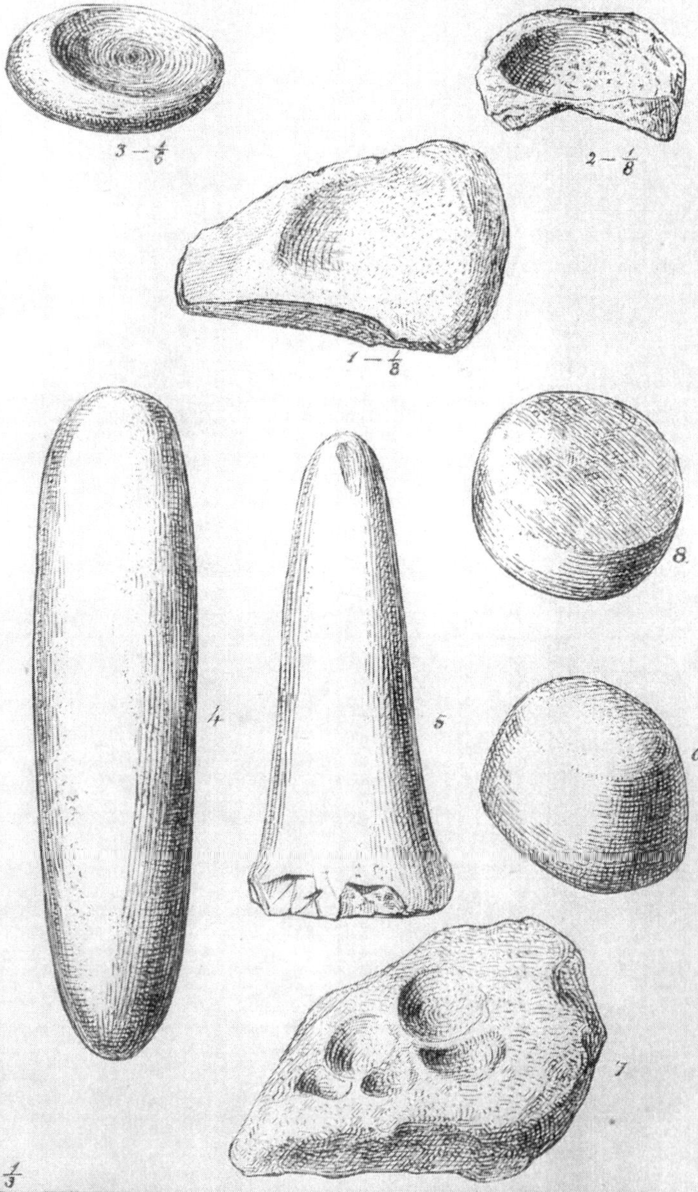

AM. PHOTO-LITHOGRAPHIC CO. N.Y. (OSBORNE'S PROCESS.)

move from the spot where it was found, and was subsequently brought to the coast by some primitive merchantman, by whom it was there exchanged for sea-shells and other articles of value native to this region. Upon its construction great time and labor must have been expended; and this relic is a remarkable illustration of the skill and patient industry of the ancient workman, who, unassisted by any metallic tools, was able from such a hard substance to fashion a mortar so serviceable and so admirable in all its proportions. A mortar not unlike in its general appearance was obtained by the Rev. George Howe, D. D., from an Indian cemetery on the bank of the Congaree River, a few miles from Columbia, South Carolina. It is figured in the plate facing page 178 of the sixth volume of Mr. Schoolcraft's "Archives of Aboriginal Knowledge." In a subsequent chapter we will observe that some of the imperforate discoidal stones clearly indicate that at some time or other they have been diverted from the original purpose for which they were manufactured, and have been treated as mortars. This secondary use entitles such to specific mention in this connection. In addition to the stone mortars described, I have seen, in the middle and upper parts of the State, large bowlders—some of them waist-high—permanent in their location, whose tops had been hollowed out for mortars. These cavities were circular in form, and capable of holding a half-peck or more. They may be regarded as public property, and afford proof of the stability of the agricultural population by which they were used. Hunter[1] alludes to the presence of wooden mortars among the tribes west of the

[1] "Manners and Customs of Several Indian Tribes located west of the Mississippi," pp. 269, 270. Philadelphia, 1823.

Mississippi, and says that, "in addition, each village has one or two large stone mortars for pounding corn; they are placed in a central situation, are public property, and are used in rotation by the different families." Mr. Bartlett counted, at El Paso, twenty-six artificial cavities in detached blocks of stone which had been hollowed out by the Indians, and served as mortars in which to pound their maize.[1] The pestles handled in connection with the wooden mortars, consisted of pieces of hard wood between three and four feet long, heavy and rounded at each end, and narrow in the middle where they were grasped.

Stone pestles—of which Figures 4 and 5, Plate XVIII., are typical representations—were both shorter and narrower, varying in length from seven to eighteen inches, and from one to three inches in diameter. Usually rounded at both ends, there are some which expand at the lower end,[2] thus affording a circular, flat crushing surface. The upper ends of others are ornamented—being sculptured after the similitude of the head of a bird, animal, or snake, and sometimes in imitation of the male organ of generation.

Figures 6 and 8, Plate XVIII., represent the customary forms of maize-crushers or triturating stones. Relics of this class are very numerous. They are generally circular in form, with two flat surfaces, or one flat and the other convex, and can be conveniently grasped and manipulated with the hand. The flat surfaces plainly indicate the use to which they were applied. Sometimes round, water-worn pebbles were employed as mealing-stones—no pains having been

[1] "Explorations," etc., vol. ii., p. 370. New York, 1854.

[2] Compare "Ancient Monuments of the Mississippi Valley," p. 220, Fig. 118. Washington, 1848.

taken to modify their natural shapes where they could be made serviceable. Diorite, quartz-rock, agate, and flint, were the favorite materials from which these pestles and maize-crushers were manufactured.

In this connection, it seems proper that we should notice a class of relics found in considerable quantities in Middle and Upper Georgia. When I first observed them upon the site of an ancient Indian village near the confluence of Great Kiokee Creek and the Savannah River, I was somewhat at a loss to comprehend their precise use. More than thirty were there seen within the space of a few acres. They consist of irregular masses of compact sandstone or soap-stone, weighing from two to ten pounds, in whose surfaces occur circular depressions from an inch to an inch and a half in diameter, and from one-quarter to three-quarters of an inch in depth. Upon the broadest and flattest sides, these depressions, from three to five in number, are located close together. (*See* Fig. 7, Plate XVIII.) To produce them the harder stones had been pecked, and the softer, gouged. Not only on one side do they appear, but frequently on both sides and often in the ends, so that the stone, when set up in the earth on any one of its faces, would always present one or more of these cup-shaped cavities, ready for use.

The Gentleman of Elvas[1] informs us that in Chiaha, "There was abundance of lard in calabashes, drawn like olive-oil, which the inhabitants said was the fat of bear. There was likewise found *much oil of walnuts*, which, like the lard, was clear and of good taste."

Biedma[2] confirms this statement, and says, "In this

[1] "Narratives of the Career of Hernando de Soto," translated by Buckingham Smith, p. 69. New York, 1866.

[2] Ibid., p. 241. New York, 1866.

province where we began to find the towns set about with fence, the *Indians get a large quantity of oil from walnuts.*" At various points reached during the progress of the expedition, walnuts were found stored in the granaries of the natives; and Cabeça de Vaca asserts that these nuts, ground with a small kind of grain, furnished subsistence for two months in the year.[1] Under the term *walnut*, the historians of the expedition probably included not only the nut which we designate by that name, but also all the varieties of the hickory-nut with which the country abounded. It is clear that in his forty-fourth chapter the Knight of Elvas confounds the pecan-nut with the walnut.[2] "Westward of the Rio Grande," says he, "the walnut differs from that which is found before coming there, being of tenderer shell, and in form like an acorn: while that behind, from the river back to the port of Espiritu Santo, is generally rather hard, the tree and the nut being in their appearance like those of Spain." Among the Indians of Louisiana so important an article of food was the walnut, that the thirteenth moon was called the *walnut moon.* It was during that month that they cracked their nuts to make bread of them by mixing them with the flour of maize.[3] Bernard Romans[4] assures us that the Florida Indians *used hickory-nuts in plenty*, making from them a milky liquor of which they were very fond, and which they ate with sweet potatoes.[5] From Bartram's Travels,[6] we extract

[1] "Relation of Alvar Nuñez Cabeça de Vaca," translated by Buckingham Smith, p. 90. New York, 1871.

[2] "Narratives of the Career of Hernando de Soto," translated by Buckingham Smith, p. 202. New York, 1866.

[3] Du Pratz' "History of Louisiana," vol. ii., p. 195. London, 1763.

[4] "A Concise Natural History of East and West Florida," etc., p. 68. New York, 1775.

[5] Page 38. London, 1792.

the following: "We then passed over large, rich savannas, or natural meadows, wide-spreading cane swamps, and frequently old Indian settlements, now deserted and overgrown with forests. These are always on or near the banks of rivers, or great swamps, the artificial mounts and terraces elevating them above the surrounding groves. I observed in the ancient cultivated fields: 1. Diospyros; 2. Gleditsia triacanthos; 3. Prunus chicasau; 4. Callicarpa; 5. Morus rubra; 6. Juglans exaltata; 7. Juglans nigra, which inform us that these trees were cultivated by the ancients on account of their fruit as being wholesome and nourishing food. Though these are natives of the forest,[1] yet they thrive better, and are more fruitful in cultivated plantations, and the fruit is in great estimation with the present generation of Indians, particularly Juglans exaltata, commonly called shell-barked hiccory. The Creeks store up the last in their towns. I have seen above an hundred bushels of these nuts belonging to one family. They pound them to pieces, and then cast them into boiling water, which, after passing through fine strainers, preserves the most oily part of the liquid; this, they call by a name which signifies hiccory milk; it is as sweet and rich as fresh cream, and is an ingredient in most of their cookery, especially homony and corn cakes." Referring to the use made of walnuts by the Virginia Indians, Hariot writes: "Besides their eating of them after our ordinarie maner, they breake them with stones, and pound them in morters with water to make a milk which they vse to put into some sorts of their spoonmeate; also among

[1] "The Chickasaw plumb, I think, must be excepted, for, though certainly a native of America, yet I never saw it wild in the forests, but always in old deserted Indian plantations: I suppose it to have been brought from the southwest beyond the Mississippi by the Chicasaws."

their sodde wheat, peaze, beanes, and pompions which maketh them haue a farre more pleasant taste."[1]

We have thus, at some length, referred to the use of nuts as an article of food among the Southern Indians, because we hence derive the meaning and employment of these cup-shaped cavities. In our judgment these relics are simply the stones upon which the Indians cracked their nuts. Their cavities are so located that one, two, three, four, five, and sometimes more nuts could be cracked at a single blow delivered by means of the circular, flat crushing-stone so common, and so often found in direct connection with the rude articles now under consideration. The cups are just large enough to hold a hickory-nut or a walnut in proper position so that, when struck, its pieces would be prevented from being widely scattered. Particularly do the soap-stones indicate the impressions left by the convex surfaces of the harder nuts. Upon some of them the depressions seem to have been caused simply by repeatedly cracking the nuts upon the same spot so that in time a concavity was produced corresponding to the half of the spherical or spheroidal nut. Such is the most natural explanation we can offer with regard to the use of these stones.

In one of the Western mounds Messrs. Squier and Davis found a block of compact sandstone, weighing between thirty and forty pounds, with several circular depressions resembling those in the work-blocks of coppersmiths in which plates of metal are hammered to give them convexity. These depressions were artificial, and possessed various diameters. It was suggested

[1] "A Briefe and True Report," etc., p. 18. Francoforti ad Mœnum. De Bry, anno 1590.

that in such moulds disks or medals of copper were formed.[1]

Colonel Charles Whittlesey, in a recent monograph,[2] alludes to the existence of hundreds of stones, in Cuyahoga Valley and throughout the northern portion of Ohio, with circular, cup-shaped cavities, sometimes on one side and again on both sides, with diameters varying from a point to an inch and a half, and half the diameter in depth, which, from the description given and from the photograph of one of them, we are inclined to regard as very similar to, if not identical with, those which have just engaged our attention. He pronounces them *spindle-socket stones.* Without a personal inspection of these relics it would not be proper to express a decided opinion; and yet, in view of the facts as they appear, we cannot resist the impression that these too are stones on which nuts were cracked by the primitive peoples who dwelt in the rich valleys of Ohio. It comports not with our present design to criticise the suggestions of Messrs. Squier and Davis, and of Colonel Whittlesey, with regard to the particular specimens which claimed their examination; nevertheless, I am free to confess, while standing upon the sites of ancient Indian villages, in Georgia, at present overshadowed by large hickory and walnut trees filled with fruit—calling to mind the recorded observations of the early travellers concurring in the statement that the red-men of this region industriously collected and hoarded these nuts, using them as a favorite article of food in connection with their corn-bread and hominy—conjecturing the method

[1] "Ancient Monuments of the Mississippi Valley," pp. 206, 207, Fig. 92. Washington, 1848.

[2] "Ancient Earth Forts of the Cuyahoga Valley, Ohio," pp. 33–35, Plate VIII. Cleveland, 1871.

in all likelihood adopted by these tribes in crushing them in order that they might conveniently avail themselves of the rich oil and sweet flavor which dwelt within the tough shells—and, upon the very spots where they had long since been abandoned, unearthing these irregularly-shaped stones with their cup-like cavities, I felt persuaded that I saw before me physical proofs of the truth of history, and discerned in the locality, in their numbers and in the peculiar conformation of these rude objects, the purpose they subserved in the olden time.

CHAPTER XIV.

Fishing.—Wears.—Nets.—Net-sinkers.—Plummets.

Before the axe of the European was lifted against the primeval trees, or that system of drainage and denudation inaugurated by which large tracts of densely-wooded lands have been gradually converted into cultivated fields and the pleasant sites of cities and villages, swamps, meadows, and forests, abounded with game of every description native to this semi-tropical region. Amid the general silence which then reigned unbroken, save by the voices of Nature and the occasional dances, festivities and war-whoops of the aborigines, there was little to terrify the wild animals at sport or pasture, scarcely any thing to affright the birds from their accustomed homes. The Indian population—limited at best and confined to chosen seats—was characterized by remarkable taciturnity. On every hand the air was vocal with the variant notes of the feathered tribe, and every brake was alive with the forms of animal life. Buffaloes, bears, deer, cougars, wild-cats, raccoons, opossums, beavers, rabbits, squirrels, and other quadrupeds, frequented the woods and congregated thickly in the moss-clad margins which environed the sluggish lagoons, undisturbed save by the noiseless yet fatal arrow of the red hunter, uninterrupted in their daily ranges except by occasional villages scattered here and there at long intervals throughout this vast domain.

The buffalo long since ceased to exist in this region. But few streams give present token of the industry of the beaver. Bears confine themselves to the vine-covered depths of unfrequented swamps. The cry of the cougar is seldom heard in the night-watches. The wolf is no longer a pest, and from whole districts the deer has been expelled. For the untamed denizens of the forest, agriculture and civilization have made no reservations. Expatriation and death have been meted out even to the hunter-tribes; and they, too, are dwellers here no longer. In that ancient time, however, there was no lack of food either in the woods or in the waters. The early narratives frequently mention presents of deer, bears, and wild-turkeys, at the hands of the Indians, and perpetuate the admiration of the Europeans as they beheld, for the first time, the pathless forests teeming with game. "The Indians never lack meat," says the Fidalgo of Elvas. "With arrows they get abundance of deer, turkeys, conies, and other wild animals, being very skilful in killing game."[1] "They are excellent Hunters," affirms Thomas Ash, "their Weapons the Bow and Arrow made of a Read pointed with sharp Stones or Fish Bones."[2] Still-hunting was the favorite style, and in plate xxv. of the "Brevis Narratio" we have a quaint picture of three Florida Indians who, concealed in the skins of stags, and with drawn bows in their hands, have crept upon

[1] "Narratives of the Career of Hernando de Soto," etc., p. 55. Translation of Buckingham Smith. New York, 1866.

[2] "Carolina," etc., by T. A., Gent., p. 35. London, 1682.

and are on the eve of discharging their barbed arrows into a herd of deer drinking at a stream.[1]

Bossu[2] thus describes the method adopted by the Alibamons in hunting the roe-deer: "An Indian takes the head of a roe-buck and dries it; he then carries it with him into the woods, where he covers his back with the skin of this animal; he puts his hand into the neck of the dried head, taking care to put little hoops under the skin to keep it firm on the hand; he then kneels down, and in that attitude, mimicking the voice of these creatures, he shews the head; the roe-deer are deceived by it and come very near the hunters, who are sure to kill them."

As the woods were well stocked with game, so also was there plenteous supply of fishes in ponds, lakes, rivers, and arms of the sea. Depending for subsistence upon wild animal, bird, and fish, the natives were compelled to devote most of their time to hunting and fishing. Certain seasons were entirely set apart to these pursuits, and with formal ceremonies and solemn invocations were the general expeditions in quest of game inaugurated. With no domesticated animal except the dog, they were not entirely improvident of the future. Public granaries[3] there were, in which were carefully stored the gathered corn and native fruits. At the appointed moons[4] the men assembled for hunting and fishing, often departing upon long journeys, and returning laden with well-dried meat and the skins of the slain.

[1] "Brevis Narratio," etc., plate xxv. Francoferti ad Mœnum. De Bry, anno 1591.

[2] "Travels through Louisiana," vol. i., p. 259. London, 1771.

[3] "Brevis Narratio," plate xxii.

[4] Generally toward the end of October. Bossu's "Travels through Louisiana," vol. i., p. 259. London, 1771.

In that remote period when rivers and bays were navigated only by light cypress canoes whose paddles scarce caused a quiver among the pliant reeds which fringed their banks, when every pond and swamp was fenced in by robust trees and penetrated by huge roots and fallen trunks affording ample protection to the finny tribe, the waters, one and all, were doubtless far more replete with animal life than they are at the present time. The appetites and the more skilful contrivances of a superior and a denser population, the destruction of forests, the drainage of natural reservoirs, and the noises of commerce, have tended materially to diminish the supply of fish. So plentiful were the fishes in the ponds and shallow puddles which were encountered along the line of De Soto's march, that they were readily killed with cudgels. The captive Indians, who, in chains, were compelled to accompany the expedition, while floundering through these lagoons, so disturbed the mud at their bottoms, that the "fish becoming stupefied, would swim to the surface, when as many were taken as were desired."[1]

Ribault says, as he ascended a goodly and great river on the Florida coast, he found its waters "boiling and roaring through the multitude of all kinds of fish."

For three or four months in the year the Indians resorted to the coast and subsisted mainly upon oysters.[2] Tribes inhabiting the interior, when in the spring the shad were running up the Savannah and other Georgia rivers, would encamp upon the bluffs, and, during the continuance of the season, devote

[1] "Narratives of the Career of Hernando de Soto," p. 121, translated by Buckingham Smith. New York, 1866.

[2] "Relation of Alvar Nuñez Cabeça de Vaca," translated by Buckingham Smith, p. 79. New York, 1871.

themselves almost exclusively to the capture of these fishes. The unios and various mussels of the fresh-water streams were eagerly collected and opened with a view to securing the pearls[1] which they contained, and for the purposes of food. Physical proofs of the habits of the natives in this regard remain to the present day. Some of the islands and headlands along the coast are dotted all over with kitchen-refuse-piles in which the shells of oysters, clams, and conchs, largely predominate. Extended artificial deposits of a similar character, composed of fresh-water shells, are still extant in many localities where the flow of the river is so interrupted by rocks or shallow places as to furnish opportunity for the facile construction of wears, or permit the eager sportsman to spear the fishes as they loitered in the eddies or concealed themselves beneath the shadows of the bowlders rising above the level of the brawling current. In these refuse-piles—the accumulation of centuries—bones of large fishes abound, and net-sinkers are not infrequent.

It is interesting to note the various methods employed by the aborigines for the capture of fish.

We have the authority of the Knight of Elvas for the statement that *fish-preserves* existed among the Southern Indians.

When De Soto entered Pacaha, he quartered himself in the town where the cacique was accustomed to reside. It was enclosed and very large. In its towers and palisade were many loop-holes. Much dry maize had been there accumulated, and the new in great quantity was growing in the adjacent fields. Near the enclosure was "a great lake, and the water entered a

[1] Garcilasso de la Vega, "Conquête de la Floride," trad. par Richelet. Leide, 1731, tome i., livre 2, chap. i., p. 296, *et seq.*

ditch that well nigh went round the town.[1] From the River Grande to the lake was a canal through which the fish came into it, and where the Chief kept them for his eating and pastime. *With nets that were found in the place* as many were taken as need required; and, however much might be the casting, there was never any lack of them. In the many other lakes about were also many fish, though the flesh was soft, and none of it so good as that which came from the river."[2]

We have here, as has already been suggested, a probable explanation of the principal purpose the reservoirs and the ditch surrounding that remarkable group of mounds near the Etowah River, on Colonel Tumlin's plantation, were designed to subserve. Through the mouth of that canal fishes could readily enter from the river. Once in, that mouth could have been closed by means of a wicker-work of cane or split wood so as to prevent their escape. Thus introduced into these artificial lakes, by a very simple contrivance they could be there detained, fed, multiplied, and kept ready for daily use. By means of nets they could be fished out as occasion required. If it be true, as we have surmised, that the large tumulus was a temple of the sun, it may be that this canal and these lakes were at great labor constructed as fish-preserves for the particular benefit of the priests who ministered and the devotees who worshipped there. Similar arrangements for pisciculture are still to be seen in other localities within the present geographical limits of Georgia.

Fishing with hook and line seems to have obtained to a very limited extent, if we may judge from the re-

[1] Biedma says the town was "situated on a plain, well fenced about, and surrounded by a water-ditch made by hand."

[2] "Narratives of the Career of Hernando de Soto," translated by Buckingham Smith, p. 112. New York, 1866.

markable absence of any thing like bone, flint, and shell hooks in the mounds and refuse-piles. Very few hooks have been found, so far as our information extends, and they were made of bone.

Fishes were often captured by means of a bright fire,[1] kindled in the canoe which was paddled by night over their feeding-grounds. Frightened, blinded, and at the same time attracted by the light, they leaped toward it, and in doing so frequently fell into the boat. This mode was particularly successful on the coast, and those who are familiar with the customs of that region will bear witness that to this day many mullets are caught in this manner by negroes carrying torches in their cypress canoes.

Of the Indians inhabiting to the south of Florida, it is said:[2] "Besides their enjoyment of the water, the natives take abundance of mullet from it, bream and other fish that breed there, as well as kinds more numerous that ascend from the sea. They come over the bar, by the mouth, in the season proper to them for casting their spawn, remaining to sport in fresh water until about summer, when the river goes down. This is the principal fishing season. Then the people of the towns, bringing great bundles of bushes, gather about the holes and pools and beat the water, when the fishes in the depths becoming intoxicated from the sap, ascend to the surface and are taken. Persons receive no harm from the poison in eating them." This method of intoxicating fishes by pound-

[1] Loskiel says: "In Carolina the Indians frequently use fire in fishing. A certain kind of fish will even leap into the boats which have fire in them."—("History of the Mission of the United Brethren," etc., p. 95. London, 1794.)

[2] "Relation of Alvar Nuñez Cabeça de Vaca," translated by Buckingham Smith, p. 181. New York, 1871.

ed horse-chestnuts and various roots was extensively adopted by the Southern tribes.[1]

A favorite and manly mode of taking fish was with the bow and arrow, and with the dart or spear. This savored of sport, and afforded ample opportunity for the display of skill. Father Hennepin pays the following compliment to the dexterity of the Southern Indians dwelling "upon the River Meschasipi." They "are very subtil and have such lively and piercing Eyes that tho' the Fishes glide very swiftly in the Waters, yet they fail not to kill them with their Darts, which they vigorously thrust a little before into the Water when they shoot out of their Bow. Moreover, they have long Poles with sharp Points which they dart from them with great Accuracy, because of their being so sharp sighted; they also kill great Sturgeons and Trouts, which are seven or eight foot under Water."[2]

Bartram[3] gives an account of the capture of a salmon-trout weighing about fifteen pounds, by a young Indian. "The Indian," says he, "struck this fish with a reed harpoon, pointed very sharp, barbed and hardened by the fire. The fish lay close under the steep bank, which the Indian discovered and struck with his reed; instantly the fish darted off with it, while the Indian pursued, without extracting the harpoon, and with repeated thrusts drowned it and then dragged it to shore."

Lawson[4] declares that the hunters of the interior were very expert in striking sturgeon and rock-fish or bass when they came up the rivers to spawn; and to

[1] *See* Adair's "History of the American Indians," p. 403. London, 1775.

[2] "A Continuation of the New Discovery," etc., p. 102. London, 1698.

[3] "Travels through North and South Carolina, Georgia," etc., p. 44. London, 1792.

[4] "History of Carolina," p. 339. Raleigh reprint, 1860.

Dr. Brickell [1]—the plagiarist—we are indebted for the ensuing mention of this particular manner of fishing as practised by the Carolina Indians: "They have *Fish-gigs* that are made of the Reeds or *Hollow Canes*; these they cut and make very sharp, with two Beards, and taper at the Point like a *Harpoon;* being thus provided, they either wade into the Water, or go into their *Canoes* and paddle about the Edges of the Rivers or Creeks, striking all the Fish they meet with in the depth of five or six Feet Water, or as far as they can see them; this they commonly do in dark, calm Nights, and whilst one attends with a Light made of the *Pitch-pine*, the other with his *Fish-gig* strikes and kills the Fish. It is diverting to see them fish after this manner, which they sometimes do in the Day; how dexterous they are in striking, is admirable, and the great Quantities they kill by this Method."

Lawson states that the "Indian boys go in the night, and one holding a lightwood torch, the other has a bow and arrows, and the fire directing him to see the fish, he shoots them with the arrows; and thus they kill a great many of the smaller fry, and sometimes, pretty large ones." [2]

In plate xiii. of the "Admiranda Narratio" six Virginia Indians are represented wading in the water and busily engaged in spearing fish. Three are discovered in plate iv., in successful pursuit of a school of fishes, while others in canoes are similarly occupied. Plate xxxvi. of the "Brevis Narratio" assures us that the Florida Indians were addicted to the same sport.

In 1805 Barker observed the Chickasaws in Duck River, pursuing, in their canoes, the large fishes which

[1] "Natural History of North Carolina," etc., p. 365. Dublin, 1737.

[2] "History of Carolina," etc., p. 341. Raleigh reprint, 1860.

swarmed in that stream, and taking great numbers of them with spears made of the long canes which grew in the river-bottoms. These spears, says the narrator, "were sixteen or eighteen feet in length, sharpened with a knife into a lancet shape at one end, and thrown with great dexterity twenty or thirty feet; seldom failing to pierce a fish through at every throw. This was doubtless an invention of great antiquity, and practised by their fathers ages before the use of iron was known amongst them."—("American Pioneer," vol. i., p. 143. Cincinnati, 1844.)

It was upon their wears, traps, set-nets, and mechanical contrivances of these sorts, however, that the natives largely depended for a constant and liberal supply of fish. Their use, in some form or other, was general. Captain Ribault informs us that the Indians of May River put as presents into his boats "sundry fishes which with mervelous speed they run to take in their packs made in the water with great reeds, so well and cunningly set together after the fashion of a Labarynthe, or Maze, with so many turns and crooks as it is impossible to do it without much consideration and industry."[1] The Carolina Indians are said to have taken the sturgeon in snares such as are used in Europe for the capture of pike. "The herrings," according to Surveyor-General Lawson, "in March and April run a great way up the rivers and fresh streams to spawn, where the savages make great wares with hedges that hinder their passage, only in the middle where an artificial pond is made to take them in so that they cannot return. This method is in use all over the fresh

[1] "The Whole and True Discoverye of Terra Florida, etc., etc., written in Frenche by Captain Ribaulde, the first that wholly discovered the same, and now newly set forth in the English, the xxx of May, 1563. Prynted at London by Rowland Hall for Thomas Hackett."

streams to catch trout and the other species of fish which those parts afford."[1]

Dr. Brickell[2] is rather more definite in his description, and advises us that these wears were constructed of "long poles or hollow canes."[3]

In plate xiii. of the "Admiranda Narratio," we find a distinct representation of one of these fish-traps, with extended wings; one of which reaches the shore, and the other far out into the water. It is made of canes or small poles firmly stuck in the mud, so as to preserve an upright position. Placed close to each other, and rising a few feet above the water-level, they are securely fastened together by parallel ropes or withes, thus forming a sort of hedge or rustic fence through which the fishes are unable to force a passage. In the middle is an opening leading into a circular enclosure. This, by a circuitous opening, communicates with a second pen, and this in like manner with a third, and that, in turn, in a similar way with a fourth—each somewhat smaller than the former.[4] Two Indians are seen in a canoe at the opening of the wear. The one in the bow with a scoop-net is dipping up the fish in the first pen, while numerous other fishes are figured making their way into the other enclosures, whence, for them, there can be little or no hope of escape. The explanatory text is as follows: "Egregiam etia habent piscandi in fluminibus rationem: cum enim ferro & chalybe careant, arundinibus aut oblongis virgis piscis cuiusdam cancro marino similis caudam concauam pro

[1] "History of Carolina," etc., p. 339. Raleigh reprint, 1860.

[2] "Natural History of North Carolina," etc., p. 366. Dublin, 1737.

[3] "Cabeça de Vaca mentions wears made of *cane*." Translation of Buckingham Smith, p. 75. New York, 1871.

[4] Here we have an explanation of what Captain Ribault calls "a Labarynthe or Maze with so many turns and crooks."

cuspide imponunt, quibus noctu vel interdiu pisces figunt, & in suas cymbas congerunt: sed aliorum piscium spinis & spiculis uti norunt. Baculis etiam seu virgultis in aquam defixis tegetes conficiunt, quas intertexentes in angustum semper contrahunt, ut ex figura apparet, nunquam apud nos conspecta est tam subtilis pisces capiendi ratio, quorum varia genera istic in fluminibus reperiuntur, nostris dis similia & boni admodum succi."

By some of the illustrations accompanying the "Brevis Narratio,"[1] we are persuaded that similar wears were constructed by the Florida Indians.

Loskiel[2] describes a particular mode of fishing which was probably adopted in some of the Georgia rivers: "When the shad fish (clupea alosa) come up the rivers, the Indians run a dam of stones across the stream, where its depth will admit of it, not in a straight line, but in two parts verging towards each other in an angle. An opening is left in the middle for the water to run off. At this opening they place a large box, the bottom of which is full of holes. They then make a rope of the twigs of the wild vine, reaching across the stream, upon which boughs of about six feet in length are fastened at the distance of about two fathoms from each other. A party is detached about a mile above the dam with this rope and its appendages, who begin to move gently down the current, some guiding one, some the opposite end, whilst others keep the branches from sinking by supporting the rope in the middle with wooden forks. Thus they proceed, frightening the fishes into the opening left in the middle of the dam, where a number of Indians are placed

[1] Plate iii.

[2] "History of the Mission of the United Brethren," etc., p. 95. London, 1794.

on each side, who, standing upon the two legs of the angles, drive the fishes with poles, and an hideous noise, through the opening into the above-mentioned box or chest. Here they lie, the water running off through the holes in the bottom, and other Indians stationed on each side of the chest, take them out, kill them and fill their canoes. By this contrivance they sometimes catch above a thousand shad and other fish in half a day."

Mr. Adair's summary[1] of the various methods adopted by the Southern Indians, and particularly the Georgia tribes, in their practice of the piscatorial art, is so interesting, minute, and appropriate, that we make no apology for repeating it *in extenso*:

"Their method of fishing may be placed among their diversions, but this is of the profitable kind. When they see large fish near the surface of the water, they fire directly upon them, sometimes only with powder, which noise and surprize, however, so stupifies them that they instantly turn up their bellies and float atop, when the fisherman secures them. If they shoot at fish not deep in the water, either with an arrow or bullet, they aim at the lower part of the belly, if they are near; and lower, in like manner, according to the distance, which seldom fails of killing. In a dry summer season, they gather horse-chesnuts and different sorts of roots, which, having pounded pretty fine, and steeped a while in a trough, they scatter this mixture over the surface of a middle-sized pond, and stir it about with poles, till the water is sufficiently impregnated with the intoxicating bittern. The fish are soon inebriated and make to the surface of the water, with their bellies uppermost. The fishers gather them

1 "History of the American Indians," pp. 402-405. London, 1765.

in baskets, and barbicue the largest, covering them carefully over at night to preserve them from the supposed putrifying influence of the moon. It seems that fish catched in this manner are not poisoned, but only stupified; for they prove very wholesome food to us, who frequently use them. By experiments, when they are speedily moved into good water, they revive in a few minutes.

"The Indians have the art of catching fish in long crails, made with canes and hiccory splinters, tapering to a point. They lay these at a fall of water, where stones are placed in two sloping lines from each bank, till they meet together in the middle of the rapid stream, where the entangled fish are soon drowned. Above such a place I have known them to fasten a wreath of long grape-vines together to reach across the river, with stones fastened at proper distances to rake the bottom: they will swim a mile with it whooping and plunging all the way, driving the fish before them into their large cane pots.[1] With this draught, which is a very heavy one, they make a town feast, or feast of love, of which every one partakes in the most social manner, and afterward they dance together, singing *Halelu-yah*, and the rest of their usual praises to the divine essence, for his bountiful gifts to the beloved people. Those Indians who are unacquainted with the use of barbed irons, are very expert in striking large fish out of their canoes, with long sharp-pointed green canes, which are well bearded, and hardened in the fire. In Savannah River I have often accompanied them in killing sturgeons with those green swamp harpoons, and which they did with much pleasure and ease; for when we discovered the fish, we soon thrust

[1] *See* also "Memoirs of Lieutenant Timberlake," p. 43. London, 1765.

into their bodies one of the harpoons. As the fish would immediately strike deep, and rush away to the bottom very rapidly, their strength was soon expended by their violent struggles against the buoyant force of the green darts: as soon as the top end of them appeared again on the surface of the water, we made up to them, renewed the attack, and in like manner continued it till we secured our game.

"They have a surprising method of fishing under the edges of rocks that stand over deep places of the river. There, they pull off their red breeches, or their long slip of Stroud cloth, and wrapping it round their arm, so as to reach to the lower part of the palm of their right hand, they dive under the rock where the large cat-fish lie to shelter themselves from the scorching beams of the sun, and to watch for prey: as soon as those fierce aquatic animals see that tempting bait, they immediately seize it with the greatest violence in order to swallow it. Then is the time for the diver to improve the favorable opportunity: he accordingly opens his hand, seizes the voracious fish by his tender parts, hath a sharp struggle with it against the crevices of the rock, and at last brings it safe ashore. Except the Choktah, all our Indians, both male and female, above the state of infancy, are in the watery element nearly equal to amphibious animals, by practice: and from the experiments necessity has forced them to, it seems as if few were endued with such strong natural abilities—very few can equal them in their wild situation of life.

"There is a favorite method among them of fishing with hand-nets. The nets are about three feet deep, and of the same diameter at the opening, made of hemp, and knotted after the usual manner of our nets.

On each side of the mouth they tie very securely a strong elastic green cane, to which the ends are fastened. Prepared with these, the warriors abreast jump in at the end of a long pond, swimming under water, with their net stretched open with both hands, and the canes in a horizontal position. In this manner they will continue either till their breath is expended by the want of respiration, or till the net is so ponderous as to force them to exonerate it ashore, or in a basket fixt in a proper place for that purpose—by removing one hand the canes instantly spring together. I have been engaged half a day at a time with the old friendly Chikkasah, and half drowned in the diversion—when any of us was so unfortunate as to catch water-snakes in our sweep, and emptied them ashore, we had the ranting voice of our friendly *posse comitatus*, whooping against us till another party was so unlucky as to meet with the like misfortune. During this exercise the women are fishing ashore with coarse baskets, to catch the fish that escape our nets. At the end of our friendly diversion, we cheerfully return home, and in an innocent and friendly manner eat together, studiously diverting each other on the incidents of the day, and make a cheerful night."

It appears that the Southern Indians were fond of crawfish as an article of food. Selecting a stream frequented by such fishes, they angled for them in the following manner: Slips of half-roasted or barbecued venison were strung, about six inches apart, upon reeds sharpened at one end. Thus baited, a great many of these reeds were stuck in the bed of the brook. Remaining near, the Indians watched these baited reeds, pulling them up at intervals, shaking into baskets the crawfish adhering to the bits of meat, and then replacing them in the water. "By this method," says Lawson, "they will in a little time catch several bushels." Blackmoor's teeth were taken in great quantities by means of oysters tied to strings. The coast Indians, carrying them into the interior, traded them away to remote tribes by whom they were held in much esteem.[1]

In addition to the modes already enumerated, it may be safely asserted that nets were also used by the natives for the capture of fish. Of their peculiar shape and construction we have no specific account. Remembering, however, the ingenuity displayed by these peoples in the fabrication of garments from the fibres of trees, mats from rushes, and ornamental coverings from feathers, it would be singular if in the silk-grass, the inner bark of the mulberry, and other natural substances of this region, they had not found convenient materials for the manufacture of substantial nets and lines. Their former existence is indicated by the presence of SINKERS and FISHING-PLUMMETS.

Of the sinkers, there are two varieties—perforated, and notched or grooved. Regarding them as a whole, we may state that they were usually made of soapstone, sometimes of slate, rarely of flint or hard stone, and occasionally of clay. All of the perforated sort that I have seen, with one exception, were formed either of soap-stone or of clay. Consisting generally of flat or rounded pieces of soapstone irregular in shape, they vary in weight from scarcely more than an ounce to a pound and upward. The perforations are from a quarter of an inch to an inch in diameter, and are indifferently located either in the centre or near the edge of the stone. Of this variety, Figs. 1, 2, 3,

[1] *See* "Lawson's History of Carolina," p. 340. Raleigh reprint, 1860. Brickell's "Natural History of North Carolina," p. 3(7. Dublin, 1737.

4, and 5, Plate XIX., may be taken as typical specimens. In this connection we would refer to an object (Fig. 6, Plate XIX.) of soap-stone, well worked in every part, which was found in a relic-bed on Price's Island, in the Savannah River, opposite Columbia County, and associated with several perforated net-sinkers of similar material. It is eight inches and a half in length, six inches and a half broad at the widest part, and about three-quarters of an inch in thickness. The perforation is three-quarters of an inch in diameter. It is suggested that this article should be classed with net-sinkers. Little labor was bestowed upon the manufacture of the notched sinkers (Figs. 7, 8, and 11, Plate XIX.), the only object being to rudely break or chip the material into convenient size, and then notch it at the opposite sides or ends so that it could be securely attached by means of a vine, a strap of deer-skin, or a thong of some kind. Such plummets are, as a rule, bulky, and were probably used to weigh down the long grape-vine ropes[1] with which the Indians were wont to drag the rivers in driving the fishes before them into their large cane traps. The noise of these stones rolling along the bottom would have materially assisted in frightening the fishes from their hiding-places and in compelling them to swim toward the desired point.

Other fishing-plummets[2] (Fig. 10, Plate XIX.) have a single groove around the middle, while others still (Fig. 9, Plate XIX.) have two or more grooves inter-

[1] *See* Adair's "History of the American Indians," p. 403. London, 1775.

[2] Prof. Rau has in his collection net-sinkers, notched and grooved, found near Muncy, on the banks of the Susquehanna River. I have seen similar ones from the shores of Rhode Island. These types are also represented in the islets and reefs of the west coast of Sweden (Nilsson's "Stone Age," p. 26, plate ii., Figs. 32, 34, 35, London, 1868), and in other localities in Europe.

Plate XIX.

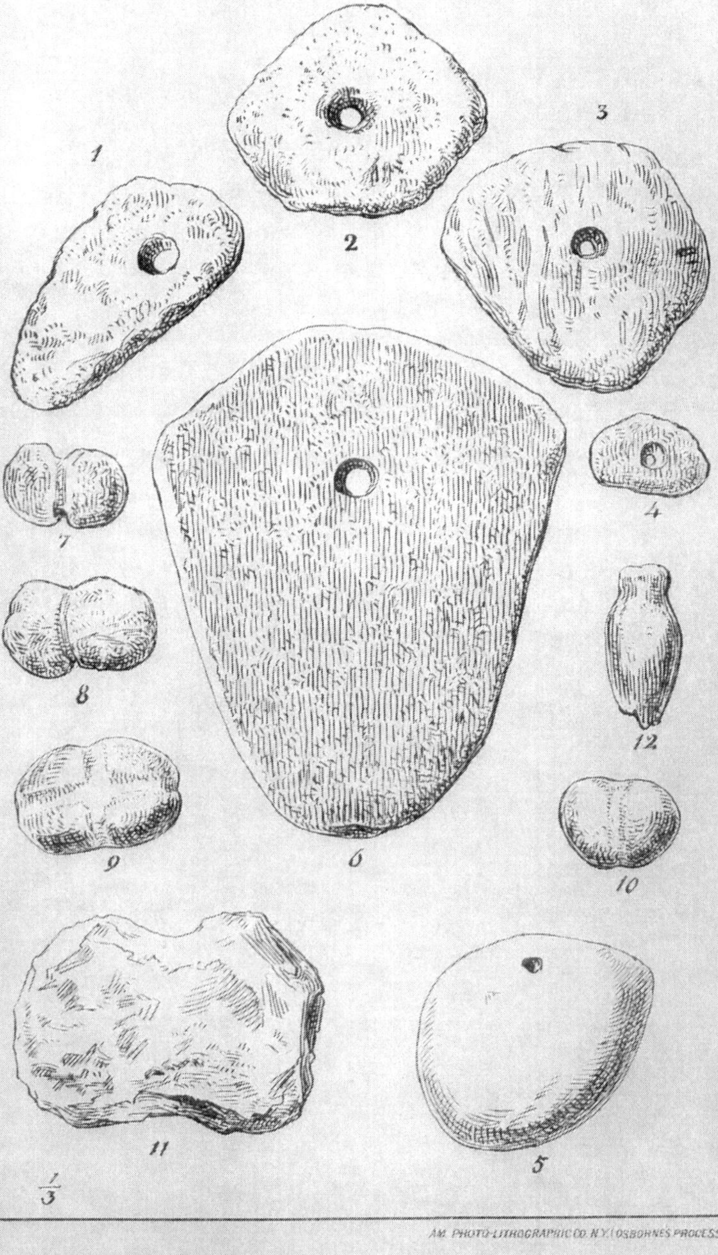

AM. PHOTO-LITHOGRAPHIC CO. N.Y. (OSBORNES PROCESS)

secting each other at right angles. These grooves are carelessly cut or pecked, and are intended to facilitate the attachment. Fig. 12, Plate XIX., illustrates a more carefully-wrought kind of plummet, which may have been employed to weight the hand-line in fishing with a hook.

These sinkers abound along the banks of the Savannah River above Augusta, and are found upon the bluffs of other streams where the Indians habitually congregated for the purpose of fishing. Near the confluence of Great Kiokee Creek and the Savannah River an extended kitchen-refuse-pile was cut in two and laid bare, some years since, by a heavy freshet. Hundreds of these perforated and notched sinkers were there unearthed, showing the great quantities manufactured and used by the natives at this point.

In his account of the fish-preserve near the village of the Cacique of Pacaha, the Gentleman of Elvas intimates that cast-nets[1] were there made and used by the natives. Cabeça de Vaca, on more than one occasion, alludes to the existence of nets, and it may be that the smaller kinds both of the perforated, and grooved or notched plummets, served as net-sinkers. It is not improbable that the Southern Indians manufactured and fished with set or gill nets, which would have proved very effective in the capture of shad. In that event these large plummets would have answered well as weights to keep the nets in proper position. In plate xiii. of the "Admiranda Narratio" two forms of nets are figured; one, the ordinary dip or scoop net, and the other, conical-shaped, its apex terminating in a long handle. The latter was made of cane or split

[1] "Narratives of the Career of Hernando de Soto," translated by Buckingham Smith, p. 112. New York, 1866.

wood—the longitudinal ribs, after leaving the handle, expanding at the bottom, where they were kept in place by means of circular and parallel cords or hoops of cane, thereby forming a stiff enclosure, open beneath, which could be thrust over a fish or crab in shallow water. Thus detained, the animal could not escape, and was subject to immediate manucaption. Nowhere, so far as our personal information goes, have either cast-nets or trolling-nets been particularly mentioned or described by the early narrators. In the present state of the inquiry, it does not become us, however, to say that such nets were not in use among the Southern Indians. The probability is that they did have some such contrivances. We would suggest, nevertheless, that the principal office of the plummets and sinkers we have been examining was either to assist in steadying and anchoring the traps, or to act as weights for set-nets; or, what is most likely, to carry to the bottom the long grape-vine ropes with which the natives dragged the streams when they wished to rout the fishes from their lurking-places and drive them into their cane labyrinths or wears.

Many of these sinkers consist simply of water-worn pebbles or irregular fragments of rock rudely notched around the centre, and sometimes longitudinally also. Little labor was expended save in the selection of stones of proper sizes, and in pecking such grooves as would permit secure attachment to the upright poles of the wears, the ends of fishing-lines, and to the short grape-vines depending from the stout mother-vine, with which the aborigines were wont to drag the rivers. Some of the heavier and rougher sort may properly be denominated anchors for wears and stationary nets, or fish-traps.

CHAPTER XV.

Discoidal Stones.—Chungke Game.

In his most interesting and valuable historical sketch of Germany, Tacitus[1] mentions the fact that the ancient Germans were so passionately addicted to a game of chance that, when all their property had been gambled away, the desperate players would hazard upon a final throw even their personal liberty.

With almost equal desperation, if we may credit Adair, did the Cherokees pursue their national game of CHUNGKE. After describing their ball-playing, he states: "The warriors have another favorite game called *Chungke*, which, with propriety of language, may be called 'Running hard labour.' They have near their state-house a square piece of ground well cleaned, and fine sand is carefully strewed over it, when requisite, to promote a swifter motion to what they throw along the surface. Only one or two on a side play at this ancient game. They have a stone about two fingers broad at the edge, and two spans round; each party has a pole of about eight feet long, smooth, and tapering at each end, the points flat. They set off

[1] "C. Cornelii Taciti Opera omnia, ad fidem editionis Orellianæ," tom. ii., p. 243. Oxonii, 1851.

abreast of each other at six yards from the end of the play-ground; then one of them hurls the stone on its edge, in as direct a line as he can, a considerable distance toward the middle of the other end of the square: when they have ran a few yards, each darts his pole anointed with bear's oil, with a proper force, as near as he can guess in proportion to the motion of the stone, that the end may lie close to the stone: when this is the case, the person counts two of the game, and, in proportion to the nearness of the poles to the mark, one is counted, unless by measuring, both are found to be at an equal distance from the stone. In this manner the players will keep running most part of the day, at half speed, under the violent heat of the sun, staking their silver ornaments, their nose-, finger-, and ear-rings; their breast-, arm-, and wrist-plates, and even all their wearing-apparel, except that which barely covers their middle. All the American Indians are much addicted to this game, which to us, appears to be a task of stupid drudgery: it seems, however, to be of early origin when their forefathers used diversions as simple as their manners. The hurling-stones they use at present were, time immemorial, rubbed smooth on the rocks, and with prodigious labour; they are kept with the strictest religious care from one generation to another, and are exempted from being buried with the dead. They belong to the town where they are used, and are carefully preserved."[1] Physical traces exist to this day, in various portions of Georgia, denoting the carefully-prepared spaces or areas dedicated in the olden time to the uses of this game. These are parallelogrammic in shape, slightly elevated, and are from sixty to ninety feet in length, and about half as wide. When Adair

[1] "History of the American Indians," etc., p. 401, *et seq.* London, 1775.

says that these "hurling-stones" were kept with the utmost religious care, from one generation to another, and were exempt from inhumation with the dead, he states a fact which was the result of his extended personal observation. His assertion, however, is not entirely correct. One of the finest discoidal stones the writer has ever seen, was taken from a mound in Cass County, near the Etowah River, about thirty feet below the upper surface of the tumulus. A similar relic lay touching it. They had both been placed on edge, and at right angles to each other. Above them was a layer of human bones in a decomposed state. From a small sepulchral mound on Pope's plantation, in the Oostenaula Valley, we obtained a discoidal stone of ferruginous quartz, almost the counterpart of those just alluded to. A little more than a year ago, a freshet in the Oconee River carried away a portion of a mound which stood upon its bank, not far from Athens, and in doing so washed out a discoidal stone of quartz, hollowed out on both sides to the depth of an inch, five inches in diameter, carefully polished and perfect in every particular. These may be exceptional cases, but they are worthy of note. In view of the special esteem in which such articles must have been held, remembering the protracted labor involved in their manufacture, and mindful of the universal fondness cherished by the natives for the game in which they were thrown, we can readily believe that these discoidal stones were carefully preserved, and, because of their great value, excused from sepulture with the general dead. If it be true, as some have asserted, that they were regarded as the common property of a town or community, we have in this circumstance additional reason for supposing that they should have escaped interment, except, perhaps, with some distinguished person or noted player of the game.

While enumerating the principal sports of the Indians of Georgia and Florida, Captain Bernard Romans[1] makes the following specific mention of the unique and absorbing game whose peculiarities are engaging our present attention: "Their favorite game of *chunké* is a plain proof of the evil consequences of a violent passion for gaming upon all kinds, classes and orders of men; at this they play from morning till night with an unwearied application, and they bet high: here you may see a savage come and bring all his skins, stake them and lose them; next his pipe, his beads, trinkets, and ornaments; at last, his blanket and other garment, and even all their arms; and, after all it is not uncommon for them to go home, borrow a gun and shoot themselves. . . . The manner of playing this game is thus: They make an alley of about two hundred feet in length, where a very smooth caly ground is laid, which when dry is very hard; they play two together, having each a streight pole of about fifteen feet long; one holds a stone, which is in shape of a truck, which he throws before him over this alley, and the instant of its departure they set off and run; in running they cast their poles after the stone; he that did not throw it endeavors to hit it, the other strives to strike the pole of his antagonist in its flight so as to prevent its hitting the stone; if the first should strike the stone, he counts one for it, and if the other by the dexterity of his cast should prevent the pole of his opponent hitting the stone, he counts one, but should both miss their aim, the throw is renewed:

[1] "A Concise Natural History of East and West Florida," etc., pp. 79, 80. New York, 1775.

and in case a score is won, the winner casts the stone and eleven is up; they hurl this stone and pole with wonderful dexterity and violence, and fatigue themselves much at it."

In describing the chunk-yards in vogue among the Creeks, Bartram expresses the opinion that they were of very ancient date, and not the work of the modern Indians. It has been supposed, and apparently with very good reason, that these areas were chiefly devoted to the practice of this favorite game; and that instead of calling them *chunk-yards*, we ought properly to denominate them *chungke-yards*.[1]

According to Du Pratz,[2] the method adopted by the Louisiana Indians in playing this game differed somewhat from that prescribed among the Indians of Georgia and Florida. "The warriors practice a diversion which is called the *game of the pole*, at which only two play together at a time. Each has a pole about eight feet long, resembling a Roman f, and the game consists in rolling a flat round stone, about three inches diameter, and an inch thick, with the edge somewhat sloping, and throwing the pole at the same time in such a manner that when the stone rests the pole may touch it or be near it. Both antagonists throw their poles at the same time, and he whose pole is nearest the stone counts one, and has the right of rolling the stone. The men fatigue themselves much at this game as they run after their poles at every throw; and, some of them are so bewitched by it that they game away one piece of furniture after another. These gamesters, however,

[1] *See* Squier's "Antiquities of the State of New York," p. 234. Buffalo, 1851. "Transactions American Ethnological Society," vol. iii., part 1, p. 34, *et seq.*

[2] "History of Louisiana," etc., p. 366. London, 1774.

are very rare and are greatly discountenanced by the rest of the people."

It would appear, from Lieutenant Timberlake's observations, that this game was also called, among some of the Cherokee tribes, *nettecawaw*, of which he gives us the following description:[1] "Each player having a pole about ten feet long, with several marks or divisions, one of them bowls a round stone, with one flat side, and the other convex, on which the players all dart their poles after it, and the nearest counts according to the vicinity of the bowl to the marks on his pole."

The Carolina Indians, as we are informed by Surveyor-General John Lawson,[2] were much addicted to a sport they called *Chenco*, "which is carried on with a staff and a bowl made of stone which they trundle upon a smooth place like a bowling green, made for that purpose." The presence of these discoidal stones in Tennessee, Alabama, Mississippi, Louisiana, Kentucky, Virginia, and elsewhere, assures us that this game of *chungke* was generally practised by all the Southern tribes. In his "Natural and Aboriginal History of Tennessee," Mr. Haywood describes several stones of this sort, and also declares that they have been found in mounds. Upon page 190 we read: "In the possession of General Cocke, of Grainger County, and in the town of Rutledge, is a circular stone found in the woods there, of three inches in diameter, resembling in colour dark yellow barber's soap. In the centre, on each side, is a small circular excavation about one inch in diameter or a little more, scooped out as far as to its circumference, extending not quite

[1] "Memoirs," etc., p. 77. London, 1765.

[2] "History of Carolina," p. 98. Raleigh reprint, 1860.

half way from the centre to the circumference of the stone itself. On both sides there is a declivity from the centre to the edge, making the extremity not more than half as thick as the stone is at the centre. It is very smoothly cut. . . .

"In the museum of a lady at Nashville is one of a similar shape; it is made of stone, very white like snow, transparent and glittering, very hard and heavy. It is about three inches in diameter, or perhaps a little less; the excavation in the centre on each side seems adapted to the thumb and finger, and at the extremity it is wider in proportion than the one before described. And, lately was taken from a mound in Maury County, a stone perfectly globular, very hard and heavy, of a variegated exterior and exceedingly well polished. It probably belonged to some employment that the other circular stones did." Again, at page 196, our historian continues: "About ten miles from Sparta, in White County, a conical mound was lately opened, and in the centre of it was found a skeleton eight feet in length. With it was found a stone of the flint kind, very hard, with two flat sides, having in the centre circular hollows exactly accommodated to the balls of the thumb and forefinger. This stone was an inch and a half in diameter—the form exactly circular. It was about one-third of an inch thick and made smooth and flat for rolling, like a grindstone, to the form of which, indeed, the whole stone was assimilated. When placed upon the floor it would roll for a considerable time without falling. The whole surface was smooth and well polished. . . . No doubt it was buried with the deceased, because for some reason he had set a great value on it in his lifetime, and had excelled in some accomplishment to which it related. The colour of the stone was a dingy white, inclining to a darkish yellow."[1]

Without multiplying these historical proofs of the presence and use of these discoidal stones among the Southern Indians, even within historic times, we proceed to consider briefly the peculiar forms of such as have been found within the present geographical limits of Georgia. It may be stated generally that they are all circular in shape, with diameters varying from one to six inches. In thickness they differ from a quarter of an inch to two inches and a quarter. Many are flat on the sides, which, as they approach the circumference, become slightly convex. Perpendicular at the edge, they are capable of standing on edge and of maintaining this upright position, with great tenacity, when rolled along the ground. Others are lenticular in shape, with oblique margins. For the manufacture of specimens of this solid type—which we presume was the common form—a hard, black, close-grained stone, capable of receiving a fine polish, formed the favorite material, especially along the coast. So nearly in outline do these frequently resemble the old-fashioned iron weights in use in country stores, that these relics are often spoken of, among the unlearned, as *Indian weights*. (*See* Figs. 1, 2, 4, 5, 7, 11, 12, 13, Plate XX.) It is probable that the smaller varieties were made for children, who, at an early age, were taught to imitate this favorite amusement of their elders. This impression is strengthened by the fact that numerous disks of pottery with the ornamentation of the vessel still upon them, are found upon the sites of old villages and at localities along the river-banks where the natives congregated from year to year to fish. It is

[1] "Natural and Aboriginal History of Tennessee," pp. 190, 196. Nashville, 1823.

Plate XX.

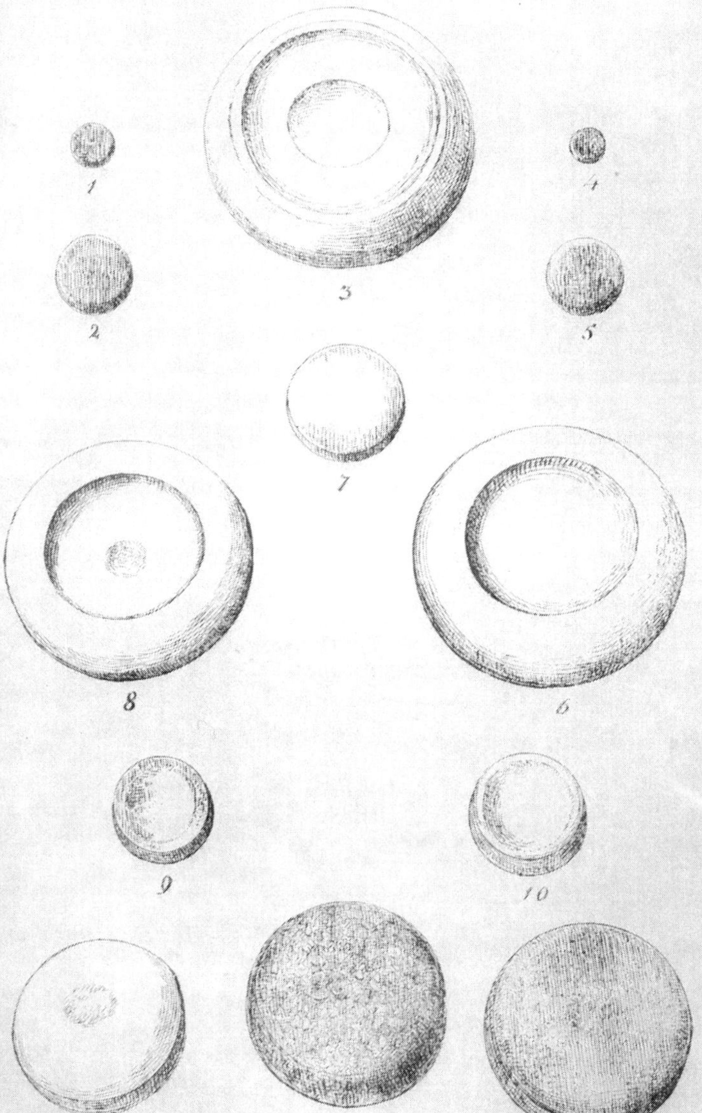

AM. PHOTO-LITHOGRAPHIC CO. N.Y. (OSBORNES PROCESS)

difficult to conjecture what uses these smaller discoidal stones and clay disks were designed to subserve except the training of the little ones in the arts and rules of this ancient and universally-esteemed game. Beautiful varieties of pudding-stone (Fig. 12, Plate XX.), greenstone (Fig. 13, Plate XX.), talcose slate, soapstone, flint, and even agate (Fig. 7, Plate XX.), were employed in the manufacture of discoidal stones of the solid type. The regularity of outline and the degree of polish are remarkable.

The first modification of this customary shape is seen in those discoidal stones whose sides are slightly concave or convex. In some instances one side appears convex, and the other concave. (Figs. 9 and 10, Plate XX.) We turn now to the more elaborate forms of these discoidal stones, three of which are represented in the accompanying plate. They are all made of ferruginous quartz, and are well polished. The first specimen (Fig. 6, Plate XX.) is evenly hollowed out on both sides to the depth of an inch and a quarter in the centre. The cavities are circular, and four inches in diameter. From the edge of each cavity toward the outer circumference, the stone is bevelled, so that the edge of the disk is just an inch in width. This discoidal stone is five inches and three-quarters in diameter, and two inches and a half in thickness at the point where the cavities begin.

The second (Fig. 3, Plate XX.), which was taken from a mound in Bullock County, is somewhat larger than the first, being exactly six inches in diameter, and a little more than two inches and a quarter thick. It has four cavities, two on each side, precisely similar, and one within the other. The diameters of the larger cavities are each four inches and a half; of the smaller, two inches and a quarter. The depth of the outer cavities is five-eighths of an inch; of the inner, three-eighths of an inch. As in the first specimen, the sides are here also bevelled toward the edge, which is rather more than three quarters of an inch in width. Between the outer circle of the concavity and the point where the bevelling commences, occurs a rim a quarter of an inch in thickness. The third specimen (Fig. 8, Plate XX.), which may justly be regarded as a wonderful illustration of the skill and protracted labor of the primitive artist working without rule or compass and unaided by a single metallic tool, was found, as we have already stated, at the bottom of a large sepulchral mound, thirty feet high, in Cass County. It is absolutely symmetrical in all its parts, being five inches and three-quarters in diameter, and one inch and seven-eighths in thickness. The cavities—which are precisely similar on both sides—are three inches and a half in diameter, and three-quarters of an inch deep. In the centre of these cavities is a slight depression an inch in diameter. The edge is slightly convex, and about an inch wide. The distance from the outer circle of the concavity to the point where the bevelling ceases toward the circumference, is a little more than an inch. The entire stone is beautifully polished. The regularity with which these relics are fashioned, challenges our admiration. Upon some of them, the workman of the present day, with all his modern implements and mechanical skill, could not improve. Adair tells us that these hurling-stones were, from "time immemorial rubbed smooth on the rocks, and with prodigious labour,"[1] and Lafitau says that a North American Indian sometimes spent his life in making a

[1] "History of the American Indians," etc., p. 402. London, 1775.

stone tomahawk, and that without finishing it.[1] Festination proceeds from the devil, is an aphorism with which the Indians offered quarrel neither in theory nor in practice. With them, time was of no consequence. It entered not as an element into their daily calculations. Consecutive labor formed no part of their ordinary occupations. Consequently, the matter on hand was readily postponed in favor of sleep, amusement, or mere idleness. We may well believe, therefore, that these discoidal stones, so carefully formed of such hard material as quartz and even agate, and fashioned into their present symmetrical shapes simply by means of attrition with other stones, and perhaps, in some measure, through the agency of large wooden drills assisted by sharp sand and water, should, in their construction, have occupied weeks, months, and even years of tedious, although desultory labor.

The general distribution of these stones shows that the game, for which they were manufactured, was in common esteem among the various Georgia tribes. Most of them are imperforate, although some have come under the writer's observation which are so thoroughly perforated that they are little more than rings of stone. In a few instances, the discoidal stones with marked cavities seem to have been put to a secondary use, and treated as mortars in which hard substances were triturated. For pulverizing clay, and perhaps some mineral substances serviceable for paint, they would have answered well. If our conjecture as to the primary use of these stones be correct, it will readily be perceived that in bowling them the outer edge only would come in contact with the surface of

[1] "Mœurs des Sauvages Amériquains," tome ii., p. 110. Paris, 1724.

the ground. The constant pressure of the thumb against the centre on one side, and of the fingers against the middle of the other side (the forefinger adapting itself to the curve of the periphery), would have exerted a decided tendency to keep the interior of the cavities smooth.

When, therefore, we perceive in the bottoms of these saucer-shaped cavities unmistakable traces of abrasion, we are persuaded that such discoidal stones have been diverted from the use they were orginally designed to subserve. Such instances are, however, rare; and, in all likelihood, afford evidence not only of desuetude, but also of perversion, at the hands of modern Indians. Occasionally we have observed a solid or lenticular-shaped stone which gave indications of its having been employed at some later period as a grinding or mealing stone.

Although it has been suggested that a similar game was practised among the ancient inhabitants of Cornwall, and perhaps at Nidau-Steinberg and Ebersberg,[1] this Chungke game, by what name soever called and however variant the rules which governed its details, was essentially an American amusement, commanding almost universal favor at the hands of the North American tribes.

In the plains and upon the mountains of Chili may be seen numbers of flat circular stones, five or six inches in diameter, made either of granite or porphyry, and with a hole drilled through their middle. While Molina supposes them to have been the clubs or maces of the ancient Chilians, it is not impossible that some of them may have been used as gaming-stones.[2] We have

[1] Keller's "Lake Dwellings," etc., pp. 135, 136. London, 1866. Plates xxxviii. and lxxxix.

[2] Stevens' "Flint Chips," p. 505. London, 1870.

seen how generally distributed these relics are through the Southern States. Several varieties, obtained by the Rev. Dr. George Howe just after a freshet in the Congaree River, which, overflowing its banks, laid bare an ancient Indian burial-ground not far from the city of Columbia, in the State of South Carolina, are represented in the plate which faces page 178 of the sixth volume of Schoolcraft's "Archives of Aboriginal Knowledge."[1] Mr. Schoolcraft[2] states that "the numerous discoidal stones that are found in the tumuli and at the sites of ancient occupancy in the Mississippi Valley, serve to denote that this amusement was practised among the earlier tribes of that valley at the mound period. These antique quoits are made with great labor and skill from very hard and heavy pieces of stone. They are generally exact disks, of a concave surface, with an orifice in the centre, and a broad rim." He expresses the opinion that the object of hurling these perforated specimens was "manifestly to cover an upright pin or peg driven into the ground." This, with all due respect, we question. The weight of authority inclines us to the belief that these stones were rolled, not pitched.

Messrs. Squier and Davis found these disks in the mounds of the West; and, in their "Ancient Monuments of the Mississippi Valley," have made us familiar with their characteristic types.[3] They are related, say they, to a very numerous class of relics scattered over the surface from the valley of the Ohio to Peru, composed of granite, porphyry, greenstone, jasper, quartz,

[1] Philadelphia, 1860.

[2] "Archives of Aboriginal Knowledge," etc., vol. i., p. 87, plate 23. Philadelphia, 1860.

[3] "Smithsonian Contributions to Knowledge," vol. i., p. 221, *et seq.*, Fig. 121. Washington, 1848.

etc. Although the opinion of these gentlemen is entitled to the highest consideration, in the light of subsequent investigations we feel constrained to differ from them when they advance the idea that discoidal stones are "of comparatively modern origin." They are old, very ancient, if we understand the record of the mounds in which they have been found, and rightly interpret the antiquity of the relics with which some of them are associated. The game, of which they are the symbols—conceived in a distant past and maintained through the intermediate centuries—was still popular within historic times. To the accounts already given, it may prove interesting to add a few other notices:

"The Rev. J. B. Finley (distinguished for his zealous efforts in Christianizing the Indian tribes of Ohio)," say Messrs. Squier and Davis,[1] "states that among the tribes with which he was acquainted, stones identical with those above described, were much used in a popular game resembling the modern game of 'ten pins.' The form of the stones suggests the manner in which they were held and thrown, or rather rolled. The concave sides received the thumb and second finger, the forefinger clasping the periphery."

Mr. Breckenridge[2] mentions a game popular among the Riccarees which was played with a ring of stone; and Lewis and Clarke assert that a similar amusement was indulged in by the Mandans. The javelin-game among the Pawnees was probably but a modification of this ancient sport.[3]

To the Abbé Em Domenech[4] we are indebted for

[1] "Smithsonian Contributions to Knowledge," vol. i., p. 223, note.

[2] "Views of Louisiana," p. 256, quoted by Squier and Davis.

[3] "Travels in North America," Hon. C. A. Murray, vol. i., p. 321. Morgan's League of the Iroquois, pp. 299–302.

[4] "Seven Years' Residence in the Great Deserts of North America," vol. ii. . 197. London, 1860.

the following: "Their game of Spear and Ring is extremely curious and difficult. The players are divided into two camps, for Indians are fond of collective parties in which are many conquerors, and consequently many conquered. The stakes and bets are deposited in the care of an old man; then a hard smooth ground, without vegetation of any kind, is chosen, in the middle of which is placed perpendicularly a stone ring of about three inches diameter. When all is prepared, the players (armed with spears six or seven feet long, furnished with small shields a little apart from each other, sometimes with bits of leather) rush forward, two at a time, one from each camp; they stoop so as to place their spears on a horizontal level with the ring, so that they may pass through it—the great test of skill being to succeed without upsetting it. Each small shield or bit of leather that passes through, counts for a point: the victory remains to the player who has most points, or he who upsets the ring at the last hit.

"Some Indians render the game still more difficult by playing it as follows: One of the players takes the ring in his hand and sends it rolling, with all his strength, as far as possible on the prepared ground; his adversary who is by his side, starts full speed after it to stop it, so as to string it on his spear as far as the last little shield.

"The Mojaves had a game so similar to the above that to avoid repetition it need only be mentioned. The Natchez favorite pastime was very like the spear game, except that it required more strength and address. Only two men could play at a time. One threw with all his strength, and as far as possible, a long stick of the shape of a bat, and before it came to the ground, rolled a huge circular stone in the same direction. His adversary then threw a stick like the first, and he whose bat came nearest the stone gained a point and the right to launch the stone in his turn: which was a great advantage, as from the impulse he gave it a player was able to guess about how far the stone would roll."

Speaking of the Mandans, Catlin[1] says: "The games and amusements of these people are in most respects like those of the other tribes, consisting of ball plays—game of the moccasin, of the platter—feats of archery—horse-racing, etc.; and they have yet another, which may be said to be their favorite amusement, and unknown to the other tribes about them—the game of Tchung-kee, a beautiful athletic exercise, which they seem to be almost unceasingly practising whilst the weather is fair, and they have nothing else of moment to demand their attention. This game is decidedly their favorite amusement, and is played near to the village on a pavement of clay, which has been used for that purpose until it has become as smooth and hard as a floor. For this game two champions form their respective parties by choosing alternately the most famous players until their requisite numbers are made up. Their bettings are then made, and their stakes are held by some of the chiefs or others present. The play commences (plate 59) with two (one from each party), who start off upon a trot, abreast of each other, and one of them rolls in advance of them, on the pavement, a little ring of two or three inches in diameter, cut out of stone; and each one follows it up with his 'tchung-kee' (a stick of six feet in length,

[1] "Illustrations of the Manners, Customs, and Conditions of the North American Indians," etc., seventh edition, vol. i., p. 132. London, 1848.

with little bits of leather projecting from its sides of an inch or more in length), which he throws before him as he runs, sliding it along upon the ground after the ring, endeavoring to place it in such a position when it stops, that the ring may fall upon it, and receive one of the little projections of leather through it, which counts for game one, or two, or four, according to the position of the leather on which the ring is lodged. The last winner always has the rolling of the ring, and both start and throw the tchung-kee together; if either fails to receive the ring or to lie in a certain position, it is a forfeiture of the amount of the number he was nearest to, and he loses his throw; when another steps into his place. This game is a very difficult one to describe, so as to give an exact idea of it, unless one can see it played—it is a game of great beauty and fine bodily exercise, and these people become excessively fascinated with it; often gambling away every thing they possess, and even sometimes, when every thing else was gone, have been known to stake their liberty upon the issue of these games, offering themselves as slaves to their opponents in case they get beaten."

No longer is this ancient game played either in Georgia or within the limits of conterminous States. Like the exercise of the discus in the heroic age, it has now become only a tradition—a shadowy memory from a nebulous past. The carefully-prepared areas over which, from morning until night, the red athletes rushed hither and thither in the enthusiastic pursuit of this sport, at the expense of time and property and personal liberty, are entirely deserted now and rugged with the trunks and roots of huge forest-trees. The anointed poles and the swift hands which launched them, have alike crumbled into nothingness. Winners and losers, forgetting their profits and losses, the exultations and the disappointments of this exciting amusement, are themselves forgotten, and but little remains to remind us of the former existence and prevalence of this great game, characterized by singular dexterity, severe exercise and desperate ventures, save these discoidal stones, often so remarkable for their symmetry, and so expressive of the skill and labor expended in their manufacture.

Plate XXI.

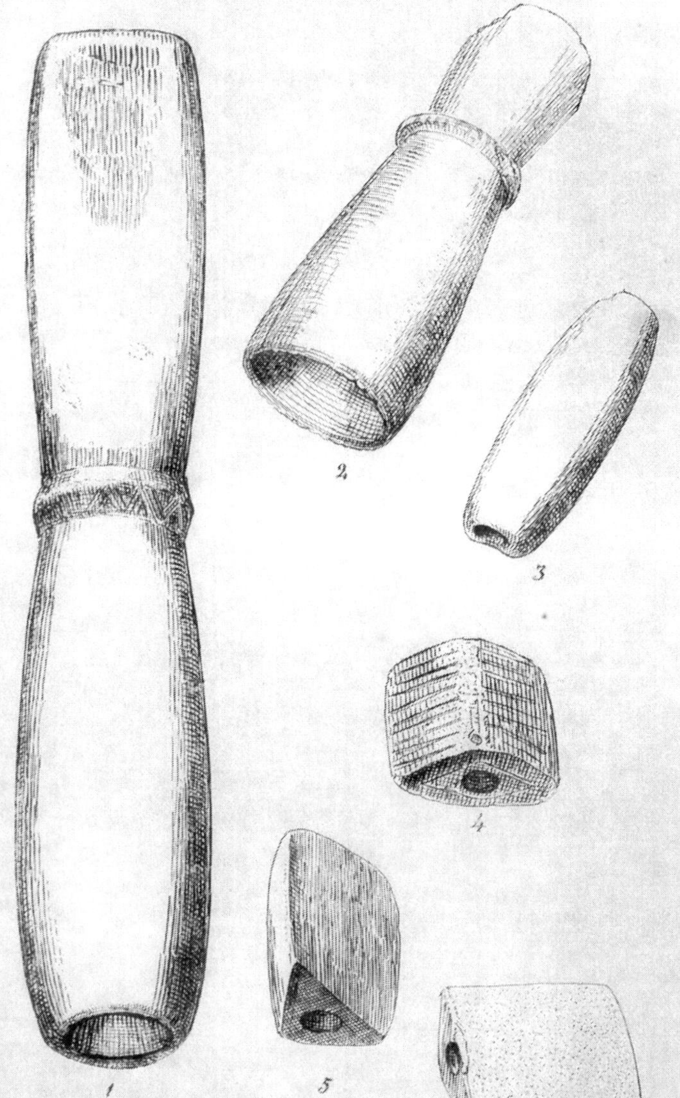

AM. PHOTO-LITHOGRAPHIC CO. N.Y. (OSBORNES PROCESS.)

CHAPTER XVI.

Stone Tubes.

The tube, of which Fig. 1, Plate XXI., is a clever representation, was found in a small burial-mound in Burke County. It is made of serpentine, is thirteen inches and a quarter in length, and weighs three pounds and a half avoirdupois. The bore at one end is circular, and an inch and three-eighths in diameter. At the other end the commencement of the aperture is elliptical in shape, the length of the major axis being an inch and three-eighths, and that of the minor one inch. At this end the exterior surface has been correspondingly flattened. The walls of the tube are about three-eighths of an inch in thickness. The perforation or bore extends longitudinally through the implement, but with diameters gradually diminishing from either end, until, at the point where they meet in the centre, the opening, which is there circular, is less than a quarter of an inch in diameter. In this tube the hollow has been compassed not by drilling but by gouging out or removing the interior particles of stone by means of some sharp-pointed instrument. Longitudinal scars, caused by the operation, are still discernible on the inner surface. No circular striæ can be perceived. The elevated ring around the central portion is rudely ornamented with zigzag lines. With this exception the exterior surface is smooth, entirely plain, and well polished.

Similar tubes of steatite (Fig. 2, Plate XXI.), soapstone, and mica slate, have been found in other localities—all, however, smaller than the specimen we have just examined. Seven inches would express the average length of such as have passed under the writer's observation. The bores of some of them are, at each end, of like diameter—say an inch and three-quarters—gradually lessening as they approach the centre, where the width of the aperture does not materially vary from a quarter of an inch. The walls are sometimes less than a quarter of an inch in thickness. Upon the ornamentation of the ends and exterior surface of these tubes, in some instances, considerable pains have been bestowed. Stone tubes not precisely similar in character, but bearing a general resemblance, have been described and figured by Mr. Schoolcraft,[1] Messrs. Squier and Davis,[2] and others. An implement very like in its conformation is thus noticed by Mr. Haywood:[3] "About eighteen miles east from Rogersville in the county of Hawkins, in East Tennessee, was ploughed up a stone trumpet. It tapers on the outside from either end to the middle, and is there surrounded by two rings of raised stone. The inside, at each end, is a hollow of an inch and a quarter in diameter; but at one end the orifice is not as large as at the other. Probably the sound is shrill and sharp when blown from one end, and more full and sonorous when

[1] "Transactions of the American Ethnological Society," vol. i., p. 406.
[2] "Ancient Monuments of the Mississippi Valley," pp. 224–227.
[3] "Natural and Aboriginal History of Tennessee," p. 210. Nashville, 1823.

blown from the other. The hollow continues throughout from the one end to the other, but in the middle, under the rings, it is not as wide as at the ends. It seems to have been made of hard soapstone; and, when blown through, makes a sound which may be heard perhaps two miles. It is very smooth on the outside, but rough within."

By some, Mr. Schoolcraft among the number, it has been suggested that these tubes were telescopic devices; and, in their construction, he pretends to trace an analogy to the tubular chambers used by the Aztec and Maya races in their astronomical observations. This notion we regard as fanciful; nor do we sympathize in the belief of those who pronounce them musical instruments. In vain have we endeavored to evoke a single sound beyond a dull, dead blast; and that incapable of transmitting itself to any practicable distance.

We know that the Southern tribes were fond of music and dancing, and that their music was both vocal and instrumental. Aside, however, from their drums, tambours, rattle-gourds, and flutes made of the joint of a reed, or of the deer's tibia, they possessed no musical instruments worth the mention.[1] So far as present recollection serves us, nowhere do we read of the use of stone trumpets, or any thing of the sort. It is entirely improbable that the Indians would have expended so much labor to such little purpose when the joint of a swamp-cane, or a large conch, would have so readily, and so much better answered the desired object. We incline to the opinion that these were medicine or cupping-tubes.

[1] *See* Bartram's "Travels through North and South Carolina, Georgia," etc., p. 502. London, 1792.

Coreal[1] mentions that when the Florida Indians "are sick, they have not their veins opened, as is done elsewhere; but they call for the *Jaoünas* who are their priests and physicians. These suck that part of the body which causes the patient most pain; and they do it either with the mouth or with a kind of shepherd's-flute (*chalumeau*), having first made a small incision near some vein."

Cabeça de Vaca[2] alludes to similar treatment of the sick: "The practitioner scarifies over the seat of pain, and then sucks about the wound. They make cauteries with fire, a remedy among them in high repute, which I have tried on myself and found benefit from it. They afterward blow on the spot, and having finished, the patient considers that he is relieved." Ribas, a century afterward, furnishes an account of this curative process: "The method of cure the possessed practitioners have, is sucking the part that aches; if it be injured, blowing on it: which, for the effort and force, may be heard many steps off. . . . They give the sick to understand that the causes of their illness are the sticks, thorns and pebbles in their bodies, which they take out. This is false. They have the things in the mouth, or held craftily in the hand, and afterwards exhibit them as our tooth-pullers do teeth, on a string, as evidences of their professional skill."[3] After enumerating the cures by burning, smoking, scarifying, and sweating, Beverly states that the Virginia Indians sometimes made use of reeds for cauter-

[1] "Voyages aux Indes Occidentales," tome i., p. 39. Amsterdam, 1722. Coreal visited Florida in 1669.

[2] "Relation of Alvar Nuñez Cabeça de Vaca," translated by Buckingham Smith, p. 81. New York, 1871.

[3] Ibid., p. 82, note. New York, 1871.

izing, which they heated over the fire until they were on the eve of ignition, and then applied, upon a piece of thin wet leather, to the part affected.[1]

In his account of the aboriginal inhabitants of the Californian Peninsula, the German Jesuit missionary Jacob Baegert, commenting upon the state of the medical art as it existed among the Indians of that region during the second half of the last century, writes: "There are many impostors among them pretending to possess the power of curing diseases, and the ignorant Indians have so much faith in their art that they send for one or more of these scoundrels whenever they are indisposed. In treating a sick person, these jugglers employ a small tube which they use for sucking or blowing the patient for a while, making also various grimaces, and muttering something which they do not understand themselves, until, finally, after much hard breathing and panting, they show the patient a flint, or some other object previously hidden about their persons, pretending to have at last removed the real cause of the disorder."[2]

Venegas[3] confirms the observation of Baegert with regard to the use of stone tubes by the medicine-men of the California Indians: "One mode was very remarkable, and the good effect it sometimes produced heightened the reputation of the physician. They applied to the suffering part of the patient's body the *chacuaco*, or a tube formed out of a very hard black stone; and through this they sometimes sucked, and other times blew, but both as hard as they were able,

[1] "History and Present State of Virginia," book iii., chap. ix., p. 49. London, 1705.

[2] Prof. Rau's "translation," etc. Annual Report of the Smithsonian Institution for 1864, p. 386.

[3] "Natural and Civil History of California," vol. i., p. 97. London, 1759.

supposing that thus the disease was either exhaled or dispersed. Sometimes the tube was filled with *cimarron* or wild tobacco lighted, and here they either sucked in or blew down the smoke, according to the physician's direction; and this powerful caustick sometimes, without any other remedy, has been known entirely to remove the disorder."

These authorities confirm our impression that tubes—like those we have been considering—were medicinal in their uses, and materially assisted the primitive physician—at once quack and conjurer—in performing his wonderful cures. The flattened end appears adapted to the lips. This, and the small hole in the centre of the bore, facilitated both the blowing and the sucking process. By the circular opening at the larger end, the seat of pain could have been conveniently covered. The weight of the instrument enhanced its efficiency, and rendered more facile its preservation in the desired position. While under treatment, Indian patients were compelled to assume more than a recumbent position. They were obliged to lie flat down, now on the back, and again on the stomach. If we go one step farther and suppose the cavity next to the flattened end filled with punk, dried tobacco-leaves, or some combustible material, the other end of the tube being firmly applied to the part affected, which had been previously scarified, we will perceive, when the contained substance was ignited, how readily this tube would have answered the purposes either of cauterization or cupping. In the one case the particles of burning matter dropping through the central opening would have blistered and burnt the diseased spot; while in the other, the active fire kindled in the upper portion of the tube—the ashes by a simple contrivance being prevented from falling through the narrow portion of the bore below—would have created and maintained during its existence a vacuum in the lower part of the tube, thus causing the blood to flow freely from the incisions made in the flesh.

Other tubes (Figs. 3, 4, 5, and 6, Platé XXI.) occur, which, apparently, were used as ornaments. These vary in length from two to three inches and a half, and in general conformation resemble triangular prisms, with convex sides, and angles slightly rounded. Steatite, talcose slate, and soapstone, were the customary materials employed in their construction. Perforated longitudinally, the average diameter of their bores may be stated at from three-eighths to one-half of an inch. Numbers of such relics have been found along the banks of the Savannah River above Augusta, and in other portions of the State. The exterior surface is not infrequently ornamented with incised lines, curved, straight, and zigzag. Ordinarily, the holes were drilled, the circular striæ being clearly defined, and the bore of equal diameter throughout the entire length of the article. Our impression is that they were worn as ornaments. In Fig. 125, of the "Ancient Monuments of the Mississippi Valley,"[1] are represented two varieties of stone tubes of this class.

[1] Page 227.

CHAPTER XVII.

Stones for rounding Arrow-shafts.—Whetstones or Sharpeners.—Pierced Tablets.—Pendants.—Slung-stones.—Amulets.—Stone Plate.—Mica Mirrors.—Sculptured Rocks.

At a large hunting-camp, which had been abandoned by the Indians, Captain Romans[1] noticed "some stones deeply marked by the savages with some uncouth marks, but most of them straight lines and crossed." He conjectured that they had been used for grinding awls. The only means the natives possessed of restoring an edge to their worn and blunted axes and other stone implements was, by rubbing them against whetstones. Hence we frequently meet with irregularly-shaped stones, grooved and scarred by this process. It will be remembered that the hard canes of the Southern swamps supplied the red hunters of this region with convenient and abundant store of arrows. The material was most suitable for this purpose, combining, as it did, requisite size, durability and lightness. No labor was necessary in shaping the arrow, save such as was expended in removing the exterior sheath, in smoothing the joints, in straightening and in cutting the reed off at the desired length.

[1] "Concise Natural History of East and West Florida," p. 327. New York, 1775.

Plate XXII

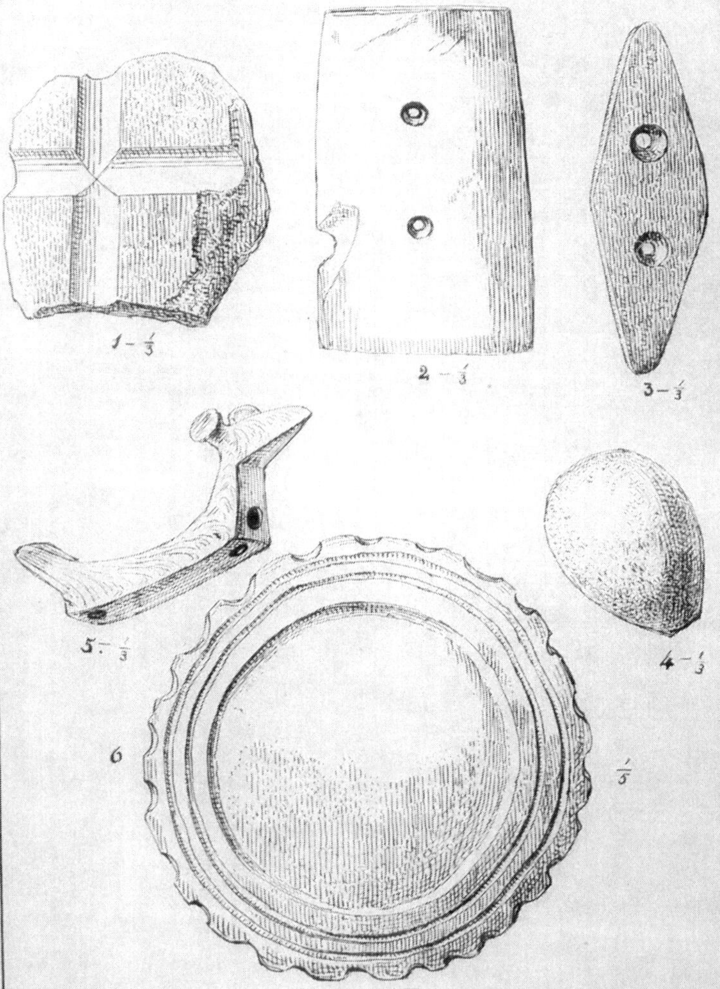

AM. PHOTO-LITHOGRAPHIC CO. N.Y. (OSBORNE'S PROCESS)

When the green cane was subjected to a certain degree of heat, its natural moisture was readily expelled, and the reed easily freed from any irregularities. If made, while heated, to assume a direct line, it would not deviate therefrom when cold and dry. In order to facilitate this straightening and polishing of the arrow, it was, while hot, passed through grooves made in sandstone or in some other coarse-grained stone. These grooves are generally carefully made in direct lines, are even in their diameters, and frequently intersect each other at right angles, thereby presenting the appearance of crosses. An example is represented in Fig. 1, Plate XXII.

It will be perceived that the heated cane arrow, when pressed and rubbed in these grooves, would not only be freed from all irregularity of surface, but would also be compelled to assume a direct line. Such a contrivance equally facilitated the manufacture and polishing of wooden arrows—the rough surface of the stone acting as a file in reducing the shaft to the desired size and roundness. These STONES FOR ROUNDING ARROW-SHAFTS are readily distinguished from the ordinary WHETSTONES, so generally employed for sharpening the edges of axes and other cutting implements. (Fig. 7, Plate XXII.)

PIERCED TABLETS.—Various as the fancies of the makers are the shapes of these relics.

The illustrations prepared by Messrs. Squier and Davis of the "gorgets" of the Mississippi Valley [1] aptly represent most of those generally found in the mounds, relic-beds, and fields of Georgia and her sister States. Many of them were made of a beautiful slate, with

[1] "Ancient Monuments of the Mississippi Valley," pp. 236, 237. Washington, D. C., 1848.

from two to five perforations, and are so thin and delicately constructed that they could have served only the purposes of ornament. Pierced tablets of this class are lozenge-shaped, oval, parallelogrammic, or fashioned after the similitude of the lid of a coffin. Others, again, are cruciform and star-shaped. In fine, their forms are varied, and in many instances quite fanciful. Many possess only a single perforation in the upper end or near the middle. Most, however, have two holes drilled about an inch apart and through the central portion. They vary in length from three to eight inches, in width from three-quarters of an inch to three inches, and in thickness from the sixteenth to a quarter of an inch. The edges are frequently ornamented with notches, and the broad surfaces are sometimes covered with incised lines. In all instances of this ornamental class it will be observed that the perforations are uniform, generally varying from the eighth to a quarter of an inch in diameter. Objects of this fragile description were, we think, intended as ornaments, and were suspended from the neck or fastened to some conspicuous part of the vestment.

There is another variety, however, so much more substantial in its character that it seems to have been designed for practical use. Relics of this class are made of serpentine, of greenstone, and of hard slate. Even jasper has been employed in their manufacture. They are thick and durable. It is not uncommon to meet with one of them fully an inch in thickness, although most of them do not attain that dimension by a half. They contain in most instances only two perforations, located in the central part of the implement, and about an inch or an inch and a quarter distant from each other. These perforations—unlike those observed in the case of the ornamental pierced tablets—are conical in form. The drilling is never done from both sides, but only from that side where the aperture is largest. The shape of the perforation is evidently not accidental, because a uniformity exists. The aperture on one side is about twice as wide as it is on the other. Such is the general rule in the case of the thicker "gorgets," and hence it has been suggested that implements of this class were employed by the Indians in the manufacture of their bow-strings. The material used for this purpose, it is believed, could be readily pressed through the wider opening and then drawn so as to make it conform to an even size. Several thongs thus passed through the two or three apertures in the same gorget, when drawn to the required length, all being of the same size, could conveniently have been twisted into one common, strong cord. Of this variety we figure two typical specimens (Figs. 2 and 3, Plate XXII.).

In response to a letter from Prof. Charles Rau, Mr. Catlin writes: "With regard to the tablets of which you speak, I have seen several, but the holes were much larger than those you describe. Those which I have seen were used by the Indians for grooving the shafts of their arrows. All arrows of the primitive Indians are found with three grooves extending from the arrow's shoulder at the fluke, to the feathers, and conducting the air between them so as to give them steadiness. These grooves, on close examination, are found to be indented by pressure, and not in any way cut out; and this pressure is produced, while forcing the arrow softened by steam through a hole in the tablet, with the incisor of a bear set firmly in a handle and projecting over the rim of the hole, as the arrow-

24

shaft is forced downward through the tablet, getting compactness and on the surface and in the groove a smoothness which no cutting, filing, or scraping can produce. It would be useless to pass the bowstring through the tablet, for the evenness and the hardness of the strings are produced much more easily and effectually by rolling them, as they do, between two flat stones whilst saturated with heated glue."

It thus appears that this extensive and venerable observer discountenances the idea that these perforated tablets were employed in the manufacture of bow-strings, thongs, and cords. Since, through the kindness of Prof. Rau, we have been made acquainted with these remarks of Mr. Catlin, we have carefully examined the tablets in our possession and have failed to note any impression produced upon the edges of the perforations by the pressure of any thing like the incisor of a bear. Remembering the rather soft material from which many of these tablets were made, we might reasonably anticipate the presence of some abrasion in the perforations if they were subjected to a constant use such as has been suggested.

PENDANTS.—The typical forms indicated by Messrs. Squier and Davis in the "Ancient Monuments of the Mississippi Valley,"[1] have their counterparts among the relics of the Southern Indians. The pear-shaped pendant, with groove around the upper end, is by no means infrequent. Brown hematite, greenstone, quartz, and a variegated jasper, were the materials selected for its manufacture. Of this variety some are so delicate, so beautiful, and so carefully polished, that they seem to have been designed for nose and ear ornaments.[2]

[1] Page 235.

[2] Adair ("History of the American Indians," pp. 170, 171. London, 1775) alludes to the use of coarse diamonds and bits of stone fastened with deer's sinew

Most of them, however, are so heavy that they could not well have answered such a purpose. May not the larger sorts have been employed—after the fashion of the modern bobbin—in twisting bow-strings, plaiting belts, and in weaving various articles for personal decoration?

From the peculiar shape and the careless manner in which many—found in the relic-beds along the river-banks—have been fashioned, it seems probable that they were intended as fishing-plummets. In their construction soapstone was the favorite material used. Often triangular in shape, sometimes they appear in the form of a double conoid, with a groove around the middle. These are usually so much lighter than the net-sinkers, and differ so essentially from them in figure, that they need not be confounded with them. Specimens of this class often resemble number 5, figure 132, "Ancient Monuments of the Mississippi Valley," although, instead of being notched at the upper end, many have a groove around the middle; while others—made of soapstone or slate—are traversed by longitudinal as well as transverse grooves.

Nearly allied to the pear-shaped pendant is an instrument which, when first observed by the writer, he regarded as a pendant whose upper end had been broken off and then flattened by attrition. Other relics, however, identical in shape, proved that the form was designed and not accidental. Carver observed among the Indians living westward of the Mississippi River a warlike implement consisting of a stone of middling size, curiously wrought and fastened

to the hair, the nose, the ear, and the maccaseene; and Lawson ("History of Carolina," p. 314, Raleigh reprint, 1860) declares that some of the Indians wore great bobs in their ears.

by a string, about a yard and a half long, to the right arm a little above the elbow. Such stones the natives carried in their hands until they approached their enemies, when, riding at full speed, they swung them with great dexterity and never failed of doing execution.[1]

Among the Shoshonee Indians, Lewis and Clarke noticed an instrument consisting of a handle about the size of a whip-handle, made of wood, twenty-two inches long and covered with leather. At one end was a thong two inches in length, to which was attached a stone weighing two pounds, enclosed in a leather cover. At the other end was a loop by means of which the implement was secured to the wrist. With this weapon they struck a powerful blow. It may be that the pear-shaped stones, now under examination, were made for some such purpose, and that they were carried and handled very much as slung-shots are used in the present day. Those in our possession are about as large as a turkey-egg, closely resembling it in shape, save that the pointed end has been cut off at right angles. (*See* Fig. 4, Plate XXII.) They have not the clearly-defined necks possessed by the relics delineated in Fig. 117, of the "Ancient Monuments of the Mississippi Valley."[2] Stones, for throwing by hand and perhaps by means of a sling, occur frequently. They are commonly round or ovoidal, and appear to have been gathered from the beds of streams —or rudely fashioned from soapstone.

Amulets.—Fig. 5, Plate XXII., represents a class of objects frequently found in Ohio and in other portions of North America, but seldom seen in that part of the

[1] "Travels," etc., pp. 294, 295. London, 1778.

[2] Page 219.

country once occupied by the Southern tribes. Generally made of a greenish striped slate, they are, in most instances, designed to represent a bird. Their use is not well understood, but it is probable that they possessed some conventional significance and importance in connection with the religious ideas of the Indians. Three of these strange articles are figured on page 239 of the "Ancient Monuments of the Mississippi Valley," and their varying forms are richly shown in the valuable collection of the Smithsonian Institution. It has been suggested by some that they were used for husking Indian-corn. This idea we regard as entirely fanciful. It appears much more probable that they were esteemed and worn as charms, as badges of distinction, or as religious tokens.

STONE PLATE.—So far as our information extends, this relic (Fig. 6, Plate XXII.) was the first of its kind found within the limits of the United States. It was ploughed up in 1859, on the lower terrace of the large temple-mound on the Etowah River, upon the plantation of Colonel Lewis Tumlin, near Cartersville. This interesting locality has proved the thesaurus of more valuable and curious aboriginal remains than any other spot in Georgia. To the companionship of the terraced mound, the stone idols, idol-pipes, simulacra of various sorts, fish-preserves, gold and pearl beads, shell ornaments, ising-glass mirrors and sundry beautiful implements of diorite, hornblend, jasper and flint, may now be added this stone plate, circular in form, eleven inches and a half in diameter, an inch and a quarter in thickness, and weighing nearly seven pounds. It is made of a close-grained, sea-green slate, and bears upon its surface the stains of centuries. Between the rim, which is scalloped, and the central portion, are two circular depressed rings, running parallel with the circumference and incised to the depth of the tenth of an inch. The central portion, or basin, is hollowed out to the depth of rather more than the eighth of an inch. This circular basin, nearly eight inches in diameter, is surrounded by a margin or rim, a little less than two inches in width, traversed by the incised rings and bevelled from the centre toward the edge. The lower surface or bottom of the plate is flat, bevelled upward, however, as it approaches the scalloped edge, which is not more than a quarter of an inch in thickness.

Two stone plates, similar in material, size, and general configuration, were unearthed in this locality. Within the past eighteen months, two relics of this class, but less elaborate in their construction and smaller, were obtained from a mound on the Black Warrior River in the State of Alabama. They now form a part of the collection of the Smithsonian Institution at Washington.

The use of these plates from the Etowah Valley may, we think, be conjectured with at least some degree of probability. It is not likely that they were employed for domestic or culinary purposes. Their weight, rarity, the care evidenced in their construction, and the amount of time and labor necessarily expended in their manufacture, forbid the belief that they were intended as ordinary dishes from which the daily meal was to be eaten, and suggest the impression that they were designed to fulfil a more unusual and important office. The common vessels from which the natives of this region ate their prepared food were bowls and pans fashioned of wood and baked clay, calabashes, pieces of bark, and large shells. Flat platters, made of an admixture of clay and pounded shells, well kneaded and burnt, were ordinarily employed for baking corn-cakes and frying meat; but it does not anywhere appear that ornamented stone plates were in general use.

It will be remembered that at some remote period idol-worship existed among many of the Southern tribes. The religious duty of offering fruits and food to these lesser deities was not neglected. We are told that the Virginia Indians represented their inferior gods by the forms of men, calling such images Kewasowok. These they placed in temples, and in their presence worshipped, prayed, sung, and made repeated offerings.[1]

The stone column which Ribault placed upon a mound to mark the limit of the French empire in the New World, was by the Florida Indians elevated into the dignity of a superior being. From top to bottom it was encircled with flowers and the branches of choicest trees, while at its base were constantly exposed offerings of fruits, corn, favorite roots, bows and arrows, and earthen vessels filled with perfumed oils.[2]

While the sun, as the most potent representative of an unseen yet acknowledged divinity with supreme powers, formed the chief object of religious worship among the ancient tribes who peopled the Etowah Valley, there existed, nevertheless, images which, perhaps at the instance of designing priests and conjurers, claimed the devotion of the masses. The precise position assigned to them in the theogony of that rude age does not fully appear; and yet, from out the depths of that dark period, comes light enough to reveal the fact that these idols—subordinate though they were to the

[1] Hariot's "Virginia," p. 26. Francoforti ad Mœnum. De Bry, anno 1590.

[2] Plate viii. of the "Brevis Narratio."

Great Spirit and to the celestial luminaries—were still invested with attributes and influences which it behooved weaker man to stand in awe of and to propitiate.

We incline to the opinion that these stone plates were designed for sacred uses, and that in them was exposed the food offered to the Dii Minores of those peoples who, antedating the modern Indians—dwellers here at the dawn of the historic period—erected the large temple-mound in honor of that great God who mingled not with men, and before whose flaming minister—the sun—they prostrated themselves in blind yet profound adoration.

MICA MEMBRANACEA.—Large plates of ising-glass are frequently found in the sepulchral tumuli of Georgia, associated with articles of use and ornament, the property of the dead at the period of the inhumation. The largest which has fallen under the observation of the writer is elliptical in form, measuring thirteen inches in length, ten inches in width, and nearly half an inch in thickness. Usually, however, these mirrors —for such it appears proper to regard them—are much smaller. The customary size may be expressed by seven inches in length and five inches in width. Often elliptical, they are sometimes square or parallelogrammic in shape, and at other times quite irregular in their outlines. Being thick, and readily reflecting the opposed image, they answered tolerably well the purposes of looking-glasses. We are not aware that any specimens have been found backed by copper plates. If originally enclosed in frames, these were fashioned of such perishable materials that they long since crumbled into nothingness, leaving no traces of their former presence or attachment. The frequent occurrence of these ising-glass mirrors, not only in the ancient graves and mounds but also upon the sites of old Indian villages and in relic-beds, attests the fact of their general use among the aborigines. Through their assistance, the process of personal decoration, of painting, and of tattooing, was materially facilitated; and it is not improbable that they formed a source of special delight to many of the softer sex, who even in that rude age were not ignorant of their personal charms, or indifferent to such artificial aids as might tend to enhance their beauty and attractions in the eyes of their savage admirers.

Occasionally a hole drilled through the lower edge of the plate—elongated after the fashion of a handle—assures us that the mirror was sometimes suspended for convenient use, and that it was thus rendered more apt for facile transportation.

Sculptured Rocks.—In Forsyth County, Georgia, is a carved or incised bowlder of fine-grained granite, about nine feet long, four feet six inches high, and three feet broad at its widest point. The figures are cut in the bowlder from one-half to three-quarters of an inch deep. (*See* illustrations, p. 378.)

As yet no interpretation of these figures has been offered, nor is it known by whom or for what purpose they were made. It is generally believed, however, that they are the work of the Cherokees. On the eastern end of the bowlder, running vertically, is a line of dots, like drill-holes, eighteen in number, connected by an incised line.

Upon the Enchanted Mountain in Union County, cut in plutonic rock, are the tracks of men, women, children, deer, bears, bisons, turkeys and terrapins, and the outlines of a snake, of two deer, and of a human hand. These sculptures—so far as they have been ascertained and counted—number one hundred and thirty-six. The most extravagant among them is that known as the footprint of the "Great Warrior." It

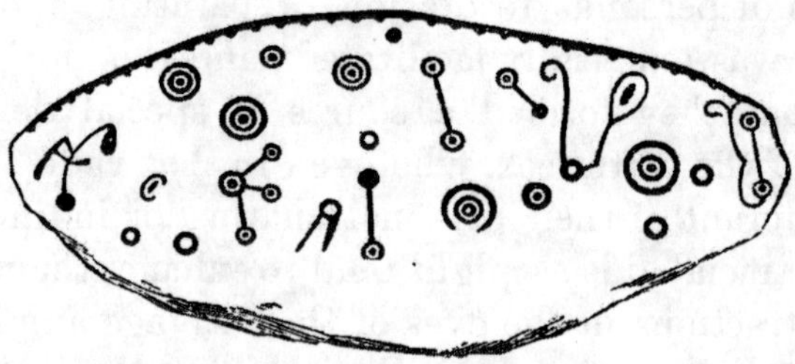

North Side of Sculptured Rock, Forsyth County, Georgia.

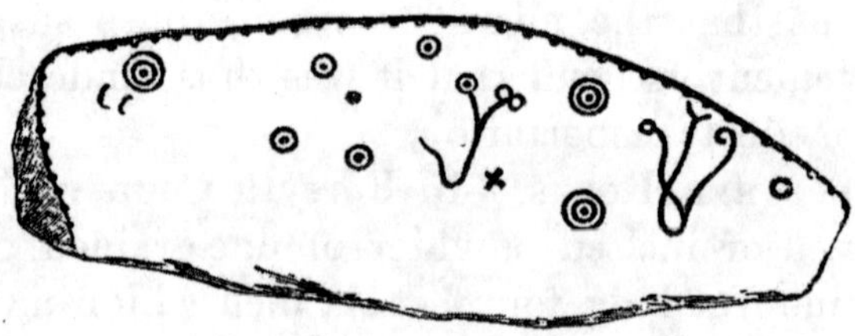

South Side of the above.

measures eighteen inches in length, and has six toes. The other human tracks and those of the animals are delineated with commendable fidelity. One track—which has been indifferently described as that of a horse and a buffalo—is seventeen inches long. These impressions are artificial, and were scraped or chiselled out of the rock apparently with the aid of cutting implements of flint. The accuracy and skill displayed in the construction of some of them challenge admiration, while others are clumsily and rudely made. Most of them present the appearance of the natural tread of the animal in plastic clay. Twenty-six of these sculptures represent impressions of human feet—varying in length from four to seventeen inches—all of them bare, save one, which was covered with a moccasin.[1]

These *intaglios* closely resemble those described by Mr. Ward as existing upon the upheaved slabs of coarse carboniferous grit, in Belmont County, Ohio, near the town of Barnesville.[2]

Among the mountains which fence in the upper portion of Georgia, in several localities, may still be seen, carved in rock, similar *intaglios* and rude representations of the sun, the human form and hand, the bow and arrow, the canoe, and various circles and irregular figures which, at the present day, seem almost meaningless exhibitions of the fancies of those by whom they were traced.

Intended, doubtless—especially when associated in groups—to perpetuate the recollection of some memorable event, the histories which they chronicled and the traditions they were designed to transmit, have, like the peoples who formed them, quite faded from the memory of succeeding generations. As yet we have seen nothing of this sort which rises above the dignity of rude picture-writing, such as at later periods has been, in a more ephemeral way, practised by the modern Indians in commemoration of an engagement, in adoration of the sun, in token of an alliance, in explanation of some marked occurrence, and in imitation of some well-known natural object. We search in vain for alphabet, lettered shaft, phonetic sign or digit. Rude representations all, they do but feebly shadow forth the earliest efforts at physical expression of common incidents, the most primitive attempts at com-

[1] Stephenson's "Geology and Mineralogy of Georgia," pp. 199, 201. Atlanta, Georgia, 1871. White's "Historical Collections of Georgia," p. 658. New York, 1854.

[2] *Journal of the Anthropological Institute of New York*, No. 1, p. 57, *et seq.*

municating thoughts and perpetuating the recollection of events by visible shapes. A few symbols there were, which possessed and retained an acknowledged significance, recognized by all.

The labors of the aborigines upon the summit of Stone Mountain, so far as we have been able to examine them, seem to have been directed not, as has been surmised, to the cutting of hieroglyphics and the fashioning of curious figures in the granite, but to the preparation of little ditches or trenches for the protection of their fires. The mountain being entirely bald and consisting of hard granite, during a storm the rain —unabsorbed by the rock—would flow freely down the sides and soon smother the fires kindled upon its surface. In order to avoid this inconvenience, the Indians resorted to the expedient of cutting in the rock circular and horseshoe-shaped troughs or trenches, which would catch the rain-water in its descent and divert it from the interior spaces upon which their fires were burning. A marked similarity exists in the sizes and shapes of these fireplaces, which are scattered in considerable numbers upon the summit and western slope of the mountain. They are generally from three to four feet in diameter, and are circular, semicircular, and elliptical in form. The incised trenches or ditches surrounding them are from four to seven inches in width, and from two to three inches deep. In the centre of almost every hearth is a fissure in the rock, which materially aided in preserving the fire. Of these fissures the natives availed themselves in the location of their fireplaces; and, in some instances, at no little labor enlarged them and formed adjacent elevations in the rock, as convenient resting-places for the earthen vessels in which they cooked their food.

We have thus, in our opinion, a simple explanation of the practical use of these incised lines, artificial elevations, and trenches cut in the rock, which have been supposed by many to possess a hidden and mysterious significance.

The delightful temperature of this mountain—a stupendous pyramid rising in austere and solitary grandeur above the plain—during the summer attracted the natives. That it was a favorite resort of the primitive peoples who in former centuries occupied this region, is attested by the presence of these laboriously-constructed fireplaces, and by mortars, permanent in their character and hollowed out of the rock. This impression is confirmed by the traces of a defensive rock-wall which at one period fortified the entire crest of the mountain.

It is above the wall, and around the summit of Stone Mountain, that the indications of long-continued occupation by the red-men are most abundant.

Returning from this digression, we would remark that in the stone images, idol, bird, and animal-shaped pipes, and in the large ornamented shell-gorgets, we trace more emphatically than in any thing else the progress made by the Southern Indians in the art of sculpture. As the distinguishing peculiarities of these relics will, however, be considered in a subsequent part of this work, it is unnecessary to anticipate what will be said on the subject. These various devices and imitations in stone and shell, while they often exhibit no little skill and ingenuity, are, after all, but rude expressions of the taste of the untaught, and fall far short of what may properly be considered works of art. Few and feeble were the attempts to transmit important memories by means of enduring physical signs and pictorial illustrations. Upon the rock-walls which guard the confines of Northern Georgia, we look in vain for any monumental traces of the history of the tribes who were native here long before the advent of the European. Among the relics intermingled with the soil upon which they dwelt, we search fruitlessly for a single tablet whereon were engraven their laws or the names of their kings, priests, and warriors. They lived and died, peoples without letters, and the Muse of History finds scarce an epitaph for their tombs. Trusting to the trembling voice of the aged warrior for a record of the brave deeds of their ancestors, and committing to the memory of the younger chieftain the story of their present achievements, they gave to the passing wind the spoken word, but carved not a line and reared not a column in commemoration either of the past or the present. History is voiceless where the use of iron and of letters is unknown. Under such circumstances, the most we can hope to discover is comprehended in vague traditions, and in the silent teachings of monuments and relics which have escaped the destructive influences of time. We compare, we conjecture, we speculate. The rest is darkness.

CHAPTER XVIII.

Pipes.—The Use of Tobacco.—Idol Pipes.—Calumets.—Common Pipes.

THE pipes of the North American Indians possess an importance, both traditional and historic, which, elevating them above the category of ordinary relics, claims for them a moral, religious, and political value, which must be duly appreciated in forming a suitable estimate of their office and in comprehending the various purposes they were intended to answer. It is not only as the media through which the narcotic influences of tobacco were imparted, nor as articles of pride and ornament upon which the protracted labor and best skill of the primitive artists were expended, nor yet as the acknowledged symbols of alternate peace and war that they are to be regarded. Combining all these, they rise higher and confess themselves, in their origin, the immediate gift of the Great Spirit by whom they were invested with certain prescribed sanctities, and, in their uses, fenced about with positive injunctions whose non-observance entailed disaster and supreme displeasure. Devotional also in their uses, their agency was invoked in solemnities which brought the red nomad face to face with his Creator. Then the puffs of smoke blown to the four quarters of the heavens were redolent of the petitions of the devotees. Taking the place of sacrifice, through them propitiation was made to an angered divinity. In sunshine and abundance they were the ministers of gratitude—the exponents of joy and thanksgiving. Among the primitive inhabitants of at least some of the Southern regions, they were elevated to the dignity of idols before whose elaborately-carved forms of man, and beast, and bird, the deluded fell down and worshipped. It is only among the North American Indians that such peculiar historic interest attaches to the Pipe—only among the ancient peoples of this region that we locate customs, ceremonies, and traditions, at once most curious and unique.

Standing on the precipice of the red-pipe-stone rock of *Coteau des Prairies*, the Great Spirit broke from it a fragment, and, by merely turning it in his hands, made out of it a huge pipe which, having smoked, he proclaimed a symbol of peace among all his children, declaring this stone common property, ordering peace-pipes to be fashioned from it, and forbidding the war-club and the scalping-knife to be lifted near it.[1] Prof. Wilson[2] very justly remarks that, "in the Old World the ideas connected with the tobacco-pipe are prosaic enough. The chibouk may, at times, be associated with the poetical reveries of the Oriental day-dreamer, and the hookah with pleasant fancies of the Anglo-Indian reposing in the shade of his bungalow; but its seductive, antique mystery, and all its symbolic significance, pertain to the New World."

Longfellow, accordingly, fitly opens his *Song of Hiawatha* with the institution of "the Peace-Pipe."

[1] *See* Stevens' "Flint Chips," p. 522. London, 1870.

[2] "Prehistoric Man," p. 312. London, 1865.

The Master of Life descends on the mountains of the prairie, breaks a fragment from the red stone of the quarry, and fashioning it with curious art into a pipe-head, fills it with the bark of the red-willow, chafes the forest into flame with the tempest of his breath, and kindling it smokes the calumet as a signal to the nations. The tribes of the ancient aborigines gather, at the divine summons, from river, lake, and prairie, to listen to the warnings and promises with which the Great Spirit seeks to guide them. This august audience concluded, the warriors having buried their war-clubs, smoke their first peace-pipe and depart:

> " While the Master of Life, ascending
> Through the opening cloud-curtains
> Through the door-ways of the heaven,
> Vanished from before their faces,
> In the smoke that rolled around him,
> The pukwana of the peace-pipe."

For tobacco a divine origin is said to have been claimed by the American Indians, who regarded it as a direct gift from the Great Spirit, for their special enjoyment. Indeed, according to Hariot, they believed that the Great Spirit was himself addicted to the habit of smoking. The pipe, therefore, came to be regarded as a sacred object, and smoking partook of the character of a moral if not a religious act.[1] The incense of tobacco was deemed pleasing to the Father of Life, and the ascending smoke was selected as the most suitable medium of communication with the world of spirits. The ordinary pipe was the constant companion and the unfailing solace of the Indian. Upon the war-path, while engaged in hunting, and

[1] Stevens' "Flint Chips," p. 318. London, 1870.

amid the lazy hours of his rude home-life, it was ever near, ministering to his pleasure and comforting him under misfortunes. Its introduction was essential to a formal declaration of war, and to the conclusion of a treaty of peace. Alternate whiffs were then tantamount to a signing and sealing by the parties in interest. Most important was the office of the *Calumet.* No tribal organization, no solemn assembly was complete without it, and the ceremonies observed in its honor were impressive and conducted with the utmost care and regularity.

"This *Calumet*," says Father Hennepin,[1] "is the most mysterious Thing in the World among the Savages of the Continent of the Northern *America;* for it is us'd in all their important Transactions: However, it is nothing else but a large Tobacco-Pipe made of Red, Black or White Marble: The Head is finely polish'd, and the Quill, which is commonly two foot and a half long, is made of a pretty strong Reed or Cane, adorn'd with Feathers of all Colours, interlac'd with Locks of Women's Hair. They tie to it two Wings of the most curious Birds they find, which makes their *Calumet* not much unlike *Mercury's* Wand, or that Staff Ambassadors did formerly carry when they went to treat of Peace. They sheath that Reed into the neck of Birds they call *Huars,* which are as big as our Geese, and spotted with Black and White; or else of a sort of Ducks who make their Nests upon Trees, tho' Water be their ordinary Element, and whose Feathers are of many different Colours. However, every Nation adorns the *Calumet* as they think according to their own *Genius* and the Birds they have in their Country.

"A Pipe such as I have describ'd it, is a Pass and

[1] "A New Discovery," etc., chapter xxiv., pp. 93, 94. London, 1698.

safe Conduct amongst all the Allies of the Nation who has given it; and in all Embassies, the Ambassadors carry that *Calumet* as the Symbol of Peace, which is always respected; for the Savages are generally persuaded that a great Misfortune would befal 'em if they violated the Publick Faith of the *Calumet*. All their Enterprizes, Declarations of War, or Conclusion of Peace, as well as all the rest of their Ceremonies are Sealed, if I may be permitted to say so, with this *Calumet*. They fill that Pipe with the best Tobacco they have, and then present it to those with whom they have concluded any great Affair, and smoak out of the same after them. I had certainly perish'd in my Voyage, had it not been for this *Calumet* or Pipe."

In Father Dablon's "Relation of the Voyages, Discoveries, and Death of Father James Marquette," we have an interesting description both of the calumet and of the dance celebrated in its honor. I adopt the translation of Mr. John Gilmary Shea:[1] "It now remains for me to speak of the calumet, than which there is nothing among them more mysterious or more esteemed. Men do not pay to the crowns and sceptres of kings the honor they pay to it; it seems to be the god of peace and war, the arbiter of life and death. Carry it about you and show it, and you can march fearlessly amid enemies who even in the heat of battle lay down their arms when it is shown. Hence the Ilinois gave me one to serve as my safeguard amid all the nations that I had to pass on my voyage. There is a calumet for peace and one for war, distinguished only by the color of the feathers with which

[1] "Discovery and Exploration of the Mississippi Valley," etc., p. 34, *et seq.* New York, 1852.

they are adorned, red being the sign of war. They use them also for settling disputes, strengthening alliances, and speaking to strangers. It is made of a polished red stone, like marble, so pierced that one end serves to hold the tobacco while the other is fastened on the stem, which is a stick two feet long, as thick as a common cane, and pierced in the middle; it is ornamented with the head and neck of different birds of beautiful plumage; they also add large feathers of red, green, and other colors, with which it is all covered. They esteem it particularly because they regard it as the calumet of the sun; and, in fact, they present it to him to smoke, when they wish to obtain calm, or rain, or fair weather. They scruple to bathe at the beginning of summer, or to eat new fruits, till they have danced it. They do it thus:—The Calumet Dance, which is very famous among these Indians, is performed only for important matters, sometimes to strengthen a peace or to assemble for some great war; at other times for a public rejoicing; sometimes they do this honor to a nation who is invited to be present; sometimes they use it to receive some important personage as if they wished to give him the entertainment of a ball or comedy. In winter the ceremony is performed in a cabin, in summer in the open fields. They select a place surrounded with trees, so as to be sheltered beneath their foliage against the heat of the sun. In the middle of the space they spread out a large party-colored mat of rushes; this serves as a carpet, on which to place with honor the god of the one who gives the dance; for every one has his own god, or manitou, as they call it, which is a snake, a bird or something of the kind, which they have dreamed in their sleep, and in which they put all their trust for the success of their wars, fishing and hunts. Near this manitou, and at its right, they put the calumet in honor of which the feast is given, making around about it a kind of trophy, spreading there the arms used by the warriors of these tribes, namely the war-club, bow, hatchet, quiver and arrows. Things being thus arranged, and the hour for dancing having arrived, those who are to sing, take the most honorable place under the foliage. They are the men and the women who have the finest voices, and who accord perfectly. The spectators then come and take their places around under the branches; but each one on arriving must salute the manitou, which he does by inhaling the smoke, and then puffing it from his mouth upon it, as if offering incense. Each one goes first, and takes the calumet respectfully, and, supporting it with both hands, makes it dance in cadence, suiting himself to the air of the song; he makes it go through various figures, sometimes showing it to the whole assembly by turning it from side to side.

"After this, he who is to begin the dance appears in the midst of the assembly, and goes first; sometimes he presents it to the sun, as if he wished it to smoke; sometimes he inclines it to the earth; and, at other times he spreads its wings as if for it to fly; at other times, he approaches it to the mouths of the spectators for them to smoke, the whole in cadence. This is the first scene of the ballet.

"The second consists in a combat, to the sound of a kind of drum, which succeeds the songs, or rather joins them, harmonizing quite well. The dancer beckons to some brave to come and take the arms on the mat, and challenges him to fight to the sound of the drums; the other approaches, takes his bow and arrow, and begins a duel against the dancer who has no defence but the calumet. This spectacle is very pleasing, especially as it is always done in time, for one attacks, the other defends; one strikes, the other parries; one flies, the othes pursues; then he who fled faces and puts his enemy to flight. This is. all done so well, with measured steps and the regular sound of voices and drums, that it might pass for a very pretty opening of a ballet in France.

"The third scene consists of a speech delivered by the holder of the calumet, for, the combat being ended without bloodshed, he relates the battles he was in, the victories he has gained; he names the nations, the places, the captives he has taken, and as a reward, he who presides at the dance presents him with a beautiful beaver robe, or something else, which he receives, and then he presents the calumet to another, who hands it to a third, and so to all the rest, till all having done their duty, the presiding chief presents the calumet itself to the nation, invited to this ceremony in token of the eternal peace which shall reign between the two tribes.

"The following is one of the songs which they are accustomed to sing; they give it a certain expression, not easily represented by notes, yet in this all its grace consists:

"'Ninahani, ninahani, ninahani,
Naniongo.'"

The calumet of peace was frequently adorned with the white feathers of the bald eagle. He who bore it passed freely, and without fear of bodily harm, wherever he pleased; because this pipe—held sacred by all the tribes—rendered the person of him who carried it —be he chief, ambassador, friend, enemy, or stranger—

inviolable. Red being the color of war, Loskiel[1] tells us that in making peace or settling alliances, the red calumet was "daubed over with white clay or chalk."

By the same author we are informed that if two Indian nations entered into a treaty of alliance, a pipe of peace was exchanged between them, which was then called the pipe of covenant. It was carefully preserved and generally lighted in council whenever any thing occurred appertaining to the alliance.[2] Then each member smoked a little out of it. This reminded them in the most impressive manner of the covenant and the time of its establishment. The greatest care was bestowed upon the construction and ornamentation of the stems of the calumets and medicine-pipes. No inconsiderable official dignity attached to the bearers of them, and their preservation was a matter of earnest solicitude. When M. D'Iberville sought his first interview with the Indians of Florida, he was received by their chiefs smoking the calumet and singing the song of peace. M. Penicaut[3] thus describes the pipe used on this occasion: "The calumet is a stick about a yard in length, or a hollow cane, ornamented with the feathers of the paroquet, birds of prey, and of the eagle. These feathers, arranged around the stick, resemble somewhat the fans used by French ladies. At the end of this stick is a pipe, to which the name of calumet is given."

From Father Charlevoix[4] we borrow the following

1 "History of the Mission of the United Brethren among the Indians in North America," part 1, p. 156. London, 1794.

2 "History of the Mission of the United Brethren," etc., part 1, page 158. London, 1794.

3 "Historical Collections of Louisiana and Florida," etc., by B. F. French. New Series, p. 38. New York, 1869.

4 "Voyage to North America," etc., vol. i., pp. 180, 181. Dublin, 1766.

interesting account of the character, uses, and importance of the calumet among the North American Indians: "The Calumet is not less sacred among these People than the Necklaces of Porcelain; if you believe them, it is derived from Heaven, for they say it is a Present which was made them by the Sun. It is more in Use with the Nations of the South and West, than those of the North and East, and it is oftener used for Peace than for War. *Calumet* is a *Norman* word, which signifies *Reed*, and the Calumet of the Savages is properly the Tube of a Pipe; but they comprehend under this Name the Pipe also, as well as its Tube. In the Calumet made for Ceremony, the Tube is very long, the Bowl of the Pipe is commonly made of a Kind of reddish Marble, very easy to work, and which is found in the Country of the *Ajouez*, beyond the *Mississippi*. The Tube is of a light Wood painted of different Colours, and adorned with the Heads, Tails and Feathers of the finest Birds, which is in all Appearance merely for Ornament. The Custom is to smoke in the Calumet when you accept it, and perhaps there is no Instance where the Agreement has been violated which was made by this Acceptation. The Savages are at least persuaded that the Great Spirit would not leave such a Breach of Faith unpunished. If in the midst of a Battle the Enemy presents a Calumet, it is allowable to refuse it, but if they receive it, they must instantly lay down their Arms. There are Calumets for every Kind of Treaty. In Trade, when they have agreed upon the Exchange, they present a Calumet to confirm it, which renders it in some Manner sacred. When it concerns War, not only the Tube, but the Feathers also that adorn it are red. Sometimes they are only set on one Side; and they say that according to the Manner in which the Feathers are disposed, they immediately know what Nation it is that presents it; and whom they intend to attack. There is scarce any Room to doubt but that the Savages in making those smoke in the Calumet with whom they would trade or treat intend to take the Sun for Witness, and in some Measure for a Guarantee of their Treaties; for they never fail to blow the Smoke towards the Planet." Overlooking or else disregarding the current tradition that the pipe was the direct gift of the Great Spirit delivered at first with specific injunctions and to be used on all important occasions with becoming solemnity, and always with the greatest good faith, our author is of opinion that the Indians "having found by Experience that the Smoke of their Tobacco draws Vapours from the Brain, makes the Head clearer, rouses the Spirits and makes us fitter to treat of Affairs," for this reason introduced its use into their councils; and that "after having gravely deliberated and taken their Resolution they thought they could never find a Symbol fitter to put a Seal to their Determinations, or any Pledge more capable of confirming the Execution of them than the Instrument which had so much Share in their Deliberations. . . . To smoke in the same Pipe therefore in Token of Alliance is the same Thing as to drink in the same Cup, as has been practised at all Times by many Nations."

When Columbus was upon the coast of Cuba he beheld several of the natives going about with firebrands in their hands, and certain dried herbs which they rolled up in a leaf, and lighting one end put the other in their mouths and continued inhaling and puffing out the smoke. A roll of this kind they called a tobacco, a name since transferred to the plant of which the rolls were made. The Spaniards, although prepared to meet with wonders, were struck with astonishment at this singular and apparently nauseous indulgence.[1]

In his chapter upon the nations and tongues of Florida, Cabeça de Vaca states that the natives everywhere "produce stupefaction with a smoke, and for that they will give whatever they possess."[2] This allusion—brief and vague although it be—has reference to the use of tobacco, and assures us emphatically both of the fondness of the Indians for that weed, and of the extravagant degree in which they subjected themselves to its narcotic influences.

One of the oldest references to Indian pipes is contained in the "Brevis Narratio" of Le Moyne de Morgues. Plate xx. represents various methods of curing the sick. An Indian is seated, smoking a pipe. A woman offers him some tobacco-leaves. The text is as follows: "Quandam etiam plantă habent cujus nomen excidit, Brasiliani PETUM, Hispani TAPACO appellant: hujus folia probè siccata laxiori tubuli parti imponunt, eorum incensorum fumum angustiore tubuli parte ori admota attrahunt tam validè, ut per os & nares illis egrediatur, & eadem opera abundè humores eliciat." This passage may be translated thus: "They have also a certain plant whose name I have forgotten—the Brazilians call it PETUM, the Spaniards TAPACO—whose well-dried leaves they place in the wider portion of a tube. Having ignited these, they apply the narrower part of the tube to the mouth and draw out the fume

[1] Irving's "Life and Voyages of Columbus," vol. i., p. 184. New York, 1849—quoting from "Navarrete," tome i., p. 51.

[2] "Relation" of Alvar Nuñez Cabeça de Vaca, translated by Buckingham Smith, p. 138. New York, 1871.

so vigorously that it escapes through the mouth and nostrils, and thus removes much humidity."

We have also, in the first volume of De Bry, another representation of an Indian pipe. It is not unlike the short clay-pipe of the present day, so much in vogue among the Irish laborers. Beverly, in his "History of the Present State of Virginia," has reproduced this illustration.[1]

The illustration which faces page 7 of the third book contains two representations of the pipe of peace; and Father Hennepin, in the frontispiece to his "New Discovery," figures a naked Indian holding in his hands the plumed calumet. Carver[2] has furnished us with a drawing of the pipe of peace.

In the early narratives smoking is alluded to rather as a curative process or public ceremony, than as a matter of habit or enjoyment among the natives. The ignorance of the times and the novelty of the custom furnish plausible excuse for the mistake.

In his "Briefe and True Report of the New-found Land of Virginia,"[3] Hariot thus quaintly describes "an herbe which is sowed apart by itselfe, and is called by the inhabitants Uppówoc: In the West Indies it hath diuers names according to the seuerall places and countries where it groweth and is vsed; The Spaniardes generally call it Tobacco. The leaues thereof being dried and brought into powder, they vse to take the fume or smoke thereof by sucking it through pipes made of claie, into their stomacke and heade; from whence it purgeth superfluous fleame and other grosse humors, openeth all the pores and passages of the

[1] *See* Tab. 10, book iii., p. 17. London, 1705.

[2] "Travels," etc., p. 296. London, 1778.

[3] Page 16. Francoforti ad Mœnum. De Bry, anno 1590.

body: by which meanes the vse thereof not only preserueth the body from obstructiōs, but also if any be so that they haue not beene of too long continuance, in short time breaketh them: wherby their bodies are notably preserued in health, and know not many greeuous diseases, wherewithall wee in England are oftentimes afflicted. This Uppówoc is of so precious estimation amongest them that they thinke their gods are maruelously delighted therewith; Whereupon sometime they make hallowed fires, and cast some of the pouder therein for a sacrifice: being in a storme uppon the waters, to pacifie their gods, they cast some vp into the aire and into the water; so a weare for fish being newly set vp, they cast some therein, and into the aire; also after an escape of danger they cast some into the aire likewise; but all done with strange gestures, stamping, sometime dauncing, clapping of hands, holding vp of hands, and staring vp into the heauens, vttering therewithal, and chattering strange words and noises."

In the voyage of Sir Francis Drake, it is mentioned that some of the North American Indians "brought a little basket made of rushes, and filled with an herbe which they called *Tobah;*" and Drake afterward adds: "They came now the second time to us, bringing with them as before had been done, feathers and bags of *Tobah* for presents, or rather indeed for sacrifices, upon this persuasion that we were gods."[1] Admitting the devotional, propitiatory, religious, political, medicinal, and social uses to which the pipe, in its various forms, was dedicated; conceding the divine origin claimed both for it and tobacco, and granting that around them clustered superstitions and ceremonies unique in

[1] Quoted in Stevens' "Flint Chips," pp. 318, 319. London, 1870.

their character and powerful in their influences, it is nevertheless true that among the North American (and particularly the Southern) Indians, smoking constituted, from the earliest times, a sensual enjoyment. Among their personal effects a pipe was frequently, if not always, reckoned; and the narcotic influences of tobacco were sought after with an avidity engendered only by confirmed habit.

The Choctaws raised tobacco to such an extent that they sometimes sold it to the traders. When using it for smoking, they mixed it with the leaves of two species of the *cariaria*, or of the *liquidambar styraciflua*. The pipe was in common use among them, and in some shape or other was the symbol of peace, friendship, and social conversation. The first civility offered by the Muscogees to a stranger was a pipe, and this, when accepted, was followed by "a dish of venison and homany."[1] Speaking of the manufacture of pipes by the Southern Indians, Mr. Adair[2] affirms that "they make beautiful stone pipes; and the Cheerake the best of any of the Indians: for their mountainous country contains many different sorts and colours of soils proper for such uses. They easily form them with their tomohawks, and afterward finish them in any desired form with their knives; the pipes being of a very soft quality till they are smoked with and used to fire, when they become quite hard. They are often a full span long, and the bowls are about half as large again as those of our English pipes. The forepart of each commonly runs out with a sharp peak, two or three fingers broad, and a quarter of an inch thick.

[1] "A Concise Natural History of East and West Florida," etc., by Captain Bernard Romans. New York, 1775.

[2] "History of the American Indians," etc., pp. 423, 424. London, 1775.

On both sides of the bowl, lengthwise, they cut several pictures with a great deal of skill and labour; such as a buffalo and a panther on the opposite sides of the bowl; a rabbit and a fox; and, very often, a man and a woman *puris naturalibus*. Their sculpture cannot much be commended for its modesty. The savages work so slow, that one of their artists is two months at a pipe with his knife, before he finishes it; indeed, as before observed, they are great enemies to profuse sweating, and are never in a hurry about a good thing. The stems are commonly made of soft wood about two feet long, and an inch thick, cut into four squares, each scooped till they join very near the hollow of the stem; the beaus always hollow the squares, except a little at each corner, to hold them together, to which they fasten a parcel of bell-buttons, different sorts of fine feathers, and several small battered pieces of copper kettles hammered round, deer-skin thongs, and a red painted scalp: this is a boasting, valuable and superlative ornament. According to their standard, such a pipe constitutes the possessor a grand beau. They so accurately carve or paint hieroglyphic characters on the stem, that all the war actions and the tribe of the owner, with a great many circumstances of things, are fully delineated."

When Lieutenant Timberlake, in 1761, was presented to the Cherokees he was complimented with many professions of friendship and a string of beads. The pipe-dance was celebrated in his honor. The bowl of the pipe used on this occasion "was of red stone, curiously cut with a knife."

He saw other pipes made of black stone, and some manufactured from "the same earth they make their pots with, but beautifully diversified. The stem is about three feet long, finely adorned with porcupine quills, dyed feathers, deer's hair, and such like gaudy trifles." Having smoked the peace-calumet, he adds, "I was almost suffocated with the pipes presented me on every hand, which I dared not to decline. They might amount to about 170 or 180; which made me so sick that I could not stir for several hours."[1]

Lawson informs us that among the Carolina Indians the women were addicted to smoking. "They have pipes," says he, "whose heads are cut out of stone, and will hold an ounce of tobacco, and some much less." The same author perpetuates the fact that by these Southern Indians tobacco-pipes were manufactured of clay with the express object of transporting them into distant regions and there exchanging them with other Indians for raw skins, etc.[2] Shortly after their primal intercourse with the whites, the red-men, in many localities, appear to have adopted the shape of the European pipe, as being more convenient than that formerly in vogue with them. As a matter of history it may be stated that the common clay pipe of commerce was, immediately upon its introduction, eagerly sought after by the Indians; and thus it came to pass that those who were visited by the traders, or who enjoyed facile communication with the colonists, speedily abandoned the general manufacture of pipes, retaining, however, their calumets, and perpetuating the different ceremonies, uses, and traditions with which they were so intimately associated.

In the olden time the Indian evidently laid great store by his pipe. For its construction the choicest material was often selected. This he collected not in-

[1] "Memoirs," etc., pp. 38, 39. London, 1765.

[2] "History of Carolina," pp. 55, 338. Raleigh reprint, 1860.

frequently at a great remove from his home, and in fashioning and polishing the bowl days and months of labor and skill were consumed. Upon the stem, also, the ingenuity and taste of the owner were exhausted. The presence of stone pipes in mounds at a distance of sometimes several hundred miles from the locality whence the material of which they were manufactured could have been procured, fully attests the fact that a trade must have existed among the aborigines in these highly-esteemed articles. It has been more than hinted by at least one person whose statement is entitled to every belief, that among the Cherokees, dwelling in the mountains, there existed certain artists whose professed occupation was the manufacture of large stone pipes, which were by them transported to the coast and there bartered away in exchange for articles of use and ornament, foreign to, and highly esteemed among, the members of their own tribe. It will be readily observed that, in selecting materials for their stone pipes, the Indians chose such varieties as were best calculated to withstand the continued action of heat. This was undoubtedly the result of actual experiment. In the absence of cutting and boring implements of metal, the construction of a pipe out of hard stone was a difficult and tedious undertaking. The constant and prolonged attrition required to reduce it to its desired proportions, the labor necessary for tracing the ornamental lines and hollowing out the bowl and the hole for the insertion of the stem simply with the aid of some rude flint implement, and the toil involved in imparting that degree of polish characteristic of so many of the more elaborate pipes, were all known to the primitive pipe-maker. In order, therefore, to avoid, as far as possible, the chances of losing his pipes at an early day by their cracking under the influence of heat, he availed himself of the experience of his forefathers, and selected such varieties of stone as would best subserve his purpose, and at the same time most certainly perpetuate the results of his taste and industry.

The mound-pipes, described by Messrs. Squier and Davis,[1] exhibit a degree of art and skill unexcelled by any other specimens of ancient pipes fashioned by the North American Indians.

Passing from these general observations we turn to an examination of the antique pipes found within the present geographical limits of Georgia. From the numbers taken from mounds, seen in refuse-piles and ploughed up in the fields, it may be confidently asserted that the Indians of this region were generally addicted to smoking. From the earliest historic period the pipe was their almost invariable companion, and its intimate association with the oldest monuments proves that there was no epoch when its use was unknown to their ancestors. These pipes may appropriately be divided into three classes: First in interest and in art is the Idol-Pipe. This is rarely seen, and only in localities where, in the distant past, dwelt peoples to all appearances more permanent in their seats and tribal organizations, more agricultural in their pursuits, more addicted to the construction of large tumuli, and superior in their degree of semi-civilization, to the nomads who occupied the soil at the date of European colonization. Specimens of such pipes are as infrequent as stone images, and it is probable that they should both be referred in their origin to the handi-

[1] "Ancient Monuments of the Mississippi Valley," vol. i.; "Smithsonian Contributions to Knowledge," pp. 251–272. Washington, 1848.

work and superstition of the primitive men who threw up those large mounds which tower along the banks of the Etowah and lift their imposing forms from out the level of several other valleys in Georgia. They are always associated, so far as our knowledge extends, with the large pentagonal and quadrangular mounds, and with those older monuments—be they watch-towers, sepulchral tumuli, temples, consecrated spaces, enclosed areas, defensive works or play-grounds—of whose age and objects the later Indian tribes cherished not even a tradition. The best idol-pipes we have seen were ploughed up near the base of the pentagonal mound, within the enclosure formed by the moat and the Etowah River, upon the plantation of Colonel Lewis Tumlin, near Cartersville, Georgia. A description of this interesting locality has already been given. Unfortunately, an opportunity for presenting a proper account and of figuring these relics is now denied. During the summer of 1859, the author enjoyed the pleasure of seeing three of these pipes at the residence of Colonel Tumlin. Amid the devastations consequent upon the invasion of Georgia by the Federal armies, in 1864, these, with other valuable relics, were either destroyed or carried away by the soldiers.

Writing from recollection, it may be stated that these particular idol-pipes were made, two of them of serpentine and the other of mica slate. They varied in height from three and a half to five inches, in breadth from two and a half to three inches, and in length from three to four inches. In each instance a human figure was represented in a sitting posture—knees drawn up—elbows resting upon the knees, and the extended hands presenting and clasping an urn-shaped bowl. These bowls were about two inches in diameter, and, disguising the sex, rested upon the abdomen and lower part of the breast. The head, rising somewhat above the level of the top of the bowl, was thrown backward. The chin and forehead were both retreating; eyes large and upturned—ears prominent. The forehead was low, broad and bald. The hair, collected from all sides, was confined at the top of the head, and thence falling backward was gathered into a sort of knot below. The countenances were decidedly idiotic, and yet the devotional idea was forcibly expressed in the attitude and general appearance of these rude idol-pipes—incense offering to an unseen yet acknowledged Deity. To these exhibitions of his skill the primitive sculptor had imparted a considerable degree of polish. The perforation for the stem passed below the shoulders through the back and belly into the bottom of the bowl. At its inception it was three-quarters of an inch in diameter, gradually lessening as it deepened, until, at the point where it entered the bowl, it was scarcely a quarter of an inch in width. These pipes were obviously very old; and in all likelihood antedated, by an indefinite period of time, the occupancy of this valley by the Cherokees. So far as recorded observation extends, nothing like them was noted in the use or possession of the modern Indians. There are at least plausible grounds for believing that the ancient peoples who piled up these august tumuli along the banks of the Etowah, and departing left behind them enduring monuments of their combined labor for a wonder and an enigma to later tribes, may have borrowed some of their ideas of sun-worship, idolatry, agriculture, and of art directly or indirectly from the Southern cradle of American civilization.

In the second class we include CALUMETS and large

pipes whose size suggests the impression that they did not generally accompany the owner, but were carried only on special occasions, and used when prescribed ceremonies of a political, religious, medicinal, or warlike character were to be observed. Varying in form and weight, such pipes are found both in the fields and in mounds. As a general rule, the more remarkable of them may be regarded as the public property of the tribe; still, their presence in conical earth-mounds containing but a single skeleton, would seem to indicate that some of them were the private property of noted personages—perhaps chiefs and medicine-men. It is scarcely probable that the public peace-pipe would have been liable to inhumation. Among the most curious of this class are the bird-shaped pipes of which Figs. 1, 2, and 3, Plate XXIII., may be regarded as interesting specimens. The first (Fig. 1) made of serpentine, is seven inches and a half from the tip of the beak to the end of the tail, three inches in height to the top of the bowl, and two inches and two-tenths in width just in rear of the bowl. The bowl is an inch and a half in diameter at the top, circular in shape, and an inch and five-eighths in depth. The walls of the bowl are three-eighths of an inch in thickness. The aperture for the stem, commencing under the tail, passes longitudinally through the body of the pipe until it intersects the bowl at its bottom. At its inception this aperture is an inch in diameter, gradually lessening as it deepens, until at the point where it communicates with the bowl it is only a quarter of an inch in width. The weight of this pipe is nearly two pounds.

The length of the second (Fig. 2) does not vary a quarter of an inch from that of the first. Its weight

Plate XXIII.

AM. PHOTO-LITHOGRAPHIC CO. N.Y. (OSBORNES PROCESS)

exceeds, however, by rather more than a quarter of a pound, and its height is three inches and three-quarters. The shape of the bowl is elliptical—its walls being half an inch thick. In depth this bowl measures two inches and a quarter. Its diameters at the top, reckoned respectively in the direction of the major and minor axes of the ellipse, are an inch and a half and an inch and three-tenths. The perforation for the stem is also elliptical, its greatest and least diameters being six-eighths and five-eighths of an inch. This aperture is half an inch in diameter where it enters the bowl. This pipe is made of serpentine, and, like the former, has been carefully polished.

The third pipe (Fig. 3) is of oolite, of a cream-color, and weighs two pounds and a half avoirdupois. It is six inches and a half in length, and about four inches high. The walls of the bowl are half an inch in thickness, and the bowl—circular in form—possesses a diameter of an inch and three-eighths, and a depth of two inches and a half. In rear of the bowl this pipe is nearly three inches in thickness. The aperture for the stem is rather more than three-quarters of an inch in diameter at its inception below the tail, and is diminished to half an inch at the point where it enters the bowl. While resting upon the flattened beak, breast, and clumsily-represented legs, this seems only a bird-pipe. If, however, we change the position, placing it upon the feet and tail, and turning the bowl away from us, this pipe at once assumes an entirely different aspect, apparently foreign to its ordinary uses, and seems to assert its right to be classed among the idol-pipes. This modified view is presented in Fig. 4, Plate XXIII. This pipe was found in the Chattahoochee Valley, several miles below the city of Columbus. The other two pipes were taken from mounds, one in Bibb County, and the other in Greene. The duck seemed to be the bird which most frequently enlisted the imitative powers of the Indians of this region. At other times the bear and the cougar, and the "human face divine," engaged the skill of the primitive artist.

Of the ordinary forms of calumets, Figs. 5, 6, 7, 8, and 9, Plate XXIII., may be regarded as typical. Fig. 5 consists of a stone composed of mica and dark brown felspar. This pipe is five inches high, nearly four inches long, and an inch and a quarter wide at the bottom, which is entirely flat, so that the pipe readily remains in an upright position. The bowl is circular, its diameter at the top being an inch and a quarter, and its depth rather more than three inches and a half. The walls of the bowl are three-quarters of an inch thick. The aperture for the stem is also circular, and three-quarters of an inch in diameter at the opening.

Number 6, composed of gneiss, is five inches in height, and five inches in length. The bowl is square, or very nearly so, the length of each side being about an inch and a quarter. Six-tenths of an inch will express the average thickness of the walls at the top. The bowl is rather more than three inches and three quarters in depth. This pipe also readily maintains an upright position, being flat at the bottom, which is an inch and three-quarters wide. The opening for the stem is circular, and, at its beginning, is an inch and a quarter in diameter. Fig. 7 represents a very fine calumet of steatite, four inches and three-quarters in height, four inches and a half in length, and about two inches wide. The circular bowl is two inches in diameter, and the walls are not less than half an inch in thickness. The bottoms of all these pipes are flat, and the bowls, with the exception of Fig. 9 (of soap-stone), are at right angles with the stem.

Many of the pipes of this class are made of mica slate and soap-stone. The latter material being easily worked and generally accessible, seems to have been held in especial esteem. Various are the devices and ornamentations traced upon the sides and faces of the soapstone pipes. Fig. 8, Plate XXIII., furnishes an example in point. Upon its bottom the paw of a bear is traced. In front are square, circular, elliptical, and parallelogrammic figures, and the upper portion and sides are ornamented with various incised lines. These calumets were taken from mounds and ploughed up in the fields.

Thus far the writer has failed to discover a single instance of the use, among the Georgia Indians, in ancient times, of the genuine red pipe stone or *Catlinite.* In the case of the softer stones there are indications that the bowls and holes for the stem were made by boring with a triangular-shaped implement, probably of flint. Upon some of the inner surfaces of these openings are annular abrasions, gradually decreasing in diameter as the end of the aperture is neared. Catlin[1] tells us that the Indians of the West shaped the bowls of their pipes from a solid stone, not quite as hard as marble, with nothing but a knife. "The stone," he continues, "which is of a cherry red, admits of a beautiful polish, and the Indian makes the hole in the bowl of the pipe by drilling into it a hard stick, shaped to the desired size, with a quantity of sharp

[1] "Illustrations of the Manners, Customs, and Condition of the North American Indians," vol. i., seventh edition, p. 234. London, 1848.

sand and water kept constantly in the hole, subjecting him, therefore, to a very great labour and the necessity of much patience."

In his account of the manners and customs of some of the Western Indians, Mr. Hunter[1] writes: "The men occasionally amuse themselves with making bowls and pipes of clay, for their individual use, which are burned as before described. They also make bowls and pipes of a kind of indurated bole, and of compact sand and limestone which are excavated and reduced to form by means of friction with harder substances and the intervention of sand and water. They generally ornament them with some figure characteristic of the owner's name; as, for instance, with that of a buffalo, elk, bear, tortoise, serpent, etc., according to the circumstance or caprice that has given rise to its assumption. In the same way they manufacture their large stone mortars for reducing corn into fine meal." In the absence of all metallic implements, it is probable that the Southern Indians gave outward shape to their harder pipes mainly by means of attrition. Sharp sand and water may have materially assisted them in drilling the holes. The drill, in all likelihood, consisted either of a piece of hard wood or of cane. As the cavity of the bowl narrowed, smaller drills were employed until the bottom was reached. Professor Rau, in his excellent article upon *drilling in stone without metal*, advances the opinion that a piece of cane will form "a regular hollow cylinder sufficiently strong to serve as a drill."[2] In this belief I fully concur, and am firmly

[1] "Memoirs of a Captivity among the Indians of North America," p. 290. London, 1823.

[2] Annual Report of the Board of Regents of the Smithsonian Institution for 1868, p. 399.

persuaded that the hard cane (*Arundinaria macrosperma*, Michaux), furnished the Southern Indians, and that abundantly, with hollow drills, which, with the aid of sharp sand and water, and a liberal expenditure of time and labor, would have compassed the perforations and hollows we observe in these pipes. Dr. Davis informed Professor Rau that a stone pipe, with an unfinished hollow partly filled with vegetable matter, was sent from Mississippi to the late Dr. Samuel G. Morton, of Philadelphia. When subjected to a microscopical examination, this vegetable substance exhibited the fibrous structure of cane, and thus appeared to be the remnant of a drill broken off in the bore.[1] Some of the bowls of the soapstone pipes were evidently hollowed or dug out with the aid of a sharp-pointed flint implement. Instances occur where the workman, neglecting to smooth or polish the inner surface, has left the marks of his rude incisive instrument. In many of these pipes the apertures for the stems appear unnecessarily large; and yet, the size of these openings, in connection with their flat bottoms, furnishes an argument in support of the principal use to which we suppose them to have been dedicated. In the deliberations of the council-lodge, or upon public occasions, it was important that the decorated stems should be long enough to be conveniently passed from one to the other, as the chief men sat around, without lifting the pipe from the ground upon which it rested. To accomplish this object, and also to afford ample opportunity for that labored ornamentation which was the pride and boast of the red-men, the stem must have been large and long. It will be remembered that the office of pipe-stem-carrier was, among many of the

[1] Annual Report of the Board of Regents of the Smithsonian Institution for 1868, p. 399.

tribes, invested with no little dignity. Swamp-canes furnished ample and convenient material, among the Southern Indians, for the facile manufacture of stems of any desired size or length. Joints of gradually-diminishing diameters could be readily adjusted the one into the other. All necessity for perforation was avoided, and thus a tapering stem, light and strong, could be easily constructed whose larger end would fit the aperture in the pipe, while its smaller extremity would admirably answer the convenience of the smoker.

The third class includes the ORDINARY PIPES in common use among the natives for smoking tobacco and other leaves, weeds, and barks, whose narcotic properties were well known to them in their primitive state. The luxury of smoking from the earliest times was recognized by nearly all the American tribes. "There is no custom," says Catlin,[1] "more uniformly in constant use amongst the poor Indians than that of smoking, nor any other more highly valued. His pipe is his constant companion through life—his messenger of peace; he pledges his friends through its stem and its bowl, and when its care-drowning fumes cease to flow, it takes a place with him in his solitary grave, with his tomahawk and war-club, companions to his long-fancied, 'mild, and beautiful hunting-grounds.'"

These common pipes were made both of stone and clay, generally of the latter material. They are usually of a size capable of being easily transported, and are not much heavier than the ordinary pipe of the present day. Some are no bigger in the bowl than a thimble. Of the stone pipes, Figs. 2 and 6, Plate XXIV., may be

[1] "Illustrations of the Manners, Customs, and Condition of the North American Indians," etc., vol. i., seventh edition, p. 235. London, 1848.

Plate XXIV.

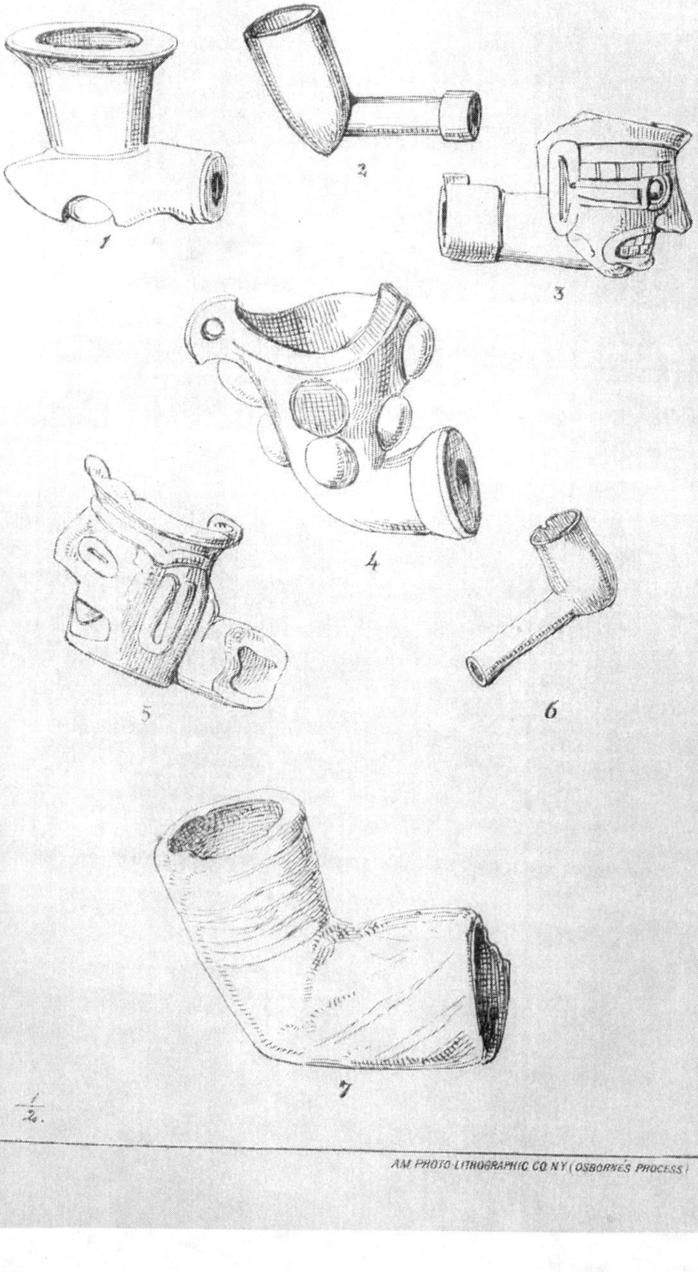

1/2.

AM. PHOTO-LITHOGRAPHIC CO. N.Y. (OSBORNE'S PROCESS)

regarded as fine specimens, perhaps rather more delicate than those in common use. The pipe represented by Fig. 2 was found near the large mound on the plantation of Mr. J. H. Nichols, in Nacoochee Valley. Made of a hard black stone, it has been formed with much regularity and delicacy. The walls of the bowl are very thin, scarcely thicker than the sides of a saddler's thimble.

The composition of the clay pipes is precisely the same as that used by the Indians of this region in the manufacture of their pottery, red and blue clay mixed with powdered shells or fine gravel.

Figs. 4 and 7, Plate XXIV., represent two pipes of this description taken from earth-mounds on the Ocmulgee River, not far from Macon; while those delineated in Figs. 3 and 5, Plate XXIV., were found in shell-mounds on the Colonel's Island. Fragments of pipes of this composition are not infrequent, and attest their general use among the ancient inhabitants of this region. Perfect specimens are rarely to be obtained. The custom of burning the dead was, at some time or other, maintained to a considerable extent on the Southern Atlantic coast. As a direct consequence, in all tumuli where cremation occurred, only fragments of pipes may now be found. From one small mound of this character the writer obtained parts of five clay pipes which had been broken in the funeral-fires. Hearne describes a custom among the Chippewas, after the shedding of blood, of throwing all their ornaments and pipes into a common fire; and Winslow narrates of the Nanohiggansets that they had a house, ordinarily frequented by priests, whither at certain times resorted all the people and offered their riches to their gods. These contributions were cast by the priests into a great fire made in the middle of that house.[1] Upon the sacrificial altars of the mounds of the West, Messrs. Squier and Davis found many beautiful pipes cracked and broken by fire. It may be that these fragmentary clay-pipes from the Georgia mounds, if rightly understood, testify the sincere affection cherished by the living for the dead when, having concluded the last funeral rites, they committed to the same fires which consumed the bones of the departed, these symbols of peace, of comfort, and of friendship.

Figure 1, Plate XXIV., is a correct delineation of a clay pipe found in a grave-mound in Tennessee.

The modern Cherokees excelled in the manufacture of bird and animal-shaped pipes—many of them large and elaborate. The nude human figure in kneeling, bending or sitting posture, frequently formed the subject of imitation; and we have seen several pipes of this description which, in the language of Adair, could not "much be commended for their modesty."

[1] *See* Wilson's "Prehistoric Man," second edition, p. 323. London, 1865.

CHAPTER XIX.

Idol-Worship among the Southern Indians.—Stone and Terra-Cotta Images.

The history of idol-worship—from its most degraded expression in the Fetichism of Congo, through all its modified forms up to its most elaborate development in the states of ancient Greece and Rome—is both curious and interesting. The stocks and stones and the senseless images of the unlearned and the base have perished, and are passing into oblivion wherever the shadows of superstition, beneath which they had their being, are dispelled by the light of a superior civilization. Even the bulls and beetles of enigmatic Egypt—overrun with gods—incurred the sneers of Juvenal. Although not a single worshipper be found among living men, the divinities of Olympus, the Muses, the Graces, the Lares and Penates, the Fates, the Furies, and the Satyrs of the classic age, and the sublime art which enthroned them on earthly pedestals, still live in the domains of literature and taste. They are as immortal as the poetry, the imagination, and the traditions, whose offspring they were. Beautifully has Coleridge testified to the permanency of this art-idolatry, and to the influence which its memories still exert over the minds of succeeding generations:

"The intelligible forms of ancient poets,
The fair humanities of old religion,
The Power, the Beauty, and the Majesty
That had their haunts in dale or piny mountain,
Or forest, by slow stream, or pebbly spring,
Or chasms and watery depths; all these have vanished;
They live no longer in the faith of reason;
But still the heart doth need a language; still
Doth the old instinct bring back the old names;
Spirits or gods that used to share this earth
With man as with their friend; and at this day
'Tis Jupiter who brings whate'er is great,
And Venus who brings every thing that's fair."

But it is not permitted us now to linger among these deifications of the unseen powers of Nature—these wonderful embodiments of the ideal and the beautiful. To humbler and more obscure investigations do our present inquiries lead.

Mr. Tylor[1] is of the opinion that idols belong to a period of transition and of growth. In support of this idea, he instances the fact that among races lowest in the scale of civilization—such as the Fuegians and many of the Indian tribes of North America—we see and hear little or nothing of idols, while in Mexico and Peru the entire apparatus of temples, idols, priests, and sacrifices, obtains in a complex and elaborate form. A belief in the existence of a Supreme Being is wellnigh universal among men, and the absence of all religious superstitions and of a conception of the immortality of the soul, is the emphatic sign of the most absolute degradation. The presence of idols among barbarians may be therefore regarded as denoting not only the entity of a religious idea, but also the coöperation of

[1] "Researches into the Early History of Mankind," etc., second edition, p. 112. London, 1870.

something like art and imagination to impart definite shape and personality to vague conceptions of superior beings.

Sympathizing with the views of Mr. Tylor, Sir John Lubbock[1] writes: "The worship of idols characterizes a somewhat higher stage of human development. We find no traces of it among the lowest races of men; and Lafitau says truly: 'On peut dire en général que le grand nombre des peuples sauvages n'a point d'idoles.' The error of regarding Idolatry as the general religion of low races, has no doubt mainly arisen from confusing the Idol and the Fetich. Fetichism, however, is an attack on the Deity; Idolatry is an act of submission to him; rude, no doubt, but yet humble. Hence, Fetichism and Idolatry are not only different, but opposite, so that the one could not be developed directly out of the other. We must, therefore, expect to find between them, as indeed we do, a stage of religion without either the one or the other."

However true it may be that idol-worship indicates a development of the religious idea as contrasted with its non-existence among peoples who give evidence either of no religious emotions whatever, or of superstitions so degraded that they do not rise above Fetichism, certain it is that a devotion which, ignoring the intervention of idols, recognizes the existence of a Supreme Being, a Great Spirit, or of two controlling divinities—the one of good and the other of evil—is still more elevated and expansive in its character. So also is that system of worship which deifies the sun and moon, and cherishes fire as an object of adoration because of its supposed direct emanation from a divine

[1] "The Origin of Civilization and the Primitive Condition of Man," p. 225. London, 1870.

source. The religion of the Southern Indians was, in some respects, not unlike that attributed by Tacitus to the ancient Germans: "Cæterum nec cohibere parietibus deos neque in ullam humani oris speciem assimulare, ex magnitudine cælestium arbitrantur. Lucos ac nemora consecrant, deorumque nominibus appellant secretum illud quod sola reverentia vident."[1]

Both the sun and moon were, among many tribes, regarded with absolute veneration; and certain seasons were set apart for special religious observances. Speaking generally, it may be stated that they recognized one great and good Spirit as the creator of all—the author of life, and light, and heat—the dispenser of rain, the provider of game, and the source of all development in plant and animal. Him they sought to propitiate on all important occasions, whether of war, the chase, or of husbandry. Subordinate to this great first cause, they reckoned other spirits, good and evil, and with them their priests, conjurers, and medicine-men were commissioned to treat. With the malign influences of the evil one—whether exerted in the form of disease, or faint-heartedness, or blight upon the zea—they were ever contending. Extravagant as were their traditions and superstitions with regard to their national or tribal origins, there was always incorporated some memory which perpetuated the primal presence and power of this Great Spirit. His intervention was admitted in the first strong wind, great fire, or dense smoke, or in the opening of some vast cave from which his children issued forth to possess the green earth he had made. Despite their curious and degraded religious notions, there can be no doubt but that many

[1] C. Cornelii Taciti Opera omnia, ad fidem editionis Orellianæ," tom. ii., p. 235. Oxonii, 1851.

of the tribes, realizing the presence of a soul or spirit in the breast of man, and appreciating the operation of natural laws, attained unto a conception not only of the immortality of that spirit, but also of the fact that in a future state good or evil fortune would betide the translated according to his conduct in this world.

That the Georgia tribes were not idol-worshippers —in the ordinary acceptation of that term—and did not fashion or reverence images at the period of our earliest acquaintance with them, may be confidently affirmed.

Speaking of the Indians who resided in the vicinity of Savannah when General Oglethorpe established the colony of Georgia beneath the pines which then crowned Yamacraw Bluff, the Reverend Mr. Bolzius[1] states: "They have some Religion, believing a Supreme Being, which they call *Sotolycate* (literally translated, *He who sitteth Above*), who is in all Places; though they would not teach us the Word by which they express the Name of GOD in their Language. They believe that from the Supreme Being comes every Thing, especially Wisdom. They use no Ceremonies, nor outward religious Exercises, except at a Solemn Festival, held once a Year. They worship no Idols; however they sing some songs about the ancient Heroes."

Equally emphatic is the testimony of Mr. Bartram:[2] "These Indians are by no means idolaters, unless their puffing the tobacco smoke towards the sun, and rejoicing at the appearance of the new moon, may be so

[1] An Extract of the Journals of Mr. Commissary Von Reck and of the Reverend Mr. Bolzius, p. 36. London, 1734.

[2] "Travels through North and South Carolina, Georgia, East and West Florida," etc., pp. 495, 496. London, 1792.

termed. So far from idolatry are they, that they have no images amongst them, nor any religious rite or ceremony that I could perceive; but adore the Great Spirit, the giver and taker away of the breath of life, with the most profound and respectful homage. They believe in a future state where the spirit exists, which they call the world of spirits, where they enjoy different degrees of tranquillity or comfort, agreeably to their life spent here; a person who in his life has been an industrious hunter, provided well for his family, an intrepid and active warrior, just, upright, and who has done all the good he could, will, they say, in the world of spirits, live in a warm, pleasant country, where are expansive, green, flowery savannas and high forests, watered with rivers of pure waters, replenished with deer and every species of game; a serene, unclouded, and peaceful sky; in short, where there is fullness of pleasure, uninterrupted."

Mr. Adair[1] is no less positive in his recorded observations on this point: "But these Indian Americans pay their religious devoir to *Loak-Ishto hoollo-Aba*, 'the great, beneficent, supreme, holy spirit of fire,' who resides (as they think) above the clouds, and on earth also, with unpolluted people. He is with them the sole author of warmth, light, and of all animal and vegetable life. They do not pay the least perceivable adoration to any images, or to dead persons; neither to the celestial luminaries, nor evil spirits, nor any created being whatsoever. They are utter strangers to all the gestures practised by the pagans in their religious rites. They kiss no idols; nor, if they were placed out of their reach, would they kiss their hands in token of reverence and a willing obedience. . . .

[1] "History of the American Indians," etc., pp. 19, 22. London, 1775.

They pay no religious worship to stocks or stones after the manner of the old Eastern pagans; neither do they worship any kind of images whatsoever. . . .

"I never heard that any of our North American Indians had images of any kind. There is a carved human statue of wood, to which, however, they pay no religious homage. It belongs to the head war-town of the Upper Muskohge country, and seems to have been originally designed to perpetuate the memory of some distinguished hero who deserved well of his country; for, when their *cusseena*, or bitter black drink, is about to be drank in the synedrion, they frequently, on common occasions, will bring it there, and honour it with the first conch-shell-full, by the hand of the chief religious attendant: and then they return it to its former place. It is observable that the same beloved waiter, or holy attendant, and his coadjutant, equally observe the same ceremony to any person of reputed merit in that quadrangular place. When I past that way, circumstances did not allow me to view this singular figure; but I am assured by several of the traders, who have frequently seen it, that the carving is modest, and very neatly finished, not unworthy of a modern civilized artist." The same author assures us that he has never seen the worship of the Priapus indulged in by the natives with whom he was acquainted.

Referring to the Cherokees, Lieutenant Timberlake[1] says: "As to religion, every one is at liberty to think for himself; whence flows a diversity of opinions amongst those that do think, but the major part do not give themselves that trouble. They generally concur, however, in the belief of one superior Being

[1] "Memoirs," etc., pp. 63–65. London, 1765.

who made them and governs all things, and are therefore never discontent at any misfortune, because they say the Man above would have it so. They believe in a reward and punishment, as may be evinced by their answer to Mr. Martin, who, having preached Scripture till both his audience and he were heartily tired, was told at last, that they knew very well that if they were good they should go up; if bad, down; that he could tell no more; that he had long plagued them with what they no ways understood, and that they desired him to depart the country. . . . They have few religious ceremonies or stated times of general worship: the green-corn dance seems to be the principal, which is, as I have been told, performed in a very solemn manner in a large square before the town-house door: the motion here is very slow, and the song in which they offer thanks to God for the corn he has sent them, far from unpleasing."

When questioned as to the origin of the new fire, and of the Boos-ke-tau, Efau Haujo,[1] the great Medal Chief of Took-au-bat-che, responded that he had been taught from his infancy to believe that there is an E-sau-ge-tuh E-mis-see (Master of Breath) who gave these customs to the Indians as necessary and suited to them; and that an observance of them entitled the red-men to his care and protection both in war and seasons of difficulty.

When asked whether the Creeks believed in a future existence, he replied: "The old notion among us is that when we die the spirit (po-yau-fic-chau) goes the way the sun goes, to the west, and there joins its family and friends who went before it." To the in-

[1] Hawkins' "Sketch of the Creek Country." Collections of the Georgia Historical Society, vol. iii., part 1, p. 80.

quiry, "Do the red people believe in a future state of rewards and punishments?" he answered: "We have an opinion that those who behaved well, are taken under the care of E-sau-ge-tuh E-mis-see and assisted; and that those who have behaved ill, are left there to shift for themselves; and that there is no other punishment."

During a conversation which occurred between Tomo-chi-chi and General Oglethorpe about prayer, the aged Mico of the Yamacraws said that the Indians never prayed to God but left it to Him to do what He thought best for them: "That the asking for any particular blessing looked to him like directing God; and if so, that it must be a very wicked thing. That for his part he thought everything that happened in the world was as it should be; that God of Himself would do for every one what was consistent with the good of the whole; and that our duty to Him was to be content with whatever happened in general, and thankful for all the good that happened in particular."[1]

In his "Philosophico-historico-hydrogeography of South Carolina, Georgia, and East Florida," De Brahm[2] says that the Indians of this region entertained a notion of immortality and of a future state wherein they expected to enjoy large hunting-grounds well stocked with deer, and also an apprehension of spirits. "The Indians have also a very scant knowledge of a Divine Being, which knowledge, or rather notion, extends no farther than that they believe he is good: the Cherakees call him (Hianequo), the great man, whom the

[1] Spence's "Anecdotes," p. 318. London, 1820. Jones' "Historical Sketch of Tomo-chi-chi," p. 105. Albany, 1868.

[2] "Documents connected with the History of South Carolina, edited by Plowden Charles, Jennett Weston, and printed for private distribution only," pp. 221, 222. London, 1856.

Catabaws call (Rivet), overseer; but they pay no manner of adoration to him, nor anything existing; nor have they any ceremony at all than to extinguish all their fires once a year in July, at the time when the Indian corn (maize) is in its milk, which they squeeze out by beating and straining; than boile that milk by a fire new caught from electrifation, which they perform with two green sticks rubd with great velocity a cross each other until they are lighted; when this milk is boiled to a consistency, they let it cool, than form it into little cakes which they fry in bear's fat, and are (whilst warm) a delicious eating; with them they keep feasting three days. To this season they postpone all elections, promotions, and their king's coronations."

"Their Religion," upon the authority of Mr. Ash,[1] "chiefly consists in the Adoration of the *Sun* and *Moon:* At the Appearance of the *New Moon* I have observed them with open extended Arms, then folded, with inclined Bodies, to make their Adorations with much Ardency and Passion."

If we may credit the narrative of Jonathan Dickenson,[2] a sort of Sabianism existed among some of the Florida tribes, and Pitchlynn once remarked: "From all I have seen and can understand of the Indians who once inhabited the portions of country covered by the Southern States of the Union, they appear to have been originally worshippers of the sun. The Chahta when he has greatly misbehaved, utters these ejaculations: When the sun forsakes a man he will do things he never thought to do! The sun is turned against me, therefore have I come to this."[3] The Fidalgo of

[1] "Carolina," etc., by T. A., Gent., p. 36. London, 1682.

[2] "God's Protecting Providence," etc., third edition, p. 13, *et aliter.* Philadelphia, 1720.

[3] "Relation of Alvar Nuñez Cabeça de Vaca," translated by Buckingham Smith, p. 171, note 3. New York, 1871.

Elvas asserts that the Indians of Florida worshipped the devil, and made sacrifices of the blood and bodies of their people whenever his satanic majesty suggested that he was athirst. It was to escape such oblation that Juan Ortiz, warned by the Indian girl, fled by night to Mococo.[1] Cabeça de Vaca mentions "gourds bored with holes and having pebbles in them," which were used by the Indians in their dances, and were supposed to possess special virtue because they were heaven-descended."[2] Elsewhere in the Spanish narratives do we read of wooden images of birds; but, so far as we now remember, no account is given of a single idol as an object of adoration among the aborigines. At Talomeco, De Soto found a large temple or mausoleum, at whose entrance were gigantic statues of wood, carved with considerable skill, the largest of which was twelve feet high. They were armed with various weapons, and "stood in threatening attitudes, with ferocious looks." The interior of the temple was decorated with statues of various shapes and sizes. There was also a great profusion of conchs and different kinds of sea and river shells. It does not appear, however, that these images were objects of religious veneration or positive worship. Like the "carved human statue of wood" in the head war-town of the upper Muskohge country, described by Adair, they seem rather to have been the effigies of heroes, the embodiments of brave memories, the symbols of tribal pomp and power.

Lawson tells us that at the corn-dances among the Carolina Indians—the one when the harvest is ended, to return thanks to the good spirit for the fruits of the

[1] "Narratives of the Career of Hernando de Soto," etc., translated by Buckingham Smith, p. 31. New York, 1866.

[2] "Relation of Alvar Nuñez Cabeça de Vaca," translated by Buckingham Smith, p. 142. New York, 1871.

earth—the other in the spring to invoke blessings upon the seed to be sown—the old men, in order to encourage the young men to labor stoutly in planting their maize, set up a sort of idol in the field, attired in the customary habit of an Indian, with strings of wampum about its neck. This image—guarded by the king and old men, who pay profound respect to it—the young ones are not permitted to approach. By the old men the young men are told that this image "is some famous Indian warrior that died a great while ago, and now is come amongst them to see if they will work well, which, if they do, he will go to the good spirit and speak to him to send them plenty of corn," and make them "expert hunters and mighty warriors."[1] Commenting upon the absurdities of their superstitions, our author asserts it to be impossible to give a true description of their religion: "I[2] have known them," says he, "amongst their idols and dead kings in their Quiogozon for several days, where I could never get admittance to see what they were doing, though I was at great friendship with the king and great men: but all my persuasions availed me nothing, neither were any, but the king, with the conjurer, and some few old men, in that house; as for the young men and chiefest numbers of the Indians, they were kept as ignorant of what the elders were doing, as myself. They all believe . . . . that there are two spirits; the one good, the other bad. The good one they reckon to be the author and maker of every thing, and say that it is he that gives them the fruits of the earth, and has taught them to hunt, fish, and be wise enough to overpower the beasts of the wilderness,

[1] "History of Carolina," pp. 285, 286. Reprint. Raleigh, 1860.
[2] Idem, p. 342.

and all other creatures that they may be assistant and beneficial to man." They declare also that the bad spirit lives apart from the good, and torments men with sickness, disappointments, losses, hunger, and all the misfortunes incident to human life. In the immortality of man they believe, and have a notion of certain rewards and punishments in another world.

Beverly[1] furnishes an account of a surreptitious visit which he paid to a Quioccosan, or house of religious worship, used by the Virginia Indians. In a mat he there found what he took to be a disjointed idol—a rude affair, scarcely justifying the elaborate representation offered in the accompanying plate. He also assures us that these peoples had altars and places of sacrifice. To the evil spirit burnt-offerings were made, and it is more than probable that on some occasions young children were immolated.

Treating of the religious belief and worship of the Virginia Indians, the author of the "Admiranda Narratio"[2] says: "Multos Deos credunt, quos Montóac appellant, diuersorum tamen generum & ordinum: unum solum primarium & Magnum Deum qui fuerit ab æterno. Is (ipsis afferentibus) mundum conditurus, initio creauit alios deos primarii ordinis, ut essent tamquam media & instrumenta, ipsi subseruientia cum ad creationem, tum ad gubernationem: deinde Solem, Lunam & Stellas tamquam Semi-Deos & instrumenta alterius ordinis præcipui. Dicunt aquas primum omnium esse factas, ex quibus Dii omnes creaturas visibiles & invisibiles condiderunt. . . .

"Omnes Deos humanam naturam habere putant,

[1] "History and Present State of Virginia," book iii., chap. viii. London, 1705.

[2] "Admiranda Narratio, fida tamen, de commodis et incolarum ritibus Virginiæ," et cæt., pp. 26, 27. Francoforti ad Mœnum. Anno 1590.

ea de causa imaginibus humanæ formæ illos exprimunt, eosque KEWASOWOK appellant, unicus KEWAS est dictus. Illis proprias ædes sine templa dicant, quæ Machicómuck nominãt, in quib, sint precationes, cantus & per multos dies oblationes ad ipsorũ Deos. In quibusdam templis nos unicum Kewas obseruauimus, in aliis binos, aliquando tres. Vulgus etiam pro Diis habet.

"Animæ immortalitatem êl credunt, eam statim atque a corpore soluta est transferri secũdum opera quæ fecit, vel ad Deorum sedes ad perpetuam felicitatem fruendam, vel ad ingentem fossam seu scrobem (quam in extremis mundi finibus procul ab ipsis versus occidentem sitis esse censent) ad perpetuum ignem: eum locum ipsi POPOGUSSO appellant."

In plate xxi., De Bry presents us with a sketch of the idol Kiwasa seated in its temple. The illustration is accompanied by the following explanatory remarks: "Idolum habent huius regionis incolæ, KIWASA appellatum, e ligneo trunco elaboratum, quatuor pedes altum, cuius caput Floridæ incolarum capita refert: facies carneo colore depicta est, pectus albo, reliquum corpus nigro, crura etiam pictura alba variegata: è collo torques pendent sphærulis albis constantes, quibus intermixtæ sunt, aliæ teretes ex ære, magis ab illis æstimato, quam aurum vel argentum. Est illud idolum in templo oppidi SECOTA repositum tamquam custos Regiorum cadauerum. Bina interdum habent in templis hujusmodi idola, nonnunquam tria, non plura; quæ cum obscuro loco sint reposita, horrenda apparent."

The following plate (xxii.) introduces us to this idol Kiwasa, seated in a sepulchre of the kings, and guarding the repose of the royal dead.

The religion of the Florida tribes is dismissed with the following brief notice:[1] "Nullam Dei habent notitiam, neque ullam religionem: quod illis conspicuum est, veluti Sol & Luna, illis Deus est. Sacrificos habent, quibus valde fidunt: magni enim sunt magi, arioli, & dæmonum invocatores. Funguntur etiam ii sacrifici medicorum & chirurgorum munere; ejus rei causa semper circumferunt saccum herbis & medicamentis plenum, ad ægros curandos, qui plerumque venerea lue laborant: nam feminarum & virginum, quas solis filias nuncupant, amoribus sunt admodum dediti."

In plate viii. of this "Brevis Narratio," we are informed that the Indians venerated as an idol the column which Ribault had placed upon a mound to mark the limit of the French empire in the New World. To this stone they offered the finest fruits, roots, corn, vessels filled with perfumed oils, and bows and arrows. The column itself was encircled from top to bottom with wreaths of flowers and branches of choicest trees.

In plate xxxv. we are made acquainted with the ceremonies attendant upon the annual offering of a stag to the sun.

Of all the Southern tribes, however, the Natchez were probably most addicted to the worship of idols. Père le Petit[2] says: "The Natchez have a temple filled with idols. These idols are different figures of men and women for which they have the deepest veneration." In another passage he is more explicit: "Their idols are *images of men and women made of stone and baked clay*, heads and tails of extraordinary serpents,

[1] "Brevis Narratio eorum quæ in Florida," etc., pp. 3, 4. Francoforti ad Mœnum. Anno 1591.

[2] Letters Ed. et Cur. iv., 261, quoted by Dr. Brinton, in the *Historical Magazine*, vol. ix., p. 300.

stuffed owls, pieces of crystal and the jaw-bones of great fishes."

Subsequently, when Father Charlevoix[1] visited this temple, its glory had departed—its stone benches were vacant, its idols gone, its altar deserted, and but little left to denote the religious uses to which it had been dedicated save the triangular fire watched by the solitary keeper and slowly burning in honor of the sun. By an old Taenca Indian the Chevalier Tonti[2] was informed that the natives of that region worshipped the sun and had temples, altars, and priests—"that in the temple there was a fire which burnt perpetually as the proper emblem of the Sun." To the moon, at certain seasons, oblations were made. Of the temple, the Chevalier has left us the following description: "The structure of it was exactly the same with that of the Prince's house. As to the out-side it is encompassed with a great high Wall, the space betwixt that and the Temple forming a kind of Court where People may walk. On the top of the Wall are several Pikes to be seen, upon which are stuck the Heads of their own most notorious Criminals, or of their Enemies. On the top of the Frontispiece there is a great Knob raised, all covered round with Hair, and above that an heap of Scalps in form of a Trophy.

"The inside of the Temple is only a *Nave*, painted on all sides, at top with all sorts of Figures; in the midst of it is an Hearth instead of an Altar, upon which there is continually three great Billets burning, standing up on end; and two Priests drest in White Vestments are ever looking after it to make up the Fire

[1] "Voyage to North America," vol. ii., p. 192, *et seq.* Dublin, 1766.

[2] "Account of Monsieur de la Salle's Last Expedition," etc., pp. 91, 94. London, 1698.

and supply it. It is round this that all the People come to say their Prayers, with strange kind of Hummings. The Prayers are three times a Day; at Sunrise, at Noon, and at Sun-set. They made me take notice of a sort of Closet cut out of the Wall, the inside of which was very fine; I could see only the Roof of it, on the top of which there hung a couple of spread Eagles which look'd towards the Sun. I wanted to go into it; but they told me that it was the Tabernacle of their God, and that it was permitted to none but their High Priest to go into it. And I was told that this was the Repository of their Wealth and Treasures; as Pearls, Gold and Silver, precious Stones, and some Goods that came out of *Europe*, which they had from their neighbours."

This sun-worship, with its attendant religious ceremonies, was not confined to the tribes who congregated along the banks of the Mississippi, but existed also among the Georgia and Florida Indians. Tradition points to a country west of the Mississippi as the original habitat of at least some of the nations composing the Creek Confederacy. We know that some of the Natchez, abandoning their former seats, joined the Creeks, and it is entirely probable that in doing so they brought with them their peculiar religious ceremonies, and perpetuated their observance among their new neighbors. Possibly this change of residence may account for the introduction of at least some idols or images within the limits of Georgia.

Without further pursuing this inquiry into the recorded observations of the early writers who have endeavored to inform us with regard to the religion of the Southern Indians, it will be perceived that, while we have thus far failed to note any emphatic account declaring the existence of idol-worship among the Georgia tribes, we are certified of the fact that idols were seen in the possession of coterminous nations, and that they were held in superstitious veneration and regarded, in some measure at least, as objects of devotion. It does appear, however, that they occupied, in the esteem of the natives, a position far inferior to that conceded to the sun or to the Great Spirit, and that they constituted only a sort of religious machinery in the hands of kings, priests, conjurers, and old men, with which to dignify temples, supplement certain sacred festivals, and operate upon the fears and credulity of the more ignorant and unthinking masses. One is tempted to regard them rather as conjurers' images, as the private property of priests, as the likenesses of famous dead, and as the potent charms of medicine-men, than as the generally acknowledged embodiments of the person and presence of unseen yet recognized divinities.

Although Bolzius, Bartram, Adair, and others, deny either positively or inferentially the existence of idols or images within the limits then occupied by the Georgia Indians, subsequent investigations prove by the discovered presence of the images themselves, that at some time or other idol-worship of some sort was here practised. The ornamented posts, the wooden images, and the questionable figures of men, birds, and animals sketched upon the white walls of the Creek houses—if any religious significance they possessed—have long since perished. Next in the order of durability are small images formed of burnt clay and modelled after the similitude of birds and animals, and of man. (*See* Plate XXV.) These occur in various parts of the State, and vary in height from

Plate XXV.

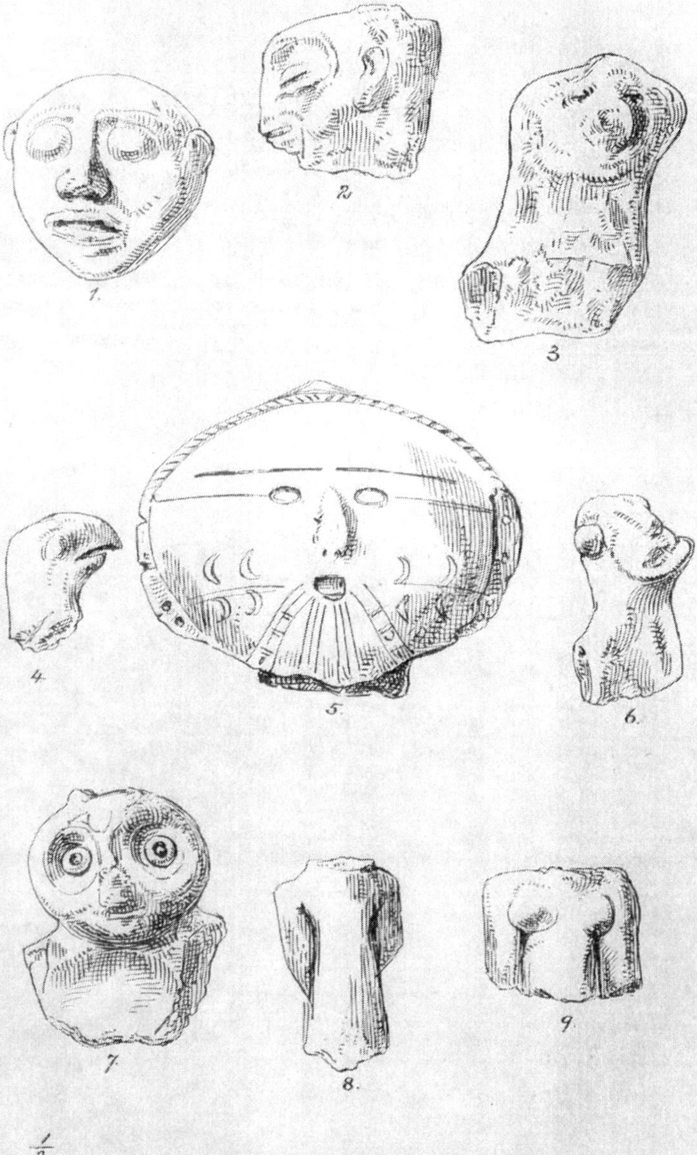

1/2.

AM. PHOTO-LITHOGRAPHIC CO. N.Y. (OSBORNE'S PROCESS)

three to seven inches. Those which represent the human figure are little more than rude terra-cotta dolls clumsily fashioned. The owl, the wild-cat, and the sun, were favorite subjects for imitation at the hands of the primitive artists. So readily could they have been made, and so little care was generally bestowed upon their construction, that it may well be questioned whether they amounted to much more than playthings for children. It may be, however, that in the repertory of the priest, the conjurer, and the medicine-man, they possessed greater dignity and were designed for more important purposes.

In a previous chapter we have described several interesting idol-pipes, and have suggested that they were in all likelihood intimately associated with the religious ceremonies of the aborigines. Whether they should properly be classed with the *simulacra* which we now proceed to consider, we do not confidently affirm or deny. So far as the writer's information extends, comparatively few stone idols have been found in Georgia. These occurred in the upper portions of the State, and chiefly in the valley of the Etowah.

In an old Indian field in Dirt-Town Valley, in Chattooga County, some years since, was ploughed up what may be termed an idol-sanctuary. It was made of a cube of limestone six inches each way. The upper portion or roof consisted of a quadrangular pyramid, with a base six inches square, terminating in an apex four inches high, thus giving to the entire object an altitude of ten inches. In one face was an aperture or doorway, arched at the top, extending almost from the bottom of the structure nearly to the base of the pyramid-shaped top. The interior of this shrine had been carefully excavated, so that its sides and bottom were not more than half an inch in thickness. In front of this arched doorway, and against the opposite wall, a little image was seated upon a pedestal. Only the countenance was visible, the figure being concealed by drapery. On either side was a pedestal similar in form to that upon which the image sat, and about half the size. In the walls to the right and left of the idol a window had been cut much smaller than, but similar in outline to, the doorway. The whole affair had been carved out of a solid block of limestone-rock.

In 1860 a stone idol was found a few miles from Catoosa Springs. It was about sixteen inches high, and represented a male figure in a sitting posture.

In the possession of Colonel Lewis Tumlin, in 1859, the writer examined an idol which had been ploughed up near the large mound on the Etowah River, upon the plantation of that gentleman. It[1] was made of a coarse dark sandstone, and was twelve inches high. It consisted of a male figure in a sitting posture. The knees were drawn up almost upon a level with the chin, the hands resting upon and clasping either knee. The chin and forehead were retreating. The hair was gathered into a knot behind. The face was upturned and the eyes were angular. Unfortunately, this image was lost or destroyed amid the desolations consequent upon Sherman's march through Georgia in 1864, but its place has been supplied by another recently found in the same neighborhood. It was ploughed up on Colonel Tumlin's plantation, near the base of the large tumulus[2] located within the area formed by the moat and the Etowah River, and

[1] Jones' "Monumental Remains of Georgia," part 1, pp. 108, 109. Savannah, 1861.

[2] Ibid., part 1, p. 27, *et seq.* Savannah, 1861.

Plate XXVI.

1. 2. 3. $\frac{1}{5}$

AM. PHOTO-LITHOGRAPHIC CO. N.Y. (OSBORNE'S PROCESS)

is certainly the most interesting idol thus far discovered in this State. The accompanying front, rear, and profile views (*see* Plate XXVI.), afford an intelligent idea of the peculiarities of this image. It is a female figure, in a sitting posture. The legs, however, are entirely rudimentary and unformed. Its height is fifteen inches and three-quarters, and its weight thirty-three and a half pounds. Cut out of a soft talcose rock, originally of a grayish hue, it has been in time so much discolored that it now presents a ferruginous appearance. Below the navel, and enveloping the buttocks and rudimentary thighs, is a hip-dress, ornamented both on the left side and behind by rectangular, circular, and irregular lines. The ears are pierced, and the head is entirely bald. In the centre of the top of the head a hole has been drilled half an inch in depth, and five-tenths of an inch in diameter. This probably formed the socket in which some head-ornament was seated. That ornament, whatever it was, had fallen out and was lost when the image was found. Springing from the back of the head and attached at the other end to the back midway between the shoulders, is a substantial handle by means of which this image could have been securely suspended or safely transported from place to place. The mammary glands are sharply defined and maidenly in their appearance. The ears, hand, and navel are rudely formed. The impression conveyed is that of a dead, young, flat-head, Indian woman. Unfortunately, the left arm has been broken off, but otherwise this idol is in a state of remarkable preservation. Dr. Berendt and Professor Rau—to whom the writer exhibited this image—concurred in opinion that this figure bears little resemblance to objects of the same class found in the more southern parts of this continent. Naked figures are rarely seen there, nearly all of them being clothed, and, generally, highly ornamented, especially about the head, which, in the present instance, is entirely bare and even without ear-ornaments. The features are more like the North American than the Central American Indian, and the remaining hand is fleshier than is usually observed among the Central American images. The marks on the back and sides also resemble more closely the North American pictographs or rock and stone inscriptions than they do the Central American hieroglyphics. We presume, with the lights now before us, it must be admitted that this is an Indian image, the handiwork of some nomadic tribe which possessed this region some time during the bygone centuries, and, in turn, was expelled from the occupancy of this beautiful valley by other and later representatives of the North American type. We are warranted in the assertion that the modern Cherokees[1] disclaimed all share in the erection of the mounds in whose proximity this idol was found. They even went so far as to declare that they possessed not even a tradition of the peoples by whom they were made, and that their forefathers saw them for the first time in a state of completion when they occupied the country. They further repudiated the idea that their nation had at any time been addicted either to the manufacture or the worship of idols. We may, therefore, safely conclude that this is not a Cherokee idol, certainly of a late date. Where there are no letters, no histories, no inscribed monuments, one wave of human life sweeps over another and the tradition of to-day is swallowed

[1] Haywood's "Natural and Aboriginal History of Tennessee," p. 226. Nashville, 1823.

up in the equally frail memory of to-morrow. Under such circumstances emphatically is it true that "one generation passeth away and another generation cometh; but the earth abideth forever. There is no remembrance of former things: neither shall there be any remembrance of things that are to come with those that shall come after."

We know not how old this Indian population was. We cannot even positively assert that it was not autochthonous. We are ignorant of the distinctive names and characteristics of the various hunter-tribes which may have succeeded each other during the lapsed ages, in the ownership of this soil. As we look upon this rude monument, we are not entirely sure that it is emblematic of a past idolatry. It may be the effort of some primitive sculptor to perpetuate in stone the form and features of some Indian maiden famous in the esteem of her family and tribe.

Various theories may be suggested, fancied analogies traced and probable origins conjectured, but, after all, the most we can confidently say with regard to the antiquity of this relic—curious and ancient as it undoubtedly appears—is that it is seemingly older than the handiwork and the superstition of any Indian tribe of which we have any knowledge as resident upon the beautiful banks of the Etowah.

If object of worship it was, this rude stone image, outliving the generation by which it was fashioned and invested with superhuman attributes, awakened from its long sleep of neglect and desuetude, conveys to us of the present day a true conception of the ignorance and the superstition of that by-gone age, affords physical insight into the condition of the sculptor's art at that remote period, and confirms the past existence of peoples whose names and origin are the subjects only of speculation—whose history is perpetuated simply by a few archaic relics which, having successfully wrestled with the disintegrating influences of time, remain uncrushed by the tread of another and a statelier civilization. But it is not alone in Georgia that these images are found. Tennessee, above all her sister States, seems to be most prolific of them. In the beginning of this century, Mr. Jefferson was presented with two "Indian busts" which were unearthed by some laborers who were excavating along the bank of the Cumberland River, near Palmyra.[1] They are described thus: "The human form extends to the middle of the body, and the figures are nearly of the natural size. The lineaments are strongly marked, and such as are peculiar to the copper-colored aboriginal inhabitants of America. It is not known of what materials they are made: some are of opinion that they have been cut with a chisel or sharp instrument out of stone: others think that they have been moulded or shaped of a soft composition, and afterwards baked. The substance is extremely hard. It has not been ascertained whether they are idols or only images of distinguished men. It will be an interesting object of research for antiquarians to discover who were the ancestors of the present Indians capable of executing such a good resemblance of the human head, face, neck, and shoulders."

In his account of the antiquities discovered in some of the Western States, Mr. Caleb Atwater[2] mentions two idols, one found in a tumulus near Nashville, Tennessee, and the other dug up on the site of an old

[1] *Monthly Magazine, or British Register*, vol. xxiv., part 1, for 1807, p. 74.
[2] "Archæologia Americana," vol. i., pp. 211, 215. Worcester, Mass., 1820.

Indian temple in Natchez, Mississippi. The first was made of clay, peculiar for its fineness, mixed with gypsum. The second was of stone. Both are figured in the first volume of the "Transactions and Collections of the American Antiquarian Society." In the writer's collection there is a clay image quite similar in appearance to Miss Clifford's drawings of the Nashville idol. The accompanying notices of antique idols are extracted from Mr. Haywood's "Natural and Aboriginal History of Tennessee."

"Upon the top of a mound at Bledsoe's Lick, in Sumner County, Tennessee, some years prior to 1823, was ploughed up an image made of sandstone. On one cheek was a mark resembling a wrinkle passing perpendicularly up and down the cheek. On the other cheek were two similar marks. The breast was that of a female, and prominent. The face was turned obliquely up towards the heavens. The palms of the hands were turned upwards before the face, and at some distance from it, in the same direction that the face was. The knees were drawn near together: and the feet, with the toes towards the ground, were separated wide enough to admit of the body being seated between them. The attitude seemed to be that of adoration. The head and upper part of the forehead were represented as covered with a cap, or mitre, or bonnet; from the lower part of which came horizontally a brim, from the extremities of which the cap extended upwards conically. The color of the image was that of a dark infusion of coffee. If the front of the image were placed to the east, the countenance—obliquely elevated—and the uplifted hands in the same direction, would be towards the meridian sun."[1]

[1] "Natural and Aboriginal History of Tennessee," etc., by John Haywood, pp. 123, 124. Nashville, 1823.

Of another image or idol dug up on the farm of Mr. McGilliam on Fall Creek, in Wilson County, Tennessee, Mr. Haywood furnishes the following description: "The figure is cut out of a hard rock, of what kind Mr. Rucker could not determine. It was designed for a female statue. The legs were not drawn. It only extends a little below the hips. It is fifteen inches long and thick in proportion. It has a flat head, broad face, a disproportionately long aquiline nose, low forehead, thick lips, and short neck. The chin and cheek bones are not prominent, but far otherwise. On the back of the head is a large projection so shaped as to show, perhaps, the manner of tying and wearing the hair. The nipples are well represented: though the breasts are not sufficiently elevated for a female of maturity. The hands are resting on the hips, the fingers in front, and the arms a-kimbo. Around the back and above the hips are two parallel lines cut, as is supposed to represent a zone, or belt. The ears project at right angles from the head, with holes through them. It was found a few inches beneath the surface of the earth. No mounds are near, but an extensive burying-ground of apparently great antiquity."[1]

To the first volume of the "Transactions of the American Ethnological Society,"[2] Dr. Troost contributed drawings of four Tennessee idols. One of them is enshrined in a large *cassis flammea*, the interior whorls and columella of which had been removed, and the front of the shell cut away so as to permit the entrance and proper location of the image. In these *simulacra* both sexes are represented. These idols are

[1] "Natural and Aboriginal History of Tennessee," pp. 162, 163. Nashville, 1823.
[2] Pp. 361, 364.

made, some of them of sandstone, and others of a mixture of clay and shells. All are rude in construction. In the same volume Mr. Schoolcraft, in an article upon the Grave-Creek mound,[1] describes and figures a stone idol in a sitting posture, thirteen inches high, which was ploughed up on the farm of a Mr. Taylor some eight miles south of the Grave-Creek Flats.

During his recent investigations, Professor Joseph Jones obtained from the tumuli and valleys of Tennessee several interesting idols both of stone, and of clay mixed with pounded shells. Without extending these observations, it may be stated that images of this archaic type have been found also in Kentucky, Virginia, South and North Carolina, Louisiana, Alabama, and Florida. The scope of the present inquiry does not lead us to an examination of such as have been observed in more northern and western localities. The worship of the Priapus probably obtained among some of the Southern Indian nations. In the collection of Dr. Troost were many carefully-carved representations in stone of the male organ of generation. They were found principally within the present limits of the State of Tennessee. But two objects of this sort, so far as our observation extends, have been noted among the relics of the Georgia tribes, and these were about twelve inches long, made of slate. In some parts of Alabama, and in Mississippi, similar objects have been exhumed from grave-mounds.

There is another class of objects which commanded the attention, and to all appearances, the veneration and perhaps worship of these ancient peoples. A stone which from some natural cause assumed the

[1] "Transactions of the American Ethnological Society," vol. i., p. 408. New York, 1845.

shape of a man or an animal was held in special esteem, and artificial means were sometimes adopted to heighten the fancied resemblance. Such objects were regarded as fit dwelling-places for some manitou or spiritual influence. To Mr. Schoolcraft we are indebted for several illustrations—one of which represents a natural idol found at the base of a mound in South Carolina.[1] From mounds and refuse-piles the writer has obtained relics of this description which doubtless answered some superstitious purpose in the hands of a conjurer, priest, or medicine-man. While the early writers discountenance the idea that idol-worship existed among the Georgia tribes at the period of our first acquaintance with them, remembering the recorded testimony with regard to the religious ceremonies, superstitions and practices of other and neighboring nations who were addicted, at least in some measure, to this sort of adoration, and appreciating the fact that stone idols and clay images have been found not only in portions of this State, but also within the limits of coterminous States, the conclusion seems irresistible that at some time or other, and among these peoples or those who preceded them in the occupancy of this region, something like the worship of idols obtained. Future and more extended observations may enable us more intelligently to comprehend the secrets of the past, and then we will be able to modify, confirm, or reject present conjectures.

[1] *See* Squier's "'Antiquities of the State of New York," etc., pp. 171, 172. Buffalo, 1851.

CHAPTER XX.

Pottery.

It has been truthfully remarked that articles of fictile ware are at once the most fragile and the most enduring of human monuments. A piece of common pottery, liable to be shivered to pieces by a slight blow, is more lasting than epitaphs in brass and effigies in bronze. These yield to the varying action of the weather; stone crumbles away, ink fades and paper decays; but the earthen vase, deposited in some quiet but forgotten receptacle, survives the changes of time and, even when broken at the moment of its discovery, affords instruction in its fragments. In their power of traversing accumulated ages and affording glimpses of ancient times and peoples, fictile articles have been compared to the fossils of animals and plants which reveal to the educated eye the former conditions of our globe.[1]

Perhaps nothing of a physical character more clearly determines the degree of civilization attained by a nation than the progress made in the fictile art. In the rudest stages of human existence vessels of some sort are required for the conveyance of water and the prep-

[1] "Encyclopædia Britannica," vol. xviii., p. 430, eighth edition.

aration of food. Hence, in those remote ages when we catch indistinct glimpses of man, as an animal, wrestling with the lowest wants of his nature and scarce able to defend himself against the inclement seasons and the attacks of wild beasts, we find only the meanest forms of domestic utensils, such as gourds, drinking-cups of conch or horn, bark basins, wooden troughs, skin bags, and coarse earthen pots and pans. The conformation and composition of such primitive pottery indicate the inexperience and awkwardness of the artificers, and convey a decided impression of the barbarity of the race to which they belonged. As the darkness of a half-clad, nomadic existence is gradually dispelled by the dawning light of civilization, and men begin to emerge from the savage state, the first step in this development is marked by a change for the better in the ceramic art. The archaic type of pottery is abandoned for forms far more graceful and intellectual, and the crude clay discarded for material more durable and attractive. From its rude beginning to its present stage of picturesque and beautiful development, the potter's art has always been invested with peculiar interest and historic value. It may be regarded as the faithful chronicler of man's progress—a fair exponent of the degree of his barbarity or civilization, and often the recorder of events and periods which would otherwise have faded from the recollection of succeeding generations. Hieroglyphically impressed upon the sun-dried bricks of Egypt are the names of a kingly series which, but for these relics, would have irretrievably perished. The sites of ancient Mesopotamia and Assyria are traced by means of the cuneiform inscriptions upon the clay bricks of which their proudest edifices were constructed. The Roman bricks have also borne their testimony. Many of them retain the names of the consuls of imperial Rome, while others prove that the proud nobility of the Eternal City derived their revenues from the kilns of their Campanian and Sabine farms.[1]

Grecian colonization and its æsthetic influences, remarks Professor Wilson,[2] are traced along the shores of the Mediterranean and the Euxine by beautiful fictile ware and sepulchral pottery. Etruria's history is written to a great extent in the same fragile yet enduring characters. The footprints of the Roman conqueror are clearly defined to the utmost limits of imperial dominion by the like evidence; and sepulchral pottery is frequently the only conclusive proof which enables the European ethnologist to discriminate between the grave of the intruding conqueror and that of the aboriginal occupant of the soil. Apart, therefore, from the exquisite beauty of many remains of fictile art, which confers on them a high intrinsic value, the works of the potter have been minutely studied by the archæologist and are constantly referred to as historical evidence of the geographical limits of ancient empires.

Few peoples, how degraded soever, have failed to bequeath some specimens of pottery—crude and misshapen though they be—to rescue the fact of their former existence from utter oblivion. The absence of pottery in the Reindeer period in France furnishes a decided exception, and affords proof alike of the great antiquity of the cave-dwellers of Dordogne and of the very low state of their civilization.[3]

In Europe, where prehistoric archæology may be

[1] Birch's "History of Ancient Pottery."
[2] "Prehistoric Man," p. 342, second edition. London, 1865.
[3] Lubbock's "Prehistoric Times," p. 326, second edition. London, 1869.

divided into four great epochs—the Palæolithic and the Neolithic periods, the Bronze and the Iron ages—careful study has been bestowed upon the peculiar characteristics of the pottery of each period. The conclusion to which this examination leads is this, that while the potter's wheel was probably unknown in both the Stone and Bronze epochs, the material of which the Stone-age pottery is composed is rougher than that which was used during the Bronze period. The ornaments of the two periods show, also, says Sir John Lubbock,[1] a great contrast. In the Stone age they consist of impressions made by the nail or the finger, and sometimes by a cord twisted round the soft clay. The lines are all straight, or, if curved, are very irregular and badly drawn. In the Bronze age all the patterns present in the Stone age are continued, but in addition we find circles and spirals; while imitations of animals and plants are characteristic of the Iron age.

In North America, where we have almost exclusively a Stone age distinguished by relics more varied than those of perhaps any other quarter of the globe, the art of pottery attained a considerable degree of perfection. The ornamentation is as diversified and comprehensive as that of all the ancient epochs of Europe combined. The manufacture of fictile articles for domestic use, devotion, and ornament, seems to have been carried on by most of the Indian tribes, from time immemorial. The Southern Indians excelled in the ceramic art, special care having been bestowed upon the selection and preparation of their clays, and no little taste displayed both in the shape and ornamentation of their vessels. The use of these frail utensils

[1] "Prehistoric Times," p. 16, second edition. London, 1869.

was, however, at an early period superseded by the employment of more serviceable articles obtained from the whites, and the fabrication of pottery was, with but few exceptions, speedily abandoned whenever ample opportunity was afforded for the purchase of European copper kettles, iron pots, and tin-ware. This fact increases our interest in these perishable relics, and causes us to cherish very tenderly all specimens of this character.

At the period of our first acquaintance with the Southern Indians, the fabrication and use of earthen vessels were very general. The Fidalgo of Elvas[1] pays high compliment to the pottery of the region when he describes it as "little differing from that of Estremoz or Montemor." He records the circumstance that the natives "had great store of walnut oil—clear as butter, and of a good taste—and of the honey of bees preserved in pots."

It would appear from Cabeça de Vaca's account[2] that some of the Southern tribes were either ignorant or neglectful of the potter's art. Of such he writes: "Their method of cooking is so new, that for its strangeness, I desire to speak of it; thus it may be seen and remarked how curious and diversified are the contrivances and ingenuity of the human family. Not having discovered the use of pipkins to boil what they would eat, they fill the half of a large calabash with water, and throw on the fire many stones of such as are most convenient and readily take the heat. When hot, they are taken up with tongs of sticks and dropped into

[1] "Narratives of the Career of Hernando dé Soto," etc., translated by Buckingham Smith, p. 165. Bradford Club Series, number five. New York, 1866.

[2] "Relation of Alvar Nuñez Cabeça de Vaca," translated from the Spanish by Buckingham Smith, p. 161. New York, 1871.

the calabash, until the water in it boils from the fervor of the stones. Then whatever is to be cooked is put in, and, until it is done they continue taking out cooled stones and throwing in hot ones. Thus they boil their food." In the "Brevis Narratio"[1] of Le Moyne de Morgues, we have several illustrations purporting to exhibit the forms of pottery in general use among the Florida Indians.

The Chevalier Tonti, in his general description of the Louisiana Indians, uses the following language: "They have Cellars or rather Holes to preserve their Corn, their Wood and other Provisions; but all their Kitchin Utensils consists in some few pieces of Earthen-Ware which they make with Clay, and harden it with the Dung of Bulls."[2]

Father Hennepin[3] asserts that before the arrival of Europeans in North America "both the Northern and Southern Salvages made use of and do to this day use Earthen Pots, especially such as have no Commerce with the Europeans from whom they may procure Kettels and other Moveables."

During Lieutenant Timberlake's sojourn among the Cherokees he observed that they used two sorts of clay from which they made excellent vessels capable of resisting the greatest heat. At a physic-dance in the town-house he saw a clay pot, set on the fire, capable of containing twenty gallons.[4]

Speaking of the same Indians Adair[5] asserts that

[1] Plates viii., xi., xx., xxviii., xxix. Francoforti ad Mœnum. De Bry, anno 1591.

[2] "An Account of Monsieur de la Salle's Last Expedition," etc., p. 12. London, 1698.

[3] "Continuation of the New Discovery of a Vast Country in America," etc., p. 102. London, 1698.

[4] "Memoirs," etc., pp. 62, 77. London, 1765.

[5] "History of the American Indians," p. 424. London, 1775.

in his day they made "earthen pots of very different sizes so as to contain from two to ten gallons; large pitchers to carry water, bowls, dishes, platters, basons, and a prodigious number of other vessels of such antiquated forms as would be tedious to describe and impossible to name. Their method of glazing them is, they place them over a large fire of smoky pitch-pine which makes them smooth, black and firm. Their lands abound with proper clay for that use; and even with porcelain, as has been proved by experiment."

Loskiel[1] tells us that the Delawares and Iroquois had pots and boilers made of clay mixed with pounded sea-shells, and burnt so hard that they were black throughout; and Joutel affirms that the Indians inhabiting the banks of the Mississippi were very skilful at making earthen vessels wherein they boiled their flesh, or roots, or sagamise.[2]

In commenting upon the customs of the Louisiana tribes, Du Pratz[3] writes: "To prepare their maiz for food and likewise their venison and game there was necessity for dressing them over the fire, and for this purpose they bethought themselves of earthen ware which is made by the women who not only form the vessel, but dig up and mix the clay. In this they are tolerable artists: they make kettles of an extraordinary size, pitchers with a small opening, gallon bottles with long necks, pots or pitchers for their bear oil which will hold forty pints; lastly, large and small plates in the French fashion. I had some made out of curiosity upon the model of my delf ware, which

[1] "History of the Mission of the United Brethren," etc., part 1, p. 54. London, 1794.

[2] "Historical Journal," etc, French's Historical Collection of Louisiana, part 1, p. 149. New York, 1846.

[3] "History of Louisiana," p. 360. London, 1774.

were a very pretty red." The kitchen utensils of the Alabama Indians consisted of dishes and pots of earthen-ware, and deep wooden dishes. "They made cups of calebashes, and spoons of the horns of wild oxen, which they cut through the middle and form into the proper shape by means of fire."[1] Haywood[2] mentions the existence in the mounds of Tennessee of fragments of pottery composed of clay and pounded cockle-shells.

It was Lawson's impression that the earthen pots found buried, and at the foot of banks whence the water had washed them, were of a sort different from those in use by the Carolina Indians when he sojourned among them. He asserts that the ancient pottery was "thicker, of another shape and composition, and nearly resembled the urns of the ancient Romans."[3]

In plate xv. of Hariot's "Virginia," we are advised of the method in which the natives seethed "their meate in earthen pottes." Says the translator: "Their woemen know how to make earthen vessells with special Cunninge, and that so large and fine, that our potters with thoye wheles can make noe better; ant then Remoue them from place to place as easelye as we can doe our brassen kettles. After they haue set them uppon an heape of erthe to stay them from fallinge, they putt wood vnder, which, being kyndled, one of them taketh great care that the fyre burne equallye Rounde abowt. They or their woemen fill the vessel with water, and then putt they in fruite, flesh, and fish, and lett all boyle together like a gallie-

[1] Bossu's "Travels through Louisiana," vol. i., p. 224. London, 1771.
[2] "Natural and Aboriginal History of Tennessee," p. 139. Nashville, 1823.
[3] "History of Carolina," pp. 278, 279. Reprint. Raleigh, 1860.

maufrye, which the Spaniarde call olla podrida. Then they putte yt out into disches, and sett before the companye, and then they make good cheere together."[1]

We conclude these citations in support of the fact that the Southern Indians at the time of primal contact between them and the whites were almost universally cognizant of and practising the potter's art, by an observation of that intelligent and entertaining traveller, William Bartram,[2] to whom we are indebted for so much valuable information respecting the Georgia tribes in 1773: "As to mechanic arts or manufactures, at present they have scarcely any thing worth observation, since they are supplied with necessaries, conveniences, and even superfluities by the white traders. The men perform nothing except erecting their mean habitations, forming their canoes, stone pipes, tambour, eagle's tail or standard, and some other trifling matters; for war and hunting are their principal employments. The women are more vigilant, and turn their attention to various manual employments: they make all their pottery or earthenware, mocasins, spin and weave the curious belts and diadems for men, fabricate lace, fringe, embroider and decorate their apparel," etc., etc.

The statement, therefore, is historically correct that until, through their intercourse with the early explorers and first settlers, the Southern Indians became convinced of the superiority of the copper and iron kettles and articles of crockery then introduced and of their

[1] "A Briefe and True Report of the New-found Land of Virginia," etc. Francoforti ad Mœnum. De Bry, anno 1590.

[2] "Travels through North and South Carolina, Georgia," etc., p. 511. London, 1792.

ability to possess them, they adhered to their primitive manufacture of clay utensils of various forms. With the general introduction of these more durable articles of European construction dates the decline of the ceramic art among the North American tribes. That decadence was more or less rapid as the intercourse between the races became partially or permanently established; and to such an extent has it progressed that, in the language of Prof. Rau, at the present time this aboriginal art may be considered as almost if not entirely extinct among the tribes still inhabiting the territory of the United States, excepting some in New Mexico and Arizona who have not yet abandoned the manufacture of earthen-ware.

In York County, South Carolina, dwell some sixty survivors of the once powerful Catawba nation. By them the fabrication of fictile articles has not been wholly discontinued. This is done, however, rather with a view to satisfying, at a good price, the demands of strangers who make frequent application for their wares, than in perpetuation of the ceramic art as it once existed among them.

The pottery of the Southern Indians is superior to that manufactured by Northern tribes. It is more varied in form, symmetrical in shape, excellent in composition, and diversified in ornamentation. The abundance of choice clay, a climate salubrious the year round, the presence of fish and game in plenty, and the fact that Nature spontaneously gratified many wants—combined with the general dissemination of art ideas apparently derived from the Natchez—afforded ample leisure and facilities for the careful fabrication of fictile ware and tended to develop a degree of taste and skill which not infrequently challenges our admiration. The presence of sherds all over the cultivated fields attests the numbers of clay vessels which were everywhere in use among the aborigines of Georgia. Especially do these fragments abound upon the sites of their villages and at the principal bluffs along the coast and water-courses whither, in ancient times, they resorted for the purposes of fishing and hunting. The refuse-piles are here filled with broken clay utensils thrown aside as they perished with the using. They form an important element in the *débris* of the encampment. Seldom are entire vessels found except in mounds and graves. Even here it is a difficult matter to secure specimens wholly free from blemish. Friable in its character, this pottery was liable to disintegration. Under the most favorable circumstances, when securely deposited in tumuli, the moisture of the soil and the weight of the superincumbent mass of earth in many instances caused the burial-urns and cooking-utensils to crack or fall to pieces. The sepulchral shell-mounds and the dry sandy tumuli of the coast were most conducive to the preservation of these frail articles. From them the best specimens have been taken.

The material employed by the Georgia Indians in the manufacture of their pottery was red, blue, yellow, and dark-colored clay. It was often used without the admixture of any foreign substance; but in many cases this clay was tempered, mixed and kneaded with powdered shells, gravel, or pulverized mica. Experience taught these primitive artificers that such a composition imparted greater consistency to the mass and rendered it more capable of resisting the action of fire.

Sometimes—as in the case of flat-bottomed vessels intended as receptacles for pounded maize—this pottery was only sun-dried, but generally the utensil was subjected to a hardening process by fire. The application of heat to the interior of the vessel was occasionally so intense as to cause a partial fusion of the inner particles. This pottery appears to have been made by hand, although, so accurate are its outlines, so homogeneous its composition, and so regular the thicknesses of the walls, that we often wonder how it could have been so skilfully formed without the aid of the potter's wheel. This earthenware was manufactured by the natives in almost every part of the State. Traces of the pits whence they dug clay, are still extant. Scattered around are fragments of pottery, masses of clay evidently intended for use, and the remains of former fires. Localities where these potters plied their trade may, to this day, be clearly noted on the coast, in the valleys of Little-Shoulder-Bone Creek, of the Etowah, Oostenaula, and Chattahoochee Rivers, and elsewhere. In Bibb and Cass Counties rude clay-hearths with elevated sides have been unearthed, which, from their form and the quantities of sherds in their vicinity, suggest the belief that they were crude kilns for baking pottery. Professor Rau, in his interesting article on "Indian Pottery," furnishes a valuable account of some localities on the left bank of Cahokia Creek, in the American Bottom, where the manufacture of earthen-ware had been carried on by the Cahokia Indians. "In some of the Southern States," remark Messrs. Squier and Davis,[1] "it is said the kilns in which the ancient pottery was baked are now occasionally to be met with. Some are represented still to contain the ware, partially burned, and retaining the rinds of the gourds, etc., over which they were modelled, and which had not been entirely removed by

[1] "Ancient Monuments of the Mississippi Valley," p. 195. Washington, 1848.

the fire." "In Panola County," says Mr. R. Morris, in a private letter, "are found great numbers of what are termed *pottery-kilns*, in which are masses of vitrified matter frequently in the form of rude bricks measuring twelve inches in length by ten in breadth."

In the Etowah Valley—a region of all others in Georgia most rich in monuments—ovens, rudely constructed of water-worn stones, have been discovered, with circular paved floorings indicating the long-continued presence of hot fires. Those which the writer examined were in ruins, but seemed to have been about five feet in diameter. The impression created by these remains and their surroundings was, that they were intended for and used as kilns for baking pottery.

Observing for a moment the general characteristics of the pottery found in Georgia, we will note that the walls or sides of the vessels vary in thickness from the eighth to the half of an inch. Some of the largest sort are thicker still, their bottoms being reënforced to insure additional strength. In size there is every variety, from the little poculum capable of holding scarce a pint, to the large pot or flat-bottomed jar whose contents may be calculated by the gallon. Most of the vessels belonging to what may be termed the archaic type, are but slightly ornamented; many of them not at all. The same may be affirmed with regard to the coarser jars designed as receptacles for pounded maize, bear-oil, walnut-oil, and honey. The rims of not a few of the larger vessels curve outward, so as to allow a vine or cord to pass round and under the projection, and thus enable them to be suspended over the fire. Others have strong ears, by means of which suspension could have been accomplished with greater facility.

Others still lack both curved rim and ears; and, with their rounded bottoms, must have been kept in an upright position through the intervention of clay rings placed beneath, or by being bolstered up with stones, fagots, or sand. One of the best specimens of ceramic art we have seen within the geographical limits of Georgia, is the burial-urn represented by Fig. 1, Plate XXVII.

It is fifteen inches and a half in height, nine inches in diameter in the widest part, and ten inches and a quarter across the top. The graceful outline and general symmetry of this vase arrest our attention. It was apparently made with the assistance of a rush or wicker basket, as its entire exterior surface is covered by impressions left by the rushes or osier-twigs upon the clay while in a plastic state. We know that some of the North American tribes adopted the custom of modelling their vessels in baskets prepared for that purpose. Either this method was used in the present case, or else the potter, with no little skill and patience, imprinted these ornamental lines while the vessel was still soft, by means of a cord or instrument of some sort. The lines are *impressed*, not *carved*. The circular ornamentation—running parallel with and half an inch distant from the rim—was doubtless made with the end of a hollow reed or bone. The hard cane abundant everywhere in the swamps of Southern Georgia and generally used by the Indians for arrows, might well have been employed for this purpose. The interior is quite smooth. This urn was fashioned of the clay common to the neighborhood in which it was found. In its composition there is an admixture of gravel, and, to a limited extent, of powdered shells. In itself considered, it is a creditable

Plate XXVII.

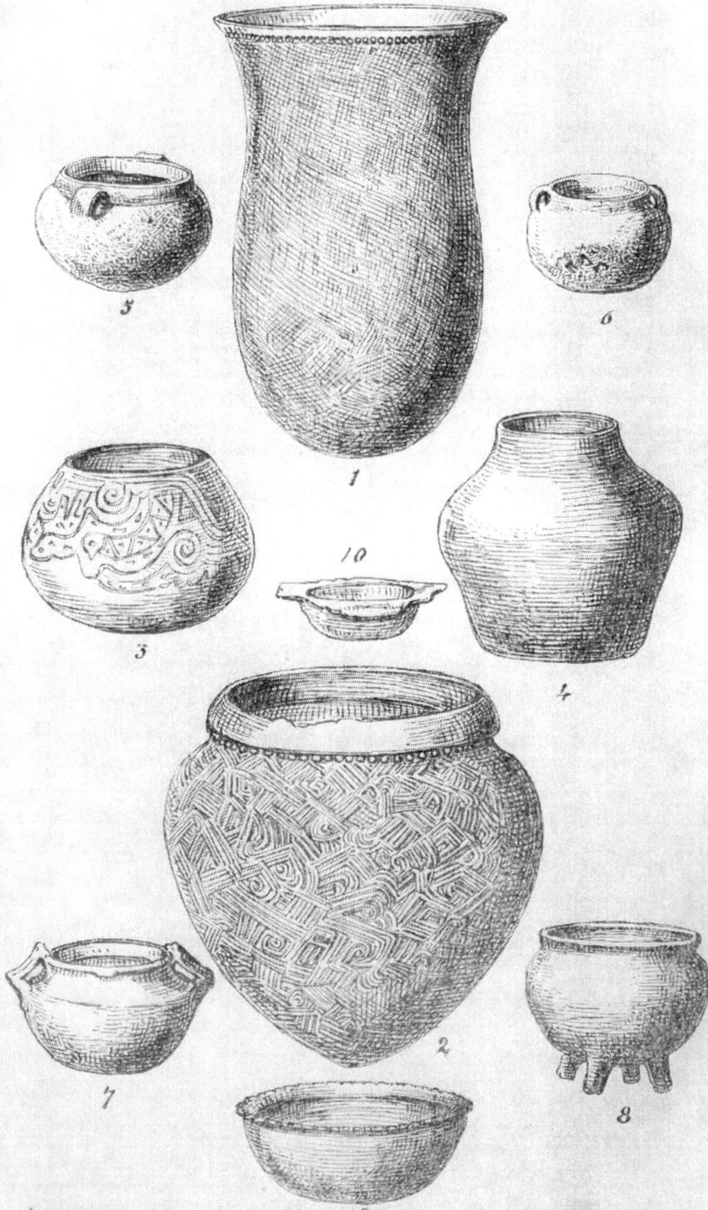

AM. PHOTO-LITHOGRAPHIC CO. N.Y. (OSBORNE'S PROCESS.)

example of the skill of the primitive potter. It possesses, however, an individual history which invests it with additional interest.

This burial-urn was found in a small shell-mound on the Colonel's Island,[1] in Liberty County. It was in an upright position and its rim was about eighteen inches below the surface. This little tumulus was evidently very old; and, although the ploughshare had not torn it asunder, the changing seasons and the merciless winds and rains had sadly wasted it. But for the quantities of stout oyster-shells which entered into its composition it would long since have been obliterated by these disintegrating influences. The remarkable state of preservation in which this vase appears is accounted for when we are made acquainted with the fact that it was guarded or enclosed by two exterior earthen vessels of ruder construction and thicker walls. Covering the top of the outer vessel and closely fitting, was a substantial lid or cap of baked clay, made for the purpose. The exterior and middle receptacles were so much softened and impaired by the moisture of the sand and shells that they crumbled into fragments in the effort to remove them and could not be restored. It was with difficulty that the innermost urn could be lifted from its position. Exposure to the sun, however, soon caused it to harden. Within this smallest and enclosed vessel, thus protected, were the bones of a young child. They had wellnigh returned to the mother-dust from which they

[1] In 1773, William Bartram, while on a visit to this island, observed among the shells of a conical mound, and about its centre, the rim of an earthen pot which he carefully removed, drawing it out almost whole. "This pot," he says, "was curiously wrought all over the outside, representing basket-work, and was undoubtedly esteemed a very ingenious performance by the people at the age of its construction."—("Travels through North and South Carolina, Georgia," etc., p. 6. London, 1792.)

sprang. No relics, save these funeral-vases, were found in this mound. This fact suggests two thoughts —one, that the tumulus was erected solely in honor of this infant, and consequently that it must have been the offspring of some noted personage of the tribe; the other, that it was too young to have come into the ownership of any articles except such as must have been very perishable in their character.

Placed here perchance by the wife of the chieftain —certainly by an affectionate mother—with the fond hope that this clay coffin, in all likelihood her own handiwork, would shield the tender form of the babe she loved so well from the chilling damp and the remorseless decay of the lonely grave, this funeral-vase affords an affecting illustration of that sincere natural attachment which leads even the uncivilized parent to wrestle with death for the preservation of her buried child. Three other instances of similar inhumations have chanced within the writer's observation, all of them occurring in mounds on the coast. It will be remarked that this sepulchral-urn is not unlike those described by Mr. Atwater and figured on pages 227 and 229 in the first volume of the "Archæologia Americana." Burial-vases enclosing human bones have occasionally been found in the grave-mounds of Tennessee, Alabama, Florida, Mississippi, and South Carolina. In ancient Greece it was customary to deposit the ashes or bones of the dead in a cinerary of baked clay, bronze, or gold, and recent investigations show that this method of protecting the dust of the departed was not confined to the limits of classic Hellas. The vessel (Fig. 2, Plate XXVII.) taken from an earth-mound near Sparta, in Hancock County, is fourteen inches high and rather more than fourteen inches in

Plate XXVIII.

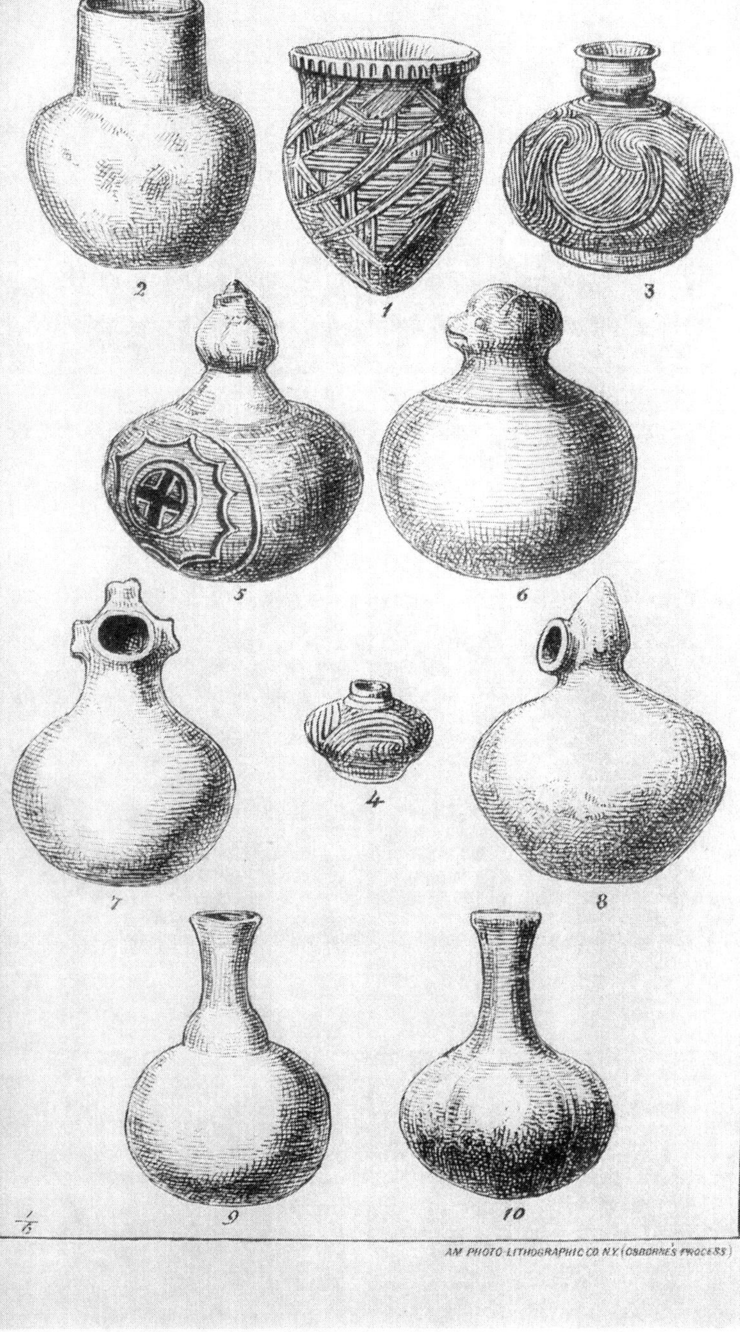

AM. PHOTO-LITHOGRAPHIC CO. N.Y. (OSBORNE'S PROCESS)

diameter. Near the rim we have a repetition of the circular or bead ornamentation noticed on the burial-vase. The ornamentation of the entire outer surface is so varied and elaborate that we are somewhat at a loss to understand precisely how it was done. If this pot was moulded in a basket, the pattern of the enclosing wicker-work was unusually elaborate and artistic. As in the case of the sepulchral urn, all these impressions were formed while the clay was still soft. There are no indications of the use of a sharp-pointed implement as in vessel Number 3, Plate XXVII., where all the lines and figures were carved after the clay had become hard.

Fig. 4, Plate XXVII., may be regarded as typical of a numerous class of flat-bottomed jars designed, as has already been intimated, as receptacles for various articles, such as pounded maize, bear-oil, walnut-oil, honey, etc. It is entirely plain both within and without, quite smooth, and measures rather more than eight inches in height and nine inches in diameter. The dark clay of which it is composed was tempered with powdered shells and mica.

Figs. 5, 6, and 7, Plate XXVII., are accurate delineations of pots with ears, while Fig. 8, in general outline, assimilates very closely to the small iron pot of the present day. The addition of legs was by no means usual. Figs. 9 and 10 of the same plate acquaint us with the shapes of the ordinary clay bowls in common use among the primitive peoples of this region. In Figs. 1 and 2, Plate XXVIII., we observe the forms of the wide-necked jars. The vessels delineated in Figs. 3 and 4, of the same Plate, were taken from an ancient burial-ground in the Mississippi Valley, near Shreveport, while those represented by the remaining Figures in this Plate were found by Professor Joseph Jones, in the stone-graves and mounds of Tennessee. Without multiplying these examples, the illustrations already furnished advise us of the prevailing types of this Southern pottery. All these vessels were taken from grave-mounds. Animal-shaped and face-vases occasionally occur. Of the latter kind the well-remembered and oft-described triune vase is a striking illustration. Professor C. Rau is now preparing a monograph upon face-vases which will prove both curious and interesting.

Upon an examination of this pottery and the many sherds which everywhere abound (some of which are figured in Plate XXIX.), we are led to believe that the ornamentation was compassed in one or the other of the following ways:

I. By modelling the vessel inside of a net-work, rush-basket, or frame made of twigs or split cane, or within a gourd, or over blocks of wood or forms of dried clay. It seems, moreover, from the delicacy of some of the impressions, that a sort of cloth must have been first spread against the sides of the enclosing basket or framework before the clay was put in and pressed against it. Perhaps in some instances the interior walls of the gourd may have been carved so as to leave raised figures and lines upon the vessel moulded within it.

II. By shaping the kneaded clay into the desired form, with the hand, leaving the outer surface smooth; and, when the pot was dry, with a sharp flint-flake or bone carving straight, curved, and zigzag lines with greater or less uniformity according to the care, patience, and skill of the artificer.

III. The circular and semicircular depressions—with or without elevated centres—could have been

Plate XXIX.

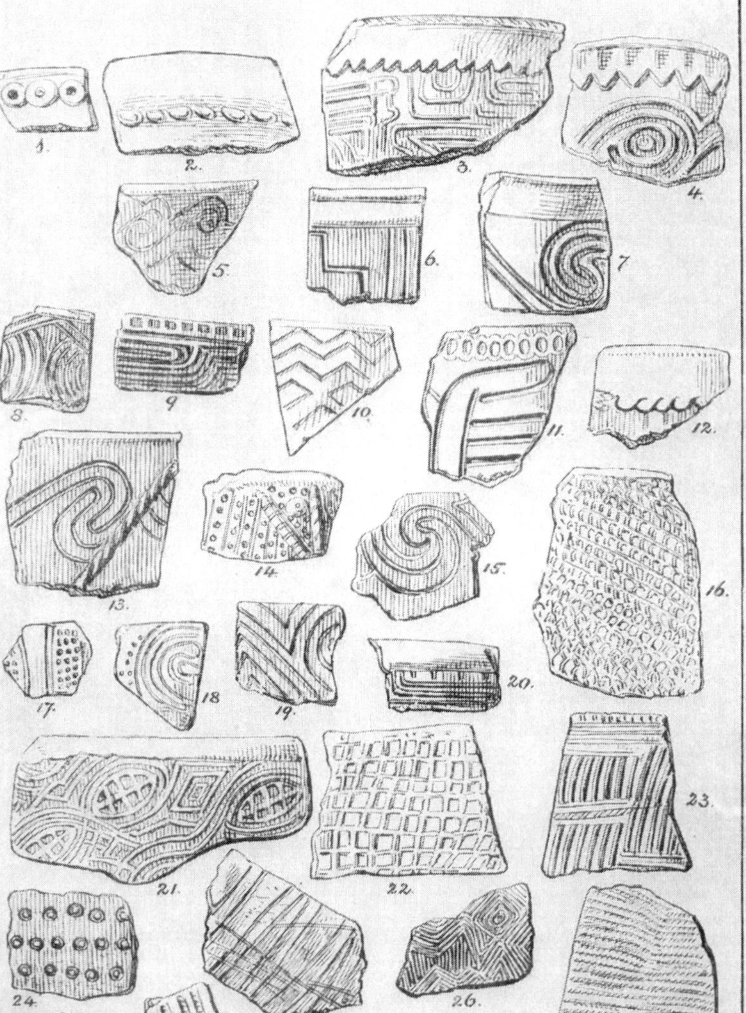

AM. PHOTO-LITHOGRAPHIC CO. N.Y. (OSBORNE'S PROCESS)

made by means of a hollow reed cut off at or near a joint, as might best indicate the artist's present fancy. It is not improbable that some of the indentations formed while the clay was still in a plastic state, were done with the finger-nail, which the Indians, in some cases and for certain purposes, permitted to grow very long.[1] Lines were impressed with the aid of a thong, while the more complicated figures may have been perpetuated with the assistance of a wooden or soapstone die in which the desired pattern was cut. Repeated applications of the same die to all the exterior portions of the vessel gave a uniform ornamentation. The use of several dies of different designs materially enhanced the variety.

IV. Frequently raised mouldings near the rims, and elevated ornaments were added while the vessel was still soft, and when the adhesion of these new parts could be readily compassed.

V. The sides of the vessels were sometimes beautified by the insertion of diamond and square-shaped, parallelogrammic, and circular pieces of mica and shell. Over the edges of these inserted or impressed ornaments the clay was slightly curved, so that when the ware was thoroughly dry these pieces of mica and shell remained permanently embedded. A beautiful drinking-cup ornamented in this way was unearthed by a freshet, which, overflowing the banks of Savannah River, cut a channel through an ancient burial-ground near the confluence of great Kiokee Creek and that stream.

VI. The ornamentation of this earthen-ware was further accomplished by means of red, blue, and black pigment.

[1] Lawson's "Carolina," p. 284. Raleigh reprint, 1860.

When completed the newly-formed vessel was either exposed in the sun, baked in a kiln or open fire, or inverted over burning coals of some hard wood, such as oak or hickory, piled up so as to fill as nearly as possible the whole interior. In the manner last mentioned was the baking process often conducted, the bed of coals being at intervals renewed and arranged in conical form so as to distribute the heat equally to every part of the pot. So intense at times was the heat employed, that the vessel glowed and a fusion of the particles on the inner surface occurred. When sufficiently baked, the vessel was allowed to cool gradually, in its hardened condition permanently retaining the impressions which had at first been made upon its plastic form.

Upon the manufacture of the ordinary cooking and domestic utensils comparatively little labor was expended. They were, however, substantially made, and answered well, both in shape and durability, the wants of this primitive period. From some of the sepulchral tumuli and refuse-piles, plates of baked clay, usually about six inches long, four inches wide, and half an inch thick, have been taken. They were used either as plates or rude baking-pans. Clay pans, with numerous holes pierced through their bottoms, thereby converting them into convenient strainers, have also been found.

In Cherokee Georgia and Alabama frequent use was made of pot-stone or soapstone for the manufacture of vessels of the largest size. Some of this kind have been exhumed fully three feet in diameter and eighteen inches deep. The walls were an inch and upward in thickness.[1]

[1] Professor Joseph Jones has a vessel of this sort in his collection, weighing nearly two hundred pounds; and one was exhumed in Alabama, large enough to permit an adult to sit and bathe in it.

We here omit a description of images, pipes, beads, and other articles of clay, as they have been noticed in another connection.

As the methods adopted by the various American nations in the manufacture of their earthen-ware were probably quite similar, in addition to the extracts already given, it is deemed proper to present the following accounts by eye-witnesses as throwing additional light upon this subject.

In his history of the manners and customs of several Indian tribes west of the Mississippi, Hunter observes:[1] "In manufacturing their pottery for cooking and domestic purposes, they collect tough clay, beat it into powder, temper it with water, and then spread it over blocks of wood which have been formed into shapes to suit their convenience or fancy. When sufficiently dried, they are removed from the moulds, placed in proper situations and burned to a hardness suitable to their intended uses. Another method practised by them is to coat the inner surface of baskets made of rushes or willows, with clay to any required thickness, and, when dry, to burn them as above described.

"In this way they construct large, handsome, and tolerably durable ware; though latterly, with such tribes as have much intercourse with the whites, it is not much used, because of the substitution of cast-iron ware in its stead.

"When these vessels are large, as is the case for the manufacture of sugar, they are suspended by grape-vines, which, wherever exposed to the fire, are constantly kept covered with moist clay.

"Sometimes, however, the rims are made strong and project a little inwardly, quite round the vessels, so as

[1] "Memoirs of a Captivity," etc., p. 288. London, 1828.

to admit of their being sustained by flattened pieces of wood, slid underneath these projections and extending across their centres."

The Mandans are reported by Mr. Catlin[1] to have fabricated their pottery in the following manner: "Earthen dishes or bowls are a familiar part of the culinary furniture of every Mandan lodge, and are manufactured by the women of this tribe in great quantities, and modelled into a thousand forms and tastes. They are made by the hands of the women from a tough, black clay, and baked in kilns, which are made for the purpose, and are nearly equal in hardness to our own manufacture of pottery; though they have not yet got the art of glazing, which would be to them a most valuable secret. They make them so strong and serviceable, however, that they hang them over the fire as we do our iron pots, and boil their meat in them with perfect success. I have seen some few specimens of such manufacture, which have been dug up in Indian mounds and tombs in the Southern and Middle States, placed in our Eastern museums, and looked upon as a great wonder, when here this novelty is at once done away with, and the whole mystery; where women can be seen handling and using them by hundreds, and they can be seen every day in the summer also, moulding them into many fanciful forms and passing them through the kiln where they are hardened."

The most minute account is that furnished by Dumont, who, in describing the customs of the Louisiana Indians, states that, "after having amassed the proper kind of clay and carefully cleaned it, the Indian

[1] "Illustrations of the Manners, Customs, and Conditions of the North American Indians," etc., vol. i., p. 116. London, 1848.

women take shells which they pound and reduce to a fine powder; they mix this powder with the clay, and having poured some water on the mass, they knead it with their hands and feet and make it into a paste, of which they form rolls, six or seven feet long, and of a thickness suitable to their purpose. If they intend to fashion a plate or a vase, they take hold of one of these rolls by the end, and, fixing here with the thumb of the left hand the centre of the vessel they are about to make, they turn the roll with astonishing quickness around this centre, describing a spiral line; now and then they dip their fingers into water and smooth with the right hand the inner and outer surface of the vase they intend to fashion, which would become ruffled or undulated without that manipulation. In this manner they make all sorts of earthen vessels, plates, dishes, bowls, pots, and jars, some of which hold from forty to fifty pints. The burning of this pottery does not cause them much trouble. Having dried it in the shade, they kindle a large fire, and, when they have a sufficient quantity of embers, they clean a space in the middle where they deposit their vessels and cover them with charcoal. Thus they bake their earthen-ware, which can now be exposed to the fire, and possesses as much durability as ours. Its solidity is doubtless to be attributed to the pulverized shells which the women mix with the *clay*."[1]

The ceramic art is no longer practised by the Indian within the limits of Georgia. Upon the removal of the Creeks and Cherokees, the last representatives of the red race departed from the beautiful valleys, the noble mountains, and luxuriant forests of this Empire State

[1] Dumont, "Mémoires Historiques sur la Louisiane," tome ii., p. 271, *et seq.* Paris, 1753.

of the South. Even before the establishment of Oglethorpe's colony at Savannah, there had occurred a by no means partial introduction of metallic vessels of European manufacture. These were furnished by traders who swarmed into the Indian country from Carolina and the Spanish settlements in Florida. Upon the general distribution of these more durable utensils, the fabrication of fictile ware gradually subsided and was at last entirely abandoned. To the industry and skill of the Indian women of those early days are we mainly indebted for these interesting relics of the past.

Roguet[1] advanced the idea that the way in which pottery came to be made was this: primitive peoples at first daubed with clay such combustible vessels as cocoa-nut shells, to protect them from the action of fire. It was found before long that the clay itself, when hardened, would retain its shape and answer the purposes of the vessels it was designed to enclose. Thus the idea of fictile ware was conceived and from time to time developed. The observations of Captain Genneville and others tend to corroborate this notion; and it may be that the early efforts of the Southern Indians in the ceramic art were confined to covering gourds with clay so as to use them for culinary purposes.

Although calabashes were long ago abandoned as unsuitable for heating water and boiling maize, the shape of many of the terra-cotta vessels of an antique type would seem to have been suggested by them.

Aside from the disintegrating influences of time and moisture, the casualties of use and accident, the operation of inherent decay and the wanton destruction of many of these frail vessels at the hands of the care-

[1] *See* Tylor's "Researches into the Early History of Mankind," etc., second edition, p. 273. London, 1870.

less and the unlearned, the Southern Indians, in observance of a custom which obtained among some ancient tribes, doomed to destruction quantities of their pottery. It will be remembered that these primitive peoples, especially along the coast of Georgia, frequently burned their dead and with them food-vessels, drinking-cups, pots, flagons, ornaments, utensils, and articles, the property of the deceased. The practice of reserving the skeletons until they had accumulated sufficiently to warrant a general inhumation was maintained among the Creeks, the Choctaws, and other Southern nations within the historic period. It was no easy task, as we have already observed, for the aborigines, with their limited means, to erect a tumulus. Hence, by an arrangement of this sort, the combined labors of the many could be secured in compassing the elevation of grave-mounds above the accumulated dead of village or tribe. Possibly, cremation was resorted to in order that the toil of mound-building might be diminished. Cremation, however, was by no means universal even in districts where the dead were frequently burned. Why these funeral customs should have thus varied in prescribed localities, we do not fully understand. Compared with each other these sepulchral tumuli differ materially in their ages, and we can only repeat what we have already suggested in explanation, that in the history of the nomadic peoples who for centuries possessed this region, one wave of human life may have swept over the other, each perpetuating its peculiar funeral-rites, and leaving in silent companionship mound-tombs similar in general aspect and yet possessing internal *indicia* which intimate that they are the creations of different hands, the offspring of varying customs—all designed, however, to honor the memory of the departed.

But a few weeks since the writer opened two grave-mounds, not more than forty yards apart, in the midst of an ancient burial-ground on the Georgia coast. In the first, the skeletons had been disposed in an horizontal position and the smell of fire had not passed upon them. In the other, after having been collected in a circle twenty feet in diameter, with all their articles of property about them, the dead, to the number of perhaps thirty, had been consumed in the flames. Charred fragments of wood and bone, broken pieces of pottery, cracked stone implements, and burnt earth, abundantly testified how complete had been the cremation. Here was a total demolition of numerous clay vessels owned by the deceased and given to the flames with the skeletons prior to the inhumation. Bushels of fragments might have been gathered, but not a vessel remained in its entirety to reward the investigation.

Upon the burning *πυραί* the Greeks cast perfumes and oils, but the beautiful vases and the property of the deceased were claimed by the living. The Southern Indian gave to one common funeral-flame the skeleton, and all the possessions of the departed.

CHAPTER XXI.

The Use of Pearls as Ornaments among the Southern Indians.

In the concession made by the King of Spain to Hernando de Soto of the government of Cuba and conquest of Florida, with the title of *Adelantado*, one-fifth of all the gold and silver, stones and *pearls*, won in battle or on entering towns, or obtained by barter with the Indians, was reserved to the crown. It was further stipulated that the "gold and silver, stones, *pearls*, and other things which might be found and taken as well in the graves, sepulchres, *ocues* or temples of the Indians as in other places where they were accustomed to offer sacrifices to idols, or in other concealed religious precincts or buried houses, or in any other public place," should be equally divided between the king and the party making the discovery.

From the special mention made of them in this royal reservation, it is evident that among the valuable trophies of the expedition precious pearls were confidently anticipated. That the Spaniards were not entirely disappointed in this expectation the early narratives abundantly testify. These relations establish the fact—and that beyond all controversy—that the use of the pearl as an ornament, among the Indians of Florida and of the South was by no means infrequent. A reference to some of these accounts—affording as they do the earliest information we possess on this subject—may prove interesting.

Near the bay of Espiritu Santo, in Florida, the followers of De Soto chanced upon the town of an Indian chief—Ucita, by name. His house stood near the beach, upon an artificial mound. At the other end of the town was a temple, on the top of which perched a wooden fowl with gilded eyes. Within these eyes, says the historian, were found pearls such as the Indians greatly value, piercing them for beads and stringing them to wear about their necks and wrists.

When the Indian queen welcomed the Spanish adventurer to the hospitalities of Cutifachiqui, she drew from over her head a long string of pearls, and, throwing it around his neck, exchanged with him gracious words of friendship and courtesy. Observing that the Christians valued these pearls, the cacica told the governor that if he would order some sepulchres, which were in the village, to be searched he would find many; and, if he chose to send to those which were in the uninhabited towns, he might load all his horses with them. The Spaniards did examine and rifle of their contents the sepulchres in Cutifachiqui; and, upon the authority of the Fidalgo of Elvas, obtained from them three hundred and fifty pounds' weight of pearls—some of them formed after the similitude of babies and birds. If the truth were known, or if an Indian had penned this account, we would be assured that De Soto and his companions, in their eager quest for treasures, without permission violated the graves and plundered the receptacles wherein were garnered the most costly possessions of the natives. As a proof that the Indians did not willingly part with these ornaments, but suffered the pillage through fear of these strange and wanton men, we are informed that when the cacica, whom De Soto compelled to accompany him with the intention of taking her to Guaxule—the farthest limit of her territory—succeeded in making her escape, she was careful to carry back with her a cane box filled with *unbored pearls*, the most precious of them all.

Luys Hernandez de Biedma says that the governor, while at this town, opened a mosque in which were interred the chief personages of that country: "From it we took a quantity of pearls of the weight of as many as six arrobas and a half, or seven, though they were injured from lying in the earth, and in the adipose substance of the dead." One of the saddest losses, in the estimation of the relator, encountered by the expedition in the bloody affair at Mauilla, was the destruction of the pearls which the Spaniards had been sedulously collecting during their wanderings in this strange land.

Fontaneda states that at the place where Lucas Vasquez went, seed-pearls were found in certain conchs; and that between Havalachi and Olagale is a river the Indians call Guasaca-esqui, which means in the Spanish language *Rio de Cañas* (river of canes). In this river, which is an arm of the sea, and along the adjacent coast, pearls are procured from certain oysters and conchs. These are carried to all the provinces and villages of Florida, but principally to Tocobaja, the nearest town. The Indians of the town of Abalachi asserted that the Spaniards hung their cacique because he would not give them a string of large pearls which he wore around his neck—the middle pearl being as big as the egg of a turtle-dove. Ribault frequently alludes to the presence of pearls in the possession of the natives of Florida, and on one occasion saw the goodliest man of a company of Indians with a collar of gold and silver about his neck from which depended a pearl "as great as an acorn, at the least."[1]

Father Hennepin[2] assures us that the Indians along the banks of the Mississippi wore "bracelets and earrings of fine pearls which they spoilt, having nothing to bore them with but fire." He adds: "They made us to understand that they have them in exchange for their *calumets* from some nations inhabiting the coast of the great lake to the southward, which I take to be the *Gulph of Florida*." A member of the expedition of Sir Walter Raleigh collected from the natives of Virginia five thousand pearls, "of which number he chose so many as made a fayre chaine, which for their likenesse, and vniformitie in roundnesse, orientnesse and pidenesse of many excellent colours, with equalitie in greatnesse, were verie fayre and rare."[3] In the plates illustrative of the "Admiranda Narratio" and the "Brevis Narratio" the natives both of Virginia and Florida are represented in the possession of numerous strings of pearls of large size; and in his description of the "treasure or riches" of the Virginia Indians, Beverly says: "They likewise have some Pearl amongst them, and formerly had many more, but where they got them is uncertain, except they found 'em in the Oyster Banks which are frequent in this Country."[4]

[1] "The Whole and True Discoverye of Terra Florida." Prynted at London by Rowland Hall for Thomas Hackett, 1563.

[2] "New Discovery," etc., p. 177. London, 1698.

[3] "A Briefe and True Report of the New-found Land of Virginia," etc., p. 11. Francoforti ad Mœnum. De Bry, anno 1590.

[4] "History and Present State of Virginia," book III., p 59. London, 1705.

Wilson asserts that he saw pearls "bigger than Rounciv̄al Pease and perfectly round," taken from oysters on the Carolina coast.[1]

By far the most minute and interesting account of the manner in which the Indians obtained pearls and converted them into beads, is that furnished by Garcilasso de la Vega. As this observation was made in the town of Ichiaha, which was in all likelihood located at or near the confluence of the Etowah and Oostenaula Rivers, and perhaps upon the very spot now occupied by the village of Rome in Georgia, the narrative becomes all the more attractive:

"On the following day the Cacique visited the General,[2] and gave him a string of pearls, two fathoms long. This present might have been considered valuable if the pearls had not been pierced, for they were all of equal size, and as large as hazel-nuts. Soto acknowledged this favor by presenting the Indian with some pieces of velvet and cloth, which were highly appreciated by him. He then made inquiry of him with regard to fishing for these pearls, upon which the Indian replied that this was done in his province: that a great many pearls were stored in the temple of the city of Ichiaha, where his ancestors were buried, and that he might take as many of them as he pleased. The General expressed his obligations, but observed that he would remove nothing from the temple, and that he had accepted his present only to please him. He desired to learn, however, in what manner the pearls were extracted from the shells. The Cacique replied he would send out people to fish for pearls all night, and that the following day at eight o'clock" (*sic*)

[1] "An Account of the Province of Carolina," etc., p. 12. London, 1682.
[2] De Soto.

"his wish should be gratified. He at once ordered four[1] boats to be dispatched for pearl-fishing, with instructions that they should be back in the morning. In the mean time much wood was burned on the bank, producing a large quantity of glowing coals. When the canoes returned, the shells were placed on the hot coals, and they opened in consequence of the heat. In the very first, ten or twelve pearls, of the size of a pea, were found and handed to the Cacique and the General, who were both present. They found them very fine, although the fire had partially deprived them of their lustre. When the General had satisfied his curiosity, he retired to take his dinner. While thus engaged a soldier came in who told him that in eating some of the oysters" (*sic*) "caught by the Indians, a pearl had got between his teeth, which pearl being very fine and brilliant, he begged him to accept as a present for the Governess of Cuba.[2] Soto very civilly declined the present, but assured the soldier that he was just as much obliged to him as if he had accepted his gift; and that he would endeavor to reward him some day for his kindness and for the regard he was exhibiting for his wife. He further advised him to keep his (intended) present and to buy horses with it at Havana. The Spaniards, who were with the General at that moment, examined the soldier's pearl, and some, who professed to be *connaisseurs* of jewelry, thought it was worth four hundred ducats. It had lost nothing of its lustre, as fire had not been employed in obtaining it."[3]

[1] Irving speaks of forty.

[2] Doña Isabel de Bobadilla, De Soto's wife.

[3] Garcilasso de la Vega, "Conquête de la Floride," trad. par Richelet. Leide, 1731, tome i., livre ii., chap. i., p. 296, *et seq.* *See* also Irving's "Conquest

During the course of the weary march of the expedition through the mountains of Upper Georgia, the following circumstance is related by the same historian as having occurred:

"A foot-soldier, calling to a horseman who was his friend, drew forth from his wallet a linen bag in which were six pounds of pearls probably filched from one of the Indian sepulchres. These he offered as a gift to his comrade, being heartily tired of carrying them on his back, though he had a pair of broad shoulders capable of bearing the burden of a mule. The horseman refused to accept so thoughtless an offer. 'Keep them yourself,' said he, 'you have most need of them. The Governor intends shortly to send messengers to Havana: you can forward these presents and have them sold, and three or four horses and mares purchased for you with the proceeds, so that you need no longer go on foot.' Juan Terron was piqued at having his offer refused. 'Well,' said he, 'if you will not have them, I swear I will not carry them, and they shall remain here.' So saying, he untied the bag, and whirling around as if he were sowing seed, scattered the pearls in all directions among the thickets and herbage. Then putting up the bag in his wallet, as if it was more valuable than the pearls, he marched on, leaving his comrade and the other by-standers astonished at his folly. The soldiers made a hasty search for the scattered pearls and recovered thirty of them. When they beheld their great size and beauty —none of them being bored or discolored—they lamented that so many of them had been lost: for the whole would have sold in Spain for more than six

of Florida," chapter li., p. 245, *et seq.* *See* also Pickett's "History of Alabama," vol. i., p. 11, *et seq.* Charleston, 1851.

thousand ducats. This egregious folly gave rise to a common proverb in the army that 'there are no pearls for Juan Terron.' The poor fellow himself became an object of constant jest and ridicule, until at last, made sensible of his absurd conduct, he implored them never to banter him further on the subject."[1]

It is the opinion of Colonel Pickett that the oyster alluded to by Garcilasso was identical with the mussel so common in all the rivers of Alabama. "Heaps of muscle-shells," says he, "are now to be seen on our river-banks where the Indians used to live. They were much used by the ancient Indians for some purpose, and old warriors have informed me that their ancestors used the shells to temper the clay with which they made their vessels. But, as thousands of the shells lie banked up—some deep in the ground—we may also suppose that the Indians in De Soto's time, everywhere in Alabama, obtained pearls from them. There can be no doubt about the quantity of pearls found in this State and Georgia in 1540, but they were of a coarser and less valuable kind than the Spaniards supposed. The Indians used to perforate them with a heated copper spindle, and string them around their necks and arms like beads."[2]

Strange to say, Cabeça de Vaca makes no specific allusion to pearls, save that he was informed by the natives that *on the coast of the South Sea there were pearls and great riches.*

At the time of the Spanish invasion the pearl, as an ornament, was held in high esteem by the Mexican peoples; and, upon occasions of state, its beauties were

[1] Garcilasso de la Vega, "Conquête de la Floride," trad. par Richelet. Leide, 1731, tome ei., livr iv., chap. xix., p. 289, *et seq.* *See* also Irving's "Conquest of Florida," p. 239, *et seq.*

[2] Pickett's "History of Alabama," vol. i., p. 12, note. Charleston, 1851.

invoked to enhance the magnificence of the apparel and lend additional lustre to the pomp of royalty. When Montezuma alighted from his regal palanquin, "blazing with burnished gold" and overshadowed by a "canopy of gaudy feather-work powdered with jewels and fringed with silver," to grant personal audience to Cortez, his ample cloak and golden-soled sandals were sprinkled with pearls and precious stones.

Morales collected large booty of gold and pearls from the Indians dwelling on the other side of the isthmus. The vanquished Cacique of Isla Rica brought as a peace-offering a basket curiously wrought and filled with pearls of great beauty. Among them were two of extraordinary size and value. One weighed twenty-five carats. The other was as "big as a muscadine pear, of Oriental color and lustre, and weighed upward of three drachms."

The natives of Paria[1] possessed such quantities of

[1] "Before the Spanish Conquest this was a smiling, happy coast, vexed occasionally by Caribs, but otherwise a bright spot on the earth, where men, without making much pretence to any thing that is elevated in human nature, lived peaceably and pleasantly enough, under the shade of their own cocoa-trees, looking out upon some of the grandest aspects of Nature. If they thought at all about the matter, they must have been delighted with the rich supplies of food which they obtained so easily from their oyster-beds. But the diseases of a creature apparently occupying a low place in the scale of creation, were fated to be the means of dissolving the whole of Indian society in these parts, and of reducing large districts from a state of cultivation into a state of Nature, so that it is only conjectured now by the skilful naturalist, founding his conjecture upon the prevalence of some particular flower, that they were once cultivated.

"It is strange that this little glistening bead, the pearl, should have been the cause of so much movement in the world as it has been. There must be something essentially beautiful in it, however, for it has been dear to the eyes both of civilized and of uncivilized people. The dark-haired Roman lady, in the palmiest days of Rome, cognizant of all the beautiful productions in the world, valued the pearl as highly as ever did the simple Indian woman; and a love for these glistening beads came upon the Spaniards from two quarters—from the Romans who had colonized them, and from the Moors they had conquered. So general, indeed, was the love for pearls that it was to be expected that whatever country in the wide circuit of the whole world was cursed with an abundance of pearl-producing fine pearls that the most sanguine anticipations were awakened in the breast of Columbus. Remembering the assertion of Pliny that pearls are generated from drops of dew which fall into the mouths of oysters, he deemed no place so propitious as this coast for their growth and multiplication. When nearing the island of Cubagua this admiral, as Charlevoix tells us, beheld a number of Indians fishing for pearls, who, at the approach of the strangers, at once made for the land. A boat being sent to communicate with them, one of the sailors noticed many strings of pearls around the neck of a female. Having a plate of Valencia-ware—a kind of porcelain painted and varnished with gaudy colors—he broke it and presented the pieces to the Indian woman, who gave him in exchange a considerable number of her pearls. These he carried to the admiral, who immediately sent persons on shore well provided with Valencian plates and hawk's-bells, for which, in a little time, he procured about three pounds' weight of pearls—some of which were of very large size, and were sent by him, afterward, to the sovereigns as specimens.[1]

To Vasco Nuñez, Túmaco gave jewels of gold, and two hundred pearls[2] of great size and beauty, although

oysters, would be sure, when the fact was discovered, to become a theatre for displaying the rapacity of the rest of mankind.

"The perilous nature, however, of his submarine possessions was not yet visible to the poor innocent Indian on the coast of Paria or Cumaná; and it was with childish delight that he threw the strings of pearls (strung in a way that would have driven the jewellers of Europe wild with vexation) on the smooth brown arm or rich brown neck of his beloved."—("*The Spanish Conquest in America*," vol. ii., p. 89. London, 1855.)

[1] "Life and Voyages of Columbus," by Washington Irving, vol. ii., p. 123. New York, 1849.

[2] Arthur Helps says: "Two hundred and forty large pearls were presented on this occasion." He continues: "The Spaniards could hardly contain their joy. One thing alone occurred to damp it. The Indians, not knowing better, were ac-

they were somewhat discolored in consequence of the fact that the oysters from which they were taken had been opened by fire. Observing the value which the Spaniards set upon these pearls, the cacique sent a number of his men to fish for them. Certain of the Indians were trained from their youth to this purpose, so as to become expert divers and acquire the power of remaining a long time beneath the water. The largest pearls were generally found in the deepest water, sometimes in three and four fathoms, and were sought only in calm weather. The smaller pearls were taken at the depth of two and three feet, and the oysters containing them were often driven in quantities on the beach during violent storms. The party of pearl-divers, sent by the cacique, consisted of thirty Indians, with whom Vasco Nuñez sent six Spaniards as eye-witnesses. The sea was so furious at that stormy season that the divers dare not venture into the deep water. Such a number of the shell-fish, however, had been driven on shore, that they collected enough to yield pearls to the value of twelve marks of gold. They were small, but exceedingly beautiful, being newly taken and uninjured by fire. Many of these shell-fish and their pearls were selected to be sent to Spain as specimens.[1]

Oviedo commemorates the circumstance that this cacique, Túmaco, subsequently furnished Vasco Nuñez with a canoe of state, formed from the trunk of an enormous tree and managed by a great number of In-

customed to open oysters by means of fire: this injured the color of the pearl; and, accordingly, the Spaniards diligently taught the Indians the art of opening oysters without fire, with far more diligence, indeed, than they expended in teaching their new friends any point of Christian doctrine."—(" *The Spanish Conquest in America*," vol. i., p. 366. London, 1855.)

[1] Irving's "Life and Voyages of Columbus and his Companions," vol. iii., p. 181. New York, 1849.

dians. The handles of the paddles were inlaid with small pearls—a fact which Vasco Nuñez caused his companions to testify before the notary that it might be reported to the sovereigns as a proof of the wealth of this newly-discovered sea.

In another bay of the Pacific coast this bold navigator saw groups of islands abounding with pearls—many of them as large as a man's eye. Davyd Ingram, during the "Land Travels" of himself and others in the years 1568 and 1569, from the Rio de Minas in the Gulf of Mexico to Cape Breton in Acadia, made the following observation: "There is in some of those Countreys great abundūnce of Pearle, for in every Cottage he founde Pearle, in some howse a quarte, in some a pottell, in some a pecke, more or lesse, where he did see some as great as an Acorn, and Richard Browne, one of his Companyons, founde one of these great Pearles in one of their Canoes, or Boates, wch Pearle he gaue to Mouns^r^ Champaine, whoe toke them aboarde his Shippe, and brought them to Newhaven in ffrūnce."[1]

Without multiplying these references, we think sufficient historical evidence has been adduced to satisfy the mind of the candid inquirer, and that beyond all reasonable doubt, that pearls were in general use among the Southern Indians; that the choicest of them were the prized ornaments of the prominent personages of the tribes; that the fluviatile mussels of various streams were constantly and extensively collected and opened for the purpose of procuring these gems, which, when obtained, were often pierced by means of heated copper spindles; that the marine shells of the Atlantic, the Gulf of Mexico, and of the

[1] "Documents connected with the History of South Carolina," edited by Plowden Charles Jennett Weston, p. 8. London, 1856.

Pacific, yielded generous and beautiful tribute to the labor, skill, and taste of numerous and well-trained pearl-divers; and that these gems were found not only in the possession of the living, but also in large quantities in the graves of chieftains and the sepulchres of the undistinguished dead. We are assured, moreover, of the eagerness with which the Spaniards sought after and preserved these treasures; and more than once do we hear expressions of disappointment at the discoloration and deterioration of the pearls caused by the action of fire, and their having been pierced. A present of pearls from the caciques to the conquerors was an earnest token of consideration, and the most acceptable pledge of friendship. It may be that the accounts which have reached us from the pens of the historians of these various expeditions and voyages, are somewhat extravagant with regard to the quantity and size of the pearls seen in the possession of the natives. It does not appear that many gems of this sort from Florida, Georgia, and Alabama, ever gladdened the eyes and enriched the coffers of the home authorities, or graced the fair necks of Spanish beauties. Most of them were observed and left amid the wilds of the Land of Flowers, where the spring of perpetual youth still conceals its life-giving waters beneath the shades of an untrodden forest. They were found and lost in that mythical region at whose upper end rose the fabled mountain from whose side flowed a stream of molten gold. And yet, in view of all the recorded observations, and in the light of subsequent investigations, we are not inclined to sympathize with those who regard with equal incredulity the story of the Abalachi pearl, and the tale told by Sinbad the sailor of the vast treasures he saw in the valley of diamonds.

With all due allowance for the scope and effect of imagination, and a tendency to exaggeration highly developed in minds naturally alive to the marvellous and eager, in this *terra incognita*, to perpetuate impressions, which, when recounted at home, would excite the cupidity and awaken the intense interest of a people already familiar with the riches of Peru and Mexico and anxious to extend the hand of conquest over other regions in this New World, there is in the narratives of the career of De Soto, and in kindred relations, ample proof that pearls of large size and of considerable value were in the possession of the Southern Indians during the sixteenth century; that their attention had been generally directed to collecting margatiferous shells; that by the simple process of heating them upon a bed of live coals they extracted the pearls from them; and that they understood the art of piercing them with heated copper spindles so that they might be strung and worn as ornaments around the neck, wrists, and ankles.

By the narrators of these primal recorded interviews between Europeans and the red-men we are informed that the Indians obtained their supplies of pearls both from marine shells and from fresh-water mussels. Some of the oysters on the Georgia and Florida coast are margatiferous. Many of them contain seed-pearls. On sundry occasions specimens have passed under the writer's observation which were symmetrical in shape, as large as pepper-corns, and not wanting in beauty. Some were quite big enough to have been perforated in the rude fashion practised by the Indians. They were, however, of a milky color and opaque. Neither in size nor quality did they answer the description of those spoken of in the Spanish narratives. We know that the Indians who inhabited the coast-regions of Carolina, Georgia, Florida, Alabama, and the more southern States, subsisted to a large extent upon oysters, clams, and conchs. This fact is to this day attested by the numerous and extensive kitchen-refuse piles and shell-heaps which abound upon the islands, along the headlands and upon the banks of salt-water creeks, and by the quantities of marine shells which were used as coverings for many of the sepulchral tumuli. These are not the abraded drift-shells cast upon the coast by the action of the waves, but are the perfect, uninjured shells from which the live animals had been artificially removed. Possessing that passion for ornament so characteristic of all barbarous tribes, it excites no surprise that the Indians should, as they opened these marine shells, have carefully watched for pearls, and that from out the vast numbers consumed, year by year, quite a store of such gems should have been accumulated. But, if the shores of Carolina, Georgia, and Florida may not have afforded specimens of the larger and more highly prized pearls, we have only to look a little nearer the equator, and we will find pearl-bearing localities whose treasures fully gratified the taste of the savage and excited the cupidity of the civilized. Pearls could have been here procured which, in size and beauty, would corroborate the statements of the early navigators and justify, at least to a large extent, the seemingly extravagant representations of the strings of these gems encircling the necks, wrists, and ankles in the oldest representations we have of the Southern Indians. In support of this opinion we have but to instance the trade in pearls which sprung up at an early period with the islet of Cubagua, and at various points in the Gulf of Mexico.

Such were the trade relations existing between the various tribes on this continent, so extensive their interchange of commodities, so general the office of runner or primitive merchantman, and so adventurous, in their larger canoes, the dwellers along the coast-regions of the South, it is not at all improbable that pearls from the islands and lower portions of the Gulf of Mexico and even from the Pacific Ocean may have found their way into the heart of Georgia and Florida and into more northern localities, to be there bartered away for skins and other articles, which, in their turn, would subserve the purposes of this rude exchange of values. If, in the same ancient stone grave in Nacoochee Valley, we find a cassis from the Gulf of Mexico, a copper axe from the shores of Lake Superior, and stone implements the material for the manufacture of which was necessarily obtained at no inconsiderable remove from this locality; if in the study of American archæology we encounter, on every hand, proofs of an extensive and varied interchange of articles for use and ornament, and the concentration in the ownership of a single individual of utensils and implements brought from places hundreds of miles apart, we surely do not overstep the bounds of probability when we suggest that the most admirable pearls among the Southern Indians once living within the present geographical limits of the United States were obtained from marine shells native to the Gulf of Mexico. The replies of the Indians to inquiries addressed to them on this subject by Hennepin and others, and the presence in remote localities of beads, ornaments, and drinking-cups—all made of marine shells and conchs to this day peculiar to the Gulf of Mexico—confirm the truthfulness of the suggestion.

But we are not confined to marine shells as the only or perhaps the chief source whence the Southern Indians derived most of their pearls. In all likelihood the fluviatile mussels contributed more freely than any other shells to the gratification of the ornament-loving masses. As we ascend the Southern rivers we observe, at various prominent points, relic-beds composed in great degree of the fresh-water shells native to the streams. It is hardly an exaggeration to assert that no prominent stream is entirely devoid of them. The inland lakes of Florida afford similar evidences of the former occupancy of their shores by the aborigines, and even some ponds in Middle Georgia and Alabama exhibit along their banks unmistakable signs of ancient refuse-piles into whose composition lacustrine shells enter largely.

As an illustration of the frequency and extent of these relic-beds along the banks of the rivers, we may instance those on the right bank of the Savannah River, above the city of Augusta. Only one need be specifically mentioned, and this will be found in Columbia County, near the confluence of Great Kiokee Creek and the Savannah River. Here, opposite a succession of rapids in the river—a locality which would have afforded marked facilities for successful fishing in the manner adopted by the Indians of this region—upon a bold bluff is an accumulation of fresh-water shells covering the surface of the ground to a depth varying from two to four feet, and extending nearly one hundred yards in length, and more than a quarter of that distance in width. Intermingled with them may still be found the bones of large fishes, deer, turkeys, raccoons, bears, bison, turtles, squirrels, rabbits, and other animals and birds, and also fragments of pottery, arrow and spear points, soapstone net-sinkers, crushing-stones, axes, chisels, rude mortars and other implements, and various ornaments of clay and soap-stone. Here, then, was one of the favorite camping-grounds of the Indians. Hither they resorted for centuries, feeding upon fish, mussels, and game. This is but one of many extensive refuse-heaps of a similar character which have attracted the notice of the writer along the banks of the fresh-water rivers not only in Georgia, but also in Florida, Carolina, Alabama, and Tennessee. In these relic-beds no two parts of the same shell are, as a general rule, found in juxtaposition. The hinge is broken, and the valves of the shell, after having been artificially torn asunder, seem to have been carelessly cast aside and allowed to accumulate at the very doors of the lodges, where, mixed with the *débris* of the encampment, in the course of time they became heaped up to such an extent as to form these large shell-banks. In these early days the Southern rivers must have abounded with mussels. Their shells were sometimes used (as were the oyster, the conch, and the clam along the coast) in the construction of burial-mounds. Take, for example, that large tumulus located on Stalling's Island, in the Savannah River, a few miles above Augusta, a description of which has already been presented. The river *unios* enter largely into its composition. The clay of which the Indians made their pottery was not infrequently mixed with particles of shells powdered for that purpose. It is also true that at least some of their shell ornaments were fashioned from the larger varieties of fluviatile shells found in the neighborhood. Evidently, therefore, the collection of fresh-water mussels must have occupied no little of the time and labor of the natives. That they subsisted largely, at certain seasons, upon them, as an article of food, admits of no doubt. Not a few of the *unios* of the Southern rivers, lakes, and swamps, are margatiferous. From the physical proofs enumerated—aside from all historical testimony—where such quantities of shells were collected and opened, we may well believe that many pearls must have been found, and we incline the more readily to give credence to the statements of the Fidalgo of Elvas and the narrative of Garcilasso de la Vega. If it be true—as some have supposed—that the town of Cutifachiqui was located on the Savannah River, not very many miles below the site at present occupied by the city of Augusta, and if De Soto was standing on the bank of the Etowah when the Cacique of Ichiaha kindly sent his men to gather the mussels, and showed him how pearls were extracted from them, we still have, in the shell-heaps extant upon the banks of these streams, physical proofs of these ancient pearl-fisheries and ocular demonstrations of the verity of those relations.

With a view to ascertaining the precise varieties of shells from which the Southern Indians obtained their pearls, the writer invited an expression of opinion from several gentlemen of intelligence whose scientific pursuits rendered them familiar with the conchology of the United States. The following extracts from some of the replies which were received, will be found interesting, as throwing light upon the inquiry:

Dr. William Stimpson, of the Chicago Academy of Sciences, expresses the opinion that the statements of the early Spanish historians with regard to the size of the pearls (as large as filberts) are incorrect. He says:

"The pearls of the *aviculæ*—our only margatiferous marine genus—are very small, and those of the oyster, valueless. The Indians must have obtained their pearls from the fresh-water bivalves (*unio* and *anodon*), which abound in the rivers of Georgia, etc. These are usually small, but, in very rare instances, examples have occurred reaching in diameter one-third of an inch."

"Most of the fresh-water mussels," writes Professor Joseph Le Conte, "contain small pearls now and then. By far the best and largest number I have seen were taken from the *Anodon Gibbosa* (Lea), a large and beautiful shell abundant in the swamps of Liberty County, Georgia—at least in Bull-town and Alatamaha Swamps. Some of the pearls taken from this species are as large as swan-shot. Of the salt-water shells. I know not if any produce pearls except the oyster (*Ostrea Virginiana*). Pearls of small size are sometimes found in them." Professor William S. Jones, of the University of Georgia, says he has seen small pearls in many of the unios in Southern Georgia. I am informed by Professor Wyman that, after a careful and extensive series of excavations in the shell-heaps of Florida, he has failed to find in them a single pearl. "It is hardly probable," he remarks, "that the Spaniards could have been mistaken as to the fact of the ornaments of the Indians being *pearls*, but in view of their frequent exaggerations, I am almost compelled to the belief that there was some mistake; and, possibly, they may not have distinguished between the pearls and the shell beads, some of which would correspond with the size and shape of the pearls mentioned by the Spaniards."

Professor Joseph Jones, whose recent investigations have thrown much valuable light upon the contents of the ancient tumuli of Tennessee, says: "I do not remember finding a genuine pearl in the many mounds which I opened in the valleys of the Tennessee, the Cumberland, the Harpeth, and elsewhere. Many of the pearls described by the Spaniards were probably little else than polished beads cut out of large sea-shells and from the thicker portions of fresh-water mussels, and prepared so as to resemble pearls. I have examined thousands of these, and they all present a laminated structure as if carved out of thick shells and sea-conchs."

Mr. Charles M. Wheatley is confident that there are "splendid pearls in Southern unios." He instances the *Unio Blandingianus* and the large old *Unio Buddianus* (Buckleyi) from Lakes George and Monroe in Florida, as pearl bearing. "In Georgia," he continues, "the large, thick shells of the Chattahoochee, such as the *Unio Elliottii*, would be the most likely to contain fine ones; but there is no positive rule, as an injured shell of any species will doubtless afford some: irregular in most cases and of no value, but in some instances worth from fifty to one hundred dollars." He mentions that he has received from the Tennessee River, in Alabama, fine round pearls both white and rose-colored.

From the response of Mr. John G. Anthony I extract the following: "I cannot so well answer your query as to what shells in Georgia and Florida are pearl-bearers, having never collected in the latter State and but little in Georgia, but I can say about Ohio what I presume will hold good in other States, that the *unios* of various species furnish them tolerably abundantly there. They are not confined to any one particular species, but are generally found in the thicker and more ponderous shells, though even the thinner shells often have small ones, especially such species as are found in canals, ponds, and places which seem to be not so healthy for the animal on account of stagnant water. I recollect taking over twenty small ones out of the mantle of one specimen of *Unio Fragilis* (Rafinesque), *Unio Gracilis* (Barnes), which I found in the Miami canal; and almost every old shell there had more or fewer pearls in it. *Unio Torsus* (Rafinesque), *Unio Orbiculatus* (Hildreth), and *Unio Costatus* (Rafinesque), *Unio Undulatus* (Barnes), also produce them in Ohio. I have seen about half a pint of beautiful pearls, regularly formed and pea-size, which were taken in one season and in one neighborhood; so you may judge of their frequency, though, as I hinted before, it is probable that a kind of disease caused by impure water may govern their production somewhat. No doubt the Southern waters are given to making pearls as well as Ohio streams. I have seen protuberances of the pearl character in Southern shells, and have no doubt that one collecting them with the animal in them would find pearls. I particularly recollect *Unio Glebulus* (Say), and *Unio Mortoni* (Conrad)—both Louisiana species—as having these protuberances in their nacreous matter. Georgia unios are generally too thin to produce any excess of pearly matter and form pearls, but the Louisiana shells from Bayou Têche, which I have seen, have a remarkably pearly nacre, quite thick, reminding one very much of the marine shell *Trigonia*, as to nacre. No doubt the bayous, which have in general no current at all, would make first-rate places for pearl-breeding."

Dr. Brinton observed many artificial shell-heaps along the Tennessee River and its tributaries. The

Tennessee mussel (*Unio Virginianus*) is margatiferous, "and there is no doubt," says the Doctor, "but that it was from this species that the early tribes obtained the hoards of pearls which the historians of De Soto's exploration estimated by bushels, and which were so much prized as ornaments."[1]

Dr. Kidder has recently pointed out the source whence at least small pearls and perhaps some fine specimens could have been obtained by the Indians of Florida, and in considerable quantities. In the *unionidæ* of some of the fresh-water lakes of that State he has of late found not less than three thousand pearls —most of them small, but many large enough to be perforated and worn as beads. From one unio he took eighty-four seed pearls; from another fifty, from a third twenty, and from several ten or twelve each. His examinations have hitherto been chiefly confined to Lake Griffin and its vicinity. He proposes soon, however, to open the shells of Lake Okeechobee, which are larger, and there hopes to find pearls of superior size and quality. It is said, but with what truth cannot now be definitely affirmed, that upon one of the islands in this lake are the remains of an old pearl-fishery.

In view of the general use of the pearl as an ornament by the Southern Indians, and of the quantities of lacustrine and fluviatile shells opened by them in various localities whither they resorted for the purpose of fishing and feeding upon these mussels, it seems singular that the pearl is not more frequently met with in the relic-beds and sepulchral tumuli of this region. We would expect to find them also in the refuse-piles, shell-heaps, and mounds of the coast. After an exami-

[1] *See* Smithsonian Report for 1866, p. 357.

nation of several fresh-water shell-heaps on the banks of the Savannah, and of others of a similar character in Alabama, Florida, and South Carolina, and after exploring many shell and earth mounds, particularly on the Georgia coast, the writer has failed, except in a few instances, to find pearls. These were obtained chiefly in an extensive relic-bed on the Savannah River, about twenty miles above Augusta, the largest being four-tenths of an inch in diameter, and all of them blackened by fire. It is, perhaps, not to be wondered at that many of the smaller earth-mounds on the Georgia coast do not contain pearls, because at the period of their construction the custom of burning the dead appears to have obtained very generally. So intense in some cases were the fires then kindled, that even hard stone axes and arrow-points were splintered. Under these circumstances it may be that the pearls were either immediately consumed or so seriously injured as soon to crumble out of sight. Excluding this class of tumuli from present consideration, and crediting the statements of the Fidalgo of Elvas and of others touching the large quantities of pearls found in Indian graves in the sixteenth century, we have been somewhat surprised that their presence has not been more frequently detected in relic-beds and tumuli in this region, in which there is no lack of shell-beads and other ornaments made of the same material. This apparent absence of pearls tends in some measure to confirm the notion of those who entertain the belief that by the imaginative Spaniards many beads and ornaments made of the thicker portions of marine and fluviatile shells—carved, perforated, and brilliant with their primal coloring—were rated as pearls. The authorities, however, are so numerous and direct, and the recent examinations into the contents of these tumuli and relic-beds have been so partial, that for one we cannot acquiesce, except to a qualified extent, in this opinion. Our impression is, that future and more minute investigations will reveal the existence of pearls, in various localities where the pearl-bearing mussels were collected, and where general inhumations occurred. Perforated pearls have been found in an ancient burial-ground, located near the bank of the Ogeechee River, in Bryan County, Georgia; and I am informed by the Reverend F. R. Goulding, that some twenty-five years ago, just after a heavy freshet in the Oconee River which had laid bare many Indian graves in the neighborhood of the large mounds on Poullain's plantation, he gathered on the spot fully a hundred pearls, of considerable size, some pierced, and others unbored.

From the "altar" or "sacrificial" mounds, Messrs. Squier and Davis took a large number of pearl beads. By exposure to the heat, they had lost their brilliancy and consequent value as ornaments. Most of them were so much injured that they crumbled under the touch. The following is the account given of them in the "Ancient Monuments of the Mississippi Valley:"[1] "The peculiarities of their form, and their concentric lamellæ, joined to the lingering lustre which some retain, place their character beyond dispute. Several hundreds in number, and not far from a quart in quantity, are in our possession, which retain their structure sufficiently well to be strung and handled. The largest of these measures two and a half inches in circumference, or upward of three-fourths of an inch in diameter. They are of all intermediate sizes, down to one-fourth

[1] Pages 232 and 233, vol. i., "Smithsonian Contributions to Knowledge."

of an inch in diameter. Most are irregular in form, or pear-shaped; yet there are many perfectly round. They have been obtained from separate localities, several miles apart, and from five distinct groups of mounds. Great numbers were so much calcined, that it was found impossible to recover them, and a large number crumbled in pieces after removal from the mounds. It is no exaggeration to say that a number of quarts of pearls were originally deposited in the mounds referred to; probably nearly two quarts were contained in a single mound."

Without expressing a decided opinion as to the precise locality whence these pearls were derived, it was evidently the impression of Messrs. Squier and Davis that for them a Southern origin should be sought.

From this examination it may, we think, be fairly concluded:

First. That the possession by the Southern Indians of pearls, bored and unbored, at the time of primal intercourse between the white and red races, is clearly proven.

Second. That the use by the Indians of such ornaments was a matter not of recent, but of long standing.

Third. That evidence of the collection and employment of these gems was furnished not only by the ownership of living Indians, but also by the large and frequent accumulations found in the graves and tumuli of the dead.

Fourth. That near the Gulf of Mexico and upon the Pacific coast lived trained divers whose occupation consisted in fishing for pearls.

Fifth. That, in view of the trade-relations existing between the various American tribes, it is not at all unlikely that the finer specimens of pearls worn as ornaments by the Indians of Florida, Georgia, Alabama, Carolina, Louisiana, and more northern localities, were obtained from the islands and shores of the Gulf of Mexico, and perhaps even from the Pacific coast.

Sixth. That the fluviatile shells and lacustrine *unios* of the Southern fresh-water rivers and lakes were extensively gathered and opened by the natives both for the purposes of food and with a view of obtaining the pearls which they produced; and that from this source the Indians probably secured their principal supply of common pearls.

Seventh. That pearls from both marine and fresh-water shells were greatly prized as ornaments by the aborigines, whose custom it was to perforate them—usually by means of heated copper spindles—and wear them on strings around the neck, wrists, waist, thighs, and ankles.

Eighth. That these gems were of such quality as to excite the cupidity of the early voyagers, and attract the marked attention of the various expeditions.

Ninth. That the marine shells of the Gulf of Mexico and of some portions of the Atlantic and Pacific coasts, as well as the *unios* of the Southern rivers and lakes, could have supplied all the pearls represented by the early narratives as having been found upon the persons and in the temples and tumuli of the natives.

Tenth. That the Spanish accounts of the quantity and size of the pearls seen in possession of the Indians during the fifteenth and sixteenth centuries, while they may be somewhat exaggerated, are not, in the main, to be regarded as unworthy of belief.

Eleventh. That the various shell-heaps along the

coast and upon the banks of Southern streams, as well as the large quantities of shells, both marine and fluviatile, employed in the construction of sepulchral tumuli, should be reckoned as proofs of the general truthfulness of those narratives, and as furnishing indications of the local sources whence large numbers of pearls were probably derived.

And, lastly, that, in all likelihood, a careful examination of these shell heaps and mounds will, even at this day, disclose the presence of pearls.

CHAPTER XXII.

Primitive Uses of Shells.—Shell-Money.—Shell Ornaments.—Personal Decorations. —Concluding Observations.

AMONG the many relics which, escaping the disintegrating influences of time and inherent decay, bear present testimony to the fact that in former times they answered various artificial uses and were freely exchanged in traffic among the Southern Indians, few are more widely distributed then those made of shell. Copper from the prehistoric mines of Lake Superior, galena from beyond the Mississippi, mica from distant hills, silver and gold in small quantities, and numerous worked flints and stones, are found in localities to which they should be utter strangers and in which their presence would never be expected but for the extensive interchange of articles which obtained among these primitive peoples. To the coast tribes the sea was the great treasure-house whence were derived abundant supplies with which they might constantly carry on a trade with interior nations, and from them secure coveted products of the mountains, chipped, rubbed, or beaten into well-known and desired forms of use and ornament. In the preceding chapter we commented at some length upon the employment of pearls as gems for personal adornment and as articles possessing the highest commercial value among the red-men of the South. We have seen how diligently they were collected, how carefully they were perforated with heated copper spindles so that they could be worn as beads, and how extensively these beautiful offerings not only of the fresh-water mussels, but also of the shells of the Gulf of Mexico and the Southern seas, were distributed among tribes remote from localities whence they were derived. These ornaments might very properly be considered in the present connection; but, in view of what has already been said on this subject, any further notice is here pretermitted. We have also observed, upon an examination of the frequent and large refuse-piles, that the coast Indians and those dwelling near rivers and lakes, relied upon oysters, mussels, clams, and conchs, as important articles of food.

Although the labors of the primitive workers in shell were chiefly expended upon the manufacture of a convenient and well-recognized medium of exchange, and the preparation of various ornaments, in the domestic economy of the natives sundry were the offices shells were made to perform. Some of these we will briefly enumerate:

I. They were employed as GOUGES, CHISELS, SCRAPERS, and KNIVES.

In that rude period when men—almost entirely ignorant of the use of metals—were compelled from such objects as Nature placed within their reach to select those materials which would most conveniently supply their mechanical requirements, the ancient artificers, avoiding the protracted labor necessary for the conversion of stone fragments into implements of serviceable shape, found in the strong shells of the ocean and in many fluviatile mussels convenient tools, well formed, edged, and ready to hand.

In plate xii. of the "Admiranda Narratio," an Indian is represented with a conch busily engaged in scraping away the charred portions of the interior of a canoe which is being hollowed out by fire. From the part of the canoe upon which he is working the fire has evidently just been removed by his assistant, who, with a fan in one hand and a stick in the other, is kindling a flame in another portion of the trough-shaped boat. The explanatory note informs us that by means of shells the bark was removed from the trunk destined for the canoe ("tunc cortice conchis quibusdam adempto"), and that, after it had been hollowed out by fire, its interior, with the aid of like implements, was scraped and rendered smooth ("restincto igne cōchis scabunt, & nouo suscitato igne denuo adurunt, atque ita deinceps pergunt, subinde urentes & scabentes donec cymba necessarium alueum nacta sit.") [1]

The wooden spades and mattocks used by the Florida Indians in the cultivation of the soil were made "with certain stones, oyster-shells, and mussels, wherewith also they made their bows and small lances, and cut and polish all sorts of wood that they employ about their buildings and necessary use." [2]

Beverly [3] asserts that before the English supplied the Virginia Indians with metallic tools, their knives

[1] "Admiranda Narratio," etc., Francoforti ad Mœnum. De Bry, anno 1590.

[2] "The Whole and True Discoverye of Terra Florida," etc., "written in French by Captain Ribaulde, the first that wholly discovered the same, and now newly set forth in the English the xxx. of May, 1563. Prynted at London by Rowland Hall, for Thomas Hackett."

[3] "History and Present State of Virginia," book iii., chap. xiii., p. 60. London, 1705.

consisted either of sharpened reeds or shells, and that with these and sharp stone-axes "bound to the end of a stick and glued in with turpentine," they formed bows of locust-wood, and cut and notched their arrows.

The oyster-shell was employed as a scraper in dressing hides.[1]

Many of the clam, oyster and mussel shells of the Southern waters were well adapted to the uses of scrapers and gouges; and the supply of such natural tools was at all times accessible, and limitless in quantity. So common were they, that near the coast they were not regarded of value sufficient to warrant their inhumation with the dead.

II. As Drinking-Cups.—The use of certain conchs as drinking-cups seems to have been general among the Southern Indians. When the Floridians, in the sixteenth century, would deliberate upon grave affairs, the chief men were wont to assemble in the public place, where, upon a semicircular wooden bench, they all took their seats. The king or mico appeared also, and occupied his place in the centre, where was a seat elevated above the rest. At his command certain women prepared the *casina*. Upon a given signal from the cacique, the cup-bearer offered this hot decoction in a capacious shell first to the king, and then to the noted personages who were present, each drinking in the order of his rank.[2]

In plate xix. of the "Brevis Narratio," widows, in token of their grief, are strewing their hair upon the graves of their dead husbands. Upon each grave are

[1] "Natural History of North Carolina," etc., Brickell, p. 365. Dublin, 1737. Lawson's "History of Carolina," etc., pp. 338, 339. Raleigh reprint, 1860.

[2] "Tum pocillator primum Regi hoc decoctum calidum in capace concha præbet, deinde (sic imperante Rege), omnibus alijs ex ordine, in illa ipsa concha." "Brevis Narratio," etc., plate xxix. Francoforti ad Mœnum. De Bry, anno 1591.

seen the bow, quiver, spear, and shell drinking-cup of the deceased.[1] Upon the demise of a king or priest, for three days did the members of his tribe gather around his tomb and mourn and fast. About the base of the tumulus numerous arrows were stuck in the ground, while upon its top was placed the shell from which he was accustomed to drink.[2]

In many of the burial-mounds of Georgia conchs are found which were doubtless used as drinking-cups, and placed there at the period of the inhumation in obedience to that well-established custom which surrounded the dead with articles of value, ornament, and convenience, that there should be no lack of them in the spirit-land. From some of them the axes have been entirely removed. In the stone graves of Nacoochee Valley more than one *cassis flammea* was seen. In each instance the interior whorls and columellas had been carefully cut away, so that these large univalves formed capacious and serviceable vessels.

Similar relics were observed by Professor Joseph Jones in the stone graves of Tennessee, and they have been found in ancient tumuli in several of the Southern States. Sometimes these shells were, at great pains, divided longitudinally. In the neighborhood of the coast the *Pyrula perversa* seems to have been the common drinking-cup, and, in its natural shape, handily supplemented the calabashes and fictile ware in ministering to the simple wants of these primitive peoples. Mr. Haywood[3] says that at the annual feast of Harvest the Southern Indians sent to those of their

[1] "Maritorum arma, concbas ex quibus bibebant."

[2] "Brevis Narratio," plate xl. "Defuncto aliquo Rege ejus Provinciæ, magna solemnitate sepelitur & ejus tumulo crater, è quo bibere solebat, imponitur, defixis circa ipsum tumulum multis sagittis."

[3] "Natural and Aboriginal History of Tennessee," p. 156. Nashville, 1823

number who were sick and unable to participate in the solemnities and festivities of the occasion, old consecrated shells, full of the sanctified, bitter casina.

III. As Spoons.—Clam and cockle shells were extensively used in this way. Generally the half-shell, in its natural state, sufficed; but, in many instances, a handle, just wide enough to be conveniently grasped by the thumb and forefinger, was cut in the side near the hinge. In this way hot food might be scooped up without bringing the fingers in contact with it.

Lying upon the mat by the side of the woman, one of these shell spoons is figured in plate xvi. of the "Admiranda Narratio."[1] Such shells also served a good turn in scaling fishes. In the writer's collection are fine specimens taken from the grave-mounds of Tennessee.

IV. As Agricultural Implements.[2]

V. As Rattles.—These were made of the shells of the land-tortoise,[3] or of conchs from which the interior whorls and columellas had been removed and pebbles, beans, or beads placed in them. By means of deer-skin thongs they were fastened to the outside of the legs. In dancing, every saltatory movement was accompanied by a corresponding jingle, and thus each motion called forth a certain sort of rude music.

VI. As Receptacles or Shrines for Idols.—Dr. Troost had in his collection a large *cassis flammea* whose interior whorls and columella had been entirely removed, and the front of the shell opened so as to permit the entrance and enshrining of a small image

[1] *See* also Beverly's "History and Present State of Virginia," book iii., chap. iv., p. 17. London, 1705.

[2] Loskiel's "North American Indians," pp. 66, 67. London, 1794.

[3] Adair's "History of the American Indians," pp. 169, 170. London, 1775.

in a kneeling posture. That idol was within the shell when it was ploughed up, and is figured *in situ* on page 361 of volume i. of the "Transactions of the American Ethnological Society."[1] This may be an exceptional case, but it is well authenticated and worthy of specific mention in this connection.

VII. As an Element of Strength and Durability in the Manufacture of Earthen-ware.—For this purpose shells were reduced, by pounding, to a fine powder and mixed with the clay. The mass, moistened with water, was then carefully kneaded and subsequently formed into the desired vessel. As we have, however, in the chapter devoted to an examination of the pottery of the Southern Indians alluded to this use of shells, we refrain from further comment.

VIII. As Money.—Ignorant of the relative worth of metals, and, in the manufacture of serviceable and ornamental articles, treating gold, silver and copper simply as malleable stones, it was necessary that the Indians in the interchange of various commodities should agree upon something which by common consent should be regarded and accepted as the representative of fixed values. Accordingly, they selected what is now generally known as wampum, or shell-money. The term *wampum* is said to be an Algonkin[2] word, signifying *white*—such being the prevailing color of the beads. The ordinary wampum beads[3] are cylindrical in shape, varying from the sixth to a quarter of an inch in length and being about the eighth of an inch in diameter. They are of two varieties, the one

[1] New York, 1845.

[2] Loskiel asserts it to be an Iroquois word, meaning a *mussel*. "History of the Mission of the United Brethren," etc., p. 26. London, 1794.

[3] These beads are variously known as wampumpeage, wampeage, peage, wampum peak, peak, seawan, seawant, ronoak, etc., etc.

white, and the other blue or purplish-black—the latter being the more valuable (*see* Figs. 1 and 2, Plate XXX.).

On the Virginia coast, as we are informed in the "Westover Papers," the species of conch-shell is found of which the Indian *peak* is made: "The extremities of these shells are blue, the rest being white, so that *peak* of both these colours are drilled out of the same shell, serving the natives both for ornament and money, and are esteemed by them beyond gold and silver."

Beverly[1] thus describes what he quaintly terms the *treasure or riches* of the Virginia Indians: "The Indians had nothing which they reckoned Riches before the *English* went among them, except *Peak*, *Roenoke*, and such-like trifles made out of the *Cunk* Shell. These past with them instead of Gold and Silver, and serv'd them both for Money and Ornament. It was the *English* alone that taught them first to put a value on their Skins and Furs, and to make a Trade of them.

"*Peak* is of two sorts, or rather of two colours, for both are made of one Shell, tho of different parts; one is a dark Purple Cylinder, and the other a white; they are both made in size and figure alike, and commonly much resembling the *English Buglas*, but not so transparent nor so brittle. They are wrought as smooth as Glass, being one-third of an inch long, and about a quarter, diameter, strung by a hole drill'd thro the center. The dark colour is the dearest, and distinguish'd by the name of *Wampom Peak*. The *English* men that are call'd *Indian* Traders value the

[1] "History and Present State of Virginia," book iii., chapter xii., p. 58. London, 1705.

Plate XXX.

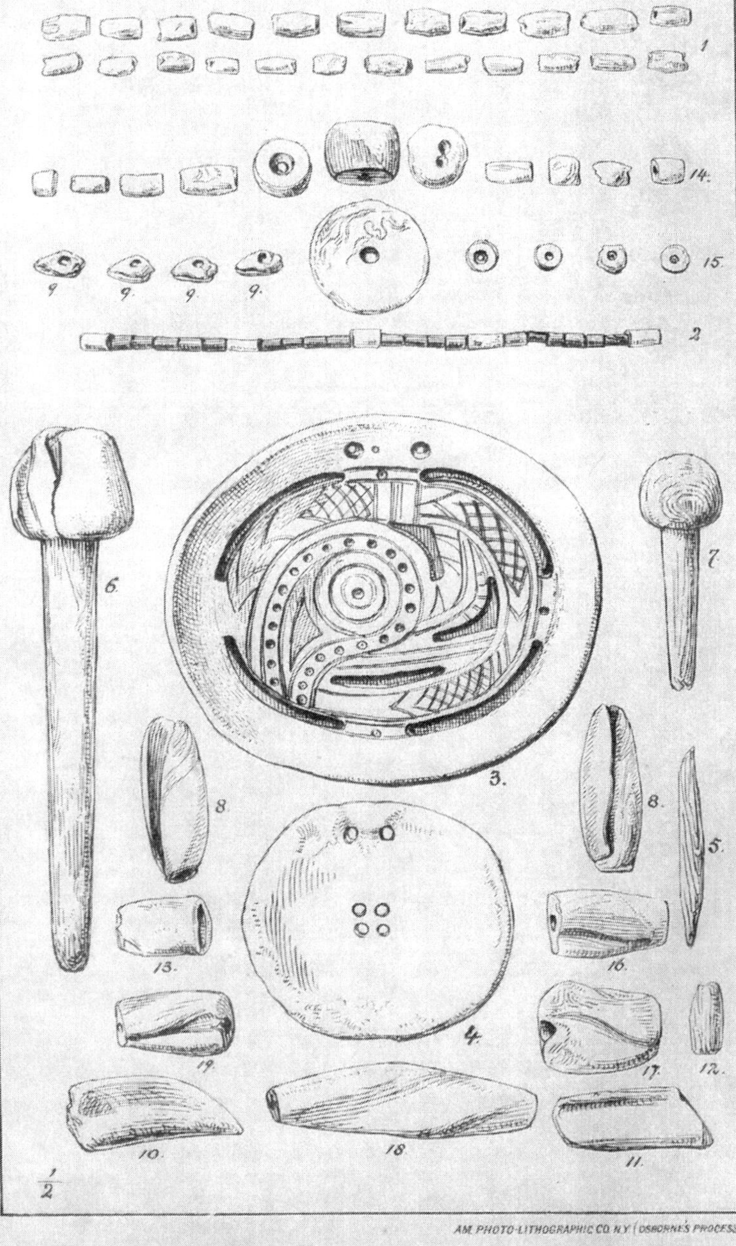

AM. PHOTO-LITHOGRAPHIC CO. N.Y. (OSBORNE'S PROCESS)

Wampom Peak at eighteen pence *per* Yard, and the white *Peak* at nine pence. The *Indians* also make Pipes of this, two or three inches long, and thicker than ordinary, which are much more valuable. They also make *Runtees* of the same Shell, and grind them as smooth as *Peak*. These are either large, like an Oval Bead, and drill'd the length of the Oval, or else they are circular and flat, almost an inch over, and one third of an inch thick, and drill'd edgeways. Of this Shell they also make round Tablets of about four inches diameter, which they polish as smooth as the other, and sometimes they etch or grave thereon Circles, Stars, a Half-Moon, or any other figure suitable to their fancy. These they wear instead of Medals before or behind their Neck, and use the *Peak*, *Runtees*, and Pipes for Coronets, Bracelets, Belts, or long Strings, hanging down before the Breast, or else they lace their Garments with them, and adorn their *Tomahawks* and every other thing that they value.

"They have also another sort which is as current among them, but of far less value; and this is made of the Cockle shell, broke into small bits with rough edges, drill'd through in the same manner as Beads, and this they call *Roenoke*, and use it as the *Peak*.

"These sorts of Money have their rates set upon them as unalterable, and current as the values of our Money are.

"The *Indians* have likewise some Pearl amongst them, and formerly had many more, but where they got them is uncertain, except they found 'em in the Oyster Banks, which are frequent in this Country."

The money of the Carolina Indians, says Lawson,[1] "is of different sorts, but all made of shells which are

[1] "History of Carolina," etc., p. 315. Raleigh reprint, 1860.

found on the coast of Carolina, which are very large and hard so that they are very difficult to cut. Some English smiths have tried to drill this sort of shell-money, and thereby thought to get an advantage; but it proved so hard that nothing could be gained. They oftentimes make of this shell a sort of gorge, which they wear about their neck in a string; so it hangs on their collar, whereon sometimes is engraven a cross or some odd sort of figure which comes next in their fancy. There are other sorts valued at a doe skin, yet the gorges will sometimes sell for three or four buck skins ready dressed. There be others, that eight of them go readily for a doe skin; but the general and current species of all the Indians in Carolina, and, I believe, all over the continent as far as the Bay of Mexico, is that which we call Peak and Ronoak; but Peak more especially. This is that which at New York they call wampum, and have used it as current money amongst the inhabitants for a great many years. This is what many writers call porcelan, and is made in New York in great quantities, and with us in some measure. Five cubits of this purchase a dressed doe skin, and seven or eight purchase a dressed buck skin. An Englishman could not afford to make so much of this wampum for five or ten times the value; for it is made out of a vast great shell, of which that country affords plenty; where it is ground smaller than the small end of a tobacco pipe, or a large wheat straw. Four or five of these make an inch, and every one is to be drilled through, and made as smooth as glass, and so strung as beads are, and a cubit of the Indian measure contains as much in length as will reach from the elbow to the end of the little finger. They never stand to question whether it is a tall man or a short man that measures it; but if this wampum peak be black or purple, as some part of that shell is, then it is twice the value. This the Indians grind on stones and other things till they make it current, but the drilling is the most difficult to the Englishmen, which the Indians manage with a nail stuck in a cane or reed. Thus they roll it continually on their thighs with their right hand, holding the bit of shell with their left; so, in time, they drill a hole quite through it, which is a very tedious work; but especially in making their ronoak, four of which will scarce make one length of wampum. The Indians are a people that never value their time, so that they can afford to make them, and never need to fear the English will take the trade out of their hands. This is the money with which you may buy skins, furs, slaves, or any thing the Indians have; it being the mammon (as our money is to us) that entices and persuades them to do any thing, and part with every thing they possess, except their children for slaves. As for their wives, they are often sold, and their daughters violated for it. With this they buy off murders; and whatsoever a man can do that is ill, this wampum will quit him of, and make him, in their opinion, good and virtuous, though never so black before."[1]

Alluding to the passion of the Southern Indians for ornaments, Adair[2] remarks: "Before we supplied them with our European beads, they had great quantities of wampum (the Buccinum of the ancients), made out of conch-shell by rubbing them on hard stones, and so they form them according to their liking.

[1] Compare Dr. Brickell's "Natural History of North Carolina," p. 337, *et seq.* Dublin, 1737.

[2] "History of the American Indians," etc., p. 170. London, 1765.

"With these they bought and sold at a stated current rate, without the least variation for circumstances either of time or place; and now they will hear nothing patiently of loss or gain, or allow us to heighten the price of our goods, be our reasons ever so strong, or though the exigencies and changes of time may require it. Formerly four deer-skins was the price of a large conch-shell bead, about the length and thickness of a man's fore-finger; which they fixed to the crown of their head as an high ornament—so greatly they valued them. Their beads bear a very near resemblance to ivory."

When Cabeça de Vaca set out upon his trading expedition he carried with him from the Gulf coast "cones and other pieces of sea-snail, conches used for cutting," and "sea-beads." These he traded away to the Indians inhabiting the interior, and in exchange received from them and brought back with him "skins, ochre with which they rub and color the face, hard canes of which to make arrows, sinews, cement and flint for the heads, and tassels of the hair of deer that by dyeing they make red." Wherever he journeyed, while thus employed, he received fair treatment at the hands of the natives, who—to use his own language—"gave me to eat out of regard to my commodities. The inhabitants were pleased when they saw me, and I had brought them what they wanted." On various occasions shell-beads were offered as presents by the Southern Indians to the Spaniards.[1] In this way they sought to propitiate their powerful invaders, and the gift was, in their estimation, among the most valuable of all their possessions. Among the articles regarded as "great riches"

[1] "Relation of Alvar Nuñez Cabeça de Vaca," translated by Buckingham Smith, pp. 85, 86, 145, 146, 150, 194. New York, 1871.

by the inhabitants of Pacaha, Biedma enumerates "beads made of sea-snails."[1]

This shell-money was also extensively manufactured by some of the Northern Indians, and for a considerable time circulated freely in the New-England colonies, in New York, Pennsylvania, and elsewhere. Several interesting accounts of the value and use of this currency in that region, during the early days of European colonization in America, have been preserved.

The New-England Indians, writes Roger Williams,[2] "are ignorant of *Europe's* Coyne; yet they have given a name to ours, and call it *Moneash* from the *English* Money. Their owne is of two sorts; one white, which they make of the stem or stocke of the *Periwincle*, which they call Meteaûhok, when all the shell is broken off: and of this sort six of their small Beads (which they make with holes to string the bracelets) are currant with the *English* for a peny. The second is black, incling to blew, which is made of the shell of a fish which some *English* call *Hens*, Poquaûhock, and of this sort three make an *English* peny. They that live upon the Sea-side generally make of it, and as many make as will.

"The *Indians* bring downe all their sorts of Furs which they take in the Countrey, both to the *Indians* and to the *English* for this *Indian* Money: this Money the *English*, *French* and *Dutch* trade to the *Indians*, six hundred miles in severall parts (North and South from *New England*) for their Furres, and whatsoever they stand in need of from them, as Corne, Venison, etc.

"This one fathom of this their stringed money,

[1] "Narratives of the Career of Hernando de Soto," translated by Buckingham Smith, p. 252. New York, 1866.

[2] "A Key into the Language of America," etc., p. 144. London, 1643.

now worth of the English but five shillings (sometimes more) some few yeeres since was worth nine and sometimes ten shillings *per* Fathome. . . . Their white they call *Wompam* (which signifies white); their black *Suckáubock* (*Súcki* signifying blacke). . . . Before ever they had *Awle-blades* from *Europe* they made shift to bore this their shell money with stone, and so fell their trees with stone set in a wooden staff, and used woden *bowes*."

The money of the Massachusetts Indians is described by the Rev. Cotton Mather as consisting of "little beads with holes in them to string them upon a bracelet, whereof some are white, and of these there go six for a penny. Some are black or blue, and of these go three for a penny. This wampum, as they call it, is made of the shell-fish which lies upon the sea-coast continually." Nathaniel Morton[1] intimates that the Plymouth colony first acquired a distinct knowledge of the value and profit of the trade in *wampampeag* from the Dutch in 1627, and denounces the "baseness of sundry unworthy persons" who, in exchange for this shell-money, furnished the Indians with "guns, powder, and shot." So firm a hold, however, did this wampum—as a standard of values and as a convenient medium of exchange—soon take upon the commercial mind of the New-Englanders, that at an early period it was, by special enactment, treated as currency and made a legal tender in payment of debts not exceeding specified amounts. The wampum-trade was also farmed out to a company which, for the privilege of the monopoly, obligated itself to pay into the colonial treasury of Massachusetts one-twentieth of all that was secured.

[1] "New England's Memoriall," etc., p. 67. Cambridge, 1669.

In his "Account of two Voyages to New England" Josselyn asserts that the natives made wampum so cunningly "that neither Jew nor devil" could counterfeit it. Subsequently, however, as Mr. Stevens [1] properly remarks, this proved to be an idle boast, for a spurious imitation, very closely resembling real wampum, was introduced by the fur-traders at so low a price that the whole Indian country was soon flooded with it, destroying at once the value and meaning of real wampum.

Burnaby,[2] who made his observations in 1759 and 1760, describes the current money among the Indians as "made of the clam-shell consisting within of two colours, purple and white, and in form not unlike a thick oyster-shell. The process of manufacture is very simple. It is first clipped to a proper size, which is that of a small oblong parallelopiped, then drilled, and afterwards ground to a round, smooth surface, and polished. The purple wampum is much more valuable than the white—a very small part of the shell being of that colour."[3]

Without multiplying authorities, it may be safely asserted that this shell-money was manufactured along the Atlantic coast from Maine to Florida, and on the Gulf coast certainly as far south as Central America. The use of this circulating medium was undoubtedly very general among the agricultural tribes east of the Mississippi River. The ancient sepulchral tumuli of Georgia, Tennessee, Florida, and of other Southern States, as well as those located in the valley of the

[1] "Flint Chips," etc., p. 458. London, 1870.

[2] "Travels through the Middle Settlements in North America," etc., p. 60. London, 1775.

[3] Compare Carver's "Travels," etc., p. 362. London, 1778. Loskiel's "History," etc., p. 26. London, 1794.

Ohio and in valleys tributary both to it and to the Mississippi from the east, when opened, fully corroborate the historical narrative, and afford physical proof that this product of the skill and the patience of the coast tribes—sought and obtained through trade-relations—was thus, and by means of subsequent migrations, widely disseminated among the red-men dwelling far in the interior. After he crossed the Mississippi, Mr. Catlin[1] saw but very little wampum among the prairie Indians. "Amongst the numerous tribes," he states, "who have formerly inhabited the Atlantic coast and that part of the country which now constitutes the principal part of the United States, wampum has been invariably manufactured and highly valued as a circulating medium."

West of the Rocky Mountains, however, some of the tribes "make use of various coloured shells, ground to an oval or nearly round shape." Belts of wampum were also regarded as standards of value, and according to these standards they exchanged property among themselves and with the traders.[2] Among the Indians of the Northwest coast the *Dentalium* formed a currency.[3]

Taking the place of money, and constituting an acknowledged medium of exchange, these wampum beads served also as favorite and valuable decorations. Broad belts, variously and elaborately ornamented with such beads, were delivered at one time as title-deeds upon the alienation of a tract of land, at another time as solemn tokens in ratification of a treaty of peace;

[1] "Illustrations of the Manners, Customs, and Condition of the North American Indians," vol. i., p. 223, note. London, 1848.

[2] Hunter, "Memoirs of a Captivity," etc., p. 294. London, 1823.

[3] J. K. Lord, "Naturalist in British Columbia," vol. ii., pp. 25, 26. Stevens' "Flint Chips," p. 468, *et seq.* London, 1870.

again, as pledges of friendship, as sacred attestations of an uttered vow, and as records of memorable events. In the latter case, each string of beads possessed an historical significance and was as intelligible as the knotted cord of the *guipu*.

IX. As Ornaments.—While the shape and characteristic peculiarities of what is commonly called the wampum bead are readily recognized and clearly defined, it seems probable, at least among the Southern Indians, that all the various forms of shell beads, pendants, and ornaments, were highly prized both for personal decoration and as objects of barter. Rarely have I seen the purple or black wampum within the limits of Georgia, while hundreds of the white have been taken from sepulchral tumuli in various portions of the State. The Southern Indians, without doubt, expended no little time and toil in the manufacture of these shell ornaments. Consequently, the results of their taste and industry are numerous and interesting. Sharing in that passion for personal decoration which, in all ages, has so thoroughly possessed the breasts of both civilized and savage, they found in the pearly nacre and bright colors of marine and fluviatile shells the choicest material for the fabrication of beads, pendants, gorgets, armlets, pins, and various ornaments with which to bedeck their persons and habits. To these ornaments a twofold value appertained—the one inherent in the intrinsic beauty and durability of the shells themselves, the other born of the skill, ingenuity, and labor involved in their manufacture. Strings[1] of these shining and carefully-polished beads adorned the ears, necks, shoulders, elbows, arms, knees, ankles,

[1] "Admiranda Narratio," plates iii., vi. vii., viii., xvi., xviii., xxi. "Brevis Narratio," plates viii., xiv., xvi., xxxiv, xxxvii., xxxviii., xxxix.

wrists, waists, and robes of these primitive peoples, and were used to enhance the beauty, dignity, and riches of their idols. Both males and females delighted in the ownership of personal ornaments; and, when the grave opened to receive those who claimed them, these prized possessions were deposited with the dead, that, amid the well-watered fields of fairer hunting-grounds, the departed might not lack the companionship of those things which pleased them most and constituted their chief treasures here. Tumuli and obliterated graves are now the storehouses whence are obtained supplies of these ornaments. Upon most of them the lapse of years, fire, and the moisture of the earth have wrought sad changes, and they are often but crumbling, discolored mockeries of former symmetry and beauty.

Dwelling under warm skies, which permitted them to pass the greater part of the year in a state of almost entire nudity, the Southern Indians delighted in painting their bodies with the most brilliant colors they could command. Their persons being uncovered, the fullest opportunity was afforded not only for the display of skin ornamentation in various lines and curious devices, but also for the exhibition upon any part of the body of necklaces, gorgets, and sundry articles of shell, bone, and stone jewelry, if indeed that word may be properly used to describe these representatives of barbaric fancy. Hence the taste for personal decoration was more general and pronounced among them, than among their more northern brethren, whose principal labor in this regard was bestowed upon the ornamentation of their clothing.

The prevailing varieties of the shell beads found within the limits of Georgia are represented in Figs. 14–19, Plate XXX.

With the exception of the disk-shaped beads, all are perforated longitudinally, the diameters of the bores varying with the size of the ornament—seldom, however, exceeding a quarter of an inch. Some of them are perforated both longitudinally and transversely. It is evident that, at the period of their manufacture, they were all carefully polished; and while many have, with the lapse of years, been converted into a soft, white, chalky substance, others still retain their smooth surfaces, and in their present appearance closely resemble ivory, for which substance they were sometimes mistaken by the early observers. The column and walls of the *Strombus gigas* were freely used in the construction of the largest of these beads, not a few of which still bear the trace of the natural canal. Those of the elongated shape vary in length from a quarter of an inch to two inches and a half, and in diameter from one-sixth of an inch to one inch. The disk-shaped beads vary in thickness from the twelfth to the sixth of an inch, and in width from a quarter of an inch to an inch and a quarter. The forms varied with the fancies of the manufacturers, some beads being round, others ovoidal, others tubular, and others still, disk-shaped.

Both Adair[1] and Lawson[2] unite in stating that the natives manufactured these beads out of conch-shells, and formed them into the desired shapes by rubbing them on hard stones. Before the introduction of metallic implements, Roger Williams[3] says the Indians "made shift to bore this their shell money with stone;"

[1] "History of the American Indians," etc., p. 170. London, 1775.

[2] "History of Carolina," p. 316. Raleigh reprint, 1860. Brickell's "Natural History of North Carolina," p. 339. Dublin, 1737.

[3] "A Key into the Language of America," etc., p. 148. London, 1643.

and, during the progress of the journey of Surveyor-General Lawson,[1] he observed the Carolina Indians drilling their beads by means of a nail stuck in the end of a cane or reed. The drill was rolled on the thigh with the right hand—the bit of shell being held in the left—and so, in the course of time, after the expenditure of much patience, the perforation was accomplished. When we consider the amount of tedious labor necessarily involved in shaping, boring, and polishing these beads, we are prepared to appreciate the reason why they came to be regarded by the natives among their most precious treasures. It is not probable that the heated copper spindles, which the Spanish historians declare were used for the perforation of pearls, could have proved serviceable in puncturing these pieces of shell. The larger beads were drilled from opposite ends, the perforation being smaller in the centre than at the inception of the bore. There is no reason why at least some of them should not have been drilled in the manner commonly adopted for boring stone. Either a solid or a hollow wooden drill, aided by sharp sand and water, would have compassed the desired object; and in the case of the disk-shaped, round, and ovoidal beads, a drill made of a triangularly-pointed flint flake would have answered every purpose.

Among the Southern Indians, upon the authority of Adair,[2] in former times "a large conch-shell bead about the length and thickness of a man's fore-finger would purchase four deer skins." Beads of this sort were greatly valued, and were "fixed to the crown of the head as high ornaments."

[1] "History of Carolina," p. 316. Raleigh reprint, 1860.

[2] "History of American Indians," etc., p. 170. London, 1774.

Du Pratz[1] describes the ear-rings of the Indian women of Louisiana as being "made of the center part of a large shell, called burgo, which is about the thickness of one's little finger;" and Father Hennepin,[2] in his account of the customs of the natives of Louisiana and Mississippi, states that "Women and Men, but above all, Young Girls, wear Necklaces of Shells about their Necks, of different Figures. They have also a sort of Shells as long as one's Finger, and hollow like Pipes, which serve them for Pendants to hang in their Ears."

While the longer varieties served as pendants and head-ornaments, the smaller were strung and worn as necklaces, bracelets, anklets, armlets, or used as decorations for moccasins, belts, and their clothing generally. The number of these beads found in a single tumulus is surprising, and shows how many of them were at times owned by one individual.[3]

In obedience to the taste and skill of the Southern Indians, the shell assumed ornamental shapes other than those represented by the beads. Prominent among them are the gorgets—two varieties of which are here represented (*see* Figs. 3 and 4, Plate XXX.). These, suspended by a string, were worn about the neck. Lawson[4] alludes to the existence of this class of ornaments among the Carolina Indians in his day, and comments upon the high commercial esteem in which they were held. He also calls attention to the fact that thereon was sometimes "engraven a cross, or some odd sort of figure which comes next in their

[1] "History of Louisiana," vol. ii., p. 232. London, 1763.

[2] "Continuation of the New Discovery," etc., p. 80. London, 1698.

[3] Compare Roger Williams' "Key into the Language of America," etc., p. 149. London, 1643.

[4] "History of Carolina," etc., p. 315. Raleigh reprint, 1860.

fancy." The Southern Indian priest wore upon his breast an ornament "made of a white conch-shell with two holes bored in the middle of it, through which he ran the ends of an otter-skin strap and fastened to the extremity of each a buck-horn white button.[1] The natives of Virginia[2] manufactured round shell "Tablets of about four inches diameter," which they polished as smooth as their *peak*, and upon which they etched or graved "Circles, Stars, a Half-Moon or any other figure suitable to their fancy." It is quite probable that the "figures of children and birds made of pearl," said by the Portuguese narrator to have been found by De Soto in the temple at Talomeco, were nothing more than beautiful gorgets, the personal ornaments of the departed caciques and chieftains of Cutifachiqui who were there interred.

The largest of these ornaments (Fig. 3, Plate XXX.), it will be perceived, is elliptical in shape—its diameters, measured in the direction of the major and minor axes, being respectively four inches and three inches and a half. It is about the eighth of an inch in thickness. In the upper edge are two holes—rather more than half an inch apart—by means of which it was suspended. The open-work and ornamentation are, we think, to be regarded rather as the expressions of the rude fancy of the workman, than as indications of any intelligent design or pictographic idea. These gorgets were, at the period of their manufacture, carefully polished, and the ornamentation occurs on the inner or concave surface. This, then, was the side intended for display. The interior of the shell being lined with an

[1] Adair's "History of the American Indians," p. 84. London, 1775.

[2] "History and Present State of Virginia," book iii., chapter xii., p. 59. London, 1705.

iridescent nacre, and that surface having been by Nature polished beyond all art, was far more beautiful than the exterior, and was consequently selected for exhibition. This we believe to be the true interpretation of the thought of these peoples in the use of such ornaments. Some of the gorgets are bored only in the centre; others have holes both in the upper edge and in the central portion, which would indicate that they were sometimes suspended, and at other times worn as fixed ornaments attached to the head-dress or clothing. In form, size, and ornamentation, these relics do but express the individual fancy of those by whom they were made; and while in the accompanying illustration we have indicated only two prevalent types, to wit, the elliptical and circular, we might mention others which are square, ovoidal, stellate, parallelogrammic and irregular in shape, some with and some without scalloped edges, and others still which, carelessly constructed and with a single hole in the centre, suggest the idea that they were designed as shell buttons.[1] Closely allied to the gorgets are the shell armlets and anklets.

Such is the peculiar shape of these ornaments that they appear by nature adapted to the curvature of the arm or leg.

By means of a thong passing round the limb and through the holes, they could have been readily worn in any desired position. Many were probably used, at pleasure, either in the manner we have suggested or as gorgets suspended from the neck or ears.

Another variety of shell ornaments found in the

[1] *See* a description of similar ornaments found in sepulchral mounds in Tennessee, Fifth Annual Report of the Trustees of the Peabody Museum, p. 16, *et seq.* Boston, 1872.

Southern mounds is that which may be designated by the general name of Pins. Two forms are here represented, the one pointed at either extremity and tumescent in the central portion (*see* Fig. 5, Plate XXX.), the other with one end terminating in a large, well-formed head, and the other tapering to a blunt point (*see* Figs. 6 and 7, Plate XXX.). Those with heads were made from the columellas of some big univalve, such as the *Strombus gigas.* The extreme length of the pin numbered 6, in Plate XXX., is five inches and a half, one inch of that distance being occupied by the head, which is an inch and a quarter in diameter. The shank is an inch and a half in circumference; and, while tapering somewhat, is blunt at the point. Relics precisely similar in shape were fashioned of soapstone. From the same tumulus pins made both of shell and stone have been taken. The pointed pins are usually smaller, seldom exceeding three inches in length, while those with heads vary in length from an inch and a half to six inches. These ornaments were at the time of their manufacture highly polished in every part. While their precise use is open to conjecture, we may safely conclude that they were intended as objects of display and personal decoration.[1]

Shells were frequently worn as ornaments without any material alteration of their natural forms. Among the Southern Indians the oliva and the marginella (*see* Figs. 8 and 9, Plate XXX.) were extensively used as necklaces, bracelets, and anklets. The apices of the former were cut or rubbed off, and the backs of the latter ground so as to make a second hole or perfora-

[1] Bone pins somewhat analogous in form have been found in the Lake Dwellings of Switzerland. "Keller's Lake Dwellings," p. 174, plate liv., Fig. 33. London, 1866.

tion by means of which a thread of some sort could be conveniently introduced, and thus any desired number of the shells securely strung.[1] In several localities we have found the columns of large sea-shells cut off at the required lengths, partially fashioned and imperforate, which were evidently obtained in this imperfect condition from the primitive shell-merchantmen and kept for polish and completion, at some future time, by the purchasers. (*See* Figs. 10, 11, and 12, Plate XXX.) Cabeça de Vaca alludes to a trade in such articles, and the banks of the Ocmulgee near Macon, and of the Chattahoochee far up among the beautiful valleys of Cherokee Georgia, as well as the sites of many old Indian villages, bear present testimony to the truth of his narrative and to the extensive character of this ancient traffic in unfinished shell beads.

We might enumerate other shell trinkets, but they are matters rather of curiosity than of archæological value.

Beads were also manufactured of stone, clay, bone, and wood. Those of stone were generally made of soapstone, are globular in shape, and about three-quarters of an inch in diameter. The clay beads are circular in form, the upper and lower sides being flat, are perforated through the centre, are from a quarter to half an inch in thickness, and vary in size from half an inch to an inch and a half in diameter. When these disk-like beads were strung in quantities, only the edges

[1] Compare "Transactions of the American Ethnological Society," vol. i., p. 360, New York, 1845. "Ancient Monuments of the Mississippi Valley," p. 233. Wilson's "Prehistoric Man," pp. 129, 141, London, 1865. Stevens' "Flint Chips," p. 454, London, 1870. "Smithsonian Report for 1868," p. 404. Venegas' "Natural and Civil History of California," vol. i., pp. 71, 73, London, 1759. Hennepin's "Continuation of the New Discovery," p. 80, London, 1698. "Narratives of the Career of Hernando de Soto," etc., translated by Buckingham Smith, p. 252, New York, 1866.

would appear. Bone beads were cut in desired lengths from the wing-bone of a large bird or from the small bone of the leg of a deer or other animal. Their perforations are longitudinal, and the ornaments when finished were carefully polished. (*See* Fig. 13, Plate XXX.)

Human teeth, and the teeth and claws of bears and the spurs of the turkey-cock, were perforated and worn as pendants. Youths frequently bedecked themselves with bracelets made of the ribs of deer, which were boiled, bent into the desired shapes, and then polished so as to look like ivory.[1]

In comparatively recent sepultures European beads of glass and porcelain are not infrequent. Black, blue, white, and red, are the predominating colors. Many are enamelled, and are evidently Venetian in their origin. With these European beads the white wampum and other shell beads are often found intermingled. Portions of strings of rosary-beads also occur, which were doubtless obtained at an early period through religious commerce with the Spanish priests.

Secondary interments upon the tops and sides of ancient tumuli, and many Indian graves in Cherokee Georgia contain ornaments of silver and brass, consisting of corrugated bracelets, ear and finger rings, pendants, buckles, clasps, bosses, and gorgets. In most of them we recognize how sedulously the European manufacturer pandered to the barbaric tastes of these primitive peoples.

In the Etowah Valley gold beads have been found which were clearly the handiwork of the natives. Copper pendants also are occasionally unearthed in Nacoochee and other valleys in Upper Georgia. In all instances of this character, as we have already re-

[1] Du Pratz, "History of Louisiana," vol. ii., p. 233. London, 1753.

marked, the metal was treated without the application of heat, and was simply hammered into the desired shape. Among the Aboriginal tribes of this region, prior to commerce with Europeans, the use of metallic ornaments and implements was limited.

Adair[1] assures us that in the olden time quartz-crystals (or, to use his own language, "such coarse diamonds as their own hilly country produced") were freely used. They were fastened by means of deer-sinews to the hair, nose, ears, moccasins, and various parts of the dress. The truth of this statement is attested by the contents of many mounds which we have opened. Mr. Atwater is correct when he supposes that the circular aggregation of crystals which he figures on page 233 of Volume I. of the "Archæologia Americana," was worn as an ornament. We have in our collection a beautiful specimen of this character taken from a Georgia burial-mound located two hundred miles away from any point whence the quartz-crystals could have been obtained. The holes in the lobes of the ears of the women were small, but the men were in the habit of cutting out the entire interior of the lobes of their ears, and then inserting large tufts of buffalo's-wool mixed with bear's-grease, so as to distend the aperture to the utmost degree.[2] Into these, when healed, they would introduce bunches of beautiful feathers, large rings, joints of cane gaudily colored, and the inflated bladders of fishes.[3] In the explanatory note accompanying plate xxxviii. of the "Brevis Narratio," we are informed that both men and women wore these fish-bladders in their ears, and that when

[1] "History of the American Indians," etc., pp. 170, 171. London, 1775.

[2] Adair's "History of the American Indians," etc., p. 171. London, 1775.

[3] "Brevis Narratio," plates viii., xi., xii., xv., xvi., xviii., xxvii., xxviii., xxxii., xxxiv., xxxv., xxxix.

inflated they shone like pearls. Sometimes they were colored red, and then they resembled carbuncles. The first joint of an eagle's leg,[1] with the talons attached, formed a favorite ear-ornament with the Southern warrior.

Cabeça de Vaca[2] observed some of the Florida Indians with their nipples and under lips bored, and wearing pieces of cane in the openings. Pendants of various sorts from the nose and under lip were customary, and it may be that lip-stones, after the fashion of the Mexicans, were also used as personal decorations.

CONCLUSION.

As it comports not with the plan proposed and adopted in the execution of this work, we refrain from entering upon a discussion of the interesting inquiry, Whence came the red-men who first peopled this portion of North America?

Our object has been to present a general description of the Southern Indians as they appeared when the Europeans first ventured among them, and to interpret their relics in the light of early recorded observations and of customs not obsolete at the date of the Spanish, French, and English colonizations.

Comparing the manners and temper of the Southern Indians with those of the more Northern tribes which he visited, Father Hennepin pronounces the former "Civil, Easie, Tractable and capable of instructions," while the latter are declared "mere Brutes as fierce and cruel as any wild Beasts."[3] Enjoying those physical blessings which are bestowed by warm skies, luxuriant vegetation and abundant animal life,

[1] "Brevis Narratio," etc., plate xiv.

[2] "Relation," etc., translated by Buckingham Smith, p. 75. New York, 1871.

[3] "New Discovery," etc., p. 157. London, 1698.

the Southern Indians were in great measure relieved of those perpetual struggles for covering and food which have such a decided tendency to harden the condition of the savage, embitter his existence, and render him an Ishmaelite even among his own fellows. To the soft airs which surrounded them and the generous trees which alike in winter and summer threw their protecting arms about them, to the food-treasures of the water and the forests—ever present to supply with little effort their simple wants—and to the spontaneous productions of a fertile soil, were these peoples largely indebted for the pleasure-loving disposition and the imaginative temperament they possessed, and for the gentle lives they were permitted to lead. Exempt from trials incident to a rigorous climate and an inhospitable country, they were able to devote much of their time to amusements and social enjoyment, and to the development of a degree of taste and skill in manufacture superior to that exhibited by their Northern neighbors. Upon a careful comparison of the antiquities of the Southern nations with those of the Northern tribes, we think a greater variety and excellence of manufacture, a more diversified expression of fancy in ornamentation, a more careful selection of beautiful material, a superior delicacy and finish in the fabrication of implements, both chipped and polished, a more pronounced exhibition of combined labor in the erection of tumuli, a more despotic form of government, a greater permanency of seats, a more liberal expenditure of care and attention in the cultivation of the soil, a more decided system of worship, and a more dignified observance of significant festivals and funeral customs may fairly be claimed for the former. We are acquainted with no region north and east of the Rio

Grande in which the earliest exhibitions of skill and taste in the manufacture of implements and ornaments of stone, shell, and bone, are more varied and attractive, where pipe-making claimed such special attention, and where the antique pottery is indicative of such diversity of form and ornamentation, and possessed of such homogeneousness of composition and durability.

Our observations have been, perhaps, too general, and not sufficiently minute, to satisfy either our own wish or the intelligent desire of those in quest of specific information touching the interesting subjects of which we have essayed to treat. Sufficient has been said, however, we trust, to afford the inquirer a tolerable conception of the antiquities of the region which has formed the field of research. So manifold are the exhibitions of fancy and use among the stone implements, so frequent the modifications of well-defined types, and so varied the traces of early constructive skill, that were we to pursue the investigation with that detail which characterizes the recent and most valuable work of Mr. Evans upon the ancient stone implements of Great Britain, we would scarcely be able to assign a reasonable limit either to the descriptions or to the illustrations which would be suggested. A particular consideration of hammer-stones, mauls, sling-stones, whet stones, and of minor relics, as well as of unfinished objects, such as flint chips, wasters, etc., has been omitted. "Flakes and splinters of silicious stone, whether flint, jasper, chert, iron-stone, quartzite, or obsidian, are to be found in almost all known countries, and belong to all ages. They are, in fact, the most catholic of all stone implements, and have been in use 'semper, ubique et ab omnibus.'"[1]

[1] Evans' "Stone Implements, etc., of Great Britain," p. 257. London, 1872.

The objects which we have selected for illustration are designed to convey a suitable idea of prevailing types, not abnormal forms. For this purpose we have used such originals as are in our own possession, refraining entirely from reproducing a single illustration which has appeared elsewhere. For the genuineness of these relics and the accuracy of the drawings we stand personally pledged. Of the relics obtained through early commerce with Europeans, and found in the graves of modern Indians, much might be said: but these belong to a transition period and do not properly claim present attention. There are other relics, the product of the labor and the ingenuity of the red-men in their effort to satisfy wants suggested by personal intercourse with these strangers. Of these a BULLET-MOULD, taken from an Indian grave in Oostenaula Valley, may be mentioned as an example. Made of soapstone, it contains thirteen matrices for running shot and balls, varying in size from a swan-shot to an ounce-ball. These cavities are carefully and regularly cut, and the entire arrangement is most creditable to the workman who, in the absence of a metallic bullet-mould, was able, in the exercise of his native ingenuity and skill, to manufacture an article out of a material with which he was entirely familiar, so cleverly answering the use which contact with the whites had taught him to understand and to require.

American archæology is as yet in its infancy, and there are, on every hand, inviting fields in which intelligent observers may reap rich harvests. If these pages shall minister to the entertainment of the general reader, and contribute aught of value to the information of the careful student, the pleasurable labors of the author will not have been entirely in vain.

GENERAL INDEX.

A.

Aconithus, mound at, 119.
Adair, James, 8, 19, 86, 115, 251, 273, 300, 309, 333, 341, 418, 505.
Adultery, punishment of, 66, 67.
Adze, 277.
Agamemnon, 119.
Agriculture, 296–320.
Agricultural implements, 301–303, 500.
Agricultural labors, 41, 307.
Alexander the Great, 120.
Alibamons, 31.
Alyattes, 119.
Amexias, 45.
Amulets, 372, 373.
Anasco, 247.
Anklets, 517.
Appalatcy, 229.
Archdale, Governor, 2.
Archery, 245–250.
Armlets, 517.
Armories, at Talomeco, 26.
Arrows, of the Florida Indians, 18; manufacture of, 245–259.
Arrow-heads, 240; general distribution of, 240–242; where manufactured, 242, 243; articles of commerce, 243; of what materials made, 244, 247, 249, 250, 256; typical forms of, 254, 265–267; size of, 257; how attached to shafts, 257; how manufactured, 259–265.
Arrow-makers, 243.
Arrow-shafts, stones for rounding, 366, 367.
Arrow-stems, of cane, 255.
Artachies, 119.
Articles of dress, 61.
Ash, Thomas, 250, 322, 422
Assembly-room, 15.
Atwater, Caleb, 436.
Awls, 291, 292.
Axes, stone, 269–286; general distribution of, 269; how made and hafted, 270–273; grooved, 274–278; size of, 275; how sharpened, 277; wedge-shaped, or stone celts, 278–281; with stone handle, 280; perforated or ceremonial, 281–284.

B.

Baegert, Jacob, 363.
Ball-play, 96–98.
Bartram, William, 3, 8, 20, 41, 123, 150, 178, 190, 216, 316, 328, 417.
Baskets, manufacture of, 225.
Beads, of European manufacture, 235–237, 520; of shell, 511–514; of stone, bone, and clay, 519; of gold, etc., 520.
Beckwith, Lieutenant, 263.
Beverley, 250, 270, 362, 470, 502.
Biedma, Luys Hernandez de, 235, 469.
Black-drink, 11, 15.
Blackmoor's teeth, 337.
Blankets, of buffalo's-wool and turkey-feathers, 87.
Blow-guns, 256, 257.
Bolzius, Rev. Martin, 417.
Bone houses, 113, 191.
Boos-ke-tau, feast of the, 99, 303–307.
Borers, 291, 292.
Borysthenes, Scythian tombs on the banks of the, 119.
Bossu, Captain, 184, 256, 271, 323.

Bows, 245–257.
Bread, preparation of maize for making, 310, 311.
Breech clouts, 74, 75, 81, 86.
Brickell, Dr. John, 329.
Brinton, Dr. D. G., 236.
Browne, Sir Thomas, 118.
Brown's Mount, fortification on, 163–165.
Bullet-mould, 525.
Burial of the dead in a sitting posture, 183–185.
Burial-ground on the Georgia coast, 205–207.
Burial-urns, 454–456.

C.

Calabashes, 445, 464.
Calumets, 386–393; typical forms of, 404–408; how drilled, 408, 409.
Calumet-dance, 388–390.
Canoe, ancient, dug up in Savannah River swamp, 53–57.
Canoes, 53–61; manufacture of, by Virginia Indians, 55.
Capital punishment, 13.
Carpets, 86.
Cassis flammea, 233.
Catawbas, 2.
Catlin, George, 261, 369, 462.
Catlinite, 407.
Celts, 278–281.
Chaouanons, 222.
Charlevoix, Father, 23, 428.
Chateaubriand, Viscount de, 204.
Chenco, game of, 346.
Cherokees, 2, 7, 8; territory of the, 6; physical characteristics of the, 9.
Cherokee chief, funeral obsequies of a, 115.
Chickasaws, 2, 3.
Chieftain-mounds, 183–188.
Chisca, 229.
Chisels, 286–288, 496.
Choctaws, 2, 256; origin of the, 5.
Chungke-game, 96, 341–346, 356, 357.
Chunky-yards, 178–181.
Circular earthwork on the headwaters of the Ogeechee River, 148.
Clavigero, 227.
Columbus, 476.
Conjurer, the office of, 28.
Cooking, 308–311.
Copper, treated as a malleable stone, 47, 227, 231; use of, among the Southern Indians, 227–233; axes of, 281; implement of, from stone grave in Nacoochee Valley, 225–227; from the Etowah Valley, 232; pendants of, 233; rods of, 232.
Coreal, François, 29, 362.
Costume, 71–89.
Council-house, 11.
Counting, 101.
Cowe, council-house of, 125.
Craven, Governor, 3.
Crawfish, mode of taking, 336.
Creeks, 2, 6.
Creek Confederacy, territory of the, 3–6; tribes composing the, 6.
Cremation, 101, 189–192, 411.
Cupping-tubes, 361.
Cutifachiqui, the Cacica of, 24, 71, 148, 149, 247.

D.

Dablon, Father, 387.
Daggers, 267.
Dances, various kinds of, 92–96, 388–390.
Davis, Dr. E. H., 232.
De Brahm, William Gerar, 6, 39, 88, 421.
De Bry, 11, 209–211.
De Soto, 24, 25, 142, 149, 235, 468.
Dentalium, use of the, 510.
Devil, worship of the, 21.
Discoidal stones, 341–358; not exempt from sepulture, 343, 346, 347; various forms of, 348–351; applied to secondary uses, 351, 352.
Divorce, 66.
Domenech, Abbé Em, 351.
Dorantes, Andres, 229.
Drift-implements, 293–295.
Drilling in stone, 408.
Drills, solid and hollow, 408–410.
Drinking-cups, 233, 498.
Drums, 90, 91.
Dug-outs, or wooden boats, manufacture and use of, by the Southern Indians, 53–61.
Dumont, 462.
Du Pratz, M. Le Page, 78, 105, 211, 272, 302, 345.
Dwellings of the Florida Indians; 35, 37; of the Virginia Indians,

36; of the Carolina tribes, 37, 38; of the Georgia tribes, 39.
Dyeing, art of, 63, 88.

E.

Ear-ornaments, 88, 515, 521.
Earth-walls, 212.
Edistoes, 2.
Efau-Haujo, 420.
Elevations for chieftain-houses, 122, 126.
Elf-stones, 251.
Elvas, the Gentleman of, 18, 25, 142, 229, 246, 300.
Emetic, prepared from calcined shells, 29.
Enchanted mountain, 377.
Enclosed work on Plunkett Creek, 147.
Etowah idol, 432–434.
Etowah mounds, 136–143.
European axes, 285.
Evans, John, 524.

F.

Family or tribal mounds, 189.
Feasts, monthly, among the Natchez, 99, 100.
Feather mantles, 61, 87.
Festivals, 99, 100.
Fire, veneration of, 21; new lighted at the feast of the Boos-ke-tau, 99.
Fishing, various modes of, 325–340.
Fish-gigs, 329, 330.
Fish-hooks, 326, 327.
Fishing-plummets, 328.
Fish-preserves, 142, 143, 156, 175, 325.
Fish-traps, 330–334.
Flutes, 90.
Fontaneda, 469.
Food, animal, 42, 43; vegetable, 44, 308, 311.
Fort James, ancient monuments near, 123.
Fortification on Brown's Mount, 163–165.
Funeral customs, 101–117, 132, 183–185, 190–192, 203; among the Choctaws, 104, 112, 113, 190; among the Natchez, 105; among the Virginia tribes, 108; among the Carolina tribes, 108–111, 184; among the Muscogulges, 113, 184; among the Alibamons, 114, 184; among the Chickasaws, 114; among the Cherokees, 114–116, 185; carefully observed, 116, 190.
Funeral-scaffolds, 112.

G.

Gallatin, Albert, 3, 6.
Galphin, Fort, 151.
Game, chungke, 96, 341–346, 356, 357; of the javelin, 354; of the pole, 345; of nettecawaw, 346; of the spear and ring, 355.
Gaming, 98, 99.
Garcilasso, 122, 471.
Gardens, private, 42, 299–301.
Georgia, original boundaries of the Colony of, 7.
Gold beads, 47.
Gorgets, 515–517.
Gouges of stone and bone, 287, 288; of shell, 496.
Government, system of, obtaining among the Southern Indians, 10.
Granaries, public, 41, 307.
Grapes, 45.
Graves, 113; veneration and attachment for, 116, 117, 204, 205.
Grave-mounds, 101–105.
Grooved axes, 274–278.
Guyachoya, Cacique of, 24.
Gygæan Lake, 119.

H.

Hammers, 265.
Hand-axes, 278–281.
Hand-nets, 335, 336.
Hariot, Thomas, 17, 26, 30, 76, 316.
Harvesting the maize, 307.
Hatchets, 281–284.
Hawkins, Colonel Benjamin, 14, 65.
Haywood, 84–86, 216, 346, 360, 437.
Head-warriors, 16.
Hennepin, Father, 230, 270, 328, 386, 470.
Hephæstion, 120.
Herodotus, 119.
Hickory-nut-oil, 45, 316.
High-priest, office and duties of the, 19.
Hired mourners, 111.
Hitchittees, origin of the, 4.
Hoes, 301.
Homer, 120.
Horn bells, 92.
Hospitality of the Southern Indians, 42.

Hot-houses, 15.
Human sacrifices, 23, 24.
Human remains found in a cave in Tennessee, 84–86.
Hunter, John D., 461.
Hunting, 322.

I.

Idol-pipes, 401–403.
Idol-shrines, 431, 500.
Images, 140, 146, 430–440.
Image-worship, 22, 413–415, 417–419, 423–430.
Immortality of the soul, belief in the, 21.
Incised trenches on Stone Mountain, 380.
Intaglios, 63, 377–399.
Iron, no knowledge of, 47.

J.

Jaoüanas, 29, 30.
Jars, 457.
Javelin-game, 354.
Jefferson, Thomas, 193, 436.
Jones, Prof. Joseph, M. D., 221–223, 233, 268, 280, 439, 458.
Jugglers, 31.

K.

Kiwasa, the idol, 26, 426.
Knives, flint, 290, 291, 496.

L.

Lafiteau, 271.
La Hontan, 192.
Lake Superior, ancient mining on the shores of, 232.
Land, tenure of, 40.
Laudonniére, 249.
Lawson, Surveyor-General, 2, 31, 80, 109, 328, 423–425, 504, 505.
Leaf-shaped implements, 291, 302.
Lee, Colonel Henry, 151.
Lip-stones, 88, 522.
Longfellow, H. W., 384.
Loskiel, 270, 332.
Lubbock, Sir John, 268, 414, 444.
Lyon, Caleb, 263.

M.

Maize, cultivation of, 297–301; harvesting of the, 307; preparation of, for food, 308–314; varieties of, 310.
Maize-crushers, 314.
Marginella, use of the, as a bead, 518.
Marriage, 65–69.
Matting, cane, 225.
Mauilla, 211.
Maxwell, Major J. A., 166.
Mechanical labor of the Southern Indians, 46–53.
Medicine-men, 28–33.
Medicine-tubes, 359–365.
Medicinal plants, 34.
Megalithic monuments, absence of, 127.
Messier's Mound, 166–174.
Mica membranacea, 376.
Mico, office and powers of the, 11–13; duties of the Creek, 14; cabin of the, 15; selection of an assistant for the, 14.
Mining, ancient, in Duke's Creek Valley, 48; in Valley-River Valley, 48.
Mirrors, 376, 377.
Moats, ancient, 136, 146, 155, 170, 171.
Money, shell, 501–511.
Mortars, 309–314.
Moscoso, Luys de, 24.
Mound-builders, 135, 161, 176; skull of one of the, 160.
Mound-building, 118; in Georgia, 121; within the historic period, 130–132.
Mounds, on the Colonel's Island, 129; in the Etowah Valley, 136–142; in the valley of Little Shoulder-bone Creek, 143; on Plunkett Creek, 147; on Mason's plantation, 153–157; on the Ocmulgee River opposite Macon, 158–162; on Lamar's plantation, 162; on Messier's plantation, 166–174; of observation and retreat, 181, 182; sepulchral, 183; chieftain or priest, 183; family or tribal, 189–192; on the low grounds of the Rivanna, 193; on Stalling's Island, 197; of shell, 195–200; of stone, 202; in Nacoochee Valley, 213; at the junction of the Etowah and Oostenaula Rivers, 253.
Muscogee Confederacy, 2.
Muscogees, origin of the, 4; physical characteristics of the, 9, 10.

Music, 90.
Musical instruments, 90–92.

N.

Nacoochee Valley, mound in, 213; stone graves in, 214–224.
Narvaez, Panphilo de, 116.
Natchez, 2; the sun among the, 22–31.
Nets, 143, 326, 335–337, 339.
Net-sinkers, 337–340.
Nettecawaw, game of, 346.
New fire, origin of, 420.
Nichols, Captain J. H., 214.
Nipples, bored, 88.
Nose-ornaments, 88.
Nuñez, Vasco, 476.
Nut-stones, 315-320.

O.

Offering of the stag, 21, 22.
Oglethorpe, General, 3, 86, 131, 188, 189, 417, 421.
Oliva, the use of the, as a bead, 518.
Open-air workshops, 242.
Orestes, 119.
Ornamental tubes, 365.
Ornamentation of primitive pottery, 444.
Ornaments, 71–89; of shell, 511–519; of European manufacture, 520.
Ortiz, Juan, 116.

P.

Pacaha, 142.
Painting, 63.
Palanquin, use of the, 72, 73.
Paria, the coast of, 475.
Patroclus, the burial of, 120.
Peace, how concluded, 15.
Pearls, 149; use of, as ornaments, among the Southern Indians, 467–494; large numbers of, found in the possession of the natives and in the graves of their dead, 467–481; method of procuring, 471, 472, 476; diving for, 477; trade in, 482; obtained from both marine and fluviatile shells, 481–490; found in relic-beds and ancient graves, 491.
Pear-shaped stones, 371, 372.
Perforated axes, 281–284.
Personal property deposited with the dead, 102, 185.
Pestles, 314.
Pendants, of copper, 233; of stone, 370, 371.
Physicians, 28–33.
Pierced tablets, 367–370.
Pins, of shell, 233, 234; of soapstone, 233, 234.
Pipe-stem carrier, 409.
Pipes, 383–412; origin and uses of, 383–385; how made, 408; how drilled, 407–410; calumets, 386–393; typical forms of, 404–407; idol-pipes, 401–403; ordinary or common pipes, 394; typical forms of, 410–412.
Pits, 187.
Plates, stone, 373–376.
Platters, 374.
Pocahontas, dance of, 94, 95.
Poisoning fish, 327, 333.
Polishing-stones, 292, 293.
Polygamy, 68.
Population, aboriginal, 123.
Pots of terra-cotta, 457.
Potter's wheel, use of the, unknown, 47.
Pottery, manufacture of, 46; general description of, among the Southern Indians, 441–466; an index of the degree of civilization, 440; historical value of, 443; ornamentation of, 444, 458, 459; use of, 445–451; manufacture of, 451, 461–464, 501; kilns for baking, 452, 453; various sizes of articles of, 453; burial-urns, 454–456; pots, 456, 457; flat-bottomed jars, 457; typical forms of Southern, 458; vessels of soapstone, 460; destroyed by cremation, 465, 466.
Priapus, worship of the, 439.
Priest-mounds, 187.
Public buildings in Creek villages, 15, 16.
Public deliberations, 15.
Public granaries, 41.
Public overseer, 41.

Q.

Quivers, 258.

R.

Rattles, 91; of gourds, 91; of terrapin-shells, 92, 500.
Rau, Prof. Charles, 64, 218–220, 302, 338, 363, 369, 408, 433, 452, 458.

Refuse-piles, 200, 201.
Religious ideas, 20–24, 416, 430.
Reynolds, Sir Joshua, 127.
Ribas, 362.
Ribault, Captain, 37, 229, 299, 330.
Rock-walls, 207–209.
Rock-writing, 62.
Roe-deer, stalking of the, 323.
Roguet, 464.
Romans, Captain Bernard, 6, 46, 83, 92, 112, 256, 344.
Rosaries, 236.

S.

Sacrifice of the first-born male child, 13.
Salt, manufacture of, 45, 46.
Savannahs, the, 2.
Saws, 292.
Scenauki, 69.
Schoolcraft, H. R., 260, 439.
Scrapers, 288–290, 496.
Sculptured rocks, 377–380.
Secondary interments, 103, 126, 131, 145, 160.
Seminoles, the, 2, 4.
Sepulchral mounds, 183.
Shawls, 61, 73.
Shawnoes, the, 7.
Shea, John Gilmary, 387.
Shell drinking-cups, 233.
Shell-heaps, 200, 201, 483.
Shell-mounds, 195–200.
Shell ornaments, 162.
Shell pins, 233, 518.
Shells, primitive uses of, 495–519; as gouges, chisels, scrapers, and knives, 496–498; as drinking-cups, 498–500; as spoons, 500; as agricultural implements, 500; as rattles, 500; as shrines for idols, 500; as an element of strength in the manufacture of earthen-ware, 501; as money, 501–511; trade in, 506; as ornaments, 511–519; beads of, 511; typical forms of shell beads, 512; how perforated, 513, 514; ear-rings, 515; gorgets, 515–517; armlets and anklets, 517; pins, 518; unfinished shell beads, as articles of commerce, 519.
Shoes, 77, 79, 81.
Sick, treatment of the, 28–33, 362–364.
Silver Bluff, 123, 148.
Sinkers, perforated and grooved, 337–340.
Skins, preparation of, 62.
Skull of modern Indian, 160; of mound-builder, 160 161.
Slave-posts in chunky-yards, 179.
Sling-stones, 371.
Slung-shots, 371, 372.
Smith, Capt. John, 76, 91, 230, 260.
Smoking, 393–399, 410.
Smoothing-stones, 292, 293.
Southern Indians, physical characteristics of the, 8.
Spades, stone, 302.
Spanish invasions, effect of the, upon the Indian population, 177.
Spears used in capturing fish, 328, 334.
Spear-heads, 240, 252, 253; typical forms of, 253, 254; how made, 259–265.
Spindle-whorls, 235.
Spinning, 87.
Spiral fire, 15.
Spoons, 500.
Squier, Hon. E. George, 232.
Squier and Davis, Messrs., 318, 354.
Stalling's Island, shell-mound on, 197.
Statues, wooden, at Talomeco, 25.
Stones for rounding arrow-shafts, 366, 367.
Stones upon which nuts were cracked, 315–320.
Stone graves, 214–238; in Nacoochee Valley, 214; age of, 238; in the environs of Keowe, 216; in Tennessee, 216–221; in Missouri, 217; in Illinois, 218–220; in Europe, 224.
Stone heaps, 114, 202.
Stone Mountain, 207, 380.
Stone tumulus near Sparta, Georgia, 148.
Stonoes, the, 2.
Storehouses, 12, 308.
Stung-Serpent, funeral obsequies of the, 105–107.
Successive inhumations, 193.
Summer-houses, 35.
Sun, office of the, among the Natchez, 23, 24; worship of the, 20, 21, 422, 427–429; truncated pyramids erected in honor of the, 22.
Supreme Being, conceptions of a, 417–419.
Sword, stone, 268.

T.

Tacitus, 341.
Talomeco, mausoleum of, 25, 230.
Tambours, 91.
Tattooing, 75, 80.
Temple of the Natchez, 427–429.
Temple-mounds, 138, 142, 158.
Terra-cotta, vessels of, 454–466.
Terron, Juan, 473.
Timberlake, Lieutenant, 251, 285, 346, 419.
Time, how reckoned, 100, 1[illegible]1.
Toalli, dwellings of, 35.
Tobacco, 44, 393–399.
Tomahawks, 277.
Tombs of the Virginia kings, 26, 27,
Tomo-chi-chi, 69, 131, 185, 188, 189, 421.
Tonti, the Chevalier, 248.
Town-plantation, 41.
Towns of the Florida Indians, 35, 37; of the Virginia Indians, 36; of the Carolina tribes, 37.
Trade relations, 63, 64, 162, 238, 243, 506.
Tribal or family mounds, 189.
Triturating-stones, 314.
Troost, Professor, 216, 438.
Tubes, stone, 359–365.
Tumlin, Colonel Lewis, 136.
Tumuli, ancient, in Georgia, 121; Bartram's account of, 123–125; secondary uses of, 126, 160; general distribution of, 127–129; associated in groups, 129; shapes and sizes of, 129, 130; few built after the advent of the Europeans, 130–132; age of, 131–135; on the Etowah River, 136–143; in the valley of Little Shoulder-bone Creek, 143–147; on the Savannah River below Augusta, 153–157; on the Ocmulgee River, opposite the city of Macon, 158–161; on Lamar's plantation, 162; on Brown's Mount, 165; on Messier's plantation, 166–174; on Woolfolk's plantation, 182; sepulchral, 183; chieftain, 183; family or tribal, 189; on the low grounds of the Rivanna, 193; of shell, 195–200; of stone, 202; on Stalling's Island, 197; in Nacoochee Valley, 213; at the confluence of the Etowah and Oostenaula Rivers, 253.
Tuscaroras, the, 7.
Tydeus, 120.
Tylor, Mr., 414.

U.

Uchees, the, 2, 3.
Undertakers, 112, 191, 223.
Uppowóc, 396.

V.

Vaca, Cabeça de, 229, 245, 362.
Venegas, Miguel, 363.
Venetian beads, 235.
Victory-stones, 285.
Virginia kings, how entombed, 108.

W.

Walled towns, 209–212.
Walnut-oil, 45, 315, 316.
Wampum, 501–511.
War, how declared, 16, 18; conduct of the Southern Indians in, 17, 18.
War-chief, the great, dignity and power of, 11, 16; represents the Mico in his absence, 16.
Warriors, cabin of the, 16; characteristics of the Southern, 19.
Wears, 330–332.
Weaving, 78, 87.
Wedge-shaped axes, 278–281.
Westoes, the, 2.
Whetstones, 277, 367.
Whittlesey, Colonel Charles, 319, 331.
Widows, the care of, 18.
Williams, Roger, 507.
Wilson, Dr. Daniel, 384.
Winter houses, 35.
Wislizenus, Dr. A., 218.
Woman-chief, among the Natchez, 23.
Woman, position of, 70.
Wrightsboro, ancient monuments near, 123.
Wyman, Prof. Jeffries, 200.

Y.

Yamasees, the, 2, 3.
Year, divisions of the, 100.